CORRECTIONS
An Issues Approach

Martin D. Schwartz
Assistant Professor, University of Cincinnati

Todd R. Clear
Assistant Professor, Rutgers University

Lawrence F. Travis III
Research Director, Oregon State Board of Parole

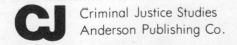
Criminal Justice Studies
Anderson Publishing Co.

CORRECTIONS: AN ISSUES APPROACH

Library of Congress Catalog Card Number: 79-54938
ISBN: 0-87084-777-5

This book was edited by Mark Evan Chimsky.
Cover design by Steve Faske.
Cover art reprinted by permission of the Bettmann Archive.

CONTENTS

PART FIVE   EMERGING ISSUES AND CHANGE

There is the institution of punishing criminals. Different people support this for different reasons, and for different reasons in different cases and at different times. Some people support it out of a desire for revenge, some perhaps out of a desire for justice, some out of a wish to prevent a repetition of the crime, and so on. And so punishments are carried out.

—*Ludwig Wittgenstein*

Reform, sir? Reform? Don't talk to me of reform. Things are bad enough as they are.

—*Henry Maudsley*

PREFACE

There is no doubt that we are in the midst of a knowledge explosion in the fields of criminology and criminal justice. Publishers of books and journals have opened a floodgate and the serious student is being inundated by a torrent of materials. Most should never have been published; some are better than adequate; and, occasionally, some very worthwhile and scholarly works find their way into print.

Until a few years ago, it was possible for the academician and practitioner alike to keep abreast of new and important publications. There just wasn't that much available. But along came LEAA—its largesse, new programs, expanded research efforts, and heightened concern over controlling crime spurred the expansion of literature in the field. With the Office of Criminal Justice Education and Training funding students through its LEEP program, more students and faculty came on the scene to do the writing. Today, as a consequence of these and other developments, one can barely keep up with what is going on.

No area has been untouched and no development is without a ripple effect. One can pity the classroom student. For that matter, one must have considerable sympathy for the responsible professor. There is just too much to learn; too much to be concerned about; too much to comprehend. Regardless of specialization, in past years one was able to be somewhat of a generalist. Currently, one is forced to carve out an area, stick to it, and, if lucky and skillful, barely maintain awareness of what is being published in that area.

This knowledge explosion has its advantages and disadvantages. One can no longer sit in a university or agency office and let the world pass by. Students and practitioners will not permit their faculty or administrators to be ignorant. Many want to learn and with the increase in knowledge available, many are indeed learning. Whether they are achieving understanding is another issue, but the foundations are being laid anyway. While some workers in the field create changes and developments in one area, others consequently become more capable of creating changes and developments in other areas. That is the whole idea of progress and that is what has been occurring in other disciplines.

Research strategies and evaluation techniques are becoming more responsible and responsive to perceived needs. Theoretical issues and conceptual developments are being addressed more so than ever before. Administrators want to be more effective and sophisticated. Professors want to be aware of new ideas. Practice and theory are no longer the strangers they once were. A significant consequence of all of the above is that criminology and criminal justice, regardless of definition and irrespective of differences, are becoming recognized and important disciplines.

Obviously, all is not perfect. There are far too many people employed in the field who think they know what they are talking about and too many publishers so eager to have titles they publish almost anything that comes along. The knowledge explosion has produced a glut on the market which can serve to confuse as well as elucidate. The quality of academic programs probably has not improved in any way proportional to their increase in numbers. Certainly, the quality of research reports and other publications are not in any way proportional to their increase in numbers.

Thus, we are confronted by a dilemma. On the one hand we can view the knowledge explosion as helpful in that we know more and understand more than was ever possible before. On the other hand, with so much irresponsible material being published, one has to develop special techniques for discerning the good from the bad. A consequence of this is that a new breed of author has emerged: a person who examines materials, reviews and synthesizes them, and alerts colleagues to what should be read and why.

I am not speaking merely of the editors of anthologies, especially those who simply collect thematic articles and reprint them between fancy covers. Rather, I am speaking of responsible editors who sift, analyze, and help the reader to interpret. It is the editor, who, not satisfied with what has been written, commissions new works to fill in the gaps. It is this editor who seeks to enlighten, who adds to knowledge, and, more particularly, helps the reader to understand.

It is my opinion that *Corrections: An Issues Approach* falls into the latter category. This collection of articles and new papers reflects careful thought about significant areas of concern in corrections. The works selected reflect serious scholarship by authors, who, for the most part, have something to say. Further, as the editors indicate, not only do they strive to enlighten the reader on current developments and philosophies, they seek to achieve understanding through the vehicle of debate.

By concentrating on corrections, the editors bring into focus several of the really important issues: sentencing, the status of prisons and imprisonment, community-based supervision of offenders, the future of parole, strategies of community involvement, the significance of probation, the problems of rehabilitation and treatment, the control of clients, and restitution.

This book represents a serious effort and deserves serious consideration by the reader. The issues presented are indeed fit topics for debate. That no answers are given by the editors to the various conflicts is certainly not a flaw. The introductory materials set the stage for learning. The authors engage in the debates and they make their points well.

In the final analysis, what the editors have done, and successfully in my opinion, is to help the reader gain new insights and new knowledge. Armed with these, understanding potentially becomes much more feasible.

Alvin W. Cohn, D. Crim.
Administration of Justice Services
Rockville, Maryland

ACKNOWLEDGMENTS

As usual, when going through the process of preparing a book, there are large numbers of persons who deserve some sort of acknowledgment, but only limited space to give these thanks. Of those who deserve special mention, some extraordinary scholars must be included for the guidance and knowledge they shared with all three of the authors. Donald Newman, for example, has been a wealth of information on all aspects of corrections, but especially prisons, and has been especially helpful in developing in us a healthy skepticism about reform. Vincent O'Leary is owed a debt by all three of us for his constant exploration of what is possible and what is important about the future of corrections. Fred Cohen is perhaps one of the greatest resources ever seen in law and its use in social control. Leslie T. Wilkins, Hans Toch, and Marguerite Warren have individually and collectively taught us much about studying and working in the field of American corrections. As is so often the case, a large number of students and colleagues have, over the years, been helpful in clarifying thoughts and providing stimuli to further thought. Following the lead of Norval Morris and Gordon Hawkins, however, we think it only fair to suggest that any omissions and errors in this book are a direct result of the influence of these people. Any credit to be bestowed, however, no doubt comes from our ability to transcend these influences.

Several persons were particularly helpful during the last minute crush of finalizing a book during busy times. Pat Travis and Deborah Lewis were both of great assistance in taking on a variety of chores. Mona Jaeger, John Tuthill, and Robert Freniere also provided timely assistance when needed. Mark Evan Chimsky, at Anderson, was for several months a most effective critic and stimulator of work, and his influence on this book was rather dramatic (for the better, one hopes). His concern and hard work were most appreciated by all three of us during those periods when we were not accusing him of nit-picking.

The University of Cincinnati's Department of Criminal Justice, particularly Chair Keith Haley, proved most helpful in providing both material and spiritual assistance and some of the time necessary to complete this book on schedule.

Finally, since we typed most of the manuscript drafts ourselves and did not pester colleagues to read various drafts and outlines, our respective secretaries and sundry colleagues have asked for equal time to thank us.

Martin D. Schwartz, Cincinnati, OH
Todd R. Clear, Newark, NJ
Lawrence F. Travis III, Salem, OR

May, 1979

INTRODUCTION

Book introductions traditionally attempt to define a book's audience, and then give some justification for the book's existence. In the case of *Corrections: An Issues Approach*, the former task seems to be the more difficult of the two.

While there are a variety of books on the market available for use in a university level corrections course, and many more available for the general public, most are written either to present the particular viewpoint of the author, or else to cover a wide variety of explanatory material. This book takes a rather different view of the field. Acknowledging that the field of corrections is currently a battlefield of ideas and ideologies, this book attempts to present basic arguments and counter-arguments in an effort to stimulate discussion around some of the "threshold" questions of our post-adjudicatory system, (e.g., should prisons exist at all?, should parole exist?, etc.).

Corrections: An Issues Approach is not intended to be easily pigeonholed for a specific audience. Obviously, it is our hope that any person who has an interest in the current debates can find something of value here to stimulate thought. The book might best be used as a "reader" supplementing a more traditional textbook, so that concepts and problems described in those books can be seen in a more direct manner.

However, there is enough descriptive material here so that *Corrections: An Issues Approach* might also be used as the main text in an issues-oriented course in corrections at any level. Even the most advanced student may not have been exposed to the hard-line, "both-sides-of-the-coin" approach taken in this book.

This is the kind of book that asks to be "put to work"—teachers and students alike will benefit from it most if they use it to generate thought, discussion and debate. Because fundamental arguments for different correctional goals are presented in a point/counterpoint format, the reader is given the opportunity to look objectively at *both* sides before taking sides. The issues highlighted are wide-ranging and crucial to the evolution of the correctional system, generally focusing on the split between those in favor of continued use of the correctional system and those in favor of major overhauls of the system.

Perhaps the most difficult decision made in preparing this book centered on whether we should cover all, or at least more than the two basic contrasting sides of each debate. Certainly advocates in the field of corrections cannot be easily classified into two opposing camps. Instead, there is a wide variety of opinion within each camp. Yet, since this book was designed to be actively used, and not become just another library resource, the final decision was made to limit the debates to easily understood, essentially polarized camps. Reality, unfortunately, is not as simple as that. Perhaps the major argument left out of these debates is the "middle of the road" position, which states that though the system is generally acceptable, changes *are* needed in order to do the same job more effectively or more efficiently.

If you look at the debate on institutions, you will see that the "pro" argument—that prisons are basically serving some useful functions—is juxtaposed with the opposing argument—that prisons should be closed down, (except to those few prisoners who do need maximum security restraint). The alternative arguments which fall in between these two positions could be listed *ad infinitum*, and a great many of these ended up on the "cutting room floor." For example, one of them is the "construction moratorium" position, which calls for an end to new construction and expansion of the network of maximum security prisons we have now, but refrains from suggesting that we close down any prisons currently in operation.

Another variant of that argument agrees with the anti-prison writers that maximum security mega-fortresses are counter-productive to our society, but sees an alternative to sending the current and future inmates of these prisons into community-based supervision. One suggested alternative was that a large network of small prisons be utilized on the theory that more humane and less crowded conditions would avoid the monolith institution's ill effects on the inmate, while still providing the same degree of protection or isolation of these prisoners.

One treatment approach which could be termed "middle of the road" argues that it is not surprising that past efforts at treatment do not work tremendously well, since very little effort has been exerted to make them work. Taking the same facts which lead some observers to conclude that treatment is not possible within a correctional setting, these persons argue instead that the facts call for an increased commitment to treatment. Certainly, only a small portion of any correctional budget has ever been dedicated to treatment endeavors in the past, and some theorists claim that a greater commitment to treatment would produce better results.

Another treatment approach argues that blanket treatment programs cannot be expected to work. Supporters of this approach state that exposing all offenders to identical "treatment" programs will help some, not affect some, and harm others. According to these supporters, the fault lies not with the treatment ideology, but with inadequate differentiation of offenders.

WHY ARE THERE ISSUES?

One of the themes of this book is that while many people understand that there are serious debates in the field of corrections, it is surprising how few realize the root cause of many of these debates: simply put, the major cause is a lack of agreement on *the purpose* of correctional agencies in our society.

As we shall see in Part One, throughout the history of corrections key themes have always defined the direction that corrections has taken. Yet, at no time did one purpose predominate above all others. Worse, as each new concept or theme emerged, the older philosophy did not disappear; it either became merged with the newer one, or else simmered below the surface, remaining as the underlying purpose of a great many people working in corrections.

Worse yet, a great many people today continue to hold two or often more conflicting concepts regarding the purpose that correctional institutions should serve. For example, in 1977 the state of Indiana introduced a new penal code, thus becoming one of the nation's first states to move toward determinate sentencing. The idea was to use the prisons to carry out a goal of retribution, or "just deserts." Such a policy holds that if a person commits a crime, that person "deserves" a set penalty. This concept is a throwback to a much earlier philosophy, in which a person "paid a debt" to society: for instance, if you committed a robbery, you "owed" the state a certain number of years in prison.

Yet, Indiana legislators were unwilling to go all the way with their new goal. They introduced a complicated set of mitigating and aggravating factors which would allow the judge to decrease or increase the "debt." One of those factors which could militate for a prison sentence is a need for treatment which can be obtained only inside the prison. So, the goal which might be considered furthest away from pure punishment—treatment and cure of a sick individual—became an established factor to consider in the doling out of prison sentences in a pure punishment system.

A similar conflict can be found in the state which has led the nation in moving toward one goal to the exclusion of all others. California recently had the most indeterminate sentence in the nation: a convicted offender could be sent to prison for a term of zero to life, with his release determined by the Adult Authority (parole board), which based its decisions on such factors as when an offender's rehabilitation was complete.

Perhaps because California was furthest along this road to rehabilitation and treatment, it also became the state most disillusioned by the failures of these goals. Recently, it made a swing far in the opposite direction and introduced "flat time," in which an offense carries a certain penalty. No longer does an inmate serve the amount of time a treatment-oriented staff feels is necessary for rehabilitation of that inmate; rather, the specific offense committed is responsible for determining the penalty.

Yet, even in California, where the penalty is based solely on the crime and not on the characteristics of the offender, treatment and rehabilitation remain a part of the process used to determine the exact release date. In determining time off for good behavior, commonly termed "good time," California computes into the calculations 25% of the possible good time to be awarded on the basis of participation in rehabilitative programs.

CHANGE AND LACK OF CHANGE

There is virtually no field of corrections in which there is complete agreement on what we should be doing to convicted offenders. In the field of prisons, one of the first two major modern prisons ever built in this country, in Auburn, New York, is still in operation after about 150 years. Yet, there is a continuing debate today as to whether we should even be using such prisons at all.

Parole has now cycled a full one hundred years, from the first state to institute parole (New York, at Elmira Reformatory in 1876) to the first state to abolish parole completely (Maine, 1976). Community supervision is perhaps the most confused area of all, with proponents of massive law enforcement control, proponents of improved delivery of services to help the offender readjust to society, and proponents of ending supervision in favor of sending offenders to already existing community agencies (outside of corrections), all vying for attention, power and dollars.

The major problems are confusion and lack of money. There is not now, nor has there ever been (except perhaps for a short time in the 1830s) agreement on exactly what the persons charged with the supervision of convicted offenders should be doing. Even when there begins to be some agreement of the one overriding goal or purpose, the correctional coffers are rarely full enough to allow a total change in practices to meet that goal.

Over the years, most of the major issues in corrections have merely gone through cosmetic changes in vocabulary (for example, "the hole" has now become "the sensory deprivation unit"). However, as a result of technology, new issues have emerged that contain far-reaching implications. The argument made in this book by Ingraham and Smith in favor of the use of electronic technology in the supervision of offenders would not have been made in 1876. There were no electronics then. Other correctional problems, because they are not technology-based, crop up throughout the history of corrections: even in the most reform-based institutions of seventy-five years ago, or in the most rehabilitation-based institutions of recent years, the concept they were supposed to be dedicated to—changing the offender from a lawbreaker to a lawabider—never gained full acceptance in the institutional field. As in many mental institutions today, the major concern often involves custody. Society as a whole is perhaps most dedicated to keeping these people off the streets, and most afraid of them escaping the institution. In virtually every penal institution in this country, the primary operational concern has ended up being control and custody, no matter what the handout from the public relations office says.

The problem for many within the field of corrections stems from a failure to view corrections as a part of a larger process. Prisons, community supervision, treatment and other aspects of corrections have been fragmented, and treated as separate fields, rather than as pieces of the whole. Innovations in probation usually have not meant corresponding innovations in prisons or parole. Certainly, correctional planning has not been characterized by an understanding of the effect of changes in prisons on the police, prosecutors, and judges, who are responsible for choosing those persons who will enter the prisons.

Rarely has any state attempted to view the criminal justice system as a process dominated by any single goal or concern, and attempted to devise a set of agencies dedicated to carrying out that goal. Even when it seems that, on the surface, one goal is dominant, further examination often shows that other, perhaps contradictory goals play an important part in the decision-making process.

For example, recently in a northern state, as part of the governor's "get tough with crime" policy, the State Division of Probation instituted a new program for intensive supervision of dangerous offenders. Officers were given decreased caseloads (to provide a greater ability to discover rules violations), and streamlined regulations were introduced to provide faster, surer disposition of probationers accused of violating probation conditions. Yet, the major thrust of the program and its operational guidelines remained delivery of services. Special intensive supervision officers were being trained and supervised in the development of objectives for changing each individual offender, and in the facilitation of that change through the use of community resources. The question arises—how does one evaluate the success of such a program? If an increased number of probationers are sent to prison for violating probation conditions, does that mean the officers were successful in discovering violations (crime control) or failures in getting the offenders to change (service delivery)? What is to be done by the officer who is having great success at changing the individual offender, but discovers an important rules violation by that offender? Which goal predominates?

All of this is not necessarily to argue that correctional systems can only operate with one major goal. It does mean that some agreement on the various goals, and the methods of providing for them, is necessary. A system today, in which an offender can be sent to prison for specific deterrence, general deterrence, rehabilitation, incapacitation and retribution, all by the same judge as part of the same sentence, is ludicrously hard to operate. Worse yet is when the judge sends different people to the same institution for different reasons, without bothering to spell out just what those reasons are. Once the prison or community agency receives that person, it still does not know whether it is supposed to "get tough" with that person, punish that person by just limiting their liberty, or give helpful, kindly assistance so that he or she can become a better individual and stop committing crimes. If the agency itself does not know what to do with the offenders it receives, imagine the position the offender is in.

Part One

Correctional Goals
and Functions

PAST TO PRESENT

CORRECTIONS AND THE CRIMINAL JUSTICE SYSTEM

Corrections is the "home stretch" of the criminal justice system. By the time that people come under correctional supervision, they have already run through most of the field: starting out as free citizens, they have gone through the roles of suspect, arrestee, defendant, and convict, before arriving at their current status (that of inmate, probationer or parolee).

This process is important to keep in mind, for while corrections can be extracted from the larger justice system for study, that extraction is artificial. It is done for ease of analysis, and does not represent actual conditions.

Just like law enforcement or criminal courts, corrections can only be understood as a component of the larger justice process. Actually, this issue of whether the criminal justice system is really a true "system" has been hotly debated in the literature of the field.[1] But no matter what conclusion one reaches on this issue, the inescapable fact remains that the agencies and offices of the criminal justice process, viewed as a whole, share certain characteristics of a systemic nature.[2] Perhaps most important among these characteristics is that these various agencies are interdependent.[3]

An example of this interdependence is the way correctional agencies rely on the criminal courts for input in terms of subject population. If convicted offenders were not sentenced to incarceration or probation, there would be very little left for the correctional bureaucracy to do.

Certainly this example is purposely extreme. But it does make the point that the correctional process is intricately bound to the rest of the criminal justice system. Interdependence, by definition, involves a "give and take" relationship among the three branches of the criminal justice system: law enforcement, courts and corrections. On the "give" side, a particularly important characteristic of the justice system is that it has a directional process. Cases "flow" from the police through the courts to corrections. This means

---

1. See Frank Remington et al., *Criminal Justice Administration: Materials and Cases*, (Indianapolis: Bobbs-Merrill, 1969), especially pp. 6-12, for a discussion of the systemic nature of criminal justice.

2. Donald J. Newman, *Introduction to Criminal Justice*, 2nd. ed., (Philadelphia: J.B. Lippincott, 1978), notes that it is the processing of persons, from investigation through to discharge from custody, that is the key to viewing the justice process as a system.

3. The interrelationship of separate parts is a primary characteristic of any system. Just as the various organs of the human body are interrelated in order to sustain life, the components of the justice process are interdependent.

that the subject populations of correctional agencies, (the input into the correctional process), are defined and controlled by agencies not identified as being in the correctional segment of the justice system. In simple language, corrections has to take whatever it is given. This fact is even more important to an understanding of American corrections once the nature of the criminal justice system is explored.

On the "take" side, there is some feedback flowing in the other direction which may have some impact on earlier sections of the system. Constant cries of overcrowding from correctional authorities may convince some courts to sentence more offenders to community supervision. A policy of early parole for some offenders, such as marijuana possessors, combined with a court movement to dismiss or lightly sentence these offenders, can convince the law enforcement component to stop "wasting time" by arresting such law violators.

Yet, while the criminal justice process is characterized by many of the attributes of a "system," as a whole it does not quite fit any common systemic model. Sheldon Glueck has characterized the American criminal justice system as "the clumsy admixture of the oil of discretion and the water of rule."[4] Because the justice system is an "open system," it interacts with its environment and not only has an impact on that environment but is also affected by it.[5] That environment is the larger "system" of American society.[6]

By design, necessity or historical development, agencies of the justice system have obtained tremendous authority to control their day to day operations. This authority, the power to choose among alternative actions or inaction, is known as discretion.[7] The importance of discretion to an understanding of the justice system cannot be overstated.

The combination of rather broad discretionary power, residing in the criminal justice agencies, with the directional flow of the justice process has important ramifications in American corrections. The police have the power to "overlook" criminal offenses. They can fail to investigate reported crime, decide not to arrest known suspects, or fail to work for convictions.[8] By simply organizing their forces in one manner or another, they can strongly affect the types of arrests made. For example, placing over half of the available of-

---

4. Sheldon Glueck, "Principles of a Rational Penal Code," *Harvard Law Review*, vol. 41 (1928), p. 480.

5. See E.L. Trist, "On Socio-Technical Systems," in *The Planning of Change*, 2nd Edition, Bennis, Benne, Chin, eds., (New York: Holt, Rinehart, Winston, 1969), p. 269, for a discussion of "open systems."

6. President's Commission on Law Enforcement and Administration of Justice, *The Challenge of Crime in a Free Society*, (Washington, D.C.: U.S. Government Printing Office, 1967), p. 7.

7. Kenneth Culp Davis, *Discretionary Justice: A Preliminary Inquiry*, (Baton Rouge, La.: Louisiana State University Press, 1969).

8. See Herman Goldstein, *Policing a Free Society*, (Cambridge, Mass.: Ballinger Publishing Co., 1976); and Wayne LaFave, *Arrest: The Decision to Take a Suspect into Custody*, (Boston: Little, Brown, 1965).

ficers in a squad established to fight organized crime would result in quite a different arrest picture than if no such squad were to be established at all.

This same discretionary power exists throughout the justice system. Prosecutors can refuse to charge suspects with any crime at all, or can change the crime for which they were arrested to one which is not as serious.[9] Grand juries can refuse to indict. Trial juries can refuse to convict, no matter how great the evidence. Sentencing judges have the discretion to, with few exceptions, suspend sentence altogether, or to impose fines, probation or incarceration.

Correctional agencies also have discretionary power, as will be demonstrated later in the book. However, at this point, the focus will be on those decision-makers who utilize discretionary power at an earlier stage of the criminal justice process.

There are two different functions that discretion can serve. First, and most commonly, it is exercised in a manner that will help to continually reduce the number of cases being processed. Thus, the number of persons sentenced is far lower than the number arrested. The justice system acts as a funnel,[10] with the result that correctional populations have been negatively selected, and are theoretically comprised of the most serious, most intractable and most dangerous offenders.

Second, the power to divert persons from the justice process necessarily involves the power to retain others. This means that some decision-maker with discretionary power has chosen to divert those people who might benefit most from diversion, and retain those who might not so benefit. Unfortunately, what has happened is that many persons sentenced to some form of correctional supervision neither "need" such supervision, nor when compared to others diverted from the process, deserve it. Such persons place an unnecessary and unwarranted burden on the finite resources of correctional agencies.

With all of these decisions being made daily, the criminal justice system has been defined as a "complex decision network."[11] Actually, it is a sequential series of decisions made by state agents (police officers, prosecutors, judges and corrections officials), in which each decision is heavily dependent on the preceding decisions. Trial judges or juries can only convict those persons who have been formally charged by prosecutors, who generally charge only those persons identified as law-breakers by the police, and so on. Probation officers only have custody over those sentenced to terms of probation. In such a system, the decision immediately preceding that to be made by any

9. See Brian A. Grosman, *The Prosecutor: An Inquiry into the Exercise of Discretion*, (Toronto: University of Toronto Press, 1969); and Arthur Rosett and Donald Cressey, *Justice by Consent*, (Philadelphia: J.B. Lippincott, 1976).

10. President's Commission, *Task Force Report: Science and Technology*, (Washington, D.C.: U.S. Government Printing Office, 1967), p. 61.

11. Newman, *Introduction to Criminal Justice*, p. 1.

official thus carries the most weight and has the greatest influence on that official's exercise of authority. For that reason alone, judicial sentencing is of vital importance to correctional agencies.

SENTENCING

In many ways, sentencing is the center of the justice system. Television and literary dramas notwithstanding, it is at the sentencing decision that the state exercises the most power over the individual. It is at this point that a decision is made which determines the conditions under which the individual will live for a period of time up to the entire remainder of his or her existence. For certain specific offenses, over 60% of the states allow the judge or jury at sentencing to decide whether or not the offender will continue to live.[12]

Up to the point of sentencing, the entire decision network operates to identify those persons who will be subjected to criminal sanctions. After sentencing, the network operates to execute the penalty imposed. Correctional agencies play a very important role in the sentencing process, and not only because a major function of all correctional agencies is the execution of judicially imposed sanctions.

Another role corrections plays in the sentencing process involves the preparation of pre-sentence investigations by probation agencies. These source documents, which often form the basis on which judges make sentencing decisions, many times even include sentence recommendations.[13] After the judge makes his sentencing determination, he or she often shares the decision-making power with another correctional agency, the parole board. Through its authority to grant release (under specified conditions) from incarceration, parole boards actually share the sentencing power with judges,[14] who often determine the exact number of years that an offender will serve in prison.

As stated before, because of the sequential nature of sentencing decisions, each authority is limited to some degree by the decision made by the last authority to process the case. The police can arrange to make an arrest (or not to make an arrest at all) in such a manner as to limit the maximum charge the system can place on the offender. Through such methods as plea bargaining, the prosecutor can have charges dropped or reduced before the judge even hears the case. In this way, the prosecutor can severely limit the sentencing power of the judge. Even where the judge can overturn a prosecutor's plea bargain, he does so only at the price of increasing his work load and alienating other people he must work with every day.

12. Ernest van den Haag, "In Defense of the Death Penalty: A Legal-Practical-Moral Analysis," *Criminal Law Bulletin*, vol. 14 (1978), p. 52.

13. Victor H. Evjen, "Some Guidelines in Preparing Presentence Reports," *Federal Rules Decision*, vol. 37 (1964), p. 177.

14. Andrew von Hirsch and Kathleen J. Hanrahan, *Abolish Parole?* (Washington, D.C.: National Institute of Law Enforcement and Criminal Justice, 1978), p. 1.

After the judge makes a sentencing determination, as limited by the legislatively set law, this determination can work to limit the activities of correctional agencies in two important ways. First, the sentence can establish or define the goals of correctional intervention. Second, the sentence imposes certain operational constraints by setting the conditions and establishing a time limit on the correctional control over the individual. With all of these results of sentencing, it is no wonder that sentencing remains presently a very controversial function in the justice system.

The current controversy surrounding sentencing, which also affects corrections, is centered on the issue of the discretionary power of judicial decision-makers. While we have just made the argument that other decision-makers serve to limit the powers of judges, the power retained by judges is sufficient enough to spur a powerful debate across the country on the question of whether judges should be allowed to keep and exercise the power they still have.

There is a justification for allowing judges to retain broad discretionary power, but it is tied to beliefs about the goals or purposes of criminal sentences. Four such goals have been identified and expounded in current literature in the criminal justice field: deterrence, incapacitation, treatment and retribution.[15]

General deterrence as a sentencing goal specifies that criminal penalties should operate in such a manner as to serve warning on the population as a whole that criminal behavior will result in official sanctions.[16] This is accomplished by making an example through punishment of those convicted of criminal ofenses. That is, the offender is sentenced to a harsh term primarily to threaten others who might be tempted to break the law. This form of deterrence is usually the rationale behind "throwing the book" at an offender.

Although general deterrence is aimed primarily at other potential offenders, many goals of the corrections system are aimed at the specific individual offender. Two somewhat similar goals are those of specific (sometimes called "special") deterrence and incapacitation. The purpose of both these goals is to prevent future criminality of the person being sentenced. The specific deterrence sentence attempts to provide a sentence which is unpleasant, such as a term in prison, in the hopes that the offender will find the experience distasteful enough that he or she will refrain from future criminality. Incapacitation, on the other hand, attempts to prevent future criminality by restraining the person either physically or through rules and regulations in order to cut off the offender's opportunity to commit more crimes.[17] Under the rather cynical incapacitative rationale, an offender may be given a long prison term not to deter others, or even to im-

---

15. Vincent O'Leary, Michael Gottfredson, and Arthur Gelman, "Contemporary Sentencing Proposals," *Criminal Law Bulletin*, vol. 11 (1975), p. 555.

16. *Ibid.*, p. 556.

17. *Ibid.*, p. 557.

press the offender with the seriousness of the crime, but solely to prevent him or her from committing crimes for at least the period that he or she is in prison.

Treatment, or rehabilitation, as it is sometimes called, seeks the same outcome as incapacitation, (the prevention of future criminal conduct by the offender), but through radically different means. Sentences based on the treatment goal are designed to change the offender's need or desire to commit crimes, and not simply to prevent the offender from having the opportunity to do so.

Retribution, which has more recently been re-termed by some as "just deserts," takes a completely different approach to the goal of sentencing. Retribution supports criminal penalties imposed as punishment for all past offenses.[18] Retributory penalties are meant to be equal to the severity of the offense for which the individual was convicted, with each offense assigned a sentence proportionate to its severity. The retribution goal is, simply put, that the offender should "pay his debt."

Thus, these four sentencing goals can be divided into two classes. The first class, involving deterrence, incapacitation and treatment, is forward-looking. All three of these goals are concerned with the prevention of future criminal conduct. Therefore, all must be based on some predictions of criminal offenses. In the second class, there is retribution, the only sentencing philosophy which is backward-looking. The single concern of the retributionists is that offenders be punished for what they have done, not what they, or others similar to them, might do in the future.

These sentencing philosophies have been presented in "pure" form. In actual practice, however, sentencing structures and procedures reflect a mix of these philosophies. Judges rarely sit back just before sentencing and decide that defendant A should get three years of incapacitation, defendant B needs three years of treatment, while defendant C merely deserves three years of retributory imprisonment.

In one recent case, for example, the defendant's lawyer entered a plea for lenience based on the argument that this was "a classic case of a young person whose early life was formulated by hanging around with the wrong people." The judge rejected the plea, stating that he saw it as "a classic case of second-degree robbery where two individuals went out and robbed another with what appeared to be a gun." The judge admonished the young man to accept culpability for his crime. In effect, he said 'You chose to do wrong, and now must pay in full for your crime. You will receive harm for harm'—that is, be punished according to a retributionist philosophy.

At the same time, however, the judge stated that a major factor in sentencing was "deterrence to others." The judge said he was giving notice to the community that those who commit crimes of violence will "not be slapped on the wrist, but will be hit hard."[19]

---

18. *Ibid.*
19. Albany, New York, *The Times Union*, 31 January 1978.

Yet, after this speech, the judge sentenced the youth to an indeterminate term of up to seven years. That means the youth will serve zero to seven years, being let out of prison when the parole board thinks that he is rehabilitated or when they judge that he has learned his lesson (specific deterrence) or when they judge that he is no longer a threat to society (incapacitation).

If a judge can be so uncertain as to the goals of the criminal justice system, and unsure of just why he is sentencing a young man to the corrections component of the system, it certainly should come as no surprise that the people who work inside corrections are similarly confused as to just what to do with this young man after they receive him.

TYPES OF SENTENCES

Because there has been so much confusion about sentencing goals, legislatures have developed, through the years, a number of structures to help facilitate and clarify the sentencing of convicted offenders. These structures reflect a balance of discretionary power between judges and parole release authorities. Each of these different sentencing structures affects the power of the corrections system, increasing this power dramatically in some cases, and drastically cutting this power short in others.

Today, there are six basic types of sentencing structures in operation in the United States,[20] with numerous variations on each. Except for the ten states in which discretionary parole release has been abandoned, each sentence has two basic outer limits. The first is the maximum term, (the longest time for which an offender can be incarcerated before the sentence expires and he or she must be released). The second is the minimum term, (the length of time an offender must serve before he or she can be released from incarceration under almost any conditions). The period between the expiration of the minimum term and the expiration of the maximum term is the period over which the parole authority is empowered, at their discretion, to grant release.

Actually, like most other aspects of the criminal justice system, incarcerative sentences are somewhat more complex than this. For example, the effect of "good time" or "time off for good behavior" complicates the issue. Depending on the provisions of each jurisdiction,[21] inmates are awarded and/or can earn reductions in the maximum and/or minimum term. Thus, as an example, if an inmate can be awarded a one-third reduction of the maximum sentence for good behavior, the maximum period of incarceration on a sentence of six years is actually only four years. One-third, or two years, has been taken off the top as a reward for obedience to institutional rules. Similarly, if the sentence was two to six years, and sentence reductions were credited against the minimum two year sentence, the in-

---

20. Newman, *Introduction to Criminal Justice*, pp. 254-262.
21. Robert R. Smith, "A Survey of Good Time Policies and Practices in American Correctional Agencies," *Journal of Criminal Justice*, vol. 3 (1975), p. 237.

mate would be eligible for parole release after serving one year and four months. One-third of the sentence (eight months on a two year term) would be credited against his two year minimum sentence.

Good time is another example of idealized goals conflicting with institutional reality. No matter what the goal of the particular corrections system might be, it makes very little sense to allow an inmate to be released early just for obeying the rules of the institution to which he or she was sentenced. If incapacitation was really needed, the smart or career criminal knows that by "playing it cool" and "doing your own time" the total sentence will be reduced, and the day when a resumption of criminal activity can take place will be that much nearer. Other idealized goals also tend to fall short of their initial promise. For example, a treatment goal which allows for the release of an inmate before it is proven that the inmate is cured makes little sense. Similarly, the power of deterrence as a sentencing goal can be seriously diminished if everyone knows that the offender will be released early. If the goal of retribution was utilized, giving "good-time" would mean that only two-thirds of the debt (retribution) would have to be paid.

But here reality enters. Once a person is placed in a maximum security prison, as the overwhelming majority of our incarcerated felons are in this country, the correctional authorities are left with very little power to force that person to obey the rules. Considering that a relatively small number of unarmed guards must police a relatively large number of convicted criminals, there is a persuasive argument that it is impossible to run prisons without the permission of the inmates. After all, the state can only so often resort to the kind of outside help and overwhelming firepower that was present, in full force, at the New York State Attica prison riots.

When an inmate breaks an institutional rule, there are only limited punishments the institution can offer. After television privileges have been taken away, gym and library time reduced, and perhaps 24-hour lockup instituted, what is next? The courts have not looked kindly upon beatings or bread-and-water diets, and have even limited the amount of solitary confinement time. What's left?

What's left is good time. For breaking the institutional rules, an inmate can forfeit some of the one-third reduction in sentence, or even all of it, depending upon the state's regulations. An inmate who receives two years off a six-year sentence for obeying the rules may have all this "good-time" taken away should he indulge in calling the guards "pigs" or screaming all night or throwing food in the cafeteria. From the inmate's point of view, one can thus receive a two-year sentence for minor misbehavior. That is substantially more than one can receive from the criminal courts on the outside. One may not approve of this tremendous dosage of discretionary justice, but it surely is one of the most effective behavioral control devices that the correctional authorities possess.

Several other sentencing factors add even more complexity to the calculation of terms of imprisonment. An offender may be granted credit for time served while awaiting trial, sentencing or transportation to prison. If the offender is convicted of more than one offense, the various sentences can be ordered to be served concurrently (which means all sentences are served simultaneously, so that 20 five-year sentences served concurrently would result in a total sentence of five years), or consecutively (which means each sentence is served independent of the other, so that an inmate would not begin to serve time for a second offense before he had completed serving his sentence for the first offense).

All of this discussion demonstrates the extreme complexity of sentencing, and the fact that some of the sentencing authority is shared by all three of the branches of government: the legislature sets the possible penalties, the judiciary does the sentencing, and then shares some of this power with the executive branch, which runs the prisons. Not only do many variables affect how long an individual will be incarcerated after sentencing but there is substantial diversity in the calculation of sentence lengths among the 52 jurisdictions in the United States.[22]

Further, while most of the above discussion has been limited to incarcerative sentences, such sentences account for less than 40% of all criminal sanctions. Actually, the sentencing decision is a two-step process.[23] The first, as the above discussion indicates, is the determination of the length of the sentence. However, for most offenders, there is also the decision of whether to impose an incarcerative sentence at all. For most offenders, the sentencing judge also has the option of imposing a non-incarcerative penalty such as a fine or probation. In fact, approximately 60% of sentences imposed by judges do not involve incarceration.[24]

The most common of these non-incarceration sentences for serious misdemeanor or felony cases is a sentence to probation. There are several ways in which a probation sentence can be ordered, but two predominate.[25] In many jurisdictions, the sentencing judge will impose a prison sentence but suspend its execution. In others, the judge will defer sentencing. For the most part, the results are the same. The offender is placed on probation, and if he or she completes the term without violating the conditions of probation, he or she is released. If the probationer does violate the terms of conditional release and probation is revoked, the probationer is returned to court.

It is after revocation that these two modes of imposing probation sentences differ. In those cases where the judge has already ordered a prison sentence, but suspended it, the judge merely orders that original sentence to begin. Where sentencing itself had been deferred, the judge may set a term of in-

22. *Ibid.*

23. Leslie T. Wilkins et al., *Sentencing Guidelines: Structuring Judicial Discretion,* (Washington, D.C.: National Institute of Law Enforcement and Criminal Justice, 1978), pp. 2-3.

24. President's Commission, *Task Force Report: Corrections,* (Washington, D.C.: U.S. Government Printing Office, 1967), pp. 27-37.

25. Newman, *Introduction to Criminal Justice,* pp. 281-82.

carceration, or else re-order the offender to probation with new, more restrictive conditions. The judge is free to make any sentence he might have originally made after the conviction.

What is unfortunately too often disregarded by most persons studying sentencing is that any penalty imposed by a judge—fine, probation or incarceration—can serve any or a combination of the four goals of corrections. While many people can easily see how a term in prison can deter, incapacitate or punish, they find it harder to see the same ability on the part of fines or probation, since these penalties are generally considered to be "lenient."[26]

Of course, it would be extremely difficult, if not impossible, to argue that in comparison to incarceration, fines or community-based sentences are not less severe. However, this fact does not render fines and probation any less capable of attaining some of the goals of sentencing. For example, a particularly hefty fine or particularly onerous conditions of probation can be both punitive and deterrent.[27] Furthermore, one of the reasons for supervision of probationers has traditionally been to reduce the opportunity for them to commit future crimes while under intensive supervision or surveillence. This constant state of being closely watched is just as much a form of incapacitation as actual imprisonment.

While sentencing decisions directly affect correctional agencies by defining their populations and guiding agency practices, the influence of sentencing decisions is not wholly controlling. Corrections has its own philosophical underpinnings, functions and authority. Often complementary to the goals of criminal sanctions, these factors can also be in conflict with them, and with each other.

THE PHILOSOPHY AND FUNCTIONS OF CORRECTIONS

The word "corrections" itself implies change. More than simple alteration, however, it implies a specific type of change activity; one that ameliorates perceived wrongs or errors, that leads to a situation that is an improvement over what existed before. In terms of criminal corrections, there are two possible beneficiaries of such change: society and the offender.

The overall purposes of the criminal justice system are the control and prevention of crime. These two goals are not only central to sentencing, but also to the correctional process. In this respect, the ultimate measure against which all of the activities of the criminal justice system can be evaluated is the amount of crime in society. Unfortunately, obtaining that measure is an extremely difficult, if not impossible task.

While these dual purposes apply to every component of the criminal justice system, they are particularly apparent in corrections. Police are

---

26. *Ibid.*
27. *Ibid.*, pp. 41-46.

evaluated by crime rates or, less often, clearance rates.[28] They are expected to control crime by arresting offenders, and to prevent crime, as measured by changes in crime rates. Prosecutors are most often evaluated in terms of crime control, as in their "batting average," or percentage of convictions. Sentencing judges are expected to prevent crime through incapacitating, or deterring criminals, and to control crime generally through the imposition of punishment.

These crime prevention expectations, however, are more implied than imposed. That is, the police are directed to arrest law breakers, prosecutors are expected to charge, try and convict offenders, and judges are empowered to punish those offenders. Correctional agencies, on the other hand, are usually *expressly charged* with the crime prevention function. While they execute the penalties imposed by judges, they are also directed to assist the offender to adapt to a law-abiding life-style.[29]

The manner in which this is accomplished, or attempted, depends on a number of factors, not the least of which is the guiding philosophy of a correctional agency.

O'Leary and Duffee have identified four "correctional policies" or philosophies: restraint, reform, rehabilitation and reintegration.[30] These policies can be distinguished from one another by the degree to which each emphasizes a concern for the community and for the offender. O'Leary and Duffee suggest that the particular staffing, programs and other operational arrangements of corrections agencies are determined, in large part, by each agency's efforts to help benefit the community and/or the offender.

An agency stressing restraint is not operating in a manner which would stimulate change on the part of the offender or society. The restraint policy demonstrates a low concern for the offender and a low concern for the community. If the offender desires to change himself, he will do so. If not, he will not change. The goals of the administrators and staff in such an agency is to keep things on an "even keel" and avoid disruptions. Everyone follows the rules, while innovation and risk-taking are not supported.

Correctional agencies, following a reform policy, place a heavy emphasis on community protection with very little concern for the offender. The goal of those working in such an agency is to train the offender to become a law-abiding, conforming citizen. This is accomplished through a total manipulation of the offender's environment. Whether or not the offender believes in the value of conformity, he is punished for non-conformity and taught to obey.

---

28. President's Commission, *Task Force: Police*, (Washington, D.C.: U.S. Government Printing Office, 1967), pp. 2-3.

29. Legislation that creates most correctional agencies normally includes a mandate that the agency provide for the "rehabilitation" or assistance of the offender.

30. Vincent O'Leary and David Duffee, "Correctional Policy: A Classification of Goals Designed for Change," *Crime and Delinquency*, vol. 18 (1972), p. 373.

TABLE I
Correctional policies*

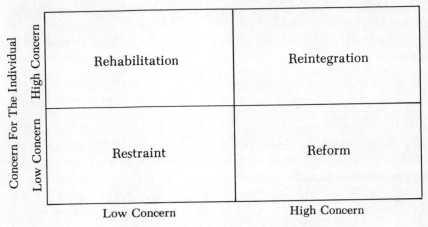

An agency operating under a rehabilitation policy is primarily concerned with the internal stability of the offender. Staffs in such agencies tend to encourage the offender to understand himself and gain "insight." The belief is that once a period of personal growth has been completed, and the offender gains insight into his behavior and motivation, he will come to terms with his criminality and choose to lead a law-abiding life. The external constraints so characteristic of a reform dominated agency are forgone, as much as possible, in the belief that only the offender can change himself.

The policy of reintegration is best exemplified by the Corrections Task Force Report of The President's Commission on Crime and Administration of Justice.[31] The report recommends that an agency espousing the philosophy of reintegration seek to achieve change in both the offender and society, for the benefit of both. Offenders are encouraged to test alternative behaviors to crime, such as employment, education, etc. In order to help offenders on the path toward these alternatives, the staff of the agency must work in an advocate role to secure social benefits for offenders. The overriding belief is that through cooperation between society and offenders, conditions can be created wherein offenders view law-abiding behavior as a viable alternative to continued criminality.

---

* Adapted, with permission of the National Council on Crime and Delinquency, from "Correctional Policy—A Classification of Goals Designed for Change" by Vincent O'Leary and David Duffee, *Crime and Delinquency*, October 1971, p. 379.

31. President's Commission, *Challenge of Crime*, note 24, pp. 1-12.

THE DEVELOPMENT OF AMERICAN CORRECTIONS

There are three basic components in the correctional process; probation, parole and prisons. All three are American inventions.[32] Like most other products of "Yankee ingenuity" and like American society itself, these correctional processes are refined versions of practices or technologies developed earlier in other countries.

Originally, "corrections" (as the word has come to be known) did not exist in any society. Those who violated the laws, mores or taboos were punished. There was no attempt to salvage the individual and return him to a constructive life-style. Punishments were of two basic types: banishment or death. Perhaps the earliest recorded penalty was banishment, the sanction imposed on Adam and Eve.[33]

Banishment was a penalty that was extreme for the simple reason that in earlier societies, removal from clan or village often meant death. It was popular in some societies because, while the result was identical to capital punishment, none of the sentencers were directly responsible for the demise of the offender.[34] In other societies, the penalty of death was imposed with some regularity, primarily because it provided an acceptable, certain solution to the problem of deviance.

In an excellent analysis of the development of the use of incarceration as a penalty for serious crime, Langbein examines the social and economic bases of criminal penalties.[35] Very briefly put, until societies are developed enough technologically, they simply do not have the capacity to hold large numbers of wrongdoers prisoner. Manpower can not be spared to guard prisoners, the logistics of housing and feeding them are impossible, and therefore, compared to banishment, capital or corporal punishments, incarceration is not a viable alternative.

As societies advance, however, the ability to hold and manage large bodies of prisoners is realized. More importantly, as Langbein noted, by the sixteenth and seventeenth centuries, there was a need for manpower. Warships were driven by oars, requiring many men to work in a very hazardous occupation for the navies of the emerging world powers. The supply of oarsmen from the free society and even from the ranks of captured enemies could not keep pace with the growing demand. Criminal offenders who would have otherwise been executed provided a work force.[36]

---

32. Prisons were established in the first quarter of the 19th century in New York and Pennsylvania; parole was initiated in New York in 1876, and about the same time, probation was initiated in Boston.

33. A vivid account of this sanction appears in the Bible, in the Book of Genesis.

34. Graeme Newman, *The Punishment Response*, (Philadelphia: J.B. Lippincott, 1978).

35. John H. Langbein, "The Historical Origins of the Sanction of Imprisonment for Serious Crime," *Journal of Legal Studies*, vol. 5 (1976), p. 35.

36. *Ibid.*

Prisoners were also very useful in the expanding mining industry, where again wretched and very hazardous working conditions inhibited the growth of any sort of volunteer labor force from developing.[37] Two new developments, however, soon decreased the need for slave labor. First, sailing vessels proved far superior to galleys as naval ships. Second, mining technology advanced reducing the need for manpower while at the same time colonies were established where indiginous workers were used to produce raw materials. Despite this movement away from the utilization of slave labor, the concept of incarceration and labor as punishments for crime had by this time become fairly well established—at least in theory, if not in practice.

The old naval galleys were retained as prison hulks where the offenders were kept during the night. In the daytime, they were set to work ashore on such public projects as road building. Those convicted of the most serious offenses however, were executed. Even when prisoner labor in mines and on naval ships was at its zenith, very serious offenses were punished by death.[38]

The fact is that most offenses were punishable by death. English penalties were uniform in their severity; hanging was the sanction specified by law for almost every serious offense.[39] This tradition of harsh penalties carried over to colonial America where death, brandings and maimings were common sanctions for felonies, with public floggings and humiliation in the stocks ordered for lesser offenses. By and large, with the exception of debtors' prisons, confinement as punishment did not then exist in the Anglo-American tradition. Jailing was used only as an intermediate step between arrest and penalty. Those offenders not executed were penalized and freed.

The rising numbers of debtors and lesser offenders not able to pay their fines began to fill English jails. In addition, public opinion began to turn away from support of capital punishment for many offenders. The result was a large number of convicts in England and not enough space or work for them. To alleviate this problem, the English hit upon the idea of transportation as punishment.

Transportation was a revised form of banishment. In essence, sentences of transportation were sentences to probation, with the one condition that the offender not return to England, or at least not return before some specified date. These convicts were first sent to America and later, to Australia, after the American colonies had gained their independence. This system of penalties worked fairly well for the English for about two centuries.[40] The

---

37. *Ibid.*

38. *Ibid.*

39. Todd R. Clear, *A Model for Supervising the Offender in the Community*, (Washington, D.C.: National Institute of Corrections, 1978), pp. 7-8.

40. See Keith O. Hawkins, "Parole Selection: *The American Experience*," (Ph.D. dissertation, University of Cambridge, England, 1971), for a history of the use of transportation by the English as a penalty for crime.

colonies, however, did not have their own outside colonies to which their convicts could be sent.

Thus, criminal punishment in early America most often took the form of what Langbein has termed "blood punishments," (that is, brandings, maimings, etc.). In time the rationale and need for such cruel penalties came to be questioned, particularly by the American Quakers, but also by other leading citizens.[41] These people desired a reform in criminal penalties. It was not until late in the eighteenth century that these reformers were able to persuade legislatures to move away from corporal and capital punishments and adopt incarceration as the penalty for crime.

This shift had no comparable predecessor in Europe because it occurred on such a broad scale. It was, however, consistent with a number of philosophical themes which were unique to the American culture. Indeed, when Patrick Henry said, "Give me liberty, or give me Death!," little did he know that his sentiment would support a vast movement towards incarcerative penalties within fifty years. The perfect punishment for those who shared Henry's philosophy was one that deprived them of *either* liberty *or* death—the prison. What more terrible punishment could there be in a nation that had recently emerged from seven years of war for independence, than to deprive an individual of his freedom?

Additionally, the Enlightenment created a belief in the ultimate perfectability of man. The idea of the social contract, so basic to the American Revolution, was aligned with an argument against the imposition of the death penalty. Cesare Beccaria, in his classic essay, "On Crimes and Punishment," argued that no man would give the state the power to take his life as part of the social contract.[42]

Thus, in the early 1800s penitentiaries sprang up across the United States. These institutions were to be more than walled penal colonies; they were to form utopian societies. As such, they drew worldwide attention and eventually, worldwide imitation.

PRISONS

The first penitentiaries were established in Pennsylvania and New York, and the two were quite dissimilar in design and daily routine. The Pennsylvania pentitentiary at Cherry Hill operated on the segregate system, while the New York institution at Auburn was run on the congregate system.

Prisoners at Cherry Hill were separated not only from the larger community, but also from each other. They were housed in separate cells, each of which had an attached, individual exercise yard. What work they did per-

41. David J. Rothman, *The Discovery of the Asylum: Social Order and Disorder in the New Republic*, (Boston: Little, Brown, 1969).
42. Cesare Beccaria, *On Crimes and Punishment*, trans. Henry Paslucci, (Indianapolis: Bobbs-Merrill, 1963).

form consisted of cottage industry tasks inside the cell. However, this system had two major drawbacks. First, since food, sanitary services, work materials and everything else had to be brought by paid personnel to each cell, it was very expensive. Second, with inmates locked for years in solitary confinement, it quite literally drove them insane.[43]

The congregate system operated on a different principle. The inmates at Auburn ate and worked in groups, although strict silence was maintained. Only at night were they placed in separate cells. The advantages of this system were that it was a bit less likely to drive prisoners insane, and perhaps more importantly, congregate work was more profitable. Because one guard could lead an entire group of inmates to the dining hall or work area, the number of prison personnel needed—as well as the salaries they would have required—was significantly reduced.

For these reasons, Auburn became the prototype penitentiary in the United States. However, perhaps because it provided a closer fit with European theories of reformation through reflection, the Cherry Hill penitentiary, a failure in this country, became the model for many European penitentiaries.

During the years 1830 to 1860, when these two penitentiary systems fought it out to prove which was more useful, much of America's attention was given over to the war between the local prototypes. A new, and perhaps slightly anxious country was a bit desperate to prove to the world that it could put into practice what Europeans had only talked about. To many, the very viability of the New World was at stake.

While there was extensive debate over which form of penitentiary would best provide a combination of reform of the inmate and profit to the sponsoring authority, the one topic that was virtually never debated was whether prisons should exist in the first place. There were high hopes and high ideals that criminals could be redeemed by these inventions. It was presumed that through hard work and regular habits, all but the worst offenders could be spiritually uplifted and eventually returned to society with better attitudes and good work habits. As the very term "penitentiary" implies, while they were being punished the offenders would become penitent, repenting and seeing the error of their ways, and therefore desiring to change themselves.

As David Rothman notes, "...the bywords of all [these] institutions became order and routine, discipline and regularity, steady work and steady habits. The inmates would be provided with a new spiritual armor, so that upon release they would go forth shielded from temptations and corruptions."[44] This was the dawning of the reform era.[45]

---

43. Newman, *Introduction to Criminal Justice*, p. 330.
44. David J. Rothman, "Of Prisons, Asylums, and Other Decaying Institutions," *Public Interest*, (1971), p. 6.
45. *Ibid.*

This belief in the ability to reform offenders began to dominate American corrections. It had been preceded by a relatively brief period when jails were first employed to hold criminal offenders as penalty for their crimes. The restraint model failed on at least two main grounds. First, the jails were run primarily as "family" style institutions. Security was lax and escapes were common, and recidivism rates were high. Second, they were very expensive to run.

The reform philosophy had a longer tenure than the restraint philosophy, but the tradition of restraint has persisted even to the present. Shortly after the opening of the penitentiaries, in the middle 1820s, problems developed. Those running the new prisons forgot that the prison was a means to an end, a setting in which reform could take place. Rather, they viewed confinement as an end, equating incarceration with reformation. They reverted to the use of severe corporal punishments to keep order in the institutions. Coupled with mismanagement, this situation led to a new reform movement in the 1850s.[46]

The failure of prisons to achieve the goal of reformation was not seen as an indictment of the concept of incarcerative penalties, but as a symptom of maladministration. What the new reformers desired was a system that operated wholly on the philosophy of reform; a correctional process that rewarded reformation with release, and which protected society from the unrepentant. To this end, penologists supported conditional pardons, sentence commutation laws and other mechanisms by which well-behaved inmates could be released.

This new reform effort was spearheaded by the New York Prison Association.[47] Their efforts attained fruition with the passage of a law creating a new type of penal institution, the reformatory. This first reformatory was constructed at Elmira, New York. It was opened in 1876, and held a select population—young, first offenders. These individuals were sentenced to a term of incarceration until reformation, with the proviso that such term not exceed five years.[48] Releasing authority was placed with the Board of Managers of the reformatory, and thus discretionary parole release was born. The age of community corrections was at hand.

PROBATION AND PAROLE

Probation and parole are the "bookends" of prison. Probation is a community-based correctional alternative that is used prior to incarceration, with imprisonment imposed on those who fail to comply with the conditions of their probation. Parole, on the other hand, can only operate after some portion of an incarcerative penalty has been served. It is supervised

---

46. Rothman, *Discovery of the Asylum*, pp. 239-42.

47. *Ibid.*, p. 249-51.

48. See Edward Lindsey, *Journal of Criminal Law and Criminology*, vol. 16 (1925), pp. 9-126, for an excellent discussion of the early development of parole in America.

release from confinement to the community, and like probation, it is conditional and can be revoked for failure to comply with the constraints imposed by the releasing body.

This distinction may seem trivial. Indeed, in light of the fact that both probation and parole officers are charged with the same general obligation to protect the public and rehabilitate the offender, it may seem artificial. However, there are two very important consequences of this distinction. Probationers are under the jurisdiction of the court; parolees are responsible to the administrative body (parole board) which released them. Additionally, since probation is a pre-incarcerative penalty, and parole is post-confinement, there are substantial differences in the populations with which each must deal. Parolees are often more seriously criminal, more dangerous, than probationers.

Given these differences, it is interesting that probation and parole began almost simultaneously in America, and that the initial form of community supervision was parole. Nonetheless, community corrections was a logical outgrowth of the reform ideal. However, whether logical or not, the idea of community supervision was radical and not quickly accepted by the public.

Parole spread fairly rapidly, and was soon enacted in some form in twenty states.[49] It was not until 1944, however, that every state had a parole system. The early years of parole were full of controversy; many attacked its use on constitutional grounds, stating that it was an illegal delegation of legislative authority, an encroachment on judicial or executive powers, and a cruel and unusual form of punishment by virtue of the uncertainty of release date.[50] With very few exceptions, appellate courts rejected these arguments and the parole system was endorsed.

While unique to America, parole drew support from a number of sources, including the well-publicized "ticket of leave" systems of the Irish and English penal systems.[51] The practice of releasing juveniles under contracts of indenture, the existence of "good time" laws, and the liberal use of executive clemency all contributed to the flourishing use of parole. The most important feature of parole release, however, was its capacity to achieve the supreme goal of the restraint philosophy—the maintenance of order.[52]

Most states followed the Elmira example and placed the power to grant release in the hands of the institutional staff, who quite understandably used that power to reward good behavior in the prison, and to control rising populations. Early parolees were not subjected to much in the way of supervision, and obtained release almost as soon as they attained eligibility.[53] This

---

49. *Ibid.*, p. 40.
50. *Ibid.*, pp. 40-52.
51. *Ibid.*, pp. 9-21.
52. W.D. Lane, "A New Day Opens for Parole," *Journal of Criminal Law and Criminology*, vol. 24 (1933), p. 90.
53. *Ibid.*, p. 108.

led to a general dissatisfaction with the operation of the parole system which mirrored the public dissatisfaction which followed the resurgence of the restraint philosophy in penitentiaries some thirty to fifty years earlier. The result was the same: a retention of the basic concept of parole and some modifications within the parole system to ensure that it was operated in a manner more consistent with the reform ideal. Primarily, this was accomplished by shifting the releasing authority from institutional staff to parole boards, and by increasing emphasis on the post-release supervision of, and assistance to, parolees.

Probation, like parole, had historical antecedents in English criminal practice. Historically, friends or family of an offender could promise to supervise the activities of the criminal and pledge to restrain him from future offenses. This peace bond could then be grounds for releasing the offender from state control.

Another ancestor to probation was "Benefit of Clergy." Initially, it was a device employed to remove clerics from the jurisdiction of the secular courts. This benefit, however, was eventually extended to all literate citizens in England, and to those who could feign literacy by memorizing Psalm 55, which, because it had become so widely associated with escape from the hangman's noose, was otherwise known as "the neck verse."[54] By demonstrating an ability to read, the offender became eligible for the benefit, and thus had the opportunity to be treated leniently. Officially, the practice of probation as we know it today (that is, the supervised release of an offender to the community as an alternate means of punishment) was started in Boston during the 1880s.

The "father of probation," John Augustus, was a Boston bootmaker who took it upon himself to reform those convicted of minor offenses. He did this by posting bond for drunks and petty criminals and then carefully watching them and assisting them in becoming law-abiding, productive citizens. This pioneering step led to enactment of laws which authorized probation as a penalty, and helped to create the first paid probation officer positions.[55]

Early release on parole, or the release of convicted offenders to community supervision on probation were radical departures from the accepted practices of the time. They were not adopted without a struggle from opponents. Nonetheless, ideologically, they were congruent with the philosophy of reform.

Another factor in the favor of community supervision as a correctional technique was that it was less expensive than incarceration. Like the congregate system in prisons, community supervision gained acceptance as the balance books were inspected. This was particularly true of parole, which

---

54. Clear, *Supervising the Offender*, p. 7.
55. Alexander Smith and Louis Berlin, *Introduction to Probation and Parole*, (St. Paul, Minn.: West Publishing Co., 1976), p. 78.

was often a mechanism used when most legislatures were unwilling to appropriate enough money to build the facilities required to control large numbers of prisoners.

By the beginning of the twentieth century, the basic components of the American correctional process were operational. Over the next thirty to forty years, probation and parole were adopted by more and more states, the authority to release prisoners from incarceration became the prerogative of boards independent of prison administrations, and other modifications in the court system and within the prison walls occurred. During this period, however, the largest change was ideological.

The rehabilitative ideal emerged as the dominant correctional philosophy. The ramifications of this shift in emphasis were tremendous. Correctional workers began an all-out push for recognition as professionals, and the discretionary powers that were granted to correctional authorities grew significantly. Treatment became the dominant goal of corrections, and of criminal sentencing.

Prisons came to be compared with mental hospitals while parole authorities were seen as diagnostic experts. The role of the parole officer was more closely linked to the counseling and treating of offenders than it was to the supervision of offenders for crime control purposes. Unfortunately, not everyone made this move from control to treatment goals at the same time. While many officers were espousing a treatment goal, remnants of the older, more coercive philosophies remained. Custody is still the primary function of institutional corrections, not treatment. From the point of view of legislatures as well as the public, community supervision is mainly meant to be used to protect the community.[56] The end result of all this is a paradox, one which plagues both correctional agencies and officers today — should parole officers treat or coerce their charges?

Contributing to this paradox is the fact that corrections serves a dual purpose: offender rehabilitation or treatment, and community protection. Is it possible to coerce and to treat someone at the same time? This dilemma is characteristic of contemporary corrections, where two goals are quite often incompatible.[57] Some commentators, having examined the effect of the community protection mandate on the operation and effectiveness of correctional treatment programs, have come to the general conclusion that these two goals cannot be reconciled.[58] In fact, the general result of this double mandate has been the delegation of broad discretionary power.

---

56. G.I. Giardini, "Adult Parole," *National Probation and Parole Association Journal*, vol. 3 (1957), pp. 375-8.
57. See Donald R. Cressey, "Limitations of Organization of Treatment in a Modern Prison," *Theoretical Studies in Social Organization of the Prison*, (New York: Social Science Research Council, 1960), pp. 93-103.
58. *Ibid.*, p. 103.

While coercive control officers can be limited easily in the amount of power they use, treatment decisions can only be made properly by correctional professionals who understand criminal behavior. In order to make these decisions, they must have discretionary power to carry out their decisions.

The existence and possiblity of abuse of this vast power has led to proposals for change in the goals and functions of correctional agencies. However, legislatures and courts have refused to interfere with the activities of corrections agencies. The result is very often a debasement of the rehabilitative ideal and the imposition of punitive sanctions, with unnecessary interference in the lives of offenders, and other hidden goals being served, all in the name of rehabilitation. For example, while society, would view with alarm the idea of giving a coercive control officer the right to dictate an offender's sexual life, marriage relations, or other private affairs, it would find it much more reasonable to allow a rehabilitative officer the right to step in with some power to help the offender change his life for the better, even though this might include dictating the offender's sexual life, marriage relations or other private affairs. If the officer is a coercive control wolf in rehabilitative sheep's clothing, that officer has just gained significant control over the life of the offender; control which he or she might not have been able to obtain otherwise.

Another problem with the treatment philosophy is that it requires two basic abilities on the part of those who administer correctional programs: the ability to "cure" offenders of their criminality, and the ability to discern when that cure has occurred. The latter, more simply stated, is the ability to accurately predict the risk posed by offenders. Contemporary scholars, as will be seen later in this book, have made very persuasive arguments that the present level of technology is incapable of performing either of these functions.

In the middle 1960s, a shift away from the rehabilitation philosophy was signalled in the report of the Task Force on Corrections of the President's Commission on Law Enforcement and Administration of Justice. That report advocated a shift to a policy of reintegration wherein correctional agencies would act to create change in both the offender and also in society.[59] Rehabilitation was considered dead, particularly because it did not place enough emphasis on the effects of the social structure on crime causation. While the offender could be considered at fault for committing crimes, it was felt that some blame should also be placed on society for creating conditions which led to the creation of criminals.

In less than a decade, however, the reintegrationist philosophy began to lose force as a new dominant philosophy began to appear: the philosophy of retribution. This philosophy states that the purpose of corrections should be to punish those convicted of criminal offenses. Those who support this idea

---

59. President's Commission, *Challenge of Crime*, note 24, pp. 11-12.

argue that change, in either the offender or in society, should not be the primary goal of correctional intervention because we are not adept enough at achieving those changes to base the assignment of penalties on our abilities to change people.[60]

This is, in short, the history of American corrections. It is interesting to note that Auburn penitentiary, which was built during the period when the dominant correctional philosophy was shifting from restraint to reform, has survived the shift from reform to rehabilitation, to reintegration, and as we currently move into a retributive policy, it is still in operation. It seems apparent that, in the area of corrections at least, our institutions and practices are far more durable than our philosophies. Or, at least the succeeding generations of prison administrators have been exceptionally adept at rolling with the punches of changing philosophies, managing to integrate the new policies into their operational procedure with minimal change. Thus, while the old penitentiary with its punitive warden ordering men to the disciplinary "hole" no longer exists, we find it replaced (although the physical facilities are still the same) by a correctional institution with a correctional superintendent ordering men to the disciplinary "behavior adjustment center." While we have generally rid the system of guards who attempt to force reform on the convict, we still have correctional officers who act as "change agents" for the "correctional client." It has been suggested that many prison administrators learned to love the rehabilitative philosophy when they discovered that the added discretionary powers it brought allowed them greater leeway in administering punishments in the name of therapy.

Hopefully, this brief examination of the development of corrections in America has lent some credence to Martinson's comment: "The history of corrections is a graveyard of abandoned fads."[61]

THE STRUCTURE OF AMERICAN CORRECTIONS

One of the supposed merits of the federalist system of government is that states are permitted to develop and run their own affairs, allowing not only for changes to meet local needs and desires, but also to do local experimentation without first obtaining the permission of the national bureaucracy. In most countries, a national agency runs the corrections system (indeed, police, courts, and virtually every phase of criminal justice work is run nationally), but under the American system, each state develops its own laws, facilities, and operating procedures. Many of these states have allowed local governments to create some of their own laws, courts, police departments, jails or community-based corrections. The only national control is that our federal courts occasionally insist that these local laws and facilities obey the mandates of the U. S. Constitution and a few national laws (such as those

---

60. See Andrew von Hirsch, *Doing Justice*, (New York: Hill and Wang, 1976).

61. Robert Martinson, "California Research at the Crossroads," *Crime and Delinquency*, vol. 22, no. 2 (April 1976), p. 181.

relating to the interstate transportation of prison industry products). Also, the courts will occasionally require local facilities to adhere to some federal standard in order to win federal grants.

The result of this system is what the National Advisory Commission on Criminal Justice Standards and Goals termed a "balkanization" of governmental agencies involved in corrections. In their 1973 publication, *Report on Corrections*, the commission noted that this balkanization "complicates police planning, impedes development of expeditious court processes, and divides responsibility for convicted offenders among a multiplicity of overlapping but barely intercommunicating agencies. The organizational structure of the criminal justice system was well suited to the frontier society in which it was implanted. It has survived in a complex, mobile, urban society for which it is grossly unsuited."[62]

Without getting involved in the argument as to whether "state's rights" or federal or state coordinated facilities are best, it is still possible to simply describe the fact that generalizations about the American corrections system are extremely difficult at best. There are, depending upon how you count them, at least fifty-two correctional systems, including the fifty states, the federal system, and the District of Columbia system. A simple and intelligent question, then, such as "Do the guards receive adequate training?" might properly receive an answer such as "Sixteen—yes, twenty-one—no, fifteen—sometimes or undecided." Admittedly, then, it is a difficult task to be a student or teacher of American corrections, for the answer to almost any question must be understood to apply, at best, only "most of the time." This warning should be carried in mind and thought of when discussing virtually any point of concern. In American corrections, exceptions do not make the rule. They *are* the rule.

PROBATION

Probation, as we have learned, most commonly means being sentenced to community-based supervision *instead of* prison or jail. Even this simple definition becomes complicated by such new innovations as "shock probation," where some jurisdictions give judges the power to sentence offenders to a short term in a local jail, to be followed by a longer term of probation. Another rule of thumb has been that probation can be differentiated from parole because probation is locally run, usually by county governments, while parole is usually state-run, often by the same Department of Corrections agency that runs the state prisons. While this may have been useful in the past it is less useful today, especially in those cases where the state government has stepped in to take partial or full control of local probation in order to standardize services across the state.

However, it can be stated that the sentence to probation supervision is available as an option to the judge for some offenders in all fifty-two

---

62. National Advisory Commission on Criminal Justice Standards and Goals, *Task Force Report on Corrections*, (Washington, D.C.: U.S. Government Printing Office, 1973), p. 11.

jurisdictions in the United States. In fact, it accounts for perhaps as much as 70% of all sentences imposed in this country, not including fines. A recent survey revealed that as of September 1, 1976 a total of 1,251,918 persons were under probation supervision across the country.[63] Of this total, 328,854 were juveniles.[64] The majority of probationers were adult males, with females comprising only 14% of the total adult probation caseload.[65] Probationers are split almost evenly between misdemeanants and felons. The usual differentiation between a misdemeanor and a felony is that a misdemeanor is a crime punishable by, *at most*, a year in a local jail, while a felony is a crime punishable by probation or *more* than a year's sentence in a state prison. This distinction can serve only as a broad generalization, however, since a particular crime—say larceny of $75—may be a misdemeanor in one state and a felony in another. Other fine-line differences between states can further complicate the matter. For example, a misdemeanor may have a longer or shorter maximum sentence attached, dependent upon the state. Even the fact that 328,854 of the probationers in the above survey were juveniles must be weighed carefully. For example, a seventeen-year-old may be an adult, in one state a juvenile in another, and in a third he may be either a juvenile or an adult, dependent upon a judge's determination of which court would be the proper place to try this particular youth.

No matter how you read these statistics, it is obvious that the lion's share of the entire correctional caseload is carried by probation agencies. However, these agencies may have very different organizational structures. For example, within each jurisdiction, the probation agency might be centrally funded and operated, as it is in twenty-seven of the fifty-two jurisdictions. Under this model, the state would have a state-wide probation service, just as the federal government runs its probation system on a national basis. In another twenty-two jurisdictions, there is local administrative control, tempered by the state, which controls much of the funding and has some power to set standards.[66] For example, the state might require a certain academic degree or a certain score on a civil service examination before the local government can appoint a probation officer. In the three remaining jurisdictions, the adult probation system is operated exclusively by local governments.

This split is also reflected in the juvenile probation field, with twenty states controlling juvenile probation, twenty-one other states where the state and local governments share the power, and ten states where the local governments exclusively run juvenile probation.[67] The major difference to be seen between adult and juvenile probation is that the courts directly operate

---

63. United States Department of Justice, *State and Local Probation and Parole Systems*, (Washington, D.C.: U.S. Government Printing Office, 1978), p. 1.
64. *Ibid.*, p. 3.
65. *Ibid.*
66. *Ibid.*, p. 6.
67. *Ibid.*, p. 103.

adult probation in seven states, while the judiciary controls juvenile probation in twenty-five states.[68]

While by definition, probation agencies are directly charged with field supervision of probationers, these same agencies are called upon to conduct pre-sentence investigations, and operate release-on-recognizance programs as well as juvenile intake programs. Although probation is usually considered a correctional function of the criminal justice system, these other services are important to remember because they are not strictly correctional services. Rather, they are programs operated for the convenience and aid of the courts. Thus, not only do probation agencies have the largest percentage of the total correctional caseload, but they also engage, on a part-time basis, in pre-sentence and pre-trial programs as well.

PAROLE

There are two distinct functions involved in parole: the granting of release from the correctional institution into the community, and then the supervision of those people so released. While previously, every state had both of these functions in their parole systems, there has been a slow process in recent years for some states to abolish one or both of these parole functions.

On May 1, 1976, the state of Maine became the first state to abolish parole release and supervision.[69] However, the parole board was retained in Maine to deal with those offenders sentenced to prison prior to that date. Since that time, six more states have passed legislation to eliminate discretionary parole release for most, and eventually all, offenders.[70] No other state, however, has taken the step of abolishing parole supervision.

Where it exists, parole is a function of the executive branch of government, and is operated exclusively at the state level, (except, of course, for the federal system which is operated at the national level). In some jurisdictions, however, the parole board has the power to grant early release to misdemeanants incarcerated in local jails as well as to those felons in state prisons. In seven states, the authority to grant parole to local jail inmates is vested in both the executive and judicial branches.[71]

Parole release from prison is an extremely important part of the system in those states where it exists. In fact, release on parole accounted for approximately 69% of all releases from prison in the United States in 1976, with an estimated population of over 173,000 on parole on December 31, 1976.[72] As can be seen, the parole population is substantially smaller than the proba-

---

68. *Ibid.*, p. 104.

69. Maine Revised Statutes, Annotated, Title 17-A, Secs. 1251-1254.

70. Those states are California, Colorado, Illinois, Indiana, New Mexico, and Alaska.

71. Department of Justice, *Probation and Parole Systems*, p. 104.

72. James Galvin et al., *Parole in the United States: 1976 and 1977*, (San Francisco: National Council on Crime and Delinquency, 1978), p. 6.

tion population. This is because, by definition, parole requires that an offender be sentenced to incarceration first, and even then, parole release is not granted to all offenders in prison.

In some correctional systems, the same officers supervise both probationers and parolees. Some agencies are responsible not only for the supervision of both probationers and parolees, but also for the supervision of juveniles and adults. Juvenile parolees numbered approximately 53,000 in 1976, bringing the total community supervision population to about 1.5 million.[73] Of all of those under parole supervision, roughly 10% are females.[74] Two things must be kept in mind about this deceptively small percentage: 1) that in order to be granted parole, an offender must first be incarcerated and 2) that relatively few females are incarcerated.

In September 1976, community supervision staff totalled 33,248, making a staff/client ratio of 1:48.[75] Less than 5% of probation and parole staff are part-time, but an interesting statistic is that these 33,248 professional staff members are supplemented by approximately 20,000 volunteers, the overwhelming majority of whom assist in the counseling of offenders.[76]

INCARCERATION

The least important segment of the correctional system, in terms of the number of "clients" under its control, is incarceration. There are two main categories of places of confinement: jails and prisons. For the juvenile system, the equivalent of adult prisons would be training schools, while the equivalent of adult jails would be juvenile detention centers. However, while adult jails hold inmates who are awaiting adjudication or sentencing, (just like juvenile detention centers do), jails are also places where some convicted misdemeanant offenders are held to serve their sentences, (whereas detention centers are not intended for the serving of sentences). Just to complicate things a little there are some jails which hold both adults and juveniles.

JAILS

Jails are a unique combination of the functions of many different types of institutions. By far, jails hold more people in any given year than prisons or training schools (sometimes called reform schools). Because of this, and the eclectic character of the inmate populations of jails, these institutions face a set of problems that are perhaps more pressing, and less easily resolved than most of the other problems encountered in the entire corrections system.

A 1972 survey of the nation's jails revealed that there were 3,921 local jails in operation at that date, with a combined population of approximately

---

73. Department of Justice, *Probation and Parole Systems*, p. 30.
74. *Ibid.*, p. 3.
75. *Ibid.*, p. 78.
76. *Ibid.*, p. 3.

141,000.[77] This type of survey is not often done, as it is an extremely difficult task. It might seem easy, to the outsider, to just count up the number of jails we have and find out how many people are locked up in them. Surely, a data-based society might ask, isn't there a computer somewhere that can simply print out this information? Unfortunately, since these are state and locally run institutions, this information is somewhat harder to obtain. Jails open and close regularly, and all too often authorities on the local level are barely aware of how many inmates they have on hand. Under these circumstances, state governments rarely know what the local authorities are doing, and there are no national figures which establish precisely how many people are locked up annually.

Further, the jail population figure just quoted, of 141,000 in 1972, does not include those "lock-ups" commonly found in police stations where suspects are detained to await processing and interrogation. In addition, that figure is only the number of persons held on one specific day. Since local jails have a rather high turnover rate—people commonly serve fairly short sentences—these local jails may well house over one million people each year.[78]

The jail populations are quite mixed, with over half of those incarcerated in jails awaiting trial or some other judicial action. Jail inmates are predominantly male, young and poor. Only 5% of jail inmates are female, and about 60% of all inmates are under 30 years old.[79] Blacks are disproportionately represented among jail populations, comprising 42% of all inmates. Nearly one-half of all jail inmates have not graduated from high school.[80]

While there are a variety of recreational, social and rehabilitative programs offered in local jails, not all jails offer these programs. Even where they are offered, only about 10% of all jail inmates participate in them.[81] The majority of local jails, at the time of the survey, held fewer than twenty-one inmates, with nearly 60% of these jails being located in buildings that also served as courthouses or law enforcement offices.[82]

Thus, local jails have two major characteristics that stand in the way of improving jail conditions. First, it is quite difficult to establish and justify costly programs for inmates. Since there is a high turnover of population, offenders are often not there long enough to take part in useful programs. Further, a large proportion of the jail population have not been convicted yet of

---

77. United States Department of Justice, *The Nation's Jails*, (Washington, D.C.: U.S. Government Printing Office, 1975), p. 1.

78. Newman, *Introduction to Criminal Justice*, p. 326.

79. U.S. Department of Justice, *Survey of Inmates of Local Jails: Advance Report*, (Washington, D.C.: U.S. Government Printing Office, 1974), p. 1.

80. *Ibid.*, p. 3.

81. *Ibid.*, p. 9.

82. Department of Justice, *The Nation's Jails*.

any crime, so it is even more difficult to create programs for them. Can you require someone to enter a rehabilitation program if that person is still "innocent until proven guilty?" What's more, since so many jails are small, or located in a portion of a major urban building, there are often no facilities to run programs of any sort. With less than twenty-one inmates in a jail located inside a courthouse, for example, even if one could locate a gym facility, there might not be enough volunteers to allow a basketball game, let alone a major reformation program.

A second problem is that most of these jails are locally run. Thus, they must compete with other necessary services for the few tax dollars available from often very limited tax bases. With such problems in urban areas as mandated tax limits, tax cutting Proposition 13 mandates, bankrupt or semibankrupt cities, and a high priority placed by local citizens on maintaining services that directly affect them, such as garbage collection and street cleaning, there is usually very little left over to finance local jails properly.

These two problems may explain the fact that while deplorable conditions in jails have often been reported, little progress has been made to reform them.[83] Complaints of inedible food, bug and rodent-infested facilities, lack of recreation—in fact lack of anything except lockup—are common, and remain common.

PRISONS AND REFORMATORIES

The part of the correctional process which touches the smallest number of convicted offenders is incarceration in prison or reformatories. However, while by comparison the numbers involved may not be very large, the impact of incarceration is tremendous. The prison is the equivalent of punishment in the public eye. It is in the prison that the full weight of the coercive power of the state is pressed on the criminal offender.

As noted previously, prisons are an American idea, and an idea which was adopted in a big way. Over 50% of all offenders are held in this country's many mammoth-like institutions which hold over 1,000 inmates each. Further, nearly half are in institutions which were constructed over fifty years ago, with fully one-third being held in facilities built at least a century ago.[84] On June 30, 1977, the number of inmates in American prisons was estimated at 283,433. For comparison, the rated capacity of all American prisons was at that time determined to be about 260,000, (which means that in 1977 there was nationwide overcrowding of at least 20,000 prison inmates).[85] This figure does not include an estimated additional 10,000 prisoners being held

---

83. Sanford Bates, *Prisons and Beyond*, (New York: Macmillan Co., 1936), p. 38; F.E. Miller, *Jail Management—Problems, Programs, and Perspectives*, (Lexington, Mass.: Lexington Books, 1978).

84. Rutherford et al., *Prison Population and Policy Choices—Volume 1: Preliminary Report to Congress*, (Washington, D.C.: National Institute of Law Enforcement and Criminal Justice, 1978), p. 97.

85. *Ibid.*, p. 107.

in local jails because overcrowded prisons did not have room for them or because they were in work-release programs or for any other number of reasons.[86] Of course, national figures do not adequately represent overcrowding since different states have different problems. One prison might be slightly under capacity, while another may be bedding down inmates in hospital rooms, corridors, and tents erected in the recreation yard.

Of those persons in prison, 4% are female,[87] 47% are black,[88] and well over half are under 30 years old.[89] Approximately two-thirds of prison inmates were convicted by pleas of guilty, and one-third of prison inmates were incarcerated for property offenses.[90] The largest single offense category for which persons were sentenced to prison was that of robbery, which accounted for 23% of all such commitments in 1974.[91]

Prisons and reformatories are usually operated by state governments, and have homogeneous populations in the sense that most inmates are young felons. However, very few juveniles are held in state prisons, and all have been convicted of crimes. Unlike local jails, prisons are normally sex-segregated, and usually more rehabilitative and recreational programs are offered to prison inmates than to inmates in local jails. To some degree, this is because prison inmates are serving enough time to afford to become seriously involved in a recreational or rehabilitative program. Further, prisons are usually large enough that even a limited-interest program might have enough of a turnout to make its operation worthwhile.

Prisons can be classified according to the level of security afforded. There are usually three categories offered: maximum, medium and minimum security institutions. Maximum security institutions are generally surrounded by an eighteen to twenty-five foot wall, with interior cell blocks and very strict regulations regarding the movement of prisoners inside the institution. An illustrative copy of regulations for a maximum security prison is included at the end of this section.

Medium and minimum security institutions are usually not walled. Alternative types of housing are available, such as rooms, or dormitories, rather than individual cells. While medium security institutions are typically enclosed by a double fence which is topped with barbed wire, the tall guard towers and heavily armed perimeter security guards, (the hallmarks of the maximum security institution), are generally not present. Minimum security institutions are normally not enclosed by a fence, and little in the way of restrictions on movement inside the institution is required. Minimum secur-

---

86. *Ibid.*, p. 88.
87. U.S. Department of Justice, *Survey of Inmates of State Correctional Facilities, 1974: Advance Report*, (Washington, D.C.: National Prisoner Statistics, 1976).
88. *Ibid.*
89. *Ibid.*
90. *Ibid.*, p. 8.
91. *Ibid.*, p. 28.

ity facilities are normally located in rural areas, as most of them are forestry camps or farms. It may be that walls and fences are unnecessary, as there may be no place to escape to. However, it is rather doubtful that geographic location has much to do with the layout of minimum security institutions, especially in light of the fact that, because of historical precedent (a desire to escape the evils of the city), high urban land values, and the lobbying of rural state legislators who desire jobs for their constituents, most maximum security prisons are also located in rural areas.

The percentage of prison inmates who are in maximum security institutions, as opposed to lesser security institutions, varies by state and region, with the country's smallest percentage of maximum security inmates (32%) being held in the federal system. This 32% figure may reflect the federal government's heavy involvement in so-called white collar crimes, such as smuggling, drug sales, interstate transport of stolen items, or other crimes where the offender is unlikely to engage in personal violence. The highest percentage of offenders in maximum security can be found in the North Central region of the country, (where the estimates reach as high as 59%, in comparison with the national average which totals about 44%).[92]

Of these maximum security institutions, most of those in operation were built over 50 years ago, while most of the minimum security institutions were built fairly recently.[93] However, the maximum security institutions tend to be quite large; some insist they are properly termed "mega-prisons." Thus, many inmates classified as requiring only minimum security have found no room available in those institutions, and have ended up instead in the maximum security monoliths.[94]

THE PROBLEMS OF INSUFFICIENT DATA

By summing the totals of those persons subject to the supervision of community corrections agencies with those incarcerated in local jails and prisons, a rough estimate of the total correctional population can be established. Approximately 1.5 million adults are under some form of correctional intervention in the United States on any given day. By far, the majority of these are on probation, with community supervision accounting for approximately 70% of the total correctional population.

The overwhelming majority of those under correctional supervision of all kinds are male and poor, with females being rather underrepresented, accounting for only about 12% of the total correctional population, and about 5% of the incarcerated population. The percentage of blacks has steadily increased, to the point where they now account for slightly less than half of all inmates.[95]

---

92. Rutherford, *Prison Population*, p. 96.

93. *Ibid.*

94. *Ibid.*, pp. 94-96.

95. Margaret Cahalan, "Trends in Incarceration in the United States since 1880," *Crime and Delinquency*, vol. 25 (January 1979), p. 39.

What is perhaps the most important fact that can be gleaned from the prior discussion is that existing data is woefully inadequate. It was necessary to report 1972 data in order to obtain an overview of jail populations.[96] It is virtually impossible to present data, as there is little available, on such questions as how many inmates are released from prison because their sentences have expired (rather than because they have been paroled), or about jurisdictions which do not have provisions for the supervision of inmates released at their "good time" dates.

However, the fact that some data was presented and obtainable gives promise that in the future the extent of our ignorance will be diminished. Data on commitment offenses, sentence type and the like is difficult to secure because of variations in definitions of those terms across jurisdictions. Some notable efforts to collect national level data have begun and should bear some fruit in the future.[97]

What does exist is information on specific programs or specific correctional components in certain states. A plethora of correctional program evaluations and descriptions have been published in the criminal justice scholarly literature. Many state and local correctional agencies publish descriptive statistics in annual reports, and a few large scale research studies gather national-level data.

USES OF DATA AND RESISTANCE TO DATA COLLECTION

The two basic types of decisions made by correctional administrators are: 1) management decisions, in which the allocation of scarce resources is determined; and 2) evaluations, in which the relative utility of operations is assessed with an eye towards increasing the benefits that may be derived from expending resources.

Of the two, management information is the most easily available, as a matter of practical necessity. Prison administrators must know how many inmates are confined in order to ensure sufficient food, beds, clothing and security forces. Likewise, probation administrators must know how many probationers are under supervision and how many presentence reports must be written in order to assign staff persons to perform these functions.

This type of information is particularly important in supporting requests for increased budget appropriations, and the retention of resources already on hand, or "system maintenance." Knowing that the prison is filled to capacity allows the prison administrator to ask for increased staff and perhaps the building of a new institution. Knowing that probation caseloads are increasing would be of similar help to the probation administrator.

---

96. The U.S. Bureau of the Census, and the National Criminal Justice Information and Statistics Service are currently conducting another survey of local jails.

97. See Carl E. Pope, *Offender Based Transaction Statistics: New Directions in Data Collection and Reporting*, (Washington, D.C.: U.S. Department of Justice, 1975).

The more important information, however, may well be that which is used for evaluation decisions. This is information relevant to program goals. This requires monitoring the outcome of correctional programs and practices and testing alternatives. By comparing observed outcomes with desired results, the administrator is able to recognize where change is needed, and where the status quo should not be disturbed. Perhaps the most well-publicized example of this type of information and decision-making is the evaluation of correctional treatment programs.

Evaluative information is more difficult to obtain than management information for a number of reasons, primary among them being that, implied in any evaluation, (if not explicitly stated), is a definition of success or failure. To the degree that a given agency or program fails to achieve its goals, it is open to attack. Evaluative information is ammunition for correctional staffs and administrators that want to make policy decisions, but it is also ammunition for critics who wish to attack those policy decisions and the people who made them.

Beyond this rather dangerous side effect of information gathering, data collection involves a great deal of work. To the extent that evaluative information is not crucial to the daily operation of the agency, the collection of such information can be viewed as an unnecessary burden. There exists, therefore, an understandable resistance to data collection.

As a result of these inadequate data bases, planning and evaluation of correctional programs or policies on a state or national level is both difficult and hazardous.[98] It will probably take years to develop data bases large enough and old enough to address some basic problem areas. A look at two of these problem areas (the American use of incarceration and our present treatment of female offenders) follows:

USE OF INCARCERATION

It often comes as quite a shock to Americans to learn that in addition to inventing the prison system, we are also perhaps the world's leader in using it. Americans tend to consider themselves rather more civilized than most of the world, and commonly believe that this sophistication results in a reduced use of prisons.[99] However, what research has been done tends to support the contention that American incarceration sentences are the longest in the world, and that we use incarceration more frequently than other societies.[100] One recent study suggests that, despite some fluctuations the American rate of incarceration has increased dramatically over the past one hundred years.[101] If

---

98. See Rutherford, *Prison Population*, pp. 5-6.
99. Eugene Doleschal, "Crime—Some Popular Briefs," *Crime and Delinquency*, vol. 25 (January 1979), p. 3.
100. Eugene Doleschal, "Rate and Length of Imprisonment," *Crime and Delinquency*, vol. 23 (January 1977), pp. 51-56.
101. Cahalan, "Trends in Incarceration," pp. 9-41.

we accept this data, and assume that prison sentences in America are more frequently imposed and lengthier than those in other countries, there is still not enough adequate prior data for one to make comparisons to the use of incarceration in America's past.

An example of insubstantial data may be found in the now fairly old argument that suggests that the adoption of the indeterminate sentence would decrease the amount of time inmates would be forced to serve before release. The feeling was that under a determinate sentencing structure, inmates were given appropriately lengthy sentences. But, by going to a sentence which was indeterminate or partially indeterminate, it was feared that sentence lengths would drop. Since an indeterminate sentence is one that allows the prison authorities to either keep the inmate for a long period of time, or to let the inmate be released if rehabilitated, deterred, or able to meet whatever other standards are set by the authorities, many were afraid that a lenient parole board would let hordes of inmates go free into the community long before they would have otherwise been released if they had received a definite determinate sentence from the judge.

The data that does exist on this subject comes mostly from very old comparisons made by persons trying to justify adoption of the indeterminate sentence. In order to pacify fears that parole was nothing more than institutionalized leniency, these studies tended to show that the indeterminate sentence actually caused inmates to serve longer sentences on the average. It was demonstrated that the parole board did not have to let the inmate go on the release date, but could keep the inmate in longer if no signs of rehabilitation or reform were shown. At the very best, the results of these old studies should be accepted with a great deal of caution.

This lack of historical data is especially important today, as many jurisdictions are adopting new penal codes with radically different penalty structures. The past decade has been a busy one for state legislatures in reforming penal codes. A growing number of mandatory sentence laws are being passed annually, and as has been noted, a number of states are moving away from indeterminate sentencing and parole to definite terms of imprisonment. The lack of detailed historical data makes it nearly impossible to ascertain the likely effects of such legislation on future prison populations, court processing, and other correctional programming.

Information on the characteristics of inmates is very difficult to obtain on a national level. Demographic variables such as age, race, sex and marital status are often easier to obtain, and probably more reliable than information regarding educational level, time served, prior record and substance abuse history. One of the reasons this data is so difficult to obtain is because the process of collecting such information is costly.

The age of the computer is upon us, however, and that fact has probably done more for the initiation of routine data collection and reporting by correctional agencies than all of the urgings of various commissions, panels, and scholars who have sought such information over the years. The utilization of computer technology for record-keeping and planning purposes by various criminal justice agencies has had the side effect of developing fairly substantial data sets in many jurisdictions. However, before computer technology is fully adopted on a national basis, the benefits must outweigh the costs. Many correctional agencies are still not making use of computerized information systems because their relatively small populations do not justify the expense.

The end result of this economic reality is that small agencies and small states are often overlooked in research. Data collection is too time-consuming to be cost-effective in those small probation agencies or prison systems while computer readable data, stored on magnetic tapes, is more easily available from some larger states. This problem arises particularly when certain types of inmates are the focus of the study.

FEMALE OFFENDERS

As was noted above, females make up a very small percentage of the total correctional population. Therefore, they are often ignored in large-scale studies of correctional programming, and reports on the correctional process.[102] The resulting lack of information about female offenders further obscures their significance, with the result that they are very often treated as an "afterthought" in a process almost entirely concerned with males. They are a group not often considered in planning; in actuality, they are a forgotten class of offenders.[103]

The historical neglect of women as an offender group and an identifiable component of the correctional population has received a great deal of attention recently.[104] The status of women in corrections, as both subjects of correctional intervention and correctional staff, is beginning to be examined. Almost invariably, the existing data is not adequate for research purposes, and a great deal of time must be spent on data collection before any analysis can be made.

As an example, there is currently a belief that more women will be sentenced to longer periods of incarceration in the future because more women are beginning to be arrested for serious crimes. The reason for this apparent rise in female criminality is unknown, but many observers feel it is the result of generally more equal treatment of males and females brought about by the women's movement.[105] For example, it might be argued that as more women are being taught to be aggressive or assertive, or to take responsibility for financial affairs, it is only natural that a certain percentage of them will turn to criminal methods in order to carry out this assertiveness or

---

102. See Rita J. Simon, *The Contemporary Woman and Crime*, (Washington, D.C.: National Institute of Mental Health, 1975), pp. 64-65.

103. *Ibid.*, p. 64; and Ray R. Price, "The Forgotten Female Offender," *Crime and Delinquency*, vol. 23 (1977), pp. 104-105.

104. Simon, *Contemporary Woman and Crime*, pp. 64-65; Price, *Forgotten Female Offender*, pp. 104-105; F. Adler, *Sisters in Crime*, (New York: McGraw-Hill, 1975).

105. Price, *Forgotten Female Offender*, pp. 102-103.

financial responsibility. Another argument has been made that women in the past have benefitted from sexism in this one aspect of society, with judges commonly assuming that a tender young lady could not possibly be as bad as the arresting officer claimed. There are certainly numerous examples of man/woman crime teams that found the man sentenced to prison because he "had to be" the brains or muscle behind the crime, while the woman either had the charges dismissed or received a light sentence.[106]

Whatever the theory, the current available data does not signal an increase in the percentage of women being incarcerated. Unfortunately, this data does not allow an examination of incarceration rates for women over a very long period of time, so this is at best a tentative conclusion.[107]

It will probably take years to develop a data base large enough to permit a sophisticated statistical examination of changes in the rate and type of female criminality, and in the justice system's response to female crime. Similarly, in most jurisdictions the number of women offenders is far too small to allow for the application of advanced statistical techniques as a means of studying factors associated with recidivism. This means that evaluation of the impact of supposedly rehabilitative programs for women must wait until a sufficiently large number of women have passed through these programs—only then will researchers have enough information to draw on for their statistical analyses.

Given the current extent (or lack) of our knowledge about women as an offender group, if female criminality is indeed on the rise, and more females are subjected to correctional intervention in the future, the correctional system will probably not be prepared to deal with them. The result will probably be unintended and unnecessary suffering by convicted female offenders at the hands of a correctional system which was supposed to help them, not hurt them further.

---

106. See Gail Armstrong, "Females Under the Law—'Protected' but Unequal," *Crime and Delinquency*, vol. 23 (1977), pp. 109-120.

107. Simon, *Contemporary Woman and Crime*, p. 69. It is worth noting, as an aside, that there have been some serious questions raised as to whether there has even been an increase in female crime rates, especially in violent or occupationally-related crimes. There is good reason to believe that all of the increase in female crime has come in petty crimes, totally unrelated to any changes in the conditions of women in this country, and that much of the argument to the contrary has come from a misunderstanding and a misuse of the available data. See, for example, Darrell J. Steffensmeier, "Sex Differences in Patterns of Adult Crime, 1965-1977: A Review and Assessment," paper presented at the 1979 annual meeting of the National Institute of Crime and Delinquency, Hartford, Conn. (June, 1979).

Indiana Prison Rules

SECTION II

Prohibited Acts:

101. Homicide.
102. Committing an assault or an assault and battery upon any person.
103. Fighting with another person.
104. Threatening another with bodily harm or with any offense against his person or property.
105. Extortion, blackmail, protection: demanding or receiving money or anything of value In return for protection against others, to avoid bodily harm, or under threat of Informing.
106. Escape.
107. Attempting to escape, or hiding out to effect an escape.
108. Engaging in sexual acts with another.
109. Making sexual proposals or threats to another.
110. Indecent exposure.
111. Wearing a disguise or mask.
112. Simulating a person (dummy).
113. Setting a fire without authorization.
114. Destroying, altering, or damaging state property, or the property of another.
115. Stealing (theft).
116. Tampering with, altering, or blocking any locking device.
117. Unauthorized alteration of any food or drink.
118. Possession or introduction of an explosive or any ammunition or literature or plans regarding same.
119. Possession or introduction of a gun, pistol, shotgun, zip gun, sling shot, revolver, knife, dagger, dirk, sword, machine gun, rifle, or other dangerous or deadly weapon or literature or plans regarding same.
120. Unauthorized possession or introduction of any device capable of being used as a weapon.
121. Possession of property belonging to another person.
122. Possession of money or currency, unless specifically authorized.
123. Possession, introduction, or use of any unauthorized narcotic, narcotic paraphernalia, drug, intoxicant, or substance controlled pursuant to the law of this state.
124. Misuse of unauthorized medication.
125. Possession of anything not authorized for retention or receipt by inmates, and not issued to the individual inmate through regular institution channels.
126. Possession of any officer's or staff clothing.
127. Possession of unauthorized clothing.
128. Loaning of property or anything of value for profit or increased return.
129. Mutilation or unauthorized alteration of clothing issued by the state.

130. Rioting.
131. Encouraging others to riot.
132. Engaging in, or encouraging others to engage in, a group demonstration.
133. Refusing to work or accept a work or program assignment.
134. Encouraging others to refuse to work or participate in a work stoppage.
135. Refusing to obey an order from any staff member.
136. Violating any rule, regulation, or condition associated with temporary leaves.
137. Violating any institutional rule, regulation, or standing order if said rule, regulation, or standing order has been communicated to the inmate.
138. Unexcused absence from work or any assignment.
139. Failing to perform work as instructed by a supervisor.
140. Insolence, vulgarity, or profanity toward staff.
141. Lying or providing a false statement to a staff member.
142. Counterfeiting, forging, or unauthorized reproduction of any document, article of identification, money, pass, security, or official paper.
143. Participating in any unauthorized meeting or gathering.
144. Being in an unauthorized area.
145. Failure to follow safety or sanitation regulations.
146. Using any equipment or machinery unless specifically authorized to do so.
147. Using any equipment or machinery contrary to instructions or posted standards.
148. Failing to stand count.
149. Interfering with the taking of count.
150. Making intoxicants.
151. Being intoxicated or under the influence of any unauthorized drug or intoxicating substance.
152. Smoking where prohibited.
153. Using abusive or obscene language.
154. Gambling.
155. Preparing or conducting a gambling pool.
156. Possession of unauthorized gambling paraphernalia.
157. Being unsanitary or untidy; failing to keep one's person or one's quarters in accordance with published standards.
158. Tattooing or self-mutilation.
159. Unauthorized use of mail or telephone.
160. Correspondence or conduct with a visitor in violation of regulations.
161. Unauthorized contacts with the public.
162. Entering into a contact without approval of the institution head or persons designated by the institution head to grant such approval.
163. Giving or offering a bribe or anything of value to a staff member.
164. Giving money or anything of value to, or

accepting same from, any person without proper authority.

165. Obstructing a cell door.

166. Any unauthorized removal, transfer, or relocation of state property or the property of another.

167. Physically resisting or fleeing a staff member in the performance of his duty.

168. Unauthorized operation of a motor vehicle.

169. Disorderly Conduct: fighting or tumultuous and violent conduct, making unreasonable noise, disturbing any lawful assembly of persons, or otherwise disturbing the peace and quiet, security, or orderly running of the institution or other area in which the inmate is located.

170. Attempting to commit any of the above offenses; aiding, commanding, inducing, counseling, or procuring another person to commit any of the above offenses; or making plans with another to commit any of the above offenses shall be considered the same as a commission of the offense itself.

Belgian Prison Rules

1. — PRACTICAL LIFE OF THE PRISONERS

A. Time-table of the day.

The time-table of the day is printed on the document you received when you came in.

When reveille sounds, the prisoners get up, dress and put their room in orderly fashion.

At bed-time, they make their bed, take their clothes off and go to bed.

They take all useful steps in order that the forecasted activities should take place normally and without delay.

B. Discipline and duties of the prisoners.

As well as in any kind of establishment the prisoners must keep some disciplinary rules, for the maintenance of order and for the good working of the services.

Here are those rules:

1) The staff must be respected and his commands quickly and indisputably executed. Politeness is a mark of good education. When a staff-member enters the cell, the good-mannered prisoner stands up, behaves himself, bares his head, takes his cigarette or pipe out of his mouth if he is smoking and keeps silence.

2) Crying and singing are unsuitable with the life in a cell; they cannot be allowed.

3) Smoking in the cell is permitted during the hereafter said time:
....
....
....

4) Climbing up the furniture to look through the window or touching the window without authorization of a staff-member is forbidden.

5) Touching the door-closing system and the light installation is also forbidden.

6) Nothing shall be placed against the wall in front of the door of the cell.

7) Walls must remain clean: writing on a wall is forbidden. Authorized pictures, reproductions, prints, drawings, etc., must be fixed on the therefore designed board only, or put on a piece of furniture.

8) Knives, razors, electric torches, bank-notes, money, credit-papers, identification papers, jewels or other valuable objects may not be kept by the prisoners, except with a special authorization of the director.

9) The cell itself, its furniture and all the objects that are in the cell must be maintained in good condition. The prisoner who is responsible for destruction or deterioration will be punished. Self-respect asks for order and tidiness.

10) A strict cleanness on body and for the clothes is also requested.

The prisoners must be shaved; beard and whiskers are allowed only by the director; the hair must be cut short.

11) In any place they stand, the prisoners shall avoid to do something against good manners. For instance, it is forbidden to lay on bed during the day.

12) When they leave the cell, the prisoners shall be correctly dressed and shall behave irreproachably: buttoned up coat, hands out of the pockets, etc.

13) In the ranks, the prisoners shall march in step, at some distance of each other. Everybody must keep silence, remain at the same place in the rank and strictly comply with the given orders.

14) Nothing may be accepted from lawyers or from other visitors. To avoid any difficulty, the prisoner who goes to the lawyers-parlour or to the visiting-room shall have nothing with him: no cigarettes, no tobacco, etc.

Without special authorization of the director, the prisoners are not allowed to give whatever to anyone.

15) Sales, exchanges, gifts, loans and other similar operations between prisoners are always a cause of difficulties. Therefore thay are not allowed.

16) The prisoners shall not leave the workshops, refectories or other meeting-rooms without the authorization of the guardian.

SELECTED BIBLIOGRAPHY

Else, John F., and Stephenson, Keith D. "Vicarious Expiation: A Theory of Prison and Social Reform." *Crime and Delinquency*, vol. 20, no. 4 (October 1974).

Gottfredson, Don M.; Wilkins, Leslie T.; and Hoffman, Peter B. *Guidelines for Parole and Sentencing: A Policy Control Method*. Lexington, Mass.: D.C. Heath and Company, 1978.

Gottfredson, Don M.; Wilkins, Leslie T.; Hoffman, Peter B.; and Singer, Susan M. *The Utilization of Experience in Parole Decision-Making: Summary Report*. Washington, D.C.: U.S. Government Printing Office, 1974.

Inciardi, J.A., and McBride, D.C. "The Parole Prediction Myth." *International Journal of Criminology and Penology*, vol. 5, no. 3 (1977).

National Council on Crime and Delinquency. *Corrections in the U.S.* Hackensack, N.J.: NCCD, 1966.

Newman, Graeme. "Theories of Punishment Reconsidered: Rationalizations for Removal." *International Journal of Criminology and Penology* 3 (1975), pp. 163-182.

Nickerson, Jeffrey. "Prisoner's Gain Time: Incentive, Deterrent, or Ritual Response?" *University of Florida Law Review*, vol. 21 (1968).

Thomas, Charles W., and Poole, Eric D. "The Consequences of Incompatible Goal Structures in Correctional Settings." *International Journal of Criminology and Penology*, vol. 3 (February 1975), pp. 27-42.

Twentieth Century Fund Task Force on Criminal Sentencing. *Fair and Certain Punishment*. New York: McGraw Hill, 1976.

von Hirsch, Andrew. *Doing Justice: The Choice of Punishments*. New York: Hill and Wang, 1976.

Wilkins, Leslie T.; Kress, Jack M.; Gottfredson, Don M.; Calpin, Joseph L.; and Gelman, Arthur M. *Sentencing Guidelines: Structuring Judicial Discretion*. Washington, D.C.: U.S. Government Printing Office, 1978.

Part Two

Correctional Institutions

1922

George Bernard Shaw, The Crime of Imprisonment, 1922.

The prisoner envies the unfortunate animals in the Zoo, watched daily by thousands of disinterested observers who never try to convert a tiger into a Quaker by solitary confinement, and would set up a resounding agitation in the papers if even the most ferocious maneater were made to suffer what the most docile convict suffers. Not only has the convict no such protection: the secrecy of his prison makes it hard to convince the public that he is suffering at all.

There is another reason for this incredulity. The vast majority of our city populations are inured to imprisonment from their childhood. The school is a prison. The office and the factory are prisons. The home is a prison. To the young who have the misfortune to be what is called well brought up it is sometimes a prison of inhuman severity. The children of John Howard, as far as their liberty was concerned, were treated very much as he insisted criminals should be treated, with the result that his children were morally disabled, like criminals. This imprisonment in the home, the school, the office, and the factory is kept up by browbeating, scolding, bullying, punishing, disbelief of the prisoner's statements and acceptance of those of the official, essentially as in a criminal prison. The freedom given by the adult's right to walk out of his prison is only a freedom to go into another or starve: he can choose the prison where he is best treated: that is all. On the other hand, the imprisoned criminal is free from care as to his board, lodging, and clothing: he pays no taxes, and has no responsibilities. Nobody expects him to work as an unconvicted man must work if he is to keep his job: nobody expects him to do his work well, or cares twopence whether it is well done or not.

Under such circumstances it is very hard to convince the ordinary citizen that the criminal is not better off than he deserves to be, and indeed on the verge of being positively pampered. Judges, magistrates, and Home Secretaries are so commonly under the same delusion that people who have ascertained the truth about prisons have been driven to declare that the most urgent necessity of the situation is that every judge, magistrate, and Home Secretary should serve a six months' sentence incognito; so that when he is dealing out and enforcing sentences he should at least know what he is doing.

Malcolm Braly, False Starts,*
(Little, Brown and Co., 1976), pp.
361-362

Since I was now a trusted old con, a willing mule, I was shipped off to one of the new conservation centers. These are modern units, designed to service and man the camp programs. No walls, no cells, no guns anywhere in sight. We lived Army style, sixteen to a barracks, and every barracks had a rec room and a TV, and if you wanted to watch *Make Room for Daddy*, instead of *The Man from U.N.C.L.E.*, you walked around from barracks to barracks until you found one where this show was playing.

The old-timers scorned these new prisons and dismissed them as Holiday Motels. We couldn't be conned by departmental window trimming. We were still under the Man, and the Man still had a gun locked away somewhere nearby. The rest was bullshit. Essentially, it was only Folsom with Muzac. We see old prisons as scars because they whisper to us of that which is ugly in our spirit, but old monasteries look much the same, and it's possible this glistening tile and gleaming Formica will someday communicate the same message we now hear from stone walls and iron bars. Those who thrill over these new prisons and exclaim, "You can do everthing but go out for a pizza!" will never understand this until they've served in one. The ways in which we are denied our own free choice are finally all the same. Simple fairness compels me to admit it's better than being beaten with a rubber hose, but not much better.

SHOULD PRISONS EXIST?

The extensive literature available on prison systems offers us innumerable suggestions on what the primary purpose of the institution is, or, more often than not, what the purpose of the institution *should be*. Perhaps the saddest commentary on our current efforts to reform our prisons is that virtually no argument for reform is new. Again and again one can find commentaries on the prison system that are relevant today, though they were published 50, 75 or 100 years ago.

For example, one former warden of three prisons, including Auburn and Sing Sing, tried to outline in a short book, published in 1924, some basic postulates of prison reform:

(1) Prisoners are human beings; for the most part remarkably like the rest of us.
(2) They can be clubbed into submission—with occasional outbreaks; but they cannot be reformed by that process.
(3) Neither can they be reformed by bribery in the shape of privileges:—special favors or tolerant treatment.
(4) They will not respond to sentimentality; they do not like gush.
(5) They appreciate a "square deal" when they get one.
(6) There are not many of them mental defectives; on the contrary, the majority are embarrassingly clever.
(7) All of these facts must be taken into consideration, if we want prisons which will protect society. Unless they are taken into consideration, our correctional institutions will continue to be what they have been in the past—costly schools of crime—monuments of wasted effort, of misguided service.[1]

Thomas Mott Osborne, who wrote those words, went on to say, "All forms of severity, all forms of kindly mental and moral pauperizing, have been tried; and all have failed."[2] Of course, he was wrong to a point. Over the past 50 years we have invented some new twists on severity and mental and moral pauperizing, and are currently in the process of working out a few new variations. Yet, although Osborne might not be unanimously acclaimed on all of his points, his basic views are repeated again and again in the current criminal justice and corrections literature.

Either the general public, the politicians, and the correctional ad-

---

1. Thomas Mott Osborne, *Prisons and Common Sense*, (Philadelphia: J.B. Lippincott Company, 1924), pp.7-8.
2. *Ibid.*, pp. 8-9.

ministrators have a remarkable ability to ignore the failure of their efforts, and to continue blundering down the same path over and over again, or there is something else going on that we are not hearing about.

To some degree, this is the question which concerns the authors in the debate which follows. Perhaps prisons don't "work" according to some measurable scale, but is it possible that they still serve some useful purpose to society that keeps them around despite generations of vicious attacks? Or are the critics correct, and is it necessary to reduce our use of prisons or change them dramatically?

Of course, in virtually all traditional literature, prisons have been defended along traditional lines: they are useful or necessary to punish offenders (retribution); to deter offenders or potential offenders (deterrence); to reform prisoners in some way (rehabilitation); or just to warehouse large numbers of bad people so they cannot prey upon the rest of society (incapacitation).

Yet there are a few authors who are beginning to take the view that prisons serve some other purposes, more deeply felt and less overtly rational, but nevertheless important enough to keep prisons around despite overwhelming evidence that the traditional goals are not being met.

Michel Foucault, the French psychologist and journalist, has come up with two different suggestions on the real utility of prisons, written at two different periods of his life. In *Madness and Civilization*, first published in 1961, Foucault describes the significance of the disappearance of the disease of leprosy in the Middle Ages. There were literally thousands of leprosariums in France in the 11th Century, for example, and society had a scapegoat to isolate. However, this isolation was in fact the proper "cure," and the disease almost completely died out in Europe. This left Western society with a moral void, and the search was on to discover some other scapegoat to punish with isolation.[3]

"What doubtless remained longer than leprosy, and would persist when the lazar houses had been empty for years, were the values and images attached to the figure of the leper as well as the meaning of his exclusion, the social importance of that insistent and fearful figure which was not driven off without first being inscribed within a sacred circle."

"Leprosy disappeared, the leper vanished, or almost, from memory; these structures remained. Often, in these same places, the formulas of exclusion would be repeated, strangely similar two or three centuries later. Poor vagabonds, criminals, and 'deranged minds' would take the place played by the leper, and we shall see what salvation was expected from this exclusion, for them and for those who excluded them as well. With an altogether new meaning and in a very different culture, the forms would

---

3. Michel Foucault, *Madness and Civilization, A History of Insanity in the Age of Reason*, (New York: Vintage Books, 1973), pp. 6-7.

remain—essentially that major form of a rigorous division which is social exclusion but spiritual reintegration."

A gross oversimplification of Foucault's argument here might be that as we ran out of lepers to vilify and exclude from society, we began to treat the mentally ill as proper scapegoats for excluson. Later, however, at the beginning of the 19th Century, just as prisons were being invented, medical thought coincidentally began to turn and the mentally ill were more and more treated as sick persons, rather than bad ones. Prisons began to spring up and a new group of persons began to be ritually excluded from society; thus the pattern was sustained and made commonplace.

If there is indeed something in human nature that requires one group of persons to be scapegoated and excluded from society by being isolated in special institutions,[4] perhaps the argument can be made that young minority males who refuse to adapt to dominant society values are today's scapegoat. This group certainly accounts for a remarkably large percentage of those persons incarcerated in America's prisons.

Foucault, however, more recently turned his attention specifically to the development of the prison, in his book, *Discipline and Punish*. Here he focuses on a different reason for the development of the prison: "the disappearance of torture as a public spectacle." Writes Foucault, "a few decades saw the disappearance of the tortured, dismembered, amputated body, symbolically branded on face or shoulder, exposed alive or dead to public view. The body as the major target of penal repression disappeared."[5] During this period, (around the beginning of the 19th Century), torture began to die out as a form of punishment, and the use of capital punishment was drastically reduced. Corporal punishments, such as whippings, also grew less and less popular. This was not a quick or radical change, but rather a long and fitful one, going faster in some countries, slower in others, but essentially completed by 1840.

Foucault asks the question, "if the penalty in its most severe forms no longer addresses itself to the body, on what does it lay hold? The answer of the theoreticians . . . is simple, almost obvious. It seems to be contained in the question itself: since it is no longer the body, it must be the soul. The expiation that once rained down upon the body must be replaced by a punishment that acts in depth on the heart, the thoughts, the will, the inclinations."[6] The focus of this kind of punishment, carried out by the prison, has also changed the focus of much of the law. Rather than simply asking if the offender is guilty, and then punishing him, legal proceedings now begin to delve into the nature of the causal processes which led to the commission of the crime.

---

4.   See Karl Menninger, *The Crime of Punishment*, (New York: Viking Press, 1968), for another psychological view of criminals as scapegoats.

5.   Michel Foucault, *Discipline and Punish, The Birth of the Prison*, (New York, Pantheon Books, 1977), pp. 7-8.

6.   *Ibid.*, p. 16.

Another modern commentator to examine this shift in "punishments" is Graeme Newman who argues that other factors were at work in this repression of public violence. Newman suggests that just as Victorian society refused to publicly acknowledge the existence of sex, it also repressed public punishment and, in search of a way to securely hide the 'base and unmannerly' element, they invented the prison system:

> "Prisons performed a major function by removing the filthy aspects of society from public view; public executions became private, prisons became places of maximum isolation and security. In addition, the systematic, rigid, and compulsive nature of [the early American types of prisons], along with the widespread use of the whip to maintain obedience (and one suspects purity), connote unmistakably their repressed sexuality. In the past 100 years, this isolation has been increased many times by the massive bureaucracies that grew up to administer these prisons, thus burying them further beneath paperwork and personnel."[7]

Newman argues that society needed to repress public punishment because of the new refinement of the culture's sensibilities, and a result of this "enlightened" repression was the prison system. The public spectacle of punishment was banished "into the unconscious of society, the prison fortresses." Newman reminds us that the squelching of this system of public brutality had its price—the development of the prison—and he insists that any massive reform of the prison system will also have its price. The problem, unfortunately, is that we do not know in advance what that price will be. Over and over again we have seen how one generation's "reform alternative" may become the next generation's problem-in-need-of-reform. It is often hard for young prison reformers to understand that prisons themselves are a reform of an earlier generation's problem. Ironically, many prison inmates today would probably prefer the original public punishment of a whipping or a branding instead of a ten to fifteen year stretch in a state prison.

Newman, however is afraid of what our punishment-oriented and repressive society would invent to replace the prison if it were abandoned as our primary means of punishment. He feels the prison

> "...should not be tampered with lightly. Those who press for abolition of prison do not understand the powder keg upon which prisons are built. To eradicate prisons would be to eradicate an important and valuable part of our culture—as seamy as it is, it is far less seamy than it might have been. We are capable of much worse, as the history of our exploits with criminals...clearly demonstrates."[8]

---

7.   Graeme Newman, *The Punishment Response*, (Philadelphia: J.B. Lippincott Company, 1978), p. 187. See Charles Berg, "The Psychology of Punishment," *British Journal of Medical Psychology*, vol. 20 (1945), pp. 295-313, for an extremely similar view.

8.   *Ibid.*, p. 286.

IMPEDIMENTS TO CHANGE

There are truckloads of books, articles, monographs and other works that document how terrible prisons are, pointing to the fact that many times inmates come out in worse condition than when they went in. Why then do prisons remain in existence?

According to one school of thought, the prison system is perpetuated because politicians and legislators are afraid that their constituents would be in strong opposition to any lessening of heavy punitive measures against offenders. Along these same lines, a traditional reason for the imposition of strict criminal penalties has been the fear that any lessening of severe sanctions would lead the general public to take the law into their own hands, and form lynch mobs or worse.[9]

Yet, there really is little evidence to support the view that the public is hard on the heels of the politician, demanding vengeance. First, one must remember that while "the public" is a convenient sounding and expedient term, our society is a diverse collection of individuals with widely differing views on the subject of punishment. One popular textbook in criminology has suggested that most crimes do not even arouse resentment in the ordinary individual, and even where such resentment is aroused, it is usually counteracted by other members of society who hold more non-punitive views.[10]

For example, one of the authors of this book has for years asked students to pick one of the traditional goals of punishment and to defend it as the only goal of the entire corrections system. In different universities, including some classes made up heavily of policemen or military police, a surprising number of students, perhaps a majority, have more or less eloquently argued in favor of rehabilitation over retaliation or incapacitation. The Harris poll conducted for the Joint Commission on Correctional Manpower and Training in 1967 showed that among the general public, at least in that time period, an even greater percentage of Americans thought that rehabilitation rather than punishment should be the goal of corrections.[11]

Of course, one of the problems of such opinion polls is that there is often a confusion between the direction of people's beliefs and the intensity of their beliefs. In other words, people can answer "yes" when an interviewer asks whether massive rehabilitation programs should be instituted, but those same people would immediately balk when asked if they would agree to have their taxes increased five cents to implement these programs. In New York State, during the 1978 campaign for governor, Republican candidate

9.   Herbert L. Packer, *The Limits of the Criminal Sanction*, (Stanford, Cal.: Stanford University Press, 1968), pp. 37-38.

10.   Edwin H. Sutherland and Donald R. Cressey, *Criminology*, 8th ed., (Philadelphia: J.B. Lippincott Company, 1970), p. 352.

11.   Louis Harris and Associates, *The Public Looks at Crime and Corrections*, (Washington, D.C.: Joint Commission on Correctional Manpower and Training, 1968), quoted in Gordon Hawkins, *The Prison*, (Chicago: The University of Chicago Press, 1976), p. 163.

Perry Duryea made the mistake of confusing direction with intensity. Acting on polls that showed New Yorkers heavily in favor of capital punishment, he based much of his campaign on that issue. Too late, he found that New Yorkers were *theoretically* in favor of it, but many were not so interested as to actually cast a ballot vote to see it implemented. Governor Hugh Carey, who had promised to veto any capital punishment bill, was re-elected.

Gordon Hawkins, while recognizing that prisons might be necessary because of a deep-seated need to punish, argues strongly that the public is at best ambiguous on the subject of penal reform, more willing to be led by the actions of legislators rather than to rise up on its own and make demands for additional severity in punishment.[12]

Hawkins states, "Of all the impediments to change...none is more fundamentally disabling than our lack of knowledge."[13] While virtually everyone agrees on the need for sound evaluation and research to guide our future actions, he states, "there is depressingly little methodologically rigorous evaluative research available."[14]

This estimate of our state of knowledge is unfortunately true. Does a movement away from prisons to more community supervision diminish the law's ability to deter? While we have some hints, we really don't know. Can we reduce the total amount of crime by repressive means? We don't know. Does the placement of more offenders in community supervision programs increase the community's fear of crime? We don't know. Is crime actually increased in those areas where community-based corrections programs have been expanded? We don't know. In Part One, we discussed the fact that it is almost impossible to determine such basic questions as how many persons are currently in prison. Imagine the state of our ignorance when it comes to the significantly more difficult questions above.

Yet, if we are to make changes in our system, evaluative research is necessary. Should we, as Graeme Newman suggests, hold onto our current system for fear of what the future might bring if we abandon it? Or should we plunge boldly ahead in ignorance and change our system because we see major problems with it? Finally, are we willing to spend the large numbers of dollars necessary to research and evaluate what the consequences of our actions would be?

PROBLEMS OF REFORM

There are a number of possible things that we can do about today's correctional institutions. Some of the more popular suggestions are:

(1) replace the maximum security mega-prison of today with some sort of network of smaller, more humane prisons;[15]

---

12. Hawkins, *The Prison*, p. 166.

13. *Ibid.*, p. 184.

14. *Ibid.*, p. 176.

15. John P. Conrad, "Which Way to the Revolution," in *Should We Build More Prisons?*, (Hackensack, N.J.: National Council on Crime and Delinquency, 1977).

(2) declare a moratorium on the construction of new prisons;[16]
(3) reduce prison populations by releasing many prisoners into alternative programs;[17]
(4) virtually abolish the use of prisons in favor of community-based corrections;[18]
(5) do more of what we are currently doing—build new maximum security prisons both to replace some of the older ones and to house the additional prisoners sent to prison by the courts;[19]
(6) ignore the problem and do nothing.

Of all of the above suggestions, the only one which is turning out to be unfeasible is the last one (6). Prison populations have continued to rise in recent years, with virtually every state showing an increase since 1975 and in many cases suffering from extremely severe overcrowding.[20] One expert is predicting that soon there will be a prison population of 380,000, an increase of 50% over the 1975 record level prison population.[21] With many states already housing up to four men in a one-man cell,[22] and others putting cots into gyms, infirmaries, tents and hallways, it is obvious that there is a limit to how long the problem can be ignored.

The one solution adopted by many correctional administrators[23] is simply more of the same—to spend enormous amounts of money in building new facilities, at an average capital construction cost of upwards of $30,000 per bed.[24]

Yet there is some opposition to this position. First, reformers who have been told for years that there could be no diversion of inmates into high

---

16. See Board of Directors, National Council on Crime and Delinquency, "Institutional Construction," *Crime and Delinquency*, vol. 18 (1972), p. 331; National Advisory Commission on Criminal Justice Standards and Goals, *A National Strategy to Reduce Crime*, (Washington, D.C.: U.S. Government Printing Office, 1973), p. 121; *Prisoners in America*, (Harriman, N.Y., Report of the 42nd American Assembly, 1972), p. 6.

17. See "Comment, Overcrowding in Prisons and Jails, Maryland Faces a Correctional Crisis," *Maryland Law Review*, vol. 36 (1976), pp. 182-211; W.G. Whitlach, "Practical Aspects of Reducing Detention Home Population," *Juvenile Justice*, vol. 24 (1973), p. 17; Howard League for Penal Reform, *Ill-Founded Premises, The Logic of Penal Policy and the Prison Building Programme*, (London, England, 1974).

18. Milton G. Rector, "The Extravagance of Imprisonment," *Crime and Delinquency*, vol. 21 (October 1975), p. 323.

19. See Steven Gettinger, "U.S. Prison Population Hits All-Time High," *Corrections Magazine*, vol. 2, no. 3 (March 1976), pp. 9-17; *American Journal of Correction*, vol. 37, no. 6 (November/December 1975), pp. 20-21, 36.

20. Gettinger, "U.S. Prison Population."

21. Rob Wilson, "U.S. Prison Population Again Hits New High," *Corrections Magazine*, vol. 3, no. 1 (March 1977), pp. 12-16, 19-22.

22. Gettinger, "U.S. Prison Population."

23. *Ibid.*

24. Carolyn Johnson and Marjorie Kravitz, *Overcrowding in Correctional Institutions*, (Washington, D.C.: National Institute of Law Enforcement and Criminal Justice, 1978), p. v.

quality community-based corrections programs because of a lack of funds, look with dismay on plans to build $30 or $50 million maximum security prisons. With some justification, they argue that if we can fund expansion of our prison network, we can equally well expand the less expensive alternatives to prison.

The other type of objection comes from those who say that expanding a failure will only create a more expensive failure. Milton Rector, for example, has argued that merely increasing the total number of prisoners in the United States will have little effect on the country's crime rate.[25] He states that we already have the Western world's highest incarceration rate, and that much of the world views our penal system as the repressive weapon of a society bent on violence. We take our strongest weapon, maximum security imprisonment, and use it easily and quickly on large numbers of people, which appears to some other societies like an assembly-line version of the frontier lynch law.

Others, such as John Conrad,[26] have tried to step a middle-ground path in this debate. Their position goes something like this: granted that society, or at least judges and legislators, will demand high levels of incarceration, there is still no reason why we have to maintain dehumanizing, brutal holding tanks for these inmates. Rather, the solution lies in designing and building smaller institutions that would reduce the inhumanity that breeds in the mega-prison. Conrad argues that continued use of brutal maximum security prisons not only affects the inmates, but degrades all of society: "When society inflicts cruel and unusual punishment, its members accustom themselves to accepting and justifying it. The whole social fabric is affected by our willingness to allow the state to do in our names what we would not ourselves do to others."[27]

This argument is underlined by a study done by Nacci, Teitelbaum and Prather. Studying thirty-seven overcrowded institutions, they discovered that the more overcrowded these institutions became, the higher the total number of assaults by inmates (particularly young adults) on other inmates and prison guards became. They predict serious problems with more overcrowding, and recommend changing institutions to at least reduce the inmates' perception of density.[28]

Yet, there is no magic solution to be found which will at one stroke solve all problems. Reading the above, particularly in combination with the rosier claims of community supervision advocates, might lead one to see the least

---

25. Milton G. Rector, "Are More Prisons Needed Now?" in *Should We Build More Prisons?*, (Hackensack, N.J.: National Council on Crime and Delinquency, 1977), p. 23.

26. Conrad, "Which Way to the Revolution."

27. *Ibid.*

28. Peter L. Nacci, Hugh E. Teitelbaum, and Jerry Prather, "Population Density and Inmate Misconduct Rates in the Federal Prison System," *Federal Probation*, vol. 41, no. 2 (June 1977), pp. 26-31.

expensive alternative as the most attractive—send large numbers of inmates back to community agencies, which are definitely cheaper, and are at least somewhat effective in reforming or controlling offenders, with the promise of becoming even more effective.

One commentator has pointed out two problems commonly ignored in this sort of approach—or any approach where large numbers of offenders are diverted into community-based corrections.

First, there must be a wide variety of services available to meet the needs of the wide variety of offenders that exists. Coates notes that "To focus only on the youth or adult who can be easily handled in the open community and ignore the needs of the more difficult individual is irresponsible and paves the way for the creation of small maximum security prisons. Although these individuals make up a very small percentage of the total population served, they ought not to be forgotten."[29]

Perhaps more importantly, however, Coates points out that there are serious dangers to be aware of when advocating an increased use of community-based corrections. Of course, there have always been a few judges or other officials who have seen prisons as a beneficial experience—one where an offender might become rehabilitated or learn a trade. But to most people, a prison is an instrument of punishment, and is to be reserved only for those people who deserve nothing more than straightforward punishment.

But community-based supervision, with its emphasis on many areas of service delivery and advocacy of offender needs, can easily become viewed by the sentencing structure or the public as something of a worthwhile experience for all people with problems. The public rationale would be, 'If the programs offered by community agencies are so good, why should we allow only the really bad people who become convicted of felonies to take part in them? The more people who are sentenced to community-based supervision, the better off we will be.' Many persons who previously received light sentences because they were not "bad" enough to deserve punishment might find themselves encouraged or coerced into participation in these programs.

Worse, as Coates points out, we as a society can get even more enthusiastic. "We may become so convinced that what we have to offer is beneficial that we are willing to coerce the *nonadjudicated* into accepting services. In accomplishing the objective of providing more services to more people individual rights are frequently disregarded."[30] A recent experience involving the Academy Award-winning film, "Scared Straight" is a perfect illustration: following the public acclaim for the film, (which depicts a proj-

---

29.   Robert B. Coates, "Community-Based Corrections: Concept, Impact, Dangers," in Lloyd E. Ohlin, Alden D. Miller, and Robert B. Coates, *Juvenile Correctional Reform in Massachusetts*, (Washington, D.C.: National Institute for Juvenile Justice and Delinquency Prevention), p. 33.

30.   *Ibid.*

ect both implemented and conducted by prison inmates, who threaten and taunt delinquent children with the bare facts of prison life as a means of scaring them into conformity behavior), the prison program was expanded to include grade-schoolers, on field-trips, who had not been accused of any crime.

Coates also warns that we must be careful to watch what we are diverting *to* as well as what we are diverting *from*. If a person is taken out of a brutal prison and sent to a mental health facility for treatment, where he is kept for a longer period of time under even less humane conditions, that can hardly be termed a reform. There is no reason to automatically assume that just because a person has been diverted from the criminal justice system, he or she is necessarily better off.

THE FUTURE

Perhaps the most depressing fact in studying the prison system is the discovery of the institution's ability to resist change. In other sections of this book we point out that there have been some changes which have had important effects upon the day to day functioning of the prison; perhaps the most important is the recognition of prisoner's rights, which has somewhat altered the power of prison administrators to arbitrarily discipline or direct their charges. In other sections, especially the Zimbardo selection which follows, the argument has been made that nothing of substance has changed at all, even if a newer breed of minority inmates are less likely to "(buy) all the bullshit we put out," as one top administrator phrased it.[31]

A former correctional administrator who became one of the nation's top corrections scholars, the late Hans Mattick, once suggested, "It is not unfair to say that if men had deliberately set themselves the task of designing an institution that would systematically maladjust men, they would have invented the large, walled, maximum security prison."[32] As Milton Rector points out in the following selection, there is a significant school of thought that argues that only a very few offenders really need to be put into such institutions in order to protect society. Yet, we still continue to prepare for the worst. Because we believe some offenders need this treatment, we sentence most incarcerated offenders to it: today as many as 90% of all prison inmates are in maximum or medium security institutions.[33]

The cry for prison reform is not a new one. Since virtually the first day of maximum security prisons, there have been dedicated prison reformers making public calls for change. The efforts of these early reformers were not only spectacularly unsuccessful, but they were also totally forgotten, even by the

31. Michael Serrill, "Procunier: A Candid Conversation," *Corrections Magazine*, vol. 1 (March/April 1975), p. 4.

32. Quoted in Hawkins, *The Prison*, p. 45.

33. Charles E. Silberman, *Criminal Violence, Criminal Justice*, (New York: Random House, 1978), p. 383.

prison reformers who followed them. Thus, a cycle of reformist efforts has taken place for more than 150 years, and continues today with a new generation. As historian David Rothman has pointed out, each of these new groups "discovers anew the scandals of incarceration, each sets out to correct them and each passes on a legacy of failure."[34]

There is at least some hope that this cycle can be broken, as more people than ever before have taken an active interest in the future of prisons. The nation's press, in the wake of the prison riots of the 1960s and 1970s, have begun to publicize the problems of prisons as never before. College students are studying corrections in numbers that would have seemed utopian only a few years ago. Theoretically, this continued development of an educated group of citizens should, over the coming years, have some impact on the future of correctional institutions. However, whether this hope translates into reality remains to be seen.

---

34.   David J. Rothman, "Decarcerating Prisoners and Patients," *Civil Liberties Review*, vol. 1 (Fall 1973), p. 8.

In Defense of Prisons*

Donald J. Newman
Dean, School of Criminal Justice
State University of New York at Albany

The War On Crime

Crime, particularly traditional street-crime, is today considered a domestic threat of the first order. We have always been plagued with crime, of course, but rarely has fear for life and limb been so pervasive or given such high priority as a cultural problem.[1] In 1965, President Johnson declared war on crime, pledging to "banish" it from our society. President Nixon—ironically it turns out—swept to office on a law and order plank. The federal government has begun to pour monies into state and local crime control and prevention programs and various commissions have issued reports and recommendations on how best to curb and control the problem.

While there is, and has long been, voices espousing major cultural changes to correct the underlying cause of crime, in general, the result of our crime war has been new demands on the agencies of crime control—the police, courts, and corrections—for greater effectiveness.[2] Control is the cry; prevention can evidently wait for more settled times. The response to demands to "do something" about crime can only be called mixed. Initially, as always, hardware was given priority. Police departments were retooled, prisons computerized, courts expanded and all-in-all a literal war on crime broke out. Commissions were formed, including two major Presidential Crime Commissions,[3] and various professional groups met and issued crime control standards and goals. Penal codes were revised and manpower recruitment became a big issue. Colleges and universities responded by creating a new field, Criminal Justice, unheard of ten years ago but now a viable program on over a thousand campuses across the nation.[4] The Supreme Court and other appellate courts sought to curb excesses in crime control efforts and were accused of "handcuffing" the police and delaying justice. Early on there was general insistence on effectiveness and efficiency

1. Richard Harris, *The Fear of Crime*, New York: Praeger, 1969.
2. Norval Morris and Gordon Hawkins, *The Honest Politician's Guide to Crime Control*, Chicago: University of Chicago Press, 1969.
3. The Johnson Crime Commission was known as the President's Commission on Law Enforcement and Administration of Justice. It reported in 1967. The Nixon Crime Commission, called the National Advisory Commission on Criminal Justice Standards and Goals, reported in 1973.
4. See Charles W. Tenney, Jr., *Higher Education Programs in Law Enforcement and Criminal Justice*, U.S. Department of Justice, 1971.

* Reprinted, with permission, from *Psychiatric Annals*, vol. 4 (March 1974).

in crime control; due process and other Constitutional protections were viewed as "technicalities" hindering the banishment of crime.[5]

There was, and continues to be, a backlash to relatively unfettered shoot 'em up crime control. The emergence of crime as a high priority domestic issue occurred at the same time and in societal context with the civil rights movement, with the political awakening of the poor, and with widespread disenchantment with governmental intervention in foreign affairs, especially the Vietnam War. The *Zeitgeist* was a mixture of demands for law and order set against a public-government credibility gap and very strong insistence on rights, opportunities, and on fair and humane treatment by the poor and by racial and ethnic minorities. It became quickly obvious that the improverished and downtrodden were the primary targets of crime control processing and rarely in a position to do the processing. Eventually both the hot eyes of those affected by crime control and the cold eyes of scholars turned to critical examination of our methods of law enforcement. To almost no one's surprise, our system of criminal justice was found to be ineffective and inequitable at least and perhaps so brutalizing and counterproductive as to be unfit for our ideology in our time.

Reaction to disenchantment with crime control efforts has taken various forms.[6] The most extreme is angry rhetoric calling not for the abolition of crime but the abolition of the criminal justice system. In effect, this is a new form of nihilism advocating the total destruction of what is perceived to be a racist, totalitarian system for the preservation of the status quo at the expense of the "people." In contrast, the mildest strategy is essentially patchwork: attract better police, reduce delay in the courts, increase rehabilitative efforts in prisons. Most of the hard realities of our societal response to crime are avoided or dismissed as irrelevant at these extremes.

A much more pervasive, middle-of-the-road stance is popular today. Its primary allegiance is toward long-range crime prevention in the classical manner, but with the immediate control of crime reluctantly conceded to be necessary. However, our present techniques of apprehending and convicting violators and putting them in prison is viewed as largely irrational, dysfunctional, endless and, perhaps, hopeless. Police are needed for a dangerous few and so are prisons or some variation in maximum restraint, but the routine formal processing of the great bulk of violators as is presently done is really unnecessary. We as a people need to find and implement more rational, more humane and more effective alternatives. In general, this attack is characterized by word slogans beginning with "d"—deemphasize, divert, decriminalize, decarcerate.

---

5.   Richard Harris, *Justice: The Crisis of Law, Order, and Freedom in America*, New York: Praeger, 1970.

6.   See for example American Friends Service Committee, *Struggle for Justice: A Report on Crime and Punishment in America*, New York: Hill and Wang, 1971, and Herbert L. Packer, *The Limits of the Criminal Sanction*, Stanford, California: Stanford University Press, 1968.

Decriminalization

This approach starts with legislative reform. Criminal behavior, after all, is a matter of definition and any reform must begin at the beginning. The prevailing view is that we have too many crimes, that we foolishly expend our criminal justice resources in an attempt to enforce morality, a task both unwise and impossible. Why should marijuana be outlawed? What of gambling, prostitution and other victimless crimes? Can't we, by removing such conduct from criminal codes, reduce our crime control efforts to manageable size and really begin to focus on serious law violation?[7]

Decriminalization, even if wildly successful, will admittedly touch only the fringes of the crime problem, leaving murder, mayhem and stick-ups on square one. Interestingly, many spokesmen for decriminalization simultaneously call for criminalization of other, emerging problems, like pollution, which only recently have been perceived as a threat to our way of life.

Diversion and Destigmatization

Apart from reducing the number and type of criminal statutes, there is major emphasis on development and use of alternatives to criminal justice processing. "Diversion" is the watchword and it applies across the system from police intake to parole.[8] Indeed, a number of observers resting their case on labelling theory research believe that full scale processing of a person from the status of suspect, through defendant, to offender, inmate and parolee, is rarely in his best interest or for that matter in the long-range interest of the social order. Having been arrested, charged, convicted, sentenced, incarcerated and released, it is sheer luck if he emerges from the process no worse, no more damaged or dangerous, than he entered. Given all this, emphasis should be placed on using the criminal process reluctantly and rarely but if necessarily invoked, then the person should be diverted from formal processing as soon as possible. Alternatives are needed and here, of course, is the rub. Are there indeed alternatives existing at present, or possible to develop, that will be more effective and at least as fitting to our ideology as full criminal justice processing?

Decarceration

Another word slogan, fully as popular as "decriminalization" has become

---

7. See Troy Duster, *The Legislation of Morality*, New York: Free Press, 1970, and Edwin Schur, *Crimes Without Victims*, Englewood Cliffs, New Jersey: Prentice-Hall, 1965.

8. See National Advisory Commission on Criminal Justice Standards and Goals, *Report on Corrections*, Washington, D.C., Government Printing Office, 1973, Chapter 3, "Diversion From The Criminal Justice Process." See, also S. Brakel, "Diversion From The Criminal Process: Informal Discretion, Motivation and Formalization." 48 *University of Denver Law Journal* 211 (1971), and Elizabeth W. Vorenberg and James Vorenberg, "Early Diversion From The Criminal Justice System: Practice in Search of a Theory," in Lloyd E. Ohlin, ed. *Prisoners in America*, Englewood Cliffs, New Jersey: Prentice-Hall, 1973.

part of this strategy. This is "decarceration" meaning, of course, the phasing-out of prisons as a method for dealing with serious criminal offenders.[9] Actually, decarceration encompasses two quite different options. The first, and most complete, calls for closing all maximum security prisons in favor of community supervision with only limited, short-term diagnostic lock-up of a few persistent or dangerous violators. These periods of brief incarceration would be effected in small community-based residential diagnostic and treatment facilities, lasting only until viable "reintegrative" plans can be worked out so that offenders can effectively be returned to unconfined but perhaps supervised community living. Chronically assaultive or otherwise dangerous offenders and those exhibiting bizarre conduct would be diverted to mental health facilities for more intensive therapy. In general, however, the maximum security prison would become a thing of the past, neither necessary nor desirable in this day and age.

A second variation on the decarceration theme rests on a belief that maximum security prisons are unnecessary and dysfunctional for the vast majority of offenders but may be necessary for a "few" very dangerous violators. How few is usually determined by asking wardens, correctional administrators and parole board members how many persons presently incarcerated really need the walls, bars and gun towers. Answers vary from one to twenty-five percent but it is believed some hard-core residue will remain after most prisoners are diverted to community alternatives. In effect, this is not truly decarceration, but merely a shrinkage of incarceration. A reduction in prisons to an "irreducible minimum."

Both decarceration options have in common dislike, distrust and disenchantment with prisons as they have been and are used. Both are predicated on belief in feasible and proper alternative methods of intervention, control and treatment. Yet the options are quite distinct in outcome for the first involves total abolition but the second leads to the creation of "maxi-maxi" prisons, smaller perhaps but otherwise not much different than now exist. As can be easily seen, this divergence is not simply one of degree but of kind. The two views, attracting quite different proponents, rest on differential beliefs about the cause and cure of criminal behavior, about the role of incarceration in our society and indeed about the basic purposes of our criminal justice system.

Decarceration, total or in significant part, is widely espoused today. There really are no informed spokesmen defending prisons as they are currently used or calling for expansion of incarceration. Yet even rudimentary attempts to decarcerate have not met with success. Some of the reasons for this are political—and this is not meant derogatively for crime control is properly a concern of our political system—and some are bureaucratic, in-

---

9.   See Ralph England, "Is The Prison Becoming Obsolete?" *Current History*, July, 1971; Erik O. Wright, *The Politics of Punishment: A Critical Analysis of Prisons*, New York: Harper and Row, 1973; and National Advisory Commission on Criminal Justice Standards and Goals, *Report on Corrections*, Chapter II, "Major Institutions."

volving entrenched resistance to abandoning capital investments and to ending the economic reliance of many small communities on prisons.

Apart from entrenched political and economic advantage there are a number of additional obstacles to decarceration which must be directly confronted if this dream is to come about. Some may be overcome but others, I am convinced, are insurmountable in the foreseeable future leaving the whole issue of incarceration one of improvement rather than abandonment. These obstacles include:

1. *Tradition*. We have had prisons for a century and a half; in fact, we invented them and the traditional ideology underlying incarceration dies slowly.[10] Criminal justice reformers have continuously come on the hard fact that any significant change from traditional ways of doing things is difficult and excruciatingly slow even in the face of overwhelming evidence and well-phrased arguments supporting the need for change. Our criminal justice system, including prisons, is by no means always rational, waiting with bated breath for the reformer and social engineer to suggest improvements. There is much of a ceremonial and symbolic nature in most crime control efforts and these are not easily dismissed by evidence of dysfunction or even of high cost.[11] Proponents of medium security "open" prisons have long been plagued by legislative and public resistance even with evidence of greater effectiveness at much less cost than walled institutions. Somehow, perhaps for reasons of deterrence, prisons are not supposed to be pastel colored but are expected to "look like" Gothic prototypes.

2. *Community Supervision*. The major difficulty with decarceration is less a matter of inertia than lack of really feasible and effective alternatives. In good part, prisons themselves were created as alternatives to overseas penal colonies, to community outlawry and to branding, flogging and hanging. If, in turn, they are abondoned, in part or in whole, something of value must be offered in their place. This something of value must not only offer promise of more effective rehabilitation or reintegration of offenders but must somehow meet the other purposes of incarceration, community protection, deterrence and even revenge, purposes less popular in professional circles, perhaps, but nonetheless operational.[12]

Setting aside for a moment punitive and deterrent purposes, a question remains of whether other methods of offender intervention are available or likely to be developed. And, as a critical corollary, whether any such alternatives, even if more effective, are proper and fitting within our political ideology. In brief there are two quesions: can we do it and might not the cure be worse than the disease?

10. David J. Rothman, *The Discovery of the Asylum*, Boston: Little, Brown, 1971.

11. Leslie T. Wilkins, "Crime and the Tender-Minded," *John Howard Society of Ontario*, Community Education Series, 1 No. 1, 1973.

12. Milton Burdman, "Realism in Community-Based Correctional Services," The *ANNALS*, 1969.

It is often stated that, in fact, we have had for some time a viable incarceration alternative, namely probation. The professional literature is replete with studies showing high "success" rates with probation, demonstrating its effectiveness over imprisonment and, perhaps most important, its success at far less cost than any form of incarceration. True, probation services are presently starved resulting in excessively large case-loads, some pro-forma supervision and limited counselling but this can be easily remedied. New forms of probation subsidies, new experiments in team supervision, including the use of paraprofessionals, matched agent-offender caseloads, new techniques of intensive supervision and similar developments hold promise beyond our wildest dreams. Even granting all this, a nagging problem remains. The fact is that probation is not and has never been an alternative to incarceration. Instead, historically and now, probation is an *additional* form of correctional intervention allowing us to keep more persons under state control.[13] It may be that probation has acted to keep prison populations in a more or less steady state. Incarceration has expanded to meet general population growth but has not proliferated beyond the gross national product of serious criminals. But an alternative? Never. The kinds of offenders placed on probation are not, in the main, of the same cut and jib as those for which prisons were designed and are currently used. Probation does act as a screening stage for the prisons and may, in fact, function to *increase* prison populations. Those offenders who initially appear to be good risks are tried out but, failing in the community, are moved into incarceration. Just as prisons must have within them deeper prisons—segregation—for those inmates who violate prison rules so probation relies on prisons in the background, the sword of Damocles that is ever ready and which not infrequently descends.

If by decarceration is really meant more limited and selected incarceration, the second option discussed above, then it may well be that probation can be more generally used than has been the case. Certainly there are some, perhaps many, present prison inmates who in a wiser court with more adequate community resources could have been effectively released to probation. But if decarceration is intended as a total stance, or even near-total, will this work? Under even ideal conditions is it feasible to suggest community supervision, counselling and the on-street application of other treatment modalities for every persistent, professional, physically dangerous, or sexually aberrant and aggressive violator now held in prisons?

3. *Community Protection: Other Alternatives.* A major, in fact a dominant, purpose of prisons is to have and to hold. True, in this day and age, we hope to rehabilitate or otherwise cure or condition those prisoners held so that they return, or perhaps first achieve, a law-abiding existence once the gates open. But restraint and incapacitation during sentence to protect the community—all of us—from further criminal acts is a fundamental purpose of incarceration. How can decarceration proposals meet this?

---

13. See David J. Rothman, "Behavior Modification in Total Instructions: An Historical Perspective" to be published as a Hastings Institute Report in 1974.

The argument, of course, is that prisons do not really protect since virtually all inmates return to civilian life, many of them more dangerous than when they entered. At best, any protection is temporary during the year or two, sometimes five, that prisoners are typically incarcerated. Of course, the average-time-in-prison statistic is somewhat deceptive; a number of violent offenders spend a much longer time in restraint and numerous lesser but persistent violators do life on an installment plan. In any case, does the argument that incapacitation is only temporary or sequential lead to the conclusion it should not be used at all?

Proponents of decarceration rarely rest their case here but instead advocate clinical and perhaps sociological intervention in community settings with an eye toward some sort of cure of the offender or improvement in his environment. They feel this is the only true path to long-range community safety. The problem with this, as reasonable as it sounds, is that at present there are only limited "cures" for serious criminal violators and even more limited opportunities for correctional services to do much about changing crime producing environments. Can a fifty year old, aggressive and persistent homosexual child molester be effectively treated? Can correctional services improve the life-chances of those in Harlem? Letting hopes run wild, assume these kinds of things could be achieved, would it be possible to accomplish them in such a short interval that the community would be continuously protected from the depredations of offenders under treatment?

Incapacitation, even temporary restraint, of offenders perceived to be dangerous is an important element in our sentencing process. If the prison alternative is removed, it may well be that other and perhaps worse alternatives will be forthcoming. Most decarceration proponents have looked in only one direction—toward community based interventions—but our social order is not ruled by social workers or clinicians. Different alternatives can be, and in fact have been, suggested by others of different orientation and political hue. To dismiss these suggestions as hardhat or irrational is to ignore political reality and the dedicated, high-minded decarceration proponent may find himself in a world he never made.

What are some of these prison alternatives? One, of course, is the death penalty. It was only yesterday that the Supreme Court in a confused and confusing opinion outlawed capital punishment.[14] Prior to this decision, the death penalty was disappearing by non-use in any event (we had no executions in the United States in a number of years, although it was still possible in the majority of our states), but since the court decision a number of jurisdictions are attempting to reinstate capital punishment by legislation conforming with the court opinion. Aside from issues of the letter of the law, there is the question of whether capital punishment is really likely to be seized upon as an alternative to incarceration. I think so. In reverse, incarceration has been a major alternative to the death sentence in serious crime cases; historically imprisonment has been a much stronger alternative

---

14. *Furman v. Georgia*, 408 U.S. 238 (1972).

to death than probation has been to imprisonment. In any event, imagine a society without prisons having instead large probation services, small residential treatment facilities and other community based correctional programs. In this society serious crimes occur: an airplane is hijacked and the pilot killed, terror bombs are mailed, kidnappings occur, children are raped and other atrocities go on, infrequent perhaps, but part of the warp and woof of living in a large complex, industrial society. It appears to me that if foreclosed from incarceration, the legislative response would inevitably be the death sentence.

Are there other alternatives less extreme than capital punishment and for less horrible crimes that might well rise to operational prominence?

One possibility, strange as it sounds in contemporary society, is vigilante justice. There is, in fact, a discernible reversal of public-witness apathy to crimes of violence, the don't-get-involved response so widely decried when a number of citizens watched without intervention the murder of Kitty Genovese in New York City a few years ago. In recent months there have been numerous examples of crowds pummeling offenders who committed crimes in the open and apparently more than one narcotics pusher has been thrown from a rooftop by citizens who object to heroin being sold in their neighborhood. Some viligante groups are organized into private neighborhood patrols; others have been co-opted by the police and made official "blockwatchers" amd "auxiliary patrolmen."[15] While a good deal of vigilante activity is a response to police ineffectiveness or inefficiency, more than simply catching perpetrators is involved. Often judgment is rendered, sentences meted and punishment carried out on the street. It has long been my contention that while the death penalty had very little deterrent effect on criminals, its potential did act to deter victims, witnesses and the police. In a jurisdiction without the ultimate penalty and where a police officer is murdered, it would seem to me that the chances of the killer being brought in alive are somewhat slimmer than if capital punishment was at least a possibility. If so, imagine the chances if both capital punishment and imprisonment are foreclosed. Another potential is electronic surveillance, perhaps combined with electronic conditioning, of persons under community supervision. A prototype form of this technique has been used with some probationers but its full potential—and all of its implications, Constitutional and otherwise—remain to be played out. Nonetheless, it is presently possible to implant electrodes into persons, as into animals, to monitor their movements and to send painful stimuli to condition them from occasions of sin.[16] According to the calendar we are within a decade of 1984;

15. See "New Yorkers Fight Back: The Tilt Toward Vigilantism," *New York* Magazine, October 15, 1973.

16. See particularly Ralph Schwitzgebel, "Issues in the Use of An Electronic Rehabilitation with Chronic Recidivists," 3 *Law and Society Review* 599 (1969); Note: "Anthropotelemetry: Dr. Schwitzgebel's Machine," 80 *Harvard L. Rev* 403 (1966); Ralph Schwitzgebel, "Electronic Innovation in the Behavioral Sciences: A Call to Responsibility," 22 *American Psychologist* 364 (1967); and Ralph Schwitzgebel, *Streetcorner Research,* (Cambridge, Mass. Harvard University Press 1964).

technologically we have arrived. Electronic control has the potential not only of supplanting prison walls, but of reducing probation staff as well. Given the great American love for gadgetry, it seems probable that a probation staff composed of a single observer and an electronic console will be most attractive to those with authority to fund and implement correctional programs.

Still another alternative might be civil commitment to mental hospitals as they exist at present or in some modified form. At best this is simply lateral transfer; at worst it is retrogressive, a return to the medical model of corrections popular in the 1940's. While it may well be that a larger proportion of offenders than at present can profit from therapy in hospital settings, if any significant number of violent and dangerous violators are hospitalized it will probably require a modification of such facilities in the direction of maximum security. Development of perimeter and internal security measures to control a mix of traditional psychotics and criminal offenders would most likely move the hospitals closer to prisons than the reverse. Furthermore, it is doubtful that many persistent and professional violators, now imprisoned, are really appropriate targets for effective clinical psychiatry. And absent significant changes in legislation, the mental hospital alternative would be reversion to a completely indeterminate—one day to life—sentencing system. With all its faults, incarceration in prisons has, for the most part, clearly specified limits based on the conduct of the offender, not on his condition.

It would be nice if prisons could be abandoned and all inmates returned to community living, staying on the path of righteousness with the aid and assistance of probation and clinical staff. But simply opening the gates may not lead in this direction; there are abroad in our land these other alternatives that, fully implemented, may well cause the decarceration proponent to look back with nostalgia to the prisons of yesteryear.

4. *The Punitive Ideal and Deterrence.* Some offenders are sent to prison not for purposes of treatment and rehabilitation, but simply as punishment and, often related, as "examples" to others. Anger, revenge, and deterrence, while not noble motives, are nonetheless part of our sentencing system. It can be argued that this is wrong: punishment should not be sanctioned as a state response and deterrence is dubious at best. In fact, both these arguments have been made in one form or another many times without, however, much effect on judges and legislatures. Operationally, a problem is presented to courts and law-making bodies, not so much by run-of-the-mill felons (most of whom have been poor and underprivileged for such a long time that their criminal activity is understandable if not permissible) but by their more socially and economically fortunate counterparts, particularly white-collar violators and by organized and professional criminals. While it is true that the wealthy and powerful have available resources to delay, obfuscate and otherwise put the whole criminal justice system fully through its own tedious tests, some are convicted and come down to the wire of sentencing. What should be the sentencing response with cases involving

willful and multiple tax evasion? embezzlement? price-fixing? What should have been done with Al Capone? Hoffa? Alger Hiss? What should have been done with former Vice President Agnew? For the most part these are not broken-home, teen-age neurotics, discriminated against, emotionally disturbed violators, but business and political leaders or their parody, the American gangster.

Part of the purpose of the sentencing ritual is affirmation of cultural norms. We express by punishment and the other aspects of this "social degredation" ceremony, the limits of our toleration of deviance. Can a social order exist without such ceremonies? Perhaps, but there are no models among large industrial societies of the world on which to rest a non-punitive hypothesis. Even Durkheim's imaginary society of saints must continuously reaffirm its outer limits by punitive sanctions.[17]

5. *The Avoidance of Due Process.* Our criminal justice system, including sentencing and post conviction processing, is cumbersome but deliberately so. We do not, and have never, advocated efficiency and effectiveness as the sole end or the primary means of crime control. Of all our systems of compulsory conformity—and there are many from the public school on—the criminal process is the most elaborate, with rigid requirements of notice, proof, procedural regularity and due process of law. The detailed stages and steps in the criminal process have evolved slowly, often at clearly recognized costs to effective crime control. Every decision about (or for) suspects, defendants, offenders, probationers, inmates and parolees is circumscribed by legislation, surrounded by appellate court decisions, with excesses forbidden by Constitutional protections afforded even the worst among us. When movement is from formal processing to diversion, out-of-court settlement, pre-trial counselling and informal post-conviction alternatives, there is invariably a reduction in procedural regularity and less attention to matters of proof and due process. We have had seventy years of experience with diversion and alternative interventions with juvenile delinquents and, in the final analysis, the juvenile court movement has been found wanting.[18] There probably never has been a more well-intentioned development than the juvenile court. Dedicated proponents sought to destigmatize criminal processing, to intervene early and informally in the best interest of Johnny Doe, to build a system of justice for children almost exactly like that imagined today by diversion and decarceration proponents for adults. The cost of the juvenile experiment was abandonment of many of the procedural safeguards of the law without accomplishing the other objectives of treatment and rehabilitation, or achieving those elusive "best interest" results. Can we really promise more with adults?

In summary, any significant moves in the direction of diversion and decarceration, as attractive as they sound, have a long way to go and

---

17.   Emile Durkheim, *The Rules of the Sociological Method*, Glencoe: Free Press, 1949, pp. 68-69.

18.   *In re Gault*, 387 U.S. 1 (1967), *In re Winship*, 397 U.S. 358 (1970).

numerous obstacles to overcome. No one, myself included, is in favor of present-day prisons, but until feasible and effective alternatives which meet all the needs of crime control and which respect all its safeguards are developed, then to simply postulate decarceration is not only foolish but dangerous.

Prisons need not and should not be human warehouses, nor ugly and brutalizing. Nor should they be used to chill political dissent or sincere efforts to change our social order in the direction of a more equitable, just and crime-free culture. Neither should they be used cosmetically, to remove "nuisances" from our streets, to hold the inept, unpleasant or unemployed who present no real physical danger to others. But until the millennium when the crime-producing factors in our world will have been eliminated, incarceration of the dangerous and the deliberate—the violent, the professional, the organized and the willful, persistent offender—is not only necessary but is itself an alternative to worse choices.

The Extravagance of Imprisonment*

Milton G. Rector
President, National Council on Crime and Delinquency

In a somewhat misleadingly titled article, the Board of Directors of the National Council on Crime and Delinquency (NCCD) proclaimed several years ago that "The Nondangerous Offender Should Not Be Imprisoned: A Policy Statement."[a] Following on the heels of another NCCD policy statement calling for a moratorium on new prison construction until "alternatives to incarceration are fully achieved,"[b] the board this time took the much more radical stance of virtually insisting that American prisons be closed down.

The question of whether the title is misleading or not hinges on the definition of the "nondangerous" offender. As will be seen later in this book, there are those who would define as dangerous anyone who might serve as a possible source of harm to anyone at any time. The NCCD Board of Directors, however, came up with an extremely narrow definition of dangerousness for their Model Sentencing Act. According to this act, the term "dangerous" may be applied only to "(1) the offender who has committed a serious crime against a person and shows a behavior pattern of persistent assaultiveness based on serious mental disturbances and (2) the offender deeply involved in organized crime."[c]

Under this definition, "only a small percentage of offenders in penal institutions today meet the criteria of dangerousness. In any state no more than one hundred persons would have to be confined in a single maximum-security institution, which, because of its small size, could be staffed for genuine treatment."[d]

The "policy statement" presented by the NCCD Board of Directors regarding imprisonment of offenders reads as follows:

"Prisons are destructive to prisoners and those charged with holding them.

---

a Board of Directors, National Council on Crime and Delinquency, "The Dangerous Offender Should Not Be Imprisoned: A Policy Statement," *Crime and Delinquency*, vol. 19 (1973), p. 449.

b Board of Directors, NCCD, "Institutional Construction," *Crime and Delinquency*, vol. 18 (1972), p. 331.

c NCCD Council of Judges, *Model Sentencing Act*, §5.

d *Ibid.*, Comment on §5, at 11.

---

* Reprinted, with permission of the National Council on Crime and Delinquency, from "The Extravagance of Imprisonment" by Milton G. Rector, *Crime and Delinquency*, October 1975, pp. 323-330.

*Confinement is necessary only for offenders who, if not confined, would
be a serious danger to the public.*

*For all others, who are not dangerous and who constitute the great ma-
jority of offenders, the sentence of choice should be one or another of the
wide variety of noninstitutional dispositions."*[e]

*In the piece which follows, Milton G. Rector, the president of the NCCD,
sets out to explain in some detail the reasoning behind the creation of this
policy statement.*

The NCCD Board of Directors' recommendation that nondangerous offenders not be imprisoned calls for a major change in public policy. Of the
broad implications and consequences of this change, the most significant is
the demise of the penal institution—the cage—as a primary means of enforcing the criminal law.

A nation founded on respect for individual liberty acknowledges that a
civilized way to deal with crime excludes exile, excludes mutilation, excludes
the death penalty.[1] The punishments of exile, mutilation, and death have
been abolished because they are excessive; imprisonment of an offender who
is not violently assaultive—not dangerous—should be abolished for the same
reason.

Adoption of the recommended policy rests on legislative initiative and
enactment. It requires leadership and courage, qualities not conspicuously
displayed by many judges and criminal justice officials, who, under present
sentencing and correctional statutes, possess but fail to exercise the broad
discretion that could sharply reduce the use of imprisonment. These judges,
and other public officials who influence prison policy, tend to be opinion-
followers, not opinion-leaders. They have endorsed proposals at all levels of
government to rebuild and expand prisons and jails and have been singularly
unreceptive to efforts to reduce unnecessary institutional commitments. In
light of the huge cost and the glaring ineffectiveness of prisons and jails, their
supine acceptance of a policy of proven waste borders on irresponsibility.
They will change their ways only when legislative debate on the extravagance of imprisonment is so loud and clear that there will be no doubt
about the need for change in sentencing and correctional practices.

Legislative prohibition of imprisonment of nondangerous offenders will
signal a basic shift to a proactive policy, a basic shift away from the almost
totally reactive policy that now determines how government responds to
crime. Law enforcement, courts, and correction are part of a reactive
system. Their principal contribution to a proactive effort to reduce crime is
thought to be deterrence, which, according to present evidence, correlates
most highly with the certainty and speed of response by each part of the

---

e   Board of Directors, NCCD, "The Dangerous Offender," p. 449.

1.   Morales v. Schmidt, 340 F. Supp. 544 (1972). See also David J. Rothman, *The Discovery of
the Asylum: Social Order and Disorder in the New Republic* (Boston: Little, Brown, 1971).

criminal justice system.[2] Individually and collectively, police, courts, and correction cannot reduce crime and violence in our society. The expectation that they can and should do so unquestionably does much to reduce the proactive planning and financing of other programs and strategies that could reduce crime. A public policy change in correction that would release 80 to 90 per cent of those now in prison would transfer hundreds of millions of correction's construction dollars to criminal justice operating funds for alternative programs and strategies and for other social service systems.[3]

Official Contribution to Violence

Government cannot give leadership to any effort to reduce violence unless it first reduces violence in its own house by adopting a policy of nonimprisonment of the nondangerous. Short of killing the offender, imprisoning him is the most violent response a government can make to crime. Despite the great cost of imprisonment and the high ratio of staff to inmate population, government has proved itself incapable of reducing violence within its prisons or of protecting those it imprisons from severe physical and psychological damage. Its rehabilitation and vocational training programs, which are supposed to return the prisoner to his home and his community better motivated and better equipped to avoid crime, have demonstrated no capacity to protect the public or to overcome the disabling effects of incarceration, despite a well-financed governmental career service for the operation of prison systems. Government itself maintains and operates a slave-labor system in which the prisoner is exploited for the production of government-purchased goods; government itself is responsible for the exclusion of the ex-prisoner from a great number of legitimate fields of employment; government itself is responsible for the civil disabilities that set the ex-prisoner apart from the rest of the population.

If a policy of nonimprisonment of the nondangerous is not adopted, the backlash of frustration over the failure of imprisonment may produce even worse results than we have already had. The inability of imprisonment thus far to improve the prisoner by a regime of "just deserts" stimulates some prison authorities to propose more of the same—despite centuries of the expensive and well-documented failure of "just deserts" penology. Others would want to retain the current large prison population (consisting mostly of persons who are not dangerous and do not have to be confined) from which they could select persistently violent offenders for experimentation in special "behavior modification" programs and to which they could return those who choose not to "volunteer" for the treatment.[4] Before wasting more

2. Eugene Doleschal, "The Deterrent Effect of Legal Punishment," *Information Review on Crime and Delinquency*, June 1969.

3. National Advisory Commission on Criminal Justice Standards and Goals, *Corrections* (Washington, D.C.: U.S. Government Printing Office, 1973); National Council on Crime and Delinquency, Board of Trustees, "Institutional Construction—A Policy Statement," *Crime and Delinquency*, October 1972; Jessica Mitford, *Kind and Usual Punishment: The Prison Business* (New York: Knopf, 1973).

4. Norval Morris, *The Future of Imprisonment* (Chicago: University of Chicago Press, 1974).

lives and public funds in new cages for the persistently violent and dangerous offender, we should direct our ingenuity and resources to the elimination of imprisonment for the nondangerous. We would then have a huge surplus of uncrowded cages to be rebuilt and refurbished for our efforts to control and change the dangerous.

Model Sentencing Act

The Model Sentencing Act, originally published in 1963 by NCCD's Council of Judges and revised in 1972, is a unique and creative document drafted by a unique and creative group of judges concerned with the need to identify the dangerous criminal who requires imprisonment. They did not pretend they had fathomed the complexities of human behavior nor did they lay a claim to scientific knowledge that could predict with accuracy the propensity of the individual for committing future crimes. They did know that judges commit far too many nondangerous offenders to jail and prison for excessively long terms and that this dispositional pattern imposes a heavy financial burden on the taxpayer. They also knew that judges are no less opinionated and prejudiced than other people and not less likely than other officials in the criminal justice system to be capricious in use of their discretion. They were aware of a prevalence of sentences which, asserting unwavering allegiance to justice, were unintelligent and irresponsible. They sensed that it was time to compose a definition of dangerousness because judges—the conscientious as well as the indifferent—had no sentencing guidelines to help them distinguish between the "ordinary" offender and the one who is dangerous and likely to repeat his violent crime.

We decided that the criteria for a determination of "dangerousness" should be defined by statute to help reduce to a minimum the disparities and inequities of sentencing. The Model Act provides for judicial discretion in fixing a maximum sentence within a statutory maximum of thirty years for dangerous offenders and five years for those who do not meet the criteria for dangerousness. It does not make prison commitment obligatory for either group, thus avoiding the injustices of mandatory sentences. It eliminates "habitual offender" sentencing, indeterminate sentences, and the death penalty.

After a decade the influence of the MSA principles was seen in the Standards for Criminal Justice of the American Bar Association and the sentencing standards recommended by the National Advisory Commission on Criminal Justice Standards and Goals. Thus far however, Oregon is the only state that has adopted the Model Sentencing Act (in slightly modified form—1971, ch. 743). Not enough time has elapsed since the new Oregon act went into effect to permit a conclusive statement on the results, but prison officials there have informed me that since 1973 the courts have reduced prison commitments from 36 per cent of total convictions to about 19 per cent and that the use of suspended sentences has increased from 7 per cent of total convictions to 14 per cent. In the first year of operation under the act, median time served dropped from two years to sixteen months. No prosecutor or judge has criticized elimination of the mandatory life sentence for habitual offenders.

The debate has been started and the NCCD Model Sentencing Act criteria for dangerousness are under attack. This is as it should be. Public debate and a better-informed public will bring a demand for anticrime policies and strategies based on research and rational assessment rather than clichés, platitudes, and law-and-order slogans. Criteria for sentencing that cannot stand the test of assessment can be changed. In the interim both the convicted offenders and the public will be the beneficiaries of legislated criteria that reduce judicial caprice and abuse of discretion to a minimum. The Council of Judges believes that public opinion will support maximum use of criminal sanctions other than imprisonment if the criminal justice system shows itself able to select for confinement those criminals who have repeatedly hurt or endangered people physically or are participants in organized criminal activity. To make this selection with reasonable accuracy requires that criteria for sentencing be established and that research back-up be instituted to monitor the use of criteria and improve the sentencing practices of judges as deficiencies appear. Guidelines should also be devised to improve the screening and diversion practices of police and prosecutors.

No research to date has corroborated anyone's ability to predict which offenders will or will not commit further violent crimes. Attempts to make such predictions have resulted in "overpredicting" and prolonged confinement of nondangerous persons. A history of violence offers the most objective data by which dangerous people can be sentenced, but even that offers no guarantee of accuracy in predicting their future violence. The performance of prisons in trying to lessen the aggression of persons who commit violent crimes is no better than their record in trying to reduce the rapacity of property offenders. Criminal justice leaders must continue to search for humane and rehabilitative programs beyond primarily custodial care for persons who commit crimes of violence and are classified as dangerous.

The rate of imprisonment in the United States, which takes pride—in orations—in its protection of liberty and freedom, is considerably higher than the rate in any other industrial nation. In proportion to population, we imprison twice as many people as New Zealand, Canada, and Great Britain; three times more than Denmark, Sweden, and France; four times more than Italy and Japan; five times more than Spain and Norway; and nine times more than the Netherlands.[5] That extraordinary rate says it all. To ignore it is to condone the flagrant waste of money and lives and the crime-producing effects of needless imprisonment; to allow it to continue would be irresponsible support of those popular politicians and criminal justice leaders who promise that extending the number and length of prison commitments will reduce crime and who perpetuate the myth that more imprisonment means better protection of the public. That is why the NCCD Board of Directors in

---

5. Irvin Waller and Janet Chan, "Prison Use: A Canadian and International Comparison," *Criminal Law Quarterly*, December 1974, p. 58.

April 1973 adopted the policy recommending nonimprisonment of the non-dangerous offender, the offender who does not meet the criteria for dangerousness set forth in the Model Sentencing Act. We and others are seeking research grants to improve these criteria, which are still too general and would imprison, up to five years, thousands of persons who are not dangerous to society.

Imprisonment Not Necessary

Retaining these criteria in its 1972 revision of the Model Sentencing Act, the Council of Judges dissented from the prohibition-of-imprisonment policy that the Board of Directors was then considering. The judges maintained that before the criminal justice system could abolish imprisonment of the nondangerous, it must first develop a set of punitive sanctions that would be not only less destructive than imprisonment but also at least equally effective. They maintained that without the threat of imprisonment, use of any less punitive alternative—a suspended sentence, a fine, probation, etc.—could not possibly be effective. The Board did not accept that reasoning: it contended that if the effectiveness of every sanction depends on the existence of a more punitive sanction as back-up, the Council of Judges' Model Sentencing Act would not have excluded the death penalty and mandatory life sentences.

The public has been told repeatedly, by officials in whom it has confidence and by others seeking public office, that crime could be stopped if the police and the judges and the parole boards performed their functions more competently. More specifically, they say crime can be stopped by, for example, throwing out the *Miranda* rule, which "prevents police from obtaining confessions"; it can be stopped by juvenile court judges who should "stop slapping young punks on the wrist and start slapping 'em in the clink"; it can be stopped by parole boards that would not release any prisoner until he was "too old and feeble to hurt anyone"; etc. But simplistic remedies, such as the death penalty, mandatory sentences, and longer prison terms—all of them resurrected periodically out of frustration—have failed in the past and there is no reason to think they will succeed in the future. The inability of the police, courts, and correction to plan and operate as a coordinated system has intensified frustration and stimulates interagency accusations of failure. In the midst of all these empty promises, panacean proposals, and angry recriminations, criminal justice expenditures have more than tripled, from $4.5-billion in 1967 to $14.5-billion in 1974. In the past five years public expenditures for the police alone have increased from three to eight billion dollars a year, with no visible effect on the crime rate. There is a general fear that urging other societal systems to attack the problems which feed the subculture of urban violence and at the same time *not* urging tougher responses to acts of violence makes one appear permissive and soft on crime. There is a supplementary fear that the shift in policy and strategy, from reacting to crime to proacting, will result in shifting public funds from criminal justice to education, health, and other human service systems.[6] The question is one of leadership and responsibility. Should a public official fashion remedies that will "give the public what it wants" or should he construct them according to what the problem demands?

The criminals who ultimately reach the courtroom for sentencing are not at all representative of all who commit crime in our society. Most persons who commit crime are not sentenced. Most are not apprehended in the first place; of those who are, many are not officially arrested. Most victims, neighbors, and employers don't press charges. Because of the discretion allowed police and prosecutors, many arrested persons are dismissed without prosecution; others are diverted from the criminal justice process without conviction; and some, including many charged with serious offenses, are sentenced on a reduced charge not at all descriptive of the crime committed. Those committed to prison are more representative of the lower socioeconomic strata of our society than of all those who commit serious crimes.

That most people who commit crimes are disposed of without being sentenced or with sentences other than imprisonment doesn't mean that the system is not working or that the goal should be to increase the number who are imprisoned. It means that we must improve the selection of those who should be imprisoned. It also means that other forces in society are working—in different ways for different people. Persons convicted of white-collar crimes are rarely sentenced to a long prison term or to a prison term of any length; for them the usual sentence is a fine and a restitution order or other conditions of probation. Why can't the same diversions from imprisonment that are now used, with general approbation, for offenders having high social status also be applied to offenders of lower social status? Research findings on the criminal behavior of children also have significance for sentencing of adults. Among them are the conclusions that the more severely punished are more likely to repeat and that those who do not go through the justice system commit fewer crimes than those who do.[7] They, too, support nonimprisonment of nondangerous offenders.

Creative Sentencing

Judges and probation officers dealing with white middle- and upper-income offenders from "good families" very often exercise considerable ingenuity in locating or creating community alternatives to imprisonment. They may not have the time to serve similarly as advocates for all the low-income nondangerous offenders from "bad families" that come before them, but with a little effort they can recruit volunteer advocates from the community. The involvement of such volunteers would enhance community sup-

6. Such a priority was recommended by the National Advisory Commission on Criminal Justice Standards and Goals, *A National Strategy to Reduce Crime* (Washington, D.C.: U.S. Government Printing Office, 1973).

7. Eugene Doleschal, "Hidden Crime," *Crime and Delinquency Literature*, October 1970. See also Jay R. Williams and Martin Gold, "From Delinquent Behavior to Official Delinquency," *Social Problems*, 20: 209-229, 1972.

port for a wide variety of alternative sentences. Communities and volunteers can devise, manage, and operate a variety of noninstitutional sanctions for all nondangerous offenders—and can do so at a cost far lower than the amount of interest now due for amortizing the construction outlay of $50,000 per cell and the annual operating expense of $10,000 per prisoner (whose theft averages about $300).

No public outrage was expressed when a heart specialist who had stolen over $200,000 was sentenced to perform free surgery for indigent children. Nor did the heavens fall when a Phoenix physician, convicted on a drug charge, was sentenced to serve as Tombstone's town doctor as a condition of probation and when a Phoenix youth convicted of armed robbery was placed on probation for five years during which he was required to complete two years of college work. Creative use of probation can find unlimited alternatives for the unskilled as well as the skilled, for nonwhite as well as white offenders. Skilled plumbers, carpenters, and painters can give their probation time on weekends and holidays to train unskilled probationers as helpers while they repair and refurbish housing for indigent and aged people in the community. England's community service law authorizing 40- to 240-hour assignments in lieu of confinement can be adapted to our sentencing alternatives within the community for offenders who cannot afford fines or restitution on the installment plan.

Implementation of the policy of nonimprisonment of the nondangerous cannot and, of course, will not take place quickly and without debate. It undoubtedly will be preceded by a gradual retreat from the present wasteful and costly use of excessively long prison sentences to the use of short terms and nighttime, weekend, and holiday sentences to jails instead of prisons. Implementation efforts should be accompanied by increased allocation of funds for research and assessment of sentencing practices and the consequences of sentences for offenders classified experimentally to test criteria for dangerousness. Assessment should include monitoring the outcome of police and prosecutor diversion practices for comparison with the outcome of similar cases that are sentenced. Monitoring of sentences judge by judge is imperative for the gathering of data that can be used to improve judicial training for better sentencing and better use of informed discretion. Sentencing outcome should be measured by cost-effectiveness factors that relate not only to the crimes committed subsequently by sentenced offenders but also to the relative costs of the sanctions used. I am willing to predict that sentencing effectiveness will correlate highly with reduction in the length of sentences and reduction in the use of imprisonment for nondangerous persons.

Holland has one-ninth the per capita prison population of the United States. Its sentences to confinement (even for crimes of violence) are for terms of a few months; ours are for many years. Holland's underlying concept is, as ours should be, that punishment should be certain but need not be destructive. Its consistently low crime rate correlates with its change to short sentences and a heavy use of volunteers in probation sentences. The change was motivated by public officials who had been imprisoned during World War II and had first-hand experience of the destructive ineffectiveness of prisons.

We should not have to endure a similar catastrophe to understand that the kinds of sentences authorized in our statutes and administered by our judges reflect the kind of society we are and the degree of civilization we have attained. We have reached the stage when imprisonment is neither socially nor economically feasible as a punitive sanction for the great majority of sentenced persons, the hundreds of thousands who can be classed as non-violent and nondangerous.

PRISONIZATION

When he was governor of Georgia, Lester Maddox once made the infamous remark that prisons in this country will not improve until we obtain a better class of prisoner. Most people in corrections laughed at him.

Yet, for some reason, no one in corrections laughs at the many people who make a parallel suggestion: that prisons in this country will not improve until we obtain a better class of prison administrator.[1]

This call is not a new one. Over thirty years ago, one writer suggested: "The surest way to increase the efficiency of criminal justice is to improve the quality of its personnel. As compared with alterations in the personnel, modernization of equipment of the institutions of criminal justice and *changes in its processes* are of slight importance."[2]

Through the past few decades, this theme has been sounded over and over again. A quick perusal of any of the leading texts, or virtually any issue of the major journals in corrections will reveal persistent calls for improved leadership, improved training, improved recruitment, and improved salaries to help attract a better class of administration and staff.

Yet, perhaps the question should at least be raised as to whether many of the problems that arise from today's prisons can, in fact, be alleviated solely by attracting better people into the field of corrections. To what extent, we might ask, is the very concept of imprisonment the cause of these problems?

Put another way, can some of the twentieth century's more puzzling behavior by large groups of people be explained by suggesting that whole groups of people went temporarily insane at the same time or, more reasonably that certain organizations tend to attract less than normal people? In Nazi Germany, for example, how was it possible that an entire nation was able to close its eyes to the mass extermination and genocide going on? Even harder to answer is the obvious question that people oftentimes forget to ask: how was it possible that the government had little or no difficulty in attracting sufficient numbers of troops and guards to carry out this genocide?

Similarly difficult to explain, although quite different in detail, might be the mass suicide in late 1978 of more than 900 followers of the Reverend Jim Jones' People's Temple, at their settlement in Guyana. Even granting that

---

1. This conjunction was first pointed out to us by Donald J. Newman.
2. Quoted in Gad Bensinger, "Training for Criminal Justice Personnel: A Case Study," *Federal Probation* 41(3) (September 1977), p. 31. (Emphasis added.)

Jones had a few armed troops to enforce his decision to commit self-genocide, many hundreds of people still went to their deaths willingly, as if offering themselves up as some kind of monumental sacrifice. How was it that Jones had little or no difficulty in convincing sufficient numbers of worshippers to carry out this bizarre self-annihilation?

There are certainly many other examples that can be given, but the basic question remains: are these select groups made up of very abnormal people, or is it possible for any of us to act in this manner given the same circumstances?

One of the first scientists to deal with this question was Stanley Milgram. In his experiments, he had an actor strapped to an electrical device, and asked a wide range of people to assist as experimentors. These people were told to administer electrical shocks to the actor, whom they believed to be another volunteer. Through some barely plausible experimental design, the assistants were asked to administer ever-increasing dosages of electrical shock to the volunteer, who acted as if he were being seriously hurt. What Milgram was really testing, of course, was whether "ordinary people" would, just because a white-smocked professional told them to, administer dangerous shocks which would cause a fellow volunteer to suffer seriously. During the early days of the concentration camps, German officers learned of their troops' limitless capacity for senseless destruction. Similarly, Milgram learned (and was appalled) at the number of seemingly "normal" people who would administer a 450-volt electrical shock, plainly labeled as extremely dangerous or possibly fatal, while the "volunteer victim" cried for mercy and begged for the experiment to stop because of his heart condition. Over the years, about 62.5% of Milgram's experimental "assistants" administered the 450-volt shock that, as far as they knew, could have been fatal.[3]

This example urges us to question the extent to which the very nature of society, or an organization to which we belong, can shape our behavior. Can membership by "ordinary people" in a certain type of organization lead these people to do extraordinary things? Even without belonging to an organization which may have taken years to build up belief patterns, can the very nature of a setting make "ordinary people" become fascist killers, commit suicide, or administer lethal shocks to a man begging for mercy, just because they are told to do so?

Some of these questions are relevant to prisons. Since the first days of American prisons, inmates have been complaining, often with excellent reason, of guard brutality. Is it that sadistic bullies are attracted to corrections work so that they might have the approval of the state for their brutal acts? Or, is there something about the very nature of the incarcerative institution that leads people, placed in authoritative positions, to act in a manner that allows, encourages or even requires participation in brutalizing experiences?

3. Stanley Milgram, *Obedience to Authority*, (New York: Harper & Row, 1974), p. 35.

Inmates seem to react to round-the-clock (or "total") institutions in similarly patterned ways. Erving Goffman,[4] John Irwin[5] and others have studied the adaptation patterns of inmates to total institutions, and found that some become completely "prisonized" while others "do their own time," while still others rebel. Since the first days of Auburn prison, almost 150 years ago, wardens and guards have spoken of "breaking" new inmates into docility, as one would break-in a wild horse, shutting it in, away from its natural environment so as to adapt it to the horse-prison, the stable. Is there a proper comparison to be made here, that suggests that prison life is arranged to break down the vitality of men and women, to make them proper inmates in an artificial environment? As many recent theorists, especially the reintegrationists, have recognized, there is a serious problem for society in getting these broken minds to operate properly once they are released into society, (and bear in mind, virtually all prison inmates are eventually released back to the "outside" world).

Philip Zimbardo is one of the few social scientists to look directly at this question, although his experiment got so far out of hand that he had to shut it down out of fear. Even though his experimental subjects were arbitrarily assigned, by the flip of a coin, to be inmates or guards in his experimental prison, the guards almost immediately became brutal or else allowed brutality to exist. The inmates became almost immediately prisonized, "servile, dehumanized robots who thought only of escape, of their own individual survival and of their mounting hatred for the guards." While Zimbardo and his associates have published the results of their experiment in more scientific form,[6] the short excerpt below gives some of the flavor of what happened.

The problem with Zimbardo's information is that we must decide what to do with it now that we have it.

A first possibility is to return to the original question above: does it make any difference who administers prisons? Perhaps the lesson to be learned is that it does not. The nature of the institution is such that it has a brutalizing effect on all concerned: inmates, guards and administrators. Only by changing the very nature of the institution can we hope to avoid this syndrome.

Yet, Zimbardo himself is unwilling to accept such a radical idea. "New management," "improved operating procedures," and "better training" for guards are his solutions to this problem.

Perhaps one additional step might be useful here—the one suggested by George Bernard Shaw almost sixty years ago (quoted above in this section). Shaw recommends that prison administrators, sentencing judges, and even

4. Erving Goffman, *Asylums*, (New York: Doubleday & Company, 1961).

5. John Irwin, *The Felon*, (Englewood Cliffs, N.J.: Prentice Hall, 1970).

6. Craig Haney, Curtis Banks and Philip G. Zimbardo, "Interpersonal Dynamics in a Simulated Prison," *International Journal of Criminology and Penology*, 1(1) (1973), pp. 69-97.

guards be required to spend some time living as inmates in order to see the incarcerative structure from the other side.

This is not a radical thought which has been totally ignored. In some states, an old jail is maintained so that state officials can "check in" for a weekend and be treated like inmates. Several years ago, a top probation official in a large industrial state commented that one of the most disorienting experiences of his life was to take his assistant to Connecticut where such a jail was operated. As in the Zimbardo experiment, this official knew he would be back at his desk Monday morning, and was not just another inmate looking forward to further dealings with the system. He could leave at any time. Yet, by the second day, he said he felt some of the reactions that Zimbardo describes. He found that he could not confide in his top assistant, whom he daily trusted with major decisions. His concern was to "do his own time," maintaining a psychological and emotional distance from everyone else in order to minimize the pains of the experience.

Perhaps a sentence in one of these institutions would be an appropriate experience for those who insist that today's prisons are merely country clubs.

Pathology of Imprisonment*

Philip G. Zimbardo
Professor of Social Psychology, Stanford University

I was recently released from solitary confinement after being held therein for 37 months [months!]. A silent system was imposed upon me and to even whisper to the man in the next cell resulted in being beaten by guards, sprayed with chemical mace, blackjacked, stomped and thrown into a strip-cell naked to sleep on a concrete floor without bedding, covering, wash basin or even a toilet. The floor served as toilet and bed, and even there the silent system was enforced. To let a moan escape your lips because of the pain and discomfort . . . resulted in another beating. I spent not days, but months there during my 37 months in solitary. . . . I have filed every writ possible against the administrative acts of brutality. The state courts have all denied the petitions. Because of my refusal to let the things die down and forget all that happened during my 37 months in solitary . . . I am the most hated prisoner in [this] penitentiary, and called a "hard-core incorrigible."

Maybe I am an incorrigible, but if true, it's because I would rather die than to accept being treated as less than a human being. I have never complained of my prison sentence as being unjustified except through legal means of appeals. I have never put a knife on a guard's throat and demanded my release. I know that thieves must be punished and I don't justify stealing, even though I am a thief myself. But now I don't think I will be a thief when I am released. No, I'm not rehabilitated. It's just that I no longer think of becoming wealthy by stealing. I now only think of killing—killing those who have beaten me and treated me as if I were a dog. I hope and pray for the sake of my own soul and future life of freedom that I am able to overcome the bitterness and hatred which eats daily at my soul, but I know to overcome it will not be easy.

This eloquent plea for prison reform—for humane treatment of human beings, for the basic dignity that is the right of every American—came to me secretly in a letter from a prisoner who cannot be identified because he is still in a state correctional institution. He sent it to me because he read of an experiment I recently conducted at Stanford University. In an attempt to understand just what it means psychologically to be a prisoner or a prison guard, Craig Haney, Curt Banks, Dave Jaffe and I created our own prison. We carefully screened over 70 volunteers who answered an ad in a Palo Alto city newspaper and ended up with about two dozen young men who were selected to be part of this study. They were mature, emotionally stable, normal, intelligent college students from middle-class homes throughout the United States and Canada. They appeared to represent the cream of the crop

---

* Reprinted, with permission, from *Society*, vol. 9, no. 2 (1972).

of this generation. None had any criminal record and all were relatively homogeneous on many dimensions initially.

Half were arbitrarily designated as prisoners by a flip of a coin, the others as guards. These were the roles they were to play in our simulated prison. The guards were made aware of the potential seriousness and danger of the situation and their own vulnerability. They made up their own formal rules for maintaining law, order and respect, and were generally free to improvise new ones during their eight-hour, three-man shifts. The prisoners were unexpectedly picked up at their homes by a city policeman in a squad car, searched, handcuffed, fingerprinted, booked at the Palo Alto station house and taken blindfolded to our jail. There they were stripped, deloused, put into a uniform, given a number and put into a cell with two other prisoners where they expected to live for the next two weeks. The pay was good ($15 a day) and their motivation was to make money.

We observed and recorded on videotape the events that occurred in the prison, and we interviewed and tested the prisoners and guards at various points throughout the study. Some of the videotapes of the actual encounters between the prisoners and guards were seen on the NBC News feature "Chronolog" on November 26, 1971.

At the end of only six days we had to close down our mock prison because what we saw was frightening. It was no longer apparent to most of the subjects (or to us) where reality ended and their roles began. The majority had indeed become prisoners or guards, no longer able to clearly differentiate between role playing and self. There were dramatic changes in virtually every aspect of their behavior, thinking and feeling. In less than a week the experience of imprisonment undid (temporarily) a lifetime of learning; human values were suspended, self-concepts were challenged and the ugliest, most base, pathological side of human nature surfaced. We were horrified because we saw some boys (guards) treat others as if they were despicable animals, taking pleasure in cruelty, while other boys (prisoners) became servile, dehumanized robots who thought only of escape, of their own individual survival and of their mounting hatred for the guards.

We had to release three prisoners in the first four days because they had such acute situational traumatic reactions as hysterical crying, confusion in thinking and severe depression. Others begged to be paroled, and all but three were willing to forfeit all the money they had earned if they could be paroled. By then (the fifth day) they had been so programmed to think of themselves as prisoners that when their request for parole was denied they returned docilely to their cells. Now, had they been thinking as college students acting in an oppressive experiment, they would have quit once they no longer wanted the $15 a day we used as our only incentive. However, the reality was not quitting an experiment but "being paroled by the parole board from the Stanford County Jail." By the last days, the earlier solidarity among the prisoners (systematically broken by the guards) dissolved into "each man for himself." Finally, when one of their fellows was put in solitary confinement (a small closet) for refusing to eat, the prisoners were given a choice by one of the guards: give up their blankets and the incorrigible prisoner would be let out, or keep their blankets and he would be kept in all night. They voted to keep their blankets and to abandon their brother.

About a third of the guards became tyrannical in their arbitrary use of power, in enjoying their control over other people. They were corrupted by the power of their roles and became quite inventive in their techniques of breaking the spirit of the prisoners and making them feel they were worthless. Some of the guards merely did their jobs as tough but fair correctional officers, and several were good guards from the prisoners' point of view since they did them small favors and were friendly. However, no good guard ever interfered with a command by any of the bad guards; they never intervened on the side of the prisoners, they never told the others to ease off because it was only an experiment, and they never even came to me as prison superintendent or experimenter in charge to complain. In part, they were good because the others were bad; they needed the others to help establish their own egos in a positive light. In a sense, the good guards perpetuated the prison more than the other guards because their own needs to be liked prevented them from disobeying or violating the implicit guards' code. At the same time, the act of befriending the prisoners created a social reality which made the prisoners less likely to rebel.

By the end of the week the experiment had become a reality, as if it were a Pirandello play directed by Kafka that just keeps going after the audience has left. The consultant for our prison, Carlo Prescott, an ex-convict with 16 years of imprisonment in California's jails, would get so depressed and furious each time he visited our prison, because of its psychological similarity to his experiences, that he would have to leave. A Catholic priest who was a former prison chaplain in Washington, D.C. talked to our prisoners after four days and said they were just like the other first-timers he had seen.

But in the end, I called off the experiment not because of the horror I saw out there in the prison yard, but because of the horror of realizing that *I* could have easily traded places with the most brutal guard or become the weakest prisoner full of hatred at being so powerless that I could not eat, sleep or go to the toilet without permission of the authorities. *I* could have become Calley at My Lai, George Jackson at San Quentin, one of the men at Attica or the prisoner quoted at the beginning of this article.

Individual behavior is largely under the control of social forces and environmental contingencies rather than personality traits, character, will power or other empirically unvalidated constructs. Thus we create an illusion of freedom by attributing more internal control to ourselves, to the individual, than actually exists. We thus underestimate the power and pervasiveness of situational controls over behavior because: a) they are often non-obvious and subtle, b) we can often avoid entering situations where we might be so controlled, c) we label as "weak" or "deviant" people in those situations who do behave differently from how we believe we would.

Each of us carries around in our heads a favorable self-image in which we are essentially just, fair, humane and understanding. For example, we could not imagine inflicting pain on others without much provocation or hurting people who had done nothing to us, who in fact were even liked by us. However, there is a growing body of social psychological research which underscores the conclusion derived from this prison study. Many people, perhaps the majority, can be made to do almost anything when put into psychologically compelling situations—regardless of their morals, ethics, values, attitudes, beliefs or personal convictions. My colleague, Stanley Milgram, has shown that more than 60 percent of the population will deliver what they think is a series of painful electric shocks to another person even after the victim cries for mercy, begs them to stop and then apparently passes out. The subjects complained that they did not want to inflict more pain but blindly obeyed the command of the authority figure (the experimenter) who said that they must go on. In my own research on violence, I have seen mild-mannered co-eds repeatedly give shocks (which they thought were causing pain) to another girl, a stranger whom they had rated very favorably, simply by being made to feel anonymous and put in a situation where they were expected to engage in this activity.

Observers of these and similar experimental situations never predict their outcomes, but estimate that it is unlikely that they themselves would behave similarly. They can afford to be so confident only when they are outside the situation. However, since the majority of people in these studies do act in non-rational, non-obvious ways, it follows that the majority of observers would also succumb to the social psychological forces in the situation.

With regard to prisons, we can state that the mere act of assigning labels to people and putting them into a situation where those labels acquire validity and meaning is sufficient to elicit pathological behavior. This pathology is not predictable from any available diagnostic indicators we have in the social sciences, and is extreme enough to modify in very significant ways fundamental attitudes and behavior. The prison situation, as presently arranged, is guaranteed to generate severe enough pathological reactions in both guards and prisoners as to debase their humanity, lower their feelings of self-worth and make it difficult for them to be part of a society outside of their prison.

For years our national leaders have been pointing to the enemies of freedom, to the fascist or communist threat to the American way of life. In so doing they have overlooked the threat of social anarchy that is building within our own country without any outside agitation. As soon as a person comes to the realization that he is being imprisoned by his society or individuals in it, then, in the best American tradition, he demands liberty and rebels, accepting death as an alternative. The third alternative, however, is to allow oneself to become a good prisoner—docile, cooperative, uncomplaining, conforming in thought and complying in deed.

Our prison authorities now point to the militant agitators who are still vaguely referred to as part of some communist plot, as the irresponsible, incorrigible troublemakers. They imply that there would be no trouble, riots, hostages or deaths if it weren't for this small band of bad prisoners. In other words, then, everything would return to "normal" again in the life of our nation's prisons if they could break these men.

The riots in prison are coming from within—from within every man and woman who refuses to let the system turn them into an object, a number, a thing or a no-thing. It is not communist inspired, but inspired by the spirit of American freedom. No man wants to be enslaved. To be powerless, to be subject to the arbitrary exercise of power, to not be recognized as a human being is to be a slave.

To be a militant prisoner is to become aware that the physical jails are but more blatant extensions of the forms of social and psychological oppression experienced daily in the nation's ghettos. They are trying to awaken the conscience of the nation to the ways in which the American ideals are being perverted, apparently in the name of justice but actually under the banner of apathy, fear and hatred. If we do not listen to the pleas of the prisoners at Attica to be treated like human beings, then we have all become brutalized by our priorities for property rights over human rights. The consequence will not only be more prison riots but a loss of all those ideals on which this country was founded.

The public should be aware that they own the prisons and that their business is failing. The 70 percent recidivism rate and the escalation in severity of crimes committed by graduates of our prisons are evidence that current prisons fail to rehabilitate the inmates in any positive way. Rather, they are breeding grounds for hatred of the establishment, a hatred that makes every citizen a target of violent assault. Prisons are a bad investment for us taxpayers. Until now we have not cared, we have turned over to wardens and prison authorities the unpleasant job of keeping people who threaten us out of our sight. Now we are shocked to learn that their management practices have failed to improve the product and instead turn petty thieves into murderers. We must insist upon new management or improved operating procedures.

The cloak of secrecy should be removed from the prisons. Prisoners claim they are brutalized by the guards, guards say it is a lie. Where is the impartial test of the truth in such a situation? Prison officials have forgotten that they work for us, that they are only public servants whose salaries are paid by our taxes. They act as if it is their prison, like a child with a toy he won't share. Neither lawyers, judges, the legislature nor the public is allowed into prisons to ascertain the truth unless the visit is sanctioned by authorities and until all is prepared for their visit. I was shocked to learn that my request to join the congressional investigating committee's tour of San Quentin and Soledad was refused, as was that of the news media.

There should be an ombudsman in every prison, not under the pay or control of the prison authority, and responsible only to the courts, state legislature and the public. Such a person could report on violations of constitutional and human rights.

Guards must be given better training than they now receive for the difficult job society imposes upon them. To be a prison guard as now constituted is to be put in a situation of constant threat from within the prison, with no social recognition from the society at large. As was shown graphically at Attica, prison guards are also prisoners of the system who can be sacrificed to the demands of the public to be punitive and the needs of politicians to preserve an image. Social scientists and business administrators should be called upon to design and help carry out this training.

The relationship between the individual (who is sentenced by the courts to a prison term) and his community must be maintained. How can a prisoner return to a dynamically changing society that most of us cannot cope with after being out of it for a number of years? There should be more community involvement in these rehabilitation centers, more ties encouraged and promoted between the trainees and family and friends, more educational opportunities to prepare them for returning to their communities as more valuable members of it than they were before they left.

Finally, the main ingredient necessary to effect any change at all in prison reform, in the rehabilitation of a single prisoner or even in the optimal development of a child is caring. Reform must start with people—especially people with power—caring about the well-being of others. Underneath the toughest, society-hating convict, rebel or anarchist is a human being who wants his existence to be recognized by his fellows and who wants someone else to care about whether he lives or dies and to grieve if he lives imprisoned rather than lives free.

SOME OTHER ISSUES*

By Val Clear of Anderson College and
    Scott Clear of Oral Roberts Law School.

INTRODUCTION

To understand the correctional system one must realize that it is only one facet of the criminal justice system. However, it is a crucial part since society expects the correctional system to be the major agent of responsibility for the convicted person. In the past, that agent has had wide latitude in dealing with the convicted; hence, the rise of such abusive institutions as Devil's Island. More recently, the pendulum has been swinging in the inmates' favor concerning the treatment of the convicted. Recent years have institutionalized "therapy" in the correctional setting to the extent that courts have viewed it as a right of the incarcerated.

The correctional system is charged with the responsibility of managing criminal offenders. The management methods used are regarded by much of the public as somewhat irrelevant; the main concern is that whatever methods are chosen prove to be workable on a practical basis. Managing the correctional system effectively is a monumental task because of the enormous number of inmates involved. In the early 1970s there were 1.3 million prisoners being managed on any given day; approximately 2.5 million admissions per year; with an annual budget of just over one billion dollars.[1] The U.S. Bureau of Prisons alone will probably add 2,000 more penal facilities and 500,000 more prison beds to the present capacity by the early 1980s. In the same period, total crime control expenditures are expected to jump from $4.5 billion to more than $20 billion. The cost of prison construction alone could reach a figure as high as $50 billion.[2] It is for these very reasons that the pendulum is beginning to swing away from "therapy" management of prisoners. In the future the management of prisoners will be done in an increasingly more economical fashion.

The unwieldiness of the current correctional system poses unique questions for the approaching decade. Conflicting pressures are being brought to bear upon a system that is already fraught with tension. The forces that act upon this system can be identified as economic, public, institutional, offender, and court pressures.

---

1. Norval Morris and Gordon Hawkins, "Rehabilitation: Rhetoric and Reality," *Federal Probation*, vol. 34, no. 4 (December 1970).

2. National Moratorium on Prison Construction, *Designs for the Caged Society: the U.S. Federal Prison System and Its Long Range Prison Construction Plan*, (Washington, D.C., 1977).

---

* Original contribution for this book

The economic pressures deal with availability and type of services in relation to population and budget. The public pressures involve citizen demands for better crime control and the need for volunteers in the correctional system. Institutional pressures deal with both the administration of institutions and the management of inmates. Offender pressures involve the interest among offenders in inmate rights. Court pressures deal with decisions which affect the entire correctional system.

ECONOMICS

Economic considerations are going to play a key role in the development of the correctional system within the next decade. With general governmental and correctional costs burgeoning, and with the public voting in favor of such issues as Proposition 13, the emphasis in corrections is going to shift increasingly from treatment to security. It can already be seen in plans, throughout the various states and within the Bureau of Prisons, to build more correctional facilities.[3] Monies are more likely to be allocated for the sole purpose of containment rather than for therapeutic approaches.

Programs already extant will probably be modified to fit the economic needs of the system. For instance, work/study release is going to be used on an increasing basis, but not primarily because it rehabilitates better. There is an increasing trend to eliminate parole from state statutes, and some states that have already eliminated parole are finding it necessary to use existing community correctional facilities to alleviate the population build-up within the high walls. The work/study release centers that were hailed as a vanguard of corrections several years ago will be used as safety valves not only for prison populations, but for prison finances as well. Some states already are beginning to finance these local programs on a subsidy basis.[4] Massachusetts has a work-release program that is financially self-sustaining.[5] Several other states are beginning to see the financial crunch coming and are implementing various low-cost work/study programs.

In Wisconsin, the well-publicized Mutual Agreement Program (MAP) may lower the incarceration time of an inmate through a two-year graduated contract model.[6] The average cost of incarceration for a youth in Colorado is $12,000 per year, and the state's Project New Pride is able to provide similar services *without incarceration* for $4,000. It is estimated that Colorado may save as much as $1.1 million through the use of New Pride.[7]

3. *Ibid.*

4. Council of State Governments, *State Subsidies to Local Corrections: A Summary of Programs*, (Lexington, Ky., 1977).

5. Ellen Chayet, *Supported Work: The Implementation of a Transitional Employment Enterprise*, (Boston, Massachusetts Correction Department, 1977).

6. Wisconsin Correction Division, Systems and Evaluation Office, *Offenders Admitted to the Mutual Agreement Program, Calendar Years 1975 and 1976 Compared*, (Madison, 1977).

7. U.S. National Institute of Law Enforcement and Criminal Justice, *An Exemplary Project: Project New Pride*, (Washington, D.C., 1977).

The correctional system will not overlook the public in its search for answers to the economic problem. Volunteers will continually be sought after, and potential employers of ex-cons will be identified and used as much as possible. Subsidizing the ex-offender for the first few months is increasingly seen as a problem, but such monies will tend to come from the private sector. However, some hope may be gained from the possibility that private enterprise may make it into the prisons in the near future, and inmates would thus have the opportunity to learn marketable skills.[8] Canada is experimenting with the elimination of governmental youth services and the contracting out of those services to private agencies—with both greater impact and lower per unit cost.[9]

The physical plants of correctional facilities are going to make major demands on available funds for several years. There is a growing movement to accredit all correctional facilities from the local jail to the maximum security prison. Along with this trend comes the standardization of all prison construction, with cell size and number of inmates per cell being strictly regulated. Those institutions not currently meeting the standards will have to be renovated or razed at a tremendous cost to the taxpayer. These standards will require fewer inmates per prison; and the result will be an inevitable growth period for prison construction. Because of the amount of money being allocated to renovation and construction, only those correctional programs considered to be economically sound will survive. Courts are going to play a significant role in determining which institutions are humane, and which are not. Correctional personnel will begin organizing, which will in turn lead to collective bargaining. Though increased wages, secured through collective bargaining, will attract better qualified staff members, it will also put increased economic stress on the correctional system.[10]

The correctional system is going to try to convince local judges to handle as many cases in the county and municipal jails as possible. However, these jails are going to be under attack from the accreditation boards. It is widely known that the worst facet of the correctional system in the United States is the county jail. Increased numbers of prisoners, however, will mean new jails. The pre-fab jail is just around the corner, one described with tongue-in-cheek as a "Ready-Mix Jail—Just Add Prisoners."[11]

More courts are taking the victim into account in sentencing procedure and are finding that restitution is a useful tool, especially when tied to part-time or week-end incarceration that enables the convicted to stay in his job

8. Cloid Schuler, Director, Adult Authority, Indiana Department of Correction. Interview with the authors, November 23, 1978.
9. Stanley C. Mounsey, "Contracting Out Government Service," *Canadian Journal of Criminology and Correction*, 19(3) (Ottawa, 1977), pp. 278-291.
10. Shuler, Interview.
11. Jean Denton, "Ready-Mix Jail—Just Add Prisoners," *American Journal of Corrections*, vol. 3, no. 4 (July/August 1974), p.41.

while serving his term.[12] This method also provides the local jails with more *per diems* with which to finance the operation. However, with the increasing number of inmates serving time in the county jails, there also will be an increasing number of law suits filed against the jails. To prevent court intervention, the use of jail ombudsmen will become increasingly popular, as will the inmate grievance system. It will be the ombudsman's job to settle disputes and keep cases out of court, thereby lowering the financial strain on the county jail.[13]

The bottom line of the future is going to be economic accountability. Is the correctional system squeezing as much out of the taxpayer's dollar as it possibly can? Are the monies going for programs that coddle prisoners, or are the monies being used to keep society safe? These are the questions that the correctional system will face in the future. Each line in the budget will have to stand on its own merits, and results must be observable.

PUBLIC PRESSURES

The above economic influences on the correctional system reflect not only the changing financial status of the taxpaying public, but also changes in the public's attitude toward treatment of offenders.

The mounting cost of government and the resultant oppressiveness of taxes, aggravated by inflation, has led to a taxpayer revolt that has direct implications for the correctional system. With the dollar shrinking in buying power, and legislatures refusing to appropriate more dollars, the correctional slice of the tax dollar will begin to get thinner and thinner.

Accompanying this trend is the public's impatience with criminal behavior and what it interprets as the criminal justice system's pampering of the offender. The mood of the public is increasingly punitive, and one has the feeling that the more oppressive the treatment of offenders, the more satisfied the average citizen will be.[14]

There seems to be a great ambivalence toward community-based corrections. Many feel it makes sense to have a community-based program in which the offender is kept in his home community, (close to both his family and his job). But the major obstacle to establishing a program usually is the unwillingness of citizens to have it in their home community. "Across town? Fine. Here? Never!" Zoning boards characteristically buckle under to citizen protest, forcing the correctional agency to look for another location. It is not likely that this reluctance to accept a local program will diminish.[15]

---

12.   Joel Hudson and Burt Galaway, eds., *Restitution in Criminal Justice: A Critical Assessment of Sanctions*, (Lexington, Mass.: Lexington Books, 1977).

13.   Paul F. Cromwell, Jr., "Needed: The Jail Ombudsman?," *American Journal of Correction*, (May/June 1974), p. 38.

14.   Shuler, Interview.

15.   Morgan V. Lewis et al., "How to Organize a Community Sponsor Project," *Prison Journal*, 56(2) (1976), pp. 18-27.

But such public reticence has been countered by the growth of a volunteer movement. Volunteers in Probation (VIP) is a highly successful part of many probation departments and it has been a commendable success. With the help of Judge Keith Leenhouts and the University of Georgia, and with Kellogg Foundation funds, a center has been set up in each state to build volunteerism in criminal justice under the National Education/Training Program. The one-to-one approach, (especially successful with juvenile delinquents but also productive with adult offenders), seems likely to grow in magnitude and effectiveness. Public interest appears likely to continue, with some citizens seeking to be an active part of the solution.[16]

INSTITUTIONAL PRESSURES

As economic restrictions and public opinion pressure the corrections system from the outside, so will there be counter pressures originating from within the system itself.

The demand for competent, trained staff members will increase in order to meet the rigid accountability requirements as well as to match the sophistication of today's inmates. Although the majority of prisoners will probably continue to be comprised of the poor and the under-educated (the John Does of the world), there will also be a periodic flow of white-collar criminals (the John Deans of the world), who will have an impact upon the system.[17]

Rights of prisoners have been endorsed by courts in recent years and can be expected to continue constricting the options of correctional managers. Censorship of reading material and mails, religious dietary requirements, the right to treatment and the right to refuse it, and general living conditions have all been modified. Still to be decided in many states are such measures as the right to parole, the right to conjugal visits or furlough, protection from assault in prison, and the federal minimum wage. (The Morrissey decision is illustrative of the kind of modification that will be changing traditional correctional methods in increasing numbers). According to Norval Morris, if by prison we mean a walled institution where adult criminals in large numbers are kept for protracted periods, then by the end of this century prisons will become extinct.[18] He sees as their successors such phenomena as halfway houses, weekend incarceration, open communities, and therapeutic communities.

The development of these alternatives to prison are favored by those who accept the "medical model," (which states that a criminal is a sick person and must be cured), because such alternatives appear to be treatment modalities. These alternatives are attractive to budget-minded legislators,

16. Robert W. Goodman, *Citizens in Corrections: An Evaluation of Thirteen Correctional Volunteer Programs*, (Sacramento, California Youth Authority, 1976).

17. Shuler, Interview.

18. Norval Morris, "Prison in Evolution," *Federal Probation*, 33(4) (1965), pp. 18-23.

also; the price tag is considerably less than the $12,000 per year in tax money required for adult males in prison.[19] But it seems to us that despite institutional pressures that tend to force the development of alternatives, the temper of the public is retributive enough to demand that large amounts continue to be spent for punitive warehouses, with a smaller amount being spent on promising alternative programs.[20]

OFFENDER PRESSURES

It was suggested above that the offender of the present is a different kind of person than past generations of offenders. Historically, inmates have tended to be from the faceless, submerged classes, although there have been a few distinguished prisoners in the past: the Apostle Paul, John Bunyan, David Thoreau, and Martin Luther King come to mind. Add the Attorney General of the United States, under somewhat different circumstances.

But a new militancy characterizes today's inmate group. Twenty-five years ago a college-educated person was a rarity in prison. The drug culture that came with Vietnam changed that; not only are today's prisoners more knowledgeable, but they are more confident. They do not hesitate to challenge the system. In many cases, they are better prepared than their keepers, and they win often enough to make it worthwhile. They have kept the correctional pot boiling, and most probably will continue to do so.[21]

Issues that the new militants can be expected to pursue include unionization of inmates, freedom from involuntary drugging, special attention to political prisoners, regularized grievance procedures, and a very busy ombudsman.[22]

We can expect to see attention focused on the claims of new minorities in prison: the elderly, the mentally retarded, women, and chicanos. The latter will probably be replacing blacks as the largest ethnic minority in prison.[23]

With the increased number of educated persons doing time and the concurrent restriction on funding for program staff, it seems likely that institutions will increasingly utilize inmates to operate directed self-help

---

19. Val Clear, Scott Clear, and Todd Clear, "Eight Million Dollars," (Anderson, Ind.: Anderson College, 1977).

20. Neil M. Singer, "Economic Implications of Standards Affecting Correctional Programs," *Crime and Delinquency*, 23(2) (1977), pp. 180-195.

21. Shuler, Interview.

22. Stephen Wolpert, *Prisoners' Unions and Inmate Militancy*, (College Park, Md.: University of Maryland Press, 1977).

23. See Joseph N. Ham, *The Forgotten Minority—An Exploration of Long-Term Institutionalized Aged and Aging Male Prisoner Inmates*, (Ph.D. Dissertation, University of Michigan, Ann Arbor, 1976); Robert Joe Lee, *Hispanics: The Anonymous Prisoners*, (Trenton, N.J.: New Jersey Correctional Master Plan Policy Council, 1976); Joann B. Morton, "Women Offenders: Fiction and Facts," *American Journal of Correction*, 38(6) (1976), p.32. Miles Santamour and Bernadette West, *The Mentally Retarded Offender and Corrections*, (Washington, D.C.: U.S. National Institute of Law Enforcement and Criminal Justice, 1977).

programs.[24] The continuing enforcement of laws related to victimless crimes will supply the educated inmates needed for this low-cost, and in many cases, highly-productive approach.

COURT PRESSURES

The major factor in the changing picture of criminal law is the development in several states of the determinate sentence.[25] Although it may vary in detail from one jurisdiction to another, in general it amounts to letting the punishment fit the crime. Emphasis is on "punish," and theoretically, the criminal knows before he commits the act just what the price will be if he is caught.

Rehabilitation would remain a part of the vocabulary of penology under determinate sentencing, but it would be a rather low priority. Each inmate would be expected to do his flat time, with some reduction if his record were clean, but he would not be required to amass a collection of brownie points to impress the parole board. (With determinate sentencing, there is no parole.) After completing his sentence (minus good time) he would be allowed out on his own.[26]

Under the determinate sentencing system, legislatures would probably continue to circumscribe the scope of judges' decisions. Criminal laws would carry clearly stated penalties for specific offenses (e.g., a third felony conviction would automatically carry a life sentence), and the main function of the judge would be to preside over a fair trial.

Currently, prosecutors are under fierce attack for their exploitive use of plea bargaining. An irate public reacts negatively to an inflammatory front-page story of a case where the prosecutor accepts an offer to plead guilty if the charge or the sentence is softened. But there is no way now open to meet the volume demanded of courts, and an uneasy tension can be expected between an overloaded court and a public exasperated with the light or suspended sentences meted out to violent criminals.[27]

With promises of lower taxes determining election returns, it is likely that courts and legislatures will find diversionary programs attractive. The arithmetic is convincing: $12,000 in tax money to keep an inmate in prison compared to $4,000 for the same individual if he is a probationer. Halfway houses and part-time incarceration would permit the convicted to continue

24. Stephen I. Hirschorn and Harman D. Burk, "Utilizing Inmates as Group Leaders in the Admissions Phase of Incarceration," *Offender Rehabilitation*, 2(1) (1977), pp.45-52.

25. Stephen P. Lagoy, Frederick A. Hussey, and John H. Kramer, "Comparative Determinate Sentencing in Four Pioneer States," *Crime and Delinquency*, 24(4) (October 1978), pp. 385-400.

26. Todd R. Clear, John D. Hewitt, and Robert M. Regoli, "Discretion and Determinate Sentencing," *Crime and Delinquency*, 24(4) (October 1978), pp. 428-445.

27. Peter F. Nardulli, "Plea Bargaining: An Organizational Perspective," *Journal of Criminal Justice*, 6(3) (Fall 1978), pp. 217-231.

to work, support his family, and pay taxes.[28]

With indeterminate sentencing, the prison population was kept in some sort of balance through the use of early release. Revolving-door operations were possible; it is said that as someone came in the front door, the officials shoved someone else out the back. With determinate sentencing, no one will be able to go through that rear exit until his day arrives—no one can move that day up to suit the convenience of the state. When prisons begin bulging—and this seems to be inevitable—pressures will be overwhelming upon courts to find alternative sentences.

Part of the problem rests with the courts themselves, which have been forcing wardens to post "Standing Room Only" at prison entrances, most notably in Florida and Kentucky. Prisoners' suits for more adequate treatment seem likely to be successful in several overloaded states where court actions are now pending.

Some courts have found enthusiastic public acceptance for plans that require public service as social restriction. PACT, a privately sponsored organization in Porter County, Indiana, runs a program funded by United Way in which young offenders (18-25) are required by the court to work for a social agency or for the county for a specified number of hours as a form of restitution to the community, for having broken its laws.

---

28. U.S. National Institute of Law Enforcement and Criminal Justice, *An Exemplary Project: Project New Pride*, (Washington, D.C., 1977).

SELECTED BIBLIOGRAPHY

Bailey, Walter C. "Correctional Outcome: An Evaluation of 100 Reports." *Journal of Criminal Law, Criminology and Police Science*, vol. 57 (1966).

Baker, J.E. *The Right to Participate: Inmate Involvement in Prison Administration. Metuchen, N.J.: Scarecrow, 1974.*

Bowker, Lee H. *Prison Subcultures*. Lexington, Mass.: Lexington Books, 1977.

Brodsky, Stanley. *Families and Friends of Men in Prison: The Uncertain Relationship*. Lexington, Mass.: Lexington Books, 1975.

Buffum, Peter C. *Homosexuality in Prisons*. Washington, D.C.: U.S. Government Printing Office, 1972.

Christianson, Scott. "Corrections Law Developments: Prisons, Prisons, and More Prisoners." *Criminal Law Bulletin*, vol. 14, no. 2 (March/April 1978), pp. 145-148.

Clemmer, Donald. *The Prison Community*. New York: Holt, Rinehart, and Winston, 1958.

Cohen, Albert K.; Cole, George F.; and Bailey, Robert G., eds. *Prison Violence*. Lexington, Mass.: D.C. Heath Books, 1976.

Cohen, Stanley, and Taylor, Laurie. *Psychological Survival: The Experience of Long Term Imprisonment*. New York: Pantheon Press, 1972.

Cressey, Donald R., ed. *The Prison: Studies in Institutional Organization and Change*. New York: Holt, Rinehart, and Winston, 1961.

Duffee, David. *Correctional Policy and Prison Organization*. New York: Sage Publications, 1975.

Econ Incorporated. *Study of the Economic and Rehabilitative Aspects of Prison Laundry, Technical Tasks and Results*. Washington, D.C., Law Enforcement Assistance Administration, 1977.

Fitzharris, Timothy L. *The Desirability of a Correctional Ombudsman*. Berkeley: University of California Institute of Governmental Studies, 1973.

Flanagan, John. "The Imminent Crisis in Prison Populations." *American Journal of Corrections*, (November/December 1975).

Fogel, David. ". . . We are the Living Proof. . ." Cincinnati, Ohio: Anderson Publishing Co., 1975).

Fox, Vernon. *Violence Behind Bars: An Explosive Report on Prison Riots in the United States.* New York: Vantage, 1956.

Giallombardo, Rose. *The Social World of Imprisoned Girls.* New York: John Wiley and Sons, 1974.

Glaser,. Daniel. *The Effectiveness of a Prison and Parole System.* Indianapolis: Bobbs-Merrill, 1964.

Glick, Ruth, and Neto, Virginia V. *National Study of Women's Correctional Programs.* Washington, D.C., National Institute of Law Enforcement and Criminal Justice, 1976.

Goldfarb, Ronald L. *Jails: The Ultimate Ghetto.* Garden City, N.Y.: Anchor Press, 1975.

Griswold, H. Jack; Misenheimer, Mike; Powers, Art; and Tromanhauser, Ed. *An Eye for an Eye.* New York: Pocket Books, 1971.

Hague, J.L. *Legal Issues for Correctional Administrators.* Richmond, Va.: Commonwealth University, 1977.

Hawkins, Gordon. *The Prison: Policy and Practice.* Chicago: University of Chicago Press, 1975.

Henderson, Thomas; Weber, J. Robert; Foster, Jack D.; Kannensohn, Michael; Werner, Stewart; and White, Joseph. *Reorganization of State Corrections Agencies: A Decade of Experience.* Lexington, Ky.: Council of State Governments, 1977.

Hirschkop, Philip J., and Millemann, Michael A. "The Unconstitutionality of Prison Life." *Virginia Law Review* 55 (June 1969), pp. 795-839.

Holland, Terrill R.; Helm, Richard B.; and Holt, Norman. "Personality Patterns Among Correctional Officer Applicants." *Journal of Clinical Psychology,* vol. 32 (October 1976), pp. 786-799.

Irwin, John. *The Felon.* Englewood Cliffs, N.J.: Prentice Hall, 1970.

Jackson, George. *Soledad Brother.* New York: Bantam, 1970.

Jacobs, James B., and Retsky, Harold G. "Prison Guard." *Urban Life and Culture,* vol. 4 (April 1975), pp. 5-29.

Johnson, Robert. *Culture and Crisis in Confinement.* Lexington, Mass.: Lexington Books, 1976.

Jones, H., and Cornes, P. *Open Prisons.* Boston, Mass.: Routledge and Kegan Paul, 1977.

Keating, Jr., J. Michael; McArthur, Virginia A.; Lewis, Michael K.; Gilligan-Sebelius, Kathleen; and Singer, Linda R. *Grievance Mechanisms in Correctional Institutions.* Washington, D.C.: U.S. Government Printing Office, 1975.

Kraft, Larry. "Prison Disciplinary Practices & Procedures: Is Due Process Provided?" *Notre Dame Law Review,* vol. 47 (1970), p. 9.

Kratz, S. *Law of Corrections and Prisoners' Rights in a Nutshell*. St. Paul, Minn.: West Publishing Co., 1976.

Langbein, John H. "The Historical Origins of the Sanction of Imprisonment for Serious Crimes." *Journal of Legal Studies*, 5 (1976), p. 35.

Martin, John Bartlow. *Break Down the Walls*. New York: Ballantine, 1954.

Mathiesen, Thomas. *The Politics of Abolition*. New York: John Wiley & Sons, 1974.

McGee, Richard A. "Our Sick Jails." *Federal Probation*, (March 1971), pp. 3-8.

Mitford, Jessica. *Kind and Usual Punishment*. New York: Alfred A. Knopf, 1971.

Morris, M. *Instead of Prisons: A Handbook for Abolitionists*. Syracuse, N.Y.: Prison Education Action Project, 1976.

Morris, Norval. *The Future of Imprisonment*. Chicago: University of Chicago Press, 1974.

Muron, Thomas. *The Dilemma of Prison Reform*. New York: Holt, Rinehart, and Winston, 1976.

Nagel, William G. *The New Red Barn: A Critical Look at the Modern American Prison*. New York: Walker and Company, 1973.

National Advisory Commission on Criminal Justice Standards and Goals. *Corrections*. Washington, D.C.: U.S. Government Printing Office, 1973.

Orland, Leonard. *Prisons: Houses of Darkness*. New York: Free Press, 1976.

Pappas, Nick, ed. *The Jail: Its Operation and Management*. Washington, D.C.: U.S. Bureau of Prisons, 1970.

President's Commission on Law Enforcement and Administration of Justice. *Task Force Report: Corrections*. Washington, D.C.: U.S. Government Printing Office, 1967.

Rothman, David J. *The Discovery of the Asylum*. Boston, Mass.: Little, Brown, and Company, 1971.

Sellin, Thorsten. *Slavery and the Penal System*. New York: Elsevier, 1976.

Singer, Neil M., and Wright, Virginia B. *Cost Analysis of Correctional Standards: Institutional Based Programs and Parole*. 2 vols. Washington, D.C.: U.S. Department of Justice, 1976.

Smith, David Lewis, and Lipsey, C. McCurdy. "Public Opinion and Penal Policy." *Criminology*, vol. 14, no. 1 (1976).

Sommer, Robert. *The End of Imprisonment*. New York: Oxford University Press, 1976.

Smith, Joan, and Fried, William. *The Uses of American Prisons: Political Theory and Penal Practice.* Cambridge, Mass.: Lexington Books, 1974.

Steele, Eric H., and Jackobs, James B. "Untangling Minimum Security: Concepts, Realities and Implications for Correctional Systems." *Journal of Research in Crime and Delinquency,* vol. 14 (1977), pp. 68-83.

Sykes, Gresham. *The Society of Captives.* Princeton, N.J.: Princeton University Press, 1958.

Takagi, Paul. "Administrative and Professional Conflicts in Modern Corrections." *Journal of Criminal Law and Criminology,* vol. 64 (1973), pp. 313-319.

Thomas, Charles W. "Prisonization and Its Consequences: An Examination of Socialization in a Coercive Setting." *Sociological Forces,* vol. 10 (January 1977), pp. 53-68.

_____. "Prisonization or Resocialization: A Study of External Factors Associated with the Impact of Imprisonment." *Journal of Research in Crime and Delinquency,* vol. 10 (January 1975), pp. 13-21.

Thomas, Charles W., and Petersen, David M. *Prison Organization and Inmate Subcultures.* Indianapolis, Ind.: Bobbs-Merrill Co., 1977.

Thomas, Charles W., and Poole, Eric D. "The Consequences of Incompatible Goal Structures in Correctional Settings." *International Journal of Criminology and Penology,* vol. 3 (1975), pp. 27-42.

Toch, Hans. *Living in Prison.* New York: The Free Press, 1977.

_____. *Men in Crisis.* Chicago: Aldine, 1976.

_____. *Police, Prisons and the Problem of Violence.* Washington, D.C.: U.S. Government Printing Office, 1977.

U.S. Law Enforcement Assistance Administration and U.S. Bureau of Census. *Local Jails.* Washington, D.C.: U.S. Government Printing Office, 1973.

Vanaguanas, Stanley. "National Standards and Goals in Corrections." *Criminology,* vol. 14 (August 1976), pp. 223-240.

Ward, David A., and Kassebaum, Gene. *Women's Prison: Sex and Social Structure.* Chicago, Ill.: Aldine, 1965.

Women Behind Bars: An Organizing Tool. Washington, D.C.: Resources for Community Change, 1975.

Wynne, J.M. *Prison Employee Unionism: Impact on Correctional Administration and Programs.* Washington, D.C.: National Institute of Law Enforcement and Criminal Justice, 1977.

Part Three

Community
Supervision

Gardiner Tufts, Superintendent of the Massachusetts Reformatory, "The Convict, Before and After Imprisonment," Proceedings of the Annual Congress of the National Prison Association, Nashville, November 16-20, 1889 (Chicago: Knight & Leonard Co., 1890), pp. 201-202.

Imprisonment, to a considerable degree, fixes the status of the ex-prisoner in the community. He is quite generally the community's dread, and it in turn is often his antipathy, because of the ill will of the one to the other, which began the moment the convict was sentenced. The great force of a community's distrust and mistrust is likely to bear against and down upon an ex-prisoner; albeit the unfriendliness of the world to him is, on the whole, less to-day than it was in the past. When the prisoner goes free from imprisonment, he generally goes burdened with poverty and a sense of disgrace; he finds it hard to make his way in the world; it frowns upon him; it does not open up its avenues of prosperity to him. In order to pass unchallenged in conduct, he must be more circumspect than other men are, for public opinion is more critical concerning his walk and conversation than concerning those who have never been convicts. Imprisonment handicaps the ex-prisoner for the new walk in life; the distressing, depressing, hindering effect of imprisonment involves the after life, position, and opportunities of the prisoner, apart from their involvement in his crime and conviction. This carrying over of the untoward things of imprisonment into the exprisoner's life is one of the evils of imprisonment.

Imprisonments are more frequent and numerous than they need be. Many an imprisoned convict could be as effectually restrained outside a prison as within; he could be better dealt with, while at the same time, the community outside could be as well protected against him. Moreover, under efficient control, in a free community, he can oftentimes be more speedily and surely reformed than if excluded from society by walls; and this being so, it goes without saying that the expense of control outside of walls will be far less than the cost of custody and maintenance within. It has been shown that restraints upon prisoners within walls can be safely lessened; that all prisoners are not criminals; that even criminals can be reformed; that treatment of prisoners should be based upon the belief that they are reformable—and reformable by the same means that make people outside prison walls, who are not convicts, better; and that considerable liberty may be given with safety to many prisoners whose reformation is attempted with the aid of the things of civilization, education and religion.

The rigors of imprisonment has been modified; the closeness of the confinement has been relaxed; many things which used to be denied to prisoners are now allowed them; there has been an enlargement of privileges, an increase of opportunities for those within prisons; in a word, there has been a quite general movement toward putting prisoners on a footing with other men, save in the fact of their imprisonment within walls, and under lock and key. There is a somewhat general feeling that the enlargement of privileges and extension of opportunities are well. The time has come for a systematic effort to keep out of prison a large class of adults who are now committed to prison. It seems to us that the least restraint upon an offender, which is sufficient to hold him from harm to himself and from harming the community, is the best to impose upon him.

National Advisory Commission on Criminal Justice Standards and Goals, Corrections, (Washington, D.C.: U.S. Government Printing Office, 1973).

Nearly two centuries of experience with the penitentiary have brought us to the realization that its benefits are transient at best. At its worst, the prison offers an insidiously false security as those who were banished return to the social scene of their former crimes. The former prisoner seldom comes back the better for the experience of confinement.... The damage the prison does is more subtle. Attitudes are brutalized, and self-confidence is lost. The prison is a place of coercion where compliance is obtained by force. The typical response to coercion is alienation, which may take the form of active hostility to all social controls or later a passive withdrawal into alcoholism, drug addiction, or dependency....

The humanitarian aspect of community-based corrections is obvious. To subject anyone to custodial coercion is to place him in physical jeopardy, to narrow drastically his access to sources of personal satisfaction, and to reduce his self-esteem. That all these unfavorable consequences are the outcome of his own criminal actions does not change their reality. To the extent that the offender can be relieved of the burden of custody, a humanitarian objective is realized. The proposition that no one should be subjected to custodial control unnecessarily is a humanitarian assertion. The key question is the definition of necessity, which must be settled by the criterion of public protection....

Broad use of probation does not increase risk to the community. Any risk increased by allowing offenders to remain in the community will be more than offset by increased safety due to offenders' increased respect for society and their maintenance of favorable community ties. Results of probation are as good, if not better, than those of incarceration. With increased concern about crime, reduction of recidivism, and allocation of limited tax dollars, more attention should be given to probation, as a system and as a sentencing disposition....

There has been a growing realization that prison commitments for most offenders can be avoided or at least abbreviated without significant loss of public protection. If the committed offender eventually returns to the community, it is best that his commitment removes him for as short a time as possible. The principle has evolved: incarcerate only when nothing less will do, and then incarcerate as briefly as possible.

SERVE OR SURVEIL?

The two most essential elements of community supervision—probation and parole—developed as penological innovations in the United States at approximately the same time in history as did the pentitentiary and the reformatory. Though it is not fair to think of community supervision as an innovation designed primarily to mitigate the incarceration of many offenders, this concept has contributed heavily to recent developments in community supervision.

In the century or so that has passed since the inception of probation and parole, the nature, philosophy and activity of American institutions have undergone numerous changes—sometimes dramatic, and sometimes merely cosmetic. Yet, the original nineteenth century community supervision techniques advocated by John Augustus, such as regular reporting, written records filed with the court, active counseling and limited direct and indirect service delivery, have not been substantially changed by those who have followed him. While this may to some degree be a result of the rather advanced thinking of John Augustus, it is probably also a result of the limitations of community supervision methods.

Even though one can argue that the basic methods of community supervision have remained stable, some subtle philosophical conflicts can be identified.[1] A brief discussion of these conflicts will provide a background for the selections that follow in this section. (Note: Some of these issues will be discussed in the section immediately following the readings.)

EARLY DEVELOPMENT

The earliest reformers were often motivated by a religious-like concern for saving their charges from immoral lives of degradation. The targets of community representatives like John Augustus were the marginal members of society: drunks, prostitutes, and vagrants. The task before these early pioneers of probation (and, to a lesser extent, parole) was to use the stong arm of strict discipline to start the wayward back on the right path. Anthony Platt, in his excellent book on the birth of the juvenile court, documents the influence of Christian reform groups in defining delinquency as a moral problem and then organizing reponses to it.[2]

---

1. See Vincent O'Leary and David Duffee, "Correctional Policy: A Classification of Goals Designed for Change," *Crime and Delinquency*, vol. 17 (1971), p. 373, for an extended discussion of issues presented here.
2. Anthony Platt, *The Child Savers: The Invention of Delinquency*, (Chicago: University of Chicago Press, 1969).

In a similar manner, the early development of probation and parole was heavily determined by both pragmatic and moralistic concerns. The early authorities were pragmatic enough to realize that institutions such as prisons had little reformative impact on the wayward. In probation, especially, there was a concern that drunks were not reformed at all by being sentenced to jail terms. In parole, however, there was a different concern. It was clear that the months immediately following release from prison were high risk months for recidivism; ex-prisoners often expressed the bitterness of their captivity (and ambivalence over their release) in the form of new crimes. It was felt that community-based supervision would provide more effective control and better reformative methods for handling certain types of offenders.

However, while these reformist concerns certainly did exist, transcending them was a less pragmatic but certainly more predominate desire to maintain a moral order. The responsibilities given to these new representatives of the state—the probation and parole officers—was not merely to insure that their charges remained crime-free, but also to enforce a morally acceptable mode of life.

Thus, these early officers were involved in all levels of the offender's lifestyle—family, religion, recreation, employment, free time, and whatever else remained. The goal of this severe intervention was the establishment of moral leadership for the marginal and criminal classes. Fittingly, two vocations produce the bulk of the early community supervision officers: the clergy and law enforcement.

THE RISE OF THERAPY

In the late nineteenth century and through the first half of the twentieth, a new set of ideals began to take hold in the community supervision professions. As the new field of psychology came to be accepted as a human science, the influence of social scientists began to be felt in corrections, most particularly in the fields of probation and parole. While casework remained the organizational model, the emphasis switched from field-based supervision to office-based "therapeutic" counseling. The rhetoric of corrections began to resemble the dogmas of psychology. The clinical method developed by Freud and refined by his followers was advocated as preferable to the more common and heavy-handed method of surveillance.[3]

This shift in emphasis was significant for a number of reasons. First, the role of community supervision changed from moral enforcement to interactive therapy. No longer did the officer represent the community, attempting to instill those values which the community-at-large esteemed. Rather, the officer came to represent the "health professions," and the new goal was to make the offender "healthy," (that is, emotionally stable, mature, rational in interpreting life, competent in living).

3. David Dressler, *Practice and Theory of Probation and Parole*, 2nd ed., (New York: Columbia University Press, 1969).

A second reason this shift was significant was that it produced a concurrent change in what the system felt was the ideal role model for the community supervision officer. The officer gradually came to be seen as a person trained in human sciences; ideally a clinical social worker. In fact, this shift has been so gradual that a certain amount of stress still exists today between probation officers who lean toward the earlier "enforcer" role and those who favor the therapy model of community supervision.

A third major change was that the offender was now expected to become involved in therapeutic activity. Soon, in many areas, this involvement came to be seen as *the* central performance expectation. The high moral ideal of living the "approved life," while still important, was no longer the dominant theme of supervision.

The one thing that did not change through all of this was the scope of the officer's authority over the offender. The new goal of improving an offender's emotional health required that discretion be given to the supervision officer. This discretion was necessary for the officer to determine the appropriate therapy and controls needed for each client.

SERVICE DELIVERY GOALS

By the 1960s, however, there was widespread dissatisfaction with the therapy model of community supervision. Part of this dissatisfaction was in reaction to the inability of therapists or clinicians to show that their methods had any more success in reducing criminal behavior or recidivism than the earlier field-based surveillance methods. Other factors leading to this dissatisfaction were the sometimes shocking abuses of discretion under the therapy model, and a questioning of some of the more untenable assumptions underlying the therapy model.

Whatever the reasons, the 1960s saw the development of a new philosophical shift from office-based counseling to the provision of other concrete services that more effectively involved not only correctional agencies themselves, but also community agencies as well.[4]

Those who supported this shift in emphasis pointed to research which had repeatedly demonstrated the limited applicability (if not the utter failure) of strategies based primarily on counseling. On the other hand, they were able to point to some limited research findings that apparently demonstrated a potential for reducing criminal behavior through those community programs (popularly known as "service delivery"). It seemed that by helping the offender in such areas as job placement, special education and training, health services, and even direct financial aid, community supervision was sometimes able to increase the chances of the offender's successful adjustment in the community.

Several key policy changes were linked to this shift in philosophy. First,

---

4. President's Commission on Law Enforcement and the Administration of Justice, *Task Force Report: Corrections,* (Washington, D.C.: U.S. Government Printing Office, 1967).

direct involvement of the officer in the life of the probationer or parolee was minimized. Conceptually, the officer was no longer the all-powerful "law enforcer," but eventually came to be seen as a resource, even as a consultant, to the offender. He or she served the vital role of linkage between the offender and the community.

Second, offenders were expected to take more control over the goals and activities of the supervision effort. The notion of client "self-determination" became a catchword representing the need for involvement of the offender in the supervision process. Rather than the older modes, where the community supervision officer told the offender how to behave, or gave therapeutic counseling on how to behave, the new model called for the offender to take an active role in determining what his or her future behavior or goals would be.

Third, it was no longer expected that supervision officers primarily needed to be counselors. Instead, a mix of professional skills was desired, with a primary emphasis on "advocacy." This new advocate position required the officer to take an active role in helping the offender meet his or her needs, and to help him or her become a functioning member of society. It was recognized that this new role might require the officer to deal more forthrightly with community institutions: schools would have to be shown how to develop truancy prevention programs, employment agencies would need to be shown how to respond to the unique needs of offenders, citizen groups would need to be urged to become more active in corrections, and so on.

WHICH WAY TO GO NOW?

The same debate going on in every other section of corrections has affected the community supervision segment of the criminal justice system. Just as people found that neither the surveillance nor the therapeutic counseling ideals of community supervision produced a magical solution to the problem of ending criminal behavior, so in recent years has there been unhappiness with service delivery. Consequently, new forms of offender supervision have begun to be implemented. Some argue that corrections must take an "advocacy" role on behalf of offenders, (that is, to lobby and work for the development of community resources and services which, in the long run, will help the offender to remain in the community).

Perhaps the most common "new" approach is that of "service-broker." Rather than attempting to be a full-time service agency to the probationer, the "advocate" correctional agency attempts to get existing community agencies to provide on-going services to correctional clients. Such services can be provided directly to the offender or as more frequently happens, the advocate agency, acting on behalf of its clients, may purchase services on a contract basis. Thus, rather than offer marriage counseling, the advocate agency may arrange for a local marriage counseling agency to provide this service to persons who are on community supervision. The reintegrative stance of the service-broker approach argues that it is better to get the offender involved in regular community agencies and services than their special correctional counterparts, since it helps the offender feel and become part of the community system.[5]

Another argument in favor of this approach is that parole officers simply can't compete with professional community agencies with staffs trained in specialized fields. For example, an employment agency is bound to have better job counselors; a mental health clinic, better therapists; a marriage counseling agency, better marriage counselors; and so on. Other reintegrative approaches include use of community volunteers, use of ex-offenders as correctional staff, and emphasis on job training and development for offenders.

Just as the primary techniques have changed from counseling to "hard" service delivery, the traditional organization of community services has also come under attack. Research has indicated that the traditional caseload is both inefficient and ineffective as a means of organizing probation services.[6] As a result, other methods of organizing community services are being attempted, including caseloads which are "specialized" on the basis of type of offender, minimum supervision caseloads, and "team supervision."[7] Thus, changes are occurring both in the way service deliveries are being organized and in the types of services being delivered. The future will require articulation of a variety of models for structuring service delivery in the community, so that agencies will have the opportunity to choose those models which best suit their own communities' resources.

Recently, some writers have begun to question whether community supervision should be legitimately involved in the business of either providing services, or even conducting surveillance.[8] One side of this argument is that probation and, particularly, parole represent further extensions of the state's power, and provide an arena for abuses of the state's social control interest.

A "middle ground" argument between those who wish to retain community supervision, yet disagree on its goals and functions, is one which argues for role specification. An example is the concept of "teaming," in which the specific skills of each officer are utilized to their fullest. Some proponents of teaming have argued that in addition to having supervision officer specialists in employment, education and counseling, each team could also have a "cop" or surveillance officer enforcing the conditions of release.

This structure of a field supervision office would free most officers from their enforcement obligations, allowing them to concentrate on providing

5. Elliot Studt, *The Reentry of the Offender Into the Community*, (Washington, D.C.: U.S. Department of Health, Education, and Welfare, 1967).

6. J. Banks et al., *Phase I Evaluation of Intensive Special Probation Projects*, (Washington, D.C.: U.S. Department of Justice, 1977).

7. Dennis C. Sullivan, *Team Management in Probation: Some Models for Implementation*, (Hackensack, N.J.: National Council on Crime and Delinquency, 1972).

8. See David T. Stanley, *Prisoners Among Us: The Problem of Parole*, (Washington, D.C.: The Brookings Institution, 1976).

assistance to their clients in a more trusting climate. The offender would not have to fear his "counselor" because his counselor would no longer also be his keeper.

Another argument questions whether there is even any need for parole to continue to exist. Traditionally, there are basically three major functions of parole: (a) to provide surveillance of former inmates and to take steps to provide for revocation of parole of those parolees who are in serious violation of the rules; (b) to provide for the delivery of services to the parolee, and (c) to provide a leveling out influence to temper inequities in sentencing between different judges or different jurisdictions in the same state.

The argument for abolition of parole requires that each of these three functions be examined in turn. First, community supervision officers have not provided very much in the way of surveillance and control. Actually, the local police departments do the lion's share of this work. Critics complain that in most cases, community supervision officers decide a revocation is in order only when they receive a telephone call from the police informing them that one of their charges has been arrested. Many suggest that since the police are already doing the surveillance and control, they should just continue doing it without being forced to add an extra level of bureaucracy—the community supervision officer.

As discussed at the beginning of this section, in the matter of delivery of services, community agencies are already being urged to provide those services which were once the parole officer's responsibility. While in the past, a parole officer had an enormous amount of power over the lives of parolees, research now proves that the delivery of services may be maintained without the assistance of the parole officer.

As to the final goal, that of leavening sentences, there is no doubt that a problem exists in many jurisdictions where two offenders, alike in virtually every respect, receive wildly divergent sentences. Critics claim that any reasonable solution to this problem doesn't involve parole. By attempting to provide early or late release dates in order to make sentences equal, the parole boards are usurping judicial functions. If there is a problem with sentencing, which is a judicial role, then it should be solved by the judiciary, through either determinate sentences (which remove discretion from the judges) or by allowing for appellate review of sentences (where an offender is given the opportunity to argue only over the length of the sentence).

Those who favor the use of some system of parole claim that it does enable the parole board to release an inmate at the proper moment in the confinement sentence. Critics argue that parole boards are ineffective, no matter which method of determining release is used. For instance, if statistical actuarial tables were used in order to predict the offender's future behavior, then a fully-empowered parole board would not be needed; a properly programmed computer would do. Also, research has shown that, though parole boards may use clinical assessments to determine an inmate's chances for success, the individual parole board members are frequently lacking in both expertise and ability when it comes to synthesizing this information.

Similar criticisms have been raised regarding probation. It is felt, for example, that the leniency of probation undercuts the deterrent potential of the law,[9] without providing the compensatory benefit of increased community protection. Probation, it is often said, becomes the sentence for white middle- and upper-class offenders because they can usually find the "resources" to assist them in staying crime-free.

An alternative method of revamping community supervision—one which also tends to place limits on the scope of that supervision—is based on the premise that parole and probation have not been effective at either 1) providing services or 2) controlling offenders. Those who take this position argue that in order to increase effectiveness, the focus of community supervision efforts will have to be narrowed, with the supervisory agency being responsible for only one of the two functions listed above.

Throughout this book, an attempt has been made to keep the debates artificially simple by presenting only two sides. Of course, there are many points of view on any issue. The goal has been to present, as closely as possible, polar opposite positions in order to clarify the arguments and stimulate thought and analysis. In the area of community supervision, however, to present only two points of view would be a gross injustice to the reader.

While some critics, like von Hirsch and Hanrahan, argue that community supervision should be abolished, others advocate a continuation of community supervision, though with a considerable amount of disagreement over how such supervision should be structured and administered. Some, like Barkdull, call for a crime control or surveillance approach. Others, such as Dell 'Apa et al. argue for a services delivery/assistance model.

Because even the broadest artificial distinction between these three points of view could not be adequately represented in only two selections, a decision was made to break with the organizational principle underlying this book, in an effort to make a more accurate presentation of current thinking about community supervision.

---

9. James Q. Wilson, *Thinking About Crime*, (New York: Basic Books, 1975).

Abolish Parole?*

Andrew von Hirsch and Kathleen J. Hanrahan

Summary of Report Submitted to the National Institute of Law Enforcement and Criminal Justice, Law Enforcement Assistance Administration, U.S. Department of Justice

Assumptions

Our analysis rests on certain general assumptions and on certain (more controversial) assumptions about the aims of punishment.

General Assumptions. First, moral assumptions. The convicted offender should retain all the rights of a free individual except those whose deprivation can affirmatively be justified by the state.[1] A related premise is that of parsimony.[2] Even where a given type of intrusion can be justified, its amount should be measured with stringent economy. The state has the burden of justifying why a given amount of intervention, not a lesser amount, is called for. Severe punishments bear an especially heavy burden of justification.

The basic conceptions of due process should apply to the convicted. If, for example, an offender is to be penalized for supposed new misconduct occurring after plea or verdict of guilt, there should be fair procedures for determining whether the individual did, in fact, commit that misconduct.

Minimum requirements of humane treatment should apply to all persons who become wards of the state, including convicted criminals. Cruel punishments, intolerable living conditions, and similarly severe deprivations are barred. This obligation of humane treatment should take precedence over whatever penal goals the state is assumed to be pursuing.[3]

Second, assumptions about controlling discretion. It was long assumed that broad, standardless discretion was necessary to allow sentences to be

---

1. Andrew von Hirsch, *Doing Justice: The Choice of Punishments* (New York: Hill and Wang, 1976), ch. 1.

2. See, Norval Morris, *The Future of Imprisonment* (Chicago: University of Chicago Press, 1974), ch.3; and *Doing Justice, supra* note 1, ch. 1.

3. The courts have not always taken this view; for an example of a case where the penal aim of the institution (in this case rehabilitation) was considered an important element in deciding whether the conditions of imprisonment constituted "cruel and unusual" punishment, see,e.g., *James* v. *Wallace*, 406 F. Supp. 318 (M.D. Ala. 1976), decided with *Pugh* v. *Locke*, 406 F. Supp. 318 (M.D. Ala. 1976).

---

* Reprinted, with permission, from *Abolish Parole?*, Summary of Report Submitted to the National Institute of Law Enforcement and Criminal Justice, September, 1978, by Andrew von Hirsch and Kathleen J. Hanrahan.

tailored to the particular offender's treatment needs.[4] But this claim does not bear analysis. Any theory of punishment, even a rehabilitatively oriented one, requires standards to insure that individual decision-makers will pursue the chosen purpose, and will do so in a reasonably consistent manner. The choice of penal philosophy concerns a different question: not whether there ought to be standards, but what their particular content should be. Thus, specific, carefully drawn standards should govern the disposition of convicted offenders. The standards should set forth the type and severity of penalties with reasonable definiteness.[5]

Third, assumptions about the severe character of imprisonment. The harshness of life in today's prisons has been too well documented to need rehearsal. Imprisonment would still be a great deprivation, even if conditions were improved—were there smaller size, better location, improved facilites, and less regimentation than is customary in prisons now.[6]

The severity of imprisonment is important, because it makes essential a careful scrutiny of each phase of the parole process. Parole release stands in need of justification, because that decision affects the duration of confinement. Parole supervision does so likewise, because (among other reasons) it may result in revocation and reimprisonment.[7]

Assumptions About the Aims of Punishment. One cannot examine the

4. See, e.g., Zebulon R. Brockway, "The Ideal of a True Prison System for a State," in *Transactions of the National Congress on Penitentiary and Reformatory Discipline*, October, 1970 (Albany, Weed, Parsons, & Co., 1871), at 38.

5. They should, in other words, be more than general exhortations such as those found in the Model Penal Code—which call on the decisionmaker to consider such factors as whether there is an "undue risk" of the offender's committing a new offense, and whether the penalty would "depreciate the seriousness of the defendant's crime." American Law Institute, *Model Penal Code: Proposed Official Draft* (Philadelphia: American Law Institute, 1962), §7.01(1).

6. See, e.g., Erving Goffman, *Asylums* (Garden City, New York: Anchor Books, 1961); David Rothman, "Decarcerating Prisoners and Patients," 1 *Civil Liberties Review* 8 (1973); Gresham M. Sykes, *The Society of Captives* (Princeton University Press, 1958); Donald Clemmer, *The Prison Community* (New York: Holt, Rinehart and Winston, 1940).

7. An obstacle to careful thinking about parole has been the notion that the offender is fortunate to be considered for release and supervision, since he otherwise would have remained in prison. Because parole was thus seen as a privilege or act of grace, the fairness of its processes was not thought to need inquiry. Our assumption about the harsh nature of imprisonment undercuts this notion. If imprisonment is as severe as we assume it is, the length sentences which judges have been accustomed to imposing are not necessarily justified—in which case earlier release is not merely a privilege.

   The Supreme Court has also questioned the notion of parole as a privilege—on grounds that it has become an institutionalized part of the punishment process. In the Courts words: "Rather than being an *ad hoc* exercise of clemency, parole is an established variation on imprisonment of convicted offenders."

   For discussion of the "grace theory," see Note. "The Parole System," 120 *University of Pennsylvania Law Review* 282, 286-300 (1971); and Fred Cohen, *The Legal Challenge to Corrections*. A consultant's Paper prepared for the Joint Commission on Correctional Manpower and Training (Washington, D.C.: March 1969).

   Morrissey v. *Brewer*, 408 U.S. 471, 477 (1972).

usefulness of parole without first asking, useful for what purpose? At least four different conceptions have been said to underlie sentencing and corrections. Three of these—rehabilitation, incapacitation, and deterrence[8] have been penologists' traditional concerns and look to reduction of crime in the future. The fourth, which the present analysis emphasizes, is desert; it looks to the blameworthiness of the offender's past criminal conduct.[9]

In punishing the convicted, we assume, the fundamental requirement of justice is the principle of *commensurate deserts:* that the severity of the punishment must be commensurate with the seriousness of the offender's criminal conduct.[10] The rationale for the principle was described in *Doing Justice,*[11] as follows:

> The severity of the penalty carries implications of degree of reprobation. The sterner the punishment, the greater the implicit blame: sending someone away for several years connotes that he is more to be condemned than does jailing him for a few months or putting him on probation. In [setting] penalties, therefore, the crime should be sufficiently serious to merit the

8. We define "rehabilitation" as changing a convicted offender's character, habits or behavior patterns so as to diminish his criminal propensities. Its success is measured by the treatment's impact on recidivism rates. It includes not only traditional correctional treatments (such as psychiatric therapy, counselling and vocational training) but also more novel techniques such as behavior modification.

   "Incapacitation," as we use the term, is restraining the convicted offender so he is unable to commit further crimes even if he were inclinded to do so. Like rehabilitation, its success is measured by recidivism rates. Unlike the latter, however, it does not involve efforts to change the offender—but only to limit his access to potential victims.

   "General deterrence" is the effect that a threat to punish has, in inducing potential offenders to desist from prohibited conduct. It seeks to alter the behavior not only of convicted criminals but also of unconvicted members of the public who otherwise might have been disposed to commit crimes. It is measured by the effects of penalties or their threat on overall crime rates—not just by recidivism rates.

   Doing Justice, supra note 1, at 11, 19, and 38.

9. For philosophical discussions, see, e.g., J.D. Mabbott, "Punishment," 48 *Mind* 152 (1939); C.W.K. Mundle, "Punishment and Desert," 4 *Philosophical Quarterly* 216 (1954); K.G. Armstrong, "The Retributist Hits Back," 70 *Mind* 471 (1961); H.J. McCloskey, "A Non-Utilitarian Approach to Punishment," 8 *Inquiry* 249 (1965); Herbert Morris, "Persons and Punishment," 52 *The Monist* 475 (1966); H.L.A. Hart, "Prolegomenon to the Principles of Punishment," in his *Punishment and Responsibility* (New York: Oxford University Press, 1968); Joel Feinberg, *Doing and Deserving* (Princeton: Princeton University Press, 1970); Claudia Card, "Retributive Penal Liability," in *Studies in Ethics,* Monograph No. 7, *American Philosophical Quarterly Monograph Series* (Oxford: Basil Blackwell, 1973); John Kleinig, *Punishment and Desert* (The Hague: Martinus Nijoff, 1973); Joel Kidder, "Requital and Criminal Justice," 15 *International Philosophical Quarterly* 235 (1975); and Andrew von Hirsch, *Doing Justice, supra* note 1.

   For discussions in the literature of penology, see, Norval Morris, *supra* note 2, ch. 3; and M. Kay Harris, "Disquisition on the Need for a New Model for Criminal Sanctioning Systems," 77 *West Virginia Law Review* 263, 297 (1975).

10. *Doing Justice, supra* note 1, ch. 8.

11. For a fuller discussion of the rationale of the commensurate-deserts principle, and of desert generally, see Andrew von Hirsch's *Doing Justice* and also the philosopher John Kleinig's valuable book, *Punishment and Desert. Doing Justice, supra* note 1; and Kleinig, *supra* note 9.

implicit reprobation.... Where an offender convicted of a minor offense is punished severely, the blame which so drastic a penalty ordinarily carries will attach to him—and unjustly so, in view of the not-so-very-wrongful character of the offense...[Conversely] imposing only a slight penalty for a serious offense treats the offender as *less* blameworthy than he deserves.[12]

To satisfy this requirement of justice, the seriousness of the criminal conduct, must determine the penalty. Seriousness, in turn, is measured, by (1) the harm done or risked, and (2) the culpability of the actor in engaging in the conduct.[13]

The principle establishes the following constraints on penal policies: First, it imposes a rank-ordering on penalties. Punishments must be arranged so that their relative severity corresponds with the comparative seriousness of offenses. Secondly, the principle limits the absolute magnitude of punishments; the penalty scale must, at all points on the scale, maintain a reasonable proportion between the quantum of punishment and the gravity of the crimes involved. The scale should not, for example, be so much inflated that less-than-serious offenses receive painful sanctions (not even if serious crimes were punished still more harshly). Finally, the principle requires that criminal behavior of equal seriousness be punished with equal severity. A specific penalty level must apply to all instances of law-breaking which involve a given degree of harmfulness and culpability.[14]

The commensurate-deserts principle, as a requirement of justice, constrains all phases of a state-inflicted criminal sanction, irrespective of whether carried out in prison or in the community. Much of our inquiry will be devoted to examining whether parole satisfies or violates commensurate-desert constraints.

For our analysis of parole, two alternative conceptual models are presented. The first is the Desert Model; it is the conception of punishment which emerges when the principle of commensurate deserts is rigorously observed. The other is the "Modified Desert Model": this is a penalty scheme based primarily on desert, but permitting limited deviations from desert constraints for rehabilitative, incapacitative, or deterrent ends.

The Desert Model. Under this model, all penalties must be commensurate in severity with the seriousness of the offense. No deviation from deserved severity would be permitted for such forward-looking ends as incapacitation

---

12. *Doing Justice, supra* note 1, at 71-73.

13. The measurement of both components of seriousness—i.e., harm and culpability—raises a number of yet unanswered questions. For discussion, see the text of the Final Report of the present project: *Abolish Parole?* (on file with NILECJ), at 21-23. (A revised version of that document was published by Ballinger Publishing Company in 1978.) See also, *Doing Justice, supra* note 1, ch. 9.

14. *Doing Justice, supra* note 1, chs. 8, 10 and 11.
   For a contrasting view, that desert should only set upper and lower limits on the amount of punishment, see Morris, *supra* note 2, ch. 3.

or rehabilitation. The salient features of such a system (as proposed in *Doing Justice*) are:

Penalties would be graded according to the gravity of the offender's criminal conduct. (This, according to *Doing Justice*, would include both the seriousness of his present crime and the seriousness of his past criminal record, if any.)[15] For each gradation of gravity, a specific penalty would be prescribed. Variations from that specific penalty would be permitted only in unusual instances where the degree of culpability of the actor or the degree of harmfulness of his conduct are greater or less than is characteristic of that kind of criminal conduct.[16]

The severe penalty of imprisonment[17] would be prescribed only for crimes that are serious—e.g., crimes of actual or threatened violence and the more grievous white-collar crimes. Penalties less severe than imprisonment would be required for nonserious crimes.[18]

It is sometimes assumed that parole must be abandoned if the rehabilitatively-oriented theory that has sustained it is no longer accepted.[19] But is it necessarily true that the assumptions of the Desert Model rule out parole? Even if parole were historically based on predictive-rehabilitative ideas, it is still a fair question to ask whether any of its features might be re-justified under a desert-oriented conception of sentencing.

The Modified Desert Model. This is an alternate model which gives somewhat greater scope to forward-looking considerations in deciding penalties. The commensurate deserts principle, as we noted, requires equal punishment of those whose offenses are equally serious: a specified level of severity must be selected for each level of seriousness. The Modified Desert Model permits some relaxation of this requirement. *Modest* upward or downward variation from the specific (deserved) penalty would be permitted, for the purpose of enhancing the rehabilitative, incapacitative or deterrent utility of the sentence. Large deviations from the requirements of the commensurate deserts principle still would be barred, however. In that sense, the model represents a compromise: the basic structure of the penalty system is shaped by the desert principle, but crime-control considerations are given some scope in the choice of the individual offender's sentence.

Of the two models, the authors strongly prefer the Desert Model. Because the commensurate deserts principle is a requirement of justice, we feel that deviations from it are undesirable even when small. The Modified Desert

---

15. *Doing Justice, supra* note 1, ch. 10.

16. *Id.*, on ch. 12.

17. *Doing Justice* argues for retaining imprisonment as the severe penalty suited to serious crimes, but would stringently limit its duration. (The report recommends that most prison terms be kept below 3 years' actual confinement). *Id.*, ch.16.

18. *Id.*, ch. 13, 14, and 16.

19. See e.g., the Citizen's Inquiry, Parole and Criminal Justice, *Prison Without Walls: Report on New York State Parole* (New York: Praeger, 1975).

Model is useful, however, as a heuristic device. It furnishes a more complex conceptual framework, in which both desert and forward-looking considerations have a role in deciding the particular offender's punishment. This allows an analysis of parole which is of wider scope than would have been possible using only the Desert Model, with the preeminence the latter gives to the single idea of desert. Besides considering whether desert requirements are met, the Modified Desert Model requires us to inquire whether and to what extent parole does actually serve the rehabilitative and incapacitative aims that traditionally were thought to provide its rationale. Yet the model shows some concern for fairness, by making the blameworthiness of the criminal conduct the primary (although not exclusive) determinant of penalties.

Parole Supervision

Parole supervision consists of a number of analytically distinct activities. In order to examine supervision, we have divided the process into three major elements: (1) the separate adjudicative system for parolees charged with new crimes; (2) supervision *per se*, which aims at preventing further criminal activity by ex-prisoners through the imposition of parole conditions, surveillance, and, if thought necessary, revocation; and, (3) the provision of services to ex-prisoners.

Parole as a Separate Adjudicative System

It is virtually always a condition of parole that the parolee refrain from new crimes.[20] Any law violation can result in revocation of parole and reimprisonment. When a parolee is suspected of new criminal activity, rather than facing criminal prosecution, his parole may be revoked.[21]*

Lower Standards of Proof. A parolee charged with violating parole by having committed a new crime can be reimprisoned on less evidence than it takes to convict. The standard of proof in revocation proceedings is not that of "beyond a reasonable doubt," constitutionally mandated in criminal

20.   A 1973 survey of parole conditions found that all but one jurisdiction had as a parole condition that the parolee abide by the law. The one jurisdiction without a "law abidingness" condition was New Hampshire. American Bar Association, *Survey of Parole Conditions in the United States* (Washington, D.C.: American Bar Association Resource Center on Correctional Law and Legal Services, 1973), at 12-13, 17-18.

A more recent survey of parole conditions (1975) found that four other States—Indiana, Oklahoma, Texas and West Virginia—eliminated this condition. William C. Parker, *Parole*, revised edition, (College Park, MD: American Correctional Association, 1975), at 201-204.

21.   Some indication of the incidence of revocation in lieu of prosecution is provided by the Uniform Parole Reports. A 3-year followup of male parolees released in 1972 showed that 15 percent were returned to prison as parole violators: 4 percent "with new minor conviction(s) or in lieu of prosecution"; 3 percent "in lieu of prosecution of a new major offense(s)"; 8 percent with "no new conviction(s) and not in lieu of prosecution" (N = 19,440; these national data do not reflect all parolees released in 1972 due to incomplete data from some jurisdictions.) Uniform Parole Reports, *Newsletter* (David, Ca.: National Council on Crime and Delinquency, December 1976).

trials, but a lower standard.[22] The procedures of parole revocation also lead to less rigor in requirements of proof. Instead of the unanimous (or near unanimous) jury required in criminal trials, only one or two board members or hearing officers need be persuaded in many jurisdictions.[23] Rights of counsel[24] and cross-examination[25] are more restricted than in a criminal trial, and evidentiary standards are less stringent.[26]

Revocation in lieu of prosecution is not the only official response to suspected criminal activity by parolees. The parolee may be prosecuted *and* his parole revoked; or else, the parolee may have his parole revoked for violation of one of the "technical" conditions of parole, rather than for the suspected crime.

It is not uncommon for boards to conduct revocation hearings even though the parolee is being prosecuted. [Vincent O'Leary and Kathleen Hanrahan, *Parole Systems in the United States* (Hackensack, N.J.: National Council on Crime and Delinquency, 1976), compiled from 88-344.] Depending upon the policy of the board, the parolee may then have to serve his new prison sentence, plus additional time for the revocation. The United States parole board sometimes had done this, and the Supreme Court has upheld the practice. See, *Moody* v. *Daggett*, 429 U.S. 78 (1976). (That case involved a parolee convicted and sentenced for two crimes while on parole. The U.S. Parole Commission issued, but did not execute a parole violator warrant. Instead, the warrant was lodged as a detainer. The parolee asserted, among other contentions, that the detainer barred him from serving the new sentences and the revocation term concurrently, affected his parole eligibility on the later convictions and denied him his constitutionally protected right to a prompt revocation hearing. The Supreme Court held that no constitutionally protected right had been denied and that the Commission need not conduct the revocation hearing until the warrant was executed and the parolee was taken into custody as a parole violator.)

22. For a description of standards of proof in revocation proceedings, see Comment, "Does Due Process Require Clear and Convincing Proof Before Life's Liberties May Be Lost?" 24 *Emory Law Journal* 103, 122-24 (1975).

23. A survey of parole practices found that at final revocation hearings, the hearing body consists of the full board in 14 jurisdictions; 2 members to a majority of the board in 23 jurisdictions; at least one member in 7 jurisdictions; hearing officer(s) in 6 jurisdictions, and "others" in 2 jurisdictions. O'Leary and Hanrahan, *supra* note 21, at 57. (The survey included the parole boards of the 50 states, the Federal and the District of Columbia parole boards.)

24. Right to counsel was determined by *Gagnon* v. *Scarpelli*, 411 U.S. 778 (1973). A survey of parole practices found that when asked *in general* if attorneys were permitted at revocation hearings (as opposed to asking about compliance with the *Gagnon* ruling) 47 boards reported that they permitted attorneys at preliminary hearings, and 25 of those appointed attorneys for indigent inmates; at final hearings, the reponses totaled to 50 and 29, respectively. O'Leary and Hanrahan, *supra* note 21, at 55, 58.

25. Cross-examination, as provided by *Morrissey*, is somewhat discretionary. At the preliminary revocation hearing, the parolee has the following right:

On request of the parolee, a person who has given adverse information on which parole revocation is to be based is to be made available for questioning in his presence. However, if the hearing officer determines that an informer would be subject to risk of harm if his identity were disclosed, he need not be subject to confrontation and cross-examination.

Similarly, at the final revocation hearing, the right to confront or cross-examine adverse witnesses can be abridged if "the hearing officer specifically finds good cause for not allowing confrontation." *Morrissey* v. *Brewer*, 408 U.S. 471 (1972), at 487, 489.

26. In *Morrissey*, the Supreme Court specifically allowed that evidence not admissible at trial is admissible at revocation proceedings:

It is true, of course, that most prosecutions do not involve an actual new trial where the state's attorney must meet traditional requirements of proof; instead a guilty plea is bargained. But at least, the defendant has some choice whether to plead guilty or demand a trial. A parolee cannot insist that there be a trial if the board prefers to pursue the revocation route. Nor can he, in cases where there is a trial, prevent the board from conducting a revocation hearing with its lower standards, and reaching its own decision as to his guilt or innocence.[27]

The high standard of proof in criminal proceedings is a fundamental requirement of fairness; it is designed to keep to a minimum the risk of punishing the innocent.[28] Any lower standard of proof, while making it easier to punish the possibly guilty, entails the unacceptable moral cost of increasing the possibility that innocent persons will be punished.[29] This principle has as much applicability to persons charged with crimes who were previously convicted and imprisoned, as it does to persons accused for the

---

We emphasize there is no thought to equate this second stage of parole revocation to a criminal prosecution in any sense. It is a narrow inquiry; the process should be flexible enough to consider evidence including letters, affidavits, and any other material that would not be admissible in an adversary criminal trial. *Morrissey* v. *Brewer*, *supra* note 25, at 489.

Evidence otherwise excludible in criminal trials under the Fourth Amendment protections against unreasonable search and seizure is usually admissible in revocation proceedings. The Fourth Amendment rights of parolees are at issue in three situations: search by the police; search by the parole officer; and joint search by the police and parole officer. Case decisions have varied, but in general, evidence secured by illegal police search is not admissible at trial, but may be introduced at revocation hearings. Searches by parole officers are usually not subject to Fourth Amendment requirements; evidence gained by parole officer search is admissible at both trial and revocation. Case decisions concerning joint searches have not been uniform.

See, e.g., Case Comment: "Constitutional Law: Warrantless Parole Officer Searches—A New Rationale," 60 *Minnesota Law Review* 805 (1976); Note, "Fourth Amendment Limitations on Probation and Parole Supervision," 1976 *Duke Law Journal* 71 (1976); and Note, "Striking the Balance Between Privacy and Supervision: The Fourth Amendment and Parole and Probation Officer Searches of Parolees and Probationers," 51 *New York University Law Review* 800 (1976).

27. In a recent case, a parolee was prosecuted for assault and acquitted. Then, his parole was revoked on the *same* evidence—and an appellate court upheld the revocation on the grounds that the applicable standard of proof was lower. [Standlee v. Smith, 83 Wash. 2d. 405, 518 P.2d. 721 (1974).] The case was later overturned by the federal district court, in a habeas corpus proceeding. *Standlee* v. *Rhay*, No. C-75-18 (E.D. Wash. Nov. 7, 1975). However, the Court specifically limited the holding to cases where the parole board "deliberately accedes to the criminal prosecution."

A practice that helps parole boards avoid the *Standlee* problem is reported by the Citizen's Inquiry, *supra* note 19 at 132.

It is the practice of the parole board that, whenever possible, revocation should be based on at least one technical violation, even if there is a new criminal arrest also. This avoids the possibility that a court could order the revoked parolee to be released because the revocation decision was based solely on a new arrest or conviction which was later dismissed or reversed on appeal.

28. *In re Winship*, 397, U.S. 358 (1970).

29. *Id.*, at 372.

first time. It is no less unfair to punish a parolee for an alleged new offense which he may, in fact, not have committed, than to punish an alleged first offender who may be innocent.

Were one to reject our assumptions about the primacy of desert and opt for a penal theory that gave more scope to predictions of dangerousness, the lower standards of proof would still be open to the charge of unfairness. Even if new criminal activity were a sign of dangerousness, it still must be established that the parolee has committed the new crime. A mistaken attribution of a new offense to the parolee will lead to an erroneous attribution of risk.[30] Lenient standards of proof increase the likelihood of such mistakes.

Standards of Disposition. The condition requiring parolees to observe the law also creates a separate system of disposition for parolees found to have committed new crimes. The parolee can have his parole revoked for any crime, irrespective of its seriousness. The maximum duration of reimprisonment, moreover, depends not on the character of the new offense, but on the amount of the parolee's unexpired sentence.[31]

Our assumptions would permit some differentiation between the penalties for repeat offenders and those for first offenders. On the Desert Model as described in *Doing Justice*, repetition is grounds for ascribing somewhat enhanced culpability to the offender.[32] On a Modified Desert Model, risk may be grounds for a modest upward adjustment in penalties—and repetition is a factor pointing toward increased risk.

Treating a new crime as a parole violation, however, leads to results that are unacceptable under either model. The penalty could be disproportionately harsh, since even minor law violations could result in revocation and reimprisonment. Conversely, the penalty could be disproportionately lenient. If the unexpired portion of the original sentence is relatively short at the time of the violation, even a serious crime could lead, via the revocation route, to a period of reconfinement insufficient to comport with the seriousness of the crime.

Abolition of the Separate System. We thus recommend abolition of the separate system of adjudication for parolees. Any ex-prisoner who is believed

---

30. See, Alan M. Dershowitz, "Preventive Confinement: A Suggested framework for Constitutional Analysis," 51 *Texas Law Review*, 1277, 1311-24 (1973).

31. The manner of computing the time remaining varies by jurisdiction. In the jurisdictions for which information is available (49), 32 boards report that the time spent under parole supervision; or "street time" is credited toward the sentence; 13 report that it is not; 3 that it may or may not be; and one, that street time is not credited toward the sentence if the parolee has been convicted of a new offense, but is if the parolee is revoked for a technical violation. O'Leary and Hanrahan, *supra* note 21, derived from 82-344.

32. *Doing Justice, supra* note 1, at 85-86. This view has been disputed by some, but it is at least an arguable position under desert theory. See, *Doing Justice,* ch. 10. See, e.g. M. K. Harris, "Disquisition on the Need for a New Model for Criminal Sanctioning Systems," 77 *West Virginia Law Review* 263, 324 (1975). See also, Stephen A. Schiller, Book review of *Doing Justice,* 67 *Journal of Criminal Law and Criminology* 356, 357 (1976).

to have committed a new crime should, instead, be criminally charged and prosecuted.

A major benefit of abolition would be fairer procedures. The requirement of "proof beyond a reasonable doubt," and the more stringent evidentiary requirements of a criminal trial, should reduce the risk of punishing the innocent.*

Practice could, concededly, prove less satisfactory. For what would be guaranteed is not a trial, but merely being put through the criminal process: which in most cases means plea-bargaining. We do not wish to underestimate the difficulties and abuses that plea-bargaining creates. But there is beginning to be an interest in reforming guilty plea practice,[33] and the traditions of the criminal trial, with its emphasis on the rights of the accused, at least make it easier to define abuses as such. Moreover, even with the criminal process as it is today, there will be cases where its more stringent standards would make a difference. Some parolees will be convinced they have a valid defense, will have the resources to hire competent counsel, and will be willing to risk a trial rather than plead guilty. Here, the higher standards could allow them to prevail, where they may have lost in a revocation proceeding.

Abolition of the separate system will also change the standards of disposition applicable to parolees found guilty of new offenses. The extent of that change, and its desirability would depend on what sentencing standards were in effect in the jurisdiction. Thus:

If a jurisdiction has adopted explicit sentencing standards, the ex-prisoner, after his new conviction, would receive the punishment prescribed in the standards. Assuming the standards were based on the Desert or Modified Desert Model, the severity of the new sentence would depend on the seriousness of the new offense and, to some extent, on the

---

* Could the revocation process be reformed to provide higher standards of proof? The high standards in criminal trials stem not only from the formal "proof beyond a reasonable doubt" standard, but from a host of ancillary protections such as strict evidentiary standards and the requirement that a jury of the defendant's peers be convinced of his guilt. To approximate these protections, parole revocation would have to be recast so as to closely approximate the criminal process, and if so, why not be done with it and require a criminal proceeding?

33. Albert Alschuler has recommended a ban on plea-bargaining, and the State of Alaska has recently begun to implement such a ban. Other, more modest proposals include express guidelines for prosecutors to follow in their bargaining decisions, and fuller judicial review of proposed plea bargains.

   Doing Justice argued that presumptive sentencing standards would make it somewhat more difficult for the prosecutor to threaten more-than-usually-severe penalties on a given charge if the defendant refuses to bargain.

   See, Stephen Gettinger, "Plea Bargaining: A Major Obstacle to True Reform in Sentencing," *Corrections Magazine* (September 1977), at 34-5 (Alaska's efforts to restrict plea bargaining); Note, "Restructuring the Plea Bargain," 82 *Yale Law Journal* 286 (1972) (procedures to follow in plea bargains); *Doing Justice, supra* note 1, at 105 (impact of presumptive sentence standards on plea-bargaining).

number and seriousness of his prior offenses. Excessive severity or leniency would be avoided: only serious new offenses could result in reimprisonment—but where the offense *is* serious, the duration of imprisonment would not be limited to the unexpired sentence for the prior offense.

If, on the other hand, the jurisdiction had not adopted such sentencing standards, the result would be less satisfactory. Instead of facing a discretionary revocation decision by the parole board, the ex-offender would face a similarly unstructured sentencing decision by a judge.

Eliminating the separate system could increase court caseloads. Charges against parolees can now be kept off court calendars and handled separately through revocation. With abolition, these cases will have to flow through the courts. Depending on how large the additional caseload is, this could add to pressures to bargain charges down.[34] The dimensions of this problem, however, will become known only as studies are done of the experience in jurisdictions where revocation has been eliminated or restricted.

Abolition of the separate system would have an impact on prehearing detention. Unlike the criminal defendant who is entitled to bail, parolees facing revocation are frequently denied prehearing release.[35] Were the separate system abolished, the parolee would have to be prosecuted, and thus he too would be eligible for bail.[36]

Parole Supervision

Besides facing a different adjudication system if accused of a new crime, a parolee is subjected to a system of supervision which supposedly will make him more likely to lead a law-abiding life. Parole conditions regulate conduct which is not criminal in itself, but is thought linked with possible future criminality.[37] To ensure compliance with these conditions, a parole agent is assigned to and maintains contact with the parolee.[38] Violation of any condition even in the absence of a new substantive criminal offense by the parolee—is grounds for revocation of parole and reimprisonment.

---

34. Caseload pressure is frequently assumed to be a major factor in the rate of cases that are decided via plea-bargaining. A study of caseload and plea-bargaining practice in Connecticut suggests, however, that caseload pressure may not, in fact, be so large a part of the explanation for plea-bargaining. See, Milton Heumann, "A Note on Plea Bargaining and Case Pressure," 9 *Law and Society Review* 515 (1975).

35. See, e.g., Sol Rubin, *The Law of Criminal Corrections* (New York: West Publishing Company, 1973), at 645. For a survey of parole board practice in allowing release pending the revocation decision, see O'Leary and Hanrahan, *supra* note 21, at 49, and 82-344.

36. For further discussion of problems of bail for parolees, were the separate system abolished, see, Final Report, *supra* note 13 at 21-23.

37. For a listing of parole conditions, see, American Bar Association, *supra* note 20; and Parker, *supra* 20.

38. For a description of parole supervision, see, Stanley, *supra* note 21, chs. 5, 6, and 7; and Elliot Studt, *Surveillance and Service in Parole* (Washington, D.C.: National Institute of Corrections, 1978).

Does Supervision Work? The ostensible purpose of parole supervision is preventive: to reduce the liklihood of further law violations by the parolee. Given this purpose, there are threshold criteria concerning whether supervision works that must be satisfied before even a *prima facie* case for this device can be made.

One such criterion may be called "rationality." It requires that parole conditions be reasonably and directly related to the prevention of future crimes by the parolee.[39] If the aim is to encourage law-abiding behavior, the means—namely, the conditions and techniques of parole supervision—should be rationally suited to that aim. Before parolees may be subjected to behavior constraints not applicable to the general population, the burden should lie on the state to give specific reasons why the behavior is linked to recidivism.

Even the most rational-seeming condition may fail when tested, however. Thus a second criterion should be empirical evidence of effectiveness. If, for example, parolees are to be routinely required to seek and hold jobs,[40] however plausible that may seem as an incentive for law abiding behavior, there should be empirical confirmation that former prisoners do offend at a lower rate when subjected to this condition.[41]

The rationality criterion would call much of present day supervision practice into question. Many of the conditions of parole have little or no perceptible relevance to criminal behavior. Periodic visits between the parole agent and the parolee—the mainstay of parole supervision—customarily are brief and superficial.[42] Little effort is made to verify in any systematic fashion what kind of behavior in the community is, in fact, connected with future criminality[43] and to relate parole conditions to such behavior. And, treatment programs are seldom made available to parole agents who wish to refer their charges to treatment.[44]

---

39. The notion that parole conditions should be reasonably related to criminality has been advanced elsewhere. See, for example, the Model Penal Code: parole conditions "should be of a nature clearly relevant to the parolee's conformity to the requirements of the criminal law." American Law Institute. *Model Penal Code, Tentative Drafts, Nos. 5, 6, and 7,* Commentary to Section 305.17 (Philadelphia: American Law Institute, 1955); and the Commission on Accreditation for Corrections, "Parole conditions...should be clearly relevant to the specific parolee's compliance with the requirements of the criminal law...[and] should be tested directly against the probability of serious criminal behavior by the individual parolee." Commission on Accreditation for Corrections, *Manual of Standards for Adult Parole Authorities,* Commentary to Standard 10.8 (Rockville, Md.: Commission on Accreditation for Corrections, 1976).

40. In 1975, that condition was reported in 33 jurisdictions. Parker, *supra* note 20, at 202-204.

41. For discussion of the link between employment and recidivism, see John Monahan and Linda Costa Monahan, "Prediction Research and the Role of Psychologists in Correctional Institutions," 14 *San Diego Law Review* 1028 (1977).

42. See, Stanley, *supra* note 21, at 95-101.

43. One notable exception is a Canadian study. See, Irwin Waller, *Men Released from Prison* (Toronto: University of Toronto Press, 1974), at 172. (Relating those findings to parole conditions is rare, however).

44. See, Studt, *supra* note 38, chs. 4 and 7.

The effectiveness of parole is also open to question. A number of studies have compared the recidivism rates of parolees with those of offenders released at expiration of sentence. Some of these are inconclusive because they do not control for possible differences in the selection of the two groups.[45] (The parolees may have recidivated less often not because of any virtues of supervision, but because the parole board has selected the better risks for release on parole.) A few studies do attempt to control for such differences in selection. Of these, some report favorable results,[46] others less favorable (albeit mixed) results.[47]

The research is too scanty and its results are too equivocal to warrant the inference that supervision succeeds—at least, if the burden of proving success rests on the proponents of supervision, as we think it should. Since there have been so few studies, it is possible that further empirical inquiry might show success, or at least, success among certain selected subcategories of offenders. But that is not what can be concluded now.

---

45. Robert Martinson and Judith Wilks, "Save Parole Supervision," *Federal Probation* (September 1977), report positive findings for supervision; James Robison, however, presents information that suggests dischargees are *less* often returned to prison than parolees. And, he summarizes the findings of another study in which dischargees had slightly more favorable disposition outcomes than did parolees for about 2 years, but by 3 years, the outcomes were virtually the same. James O. Robison, "The California Prison Parole and Probation System: It's Time to Stop Counting," *Technical Supplement No. 2;* A Special Report to the Assembly (April 1969), at 72-74.

46. One study reported by Gottfredson, which did control for risk, found that Federal parolees perform better than inmates discharged without supervision at expiration of sentence. See, Don M. Gottfredson, "Some Positive Changes in the Parole Process." Paper presented at the panel on "Successes and Failures of Parole," at the American Society of Criminology meeting; November 1, 1975, Toronto, Canada, at 10-14. Another found that misdemeanants released on parole did better than those discharged. See, Mark Jay Lerner, "The Effectiveness of a Definite Sentence Parole Program," 15 *Criminology* 211 (1977); and in addition, one study not yet available has apparently found positive results for parole supervision. The study, conducted by Howard R. Sacks of the University of Connecticut School of Law and Charles Logan of the Department of Sociology at that university, is expected to be available early in 1978. *News Release,* Department of Correction (Hartford, Connecticut, n.d.), released October 1977.

47. A Canadian study, conducted by Irwin Waller, compared the arrest rates of parolees and dischargees (after controlling for risk) at 6, 12, and 24 months. Some difference was found at 6 months, but none at 12 and 24. The author concludes:

> The effectiveness of parole in terms of reducing recidivism within 12 and 24 months, or in the long run generally, is an illusion. First, those selected for parole are no less likely to be rearrested than predicted...though parole is, however, granted in the first place to those with lower probabilities...it does appear that parole delays the arrest of a parolee from the first 6 months to a later period within 24 months....

Waller, *supra* note 43, at 190.

Preliminary findings of another study—of juvenile offenders, conducted by the California Youth Authority—found there were no difference in arrest rates for parolees and dischargees. The groups did however, differ in types of offenses for both the first and most serious arrest; dischargees were more likely to be arrested for crimes against the person and drug and alcohol offenses, while parolees were more likely to be arrested for property offenses. "Bay Area Discharge Study: Preliminary Summary of Findings," (Sacramento: Department of Youth Authority, Research Division, 1977).

Were further research to yield positive results, empirical data on what specific components of the supervision accounted for the outcome would also be necessary. It is possible, for example, that any successes are due to the lower standard of proof in revocation proceedings: e.g., parolees may be more reluctant to risk new crimes because they can be reimprisoned more easily. This would be a troublesome result because, as we pointed out in the previous section, a low standard of proof—whatever its usefulness as an inducement to law-abiding behavior—entails greater danger of penalizing the innocent.

Is Supervision Just?—Desert Constraints. Can supervision be squared with the requirements of desert? Although preventive in aim, supervision is unpleasant, and so we must ask whether it enhances the severity of the punishment in ways prohibited by the commensurate-deserts principle.

In assessing supervision, one should distinguish between (1) the contribution of supervision *per se* to severity, and (2) the contribution of the revocation sanction. Supervision may not (depending upon its content) enhance severity by much; and any such enhancement in severity could, in any event, be offset by appropriately scaling down the duration of the original confinement. Revocation, on the other hand, presents the following, more serious difficulty.

Revocation can result in substantial periods of reimprisonment, although no new criminal act has been committed. (Not all revocations result in lengthy terms, of course. But the potential exists, since the parolee can be reconfined, at the board's discretion, until his sentence expires.)[48] As a result

---

48. Information on duration of imprisonment for revoked parolees is scarce.
     The following table represents the amount of unexpired parole periods for New York parolees revoked in 1975:

Parole Violators From New York State Correctional Facilities Declared Delinquent During 1976—Unexpired Parole Period:

Unexpired Parole Period	Total	Percent
Total:	2,036	100.00
Less than 3 months	23	1.1
3 months but less than 6 months	151	7.4
6 months but less than 9 months	254	12.5
9 months but less than 1 year	298	14.7
1 year but less than 1-½ years	503	24.7
1-½ years but less than 2 years	245	12.0
2 years but less than 2-½ years	180	8.9
2-½ years but less than 3 years	82	4.0
3 years but less than 4 years	80	3.9
4 years but less than 5 years	39	1.9
5 years and over	158	7.8
Life	23	1.1

Source: State of New York, Department of Correctional Services, *Annual Statistical Report: 1975 Data, Inmate and Parole Populations* (Albany, New York: Division of Program Planning, Evaluation and Research, n.d.), at Table D-10, p. 90.

In Oregon, the parole board has issued guidelines concerning duration of reimprisonment

of revocation, offenders sentenced for the same original crime and serving initial terms of the same duration ultimately may serve very disparate terms of confinement, depending on whether or not they are reimprisoned for parole violations that are not in themselves criminal acts. And the additional confinement can render the total punishment inflicted disproportionately severe in relation to the seriousness of the original crime. This objection holds not only under the strict Desert Model, but under the Modified Desert Model as well. The latter, as we saw, permits a limited amount of variation from deserved severity for crime-control ends, and this could conceivably allow a modest amount of added confinement. But revocation could involve a *large* amount of extra imprisonment.

We have spoken only of whether the revocation sanction can be justified as deserved for the original offense. But might not the sanction be defended instead as a penalty deserved for the parole violation itself? If a parole condition is imposed as part of one's punishment for a crime, why shouldn't the flouting of that requirement be deserving of extra punishment? There are two reasons why this argument will not sustain parole revocation:

Standards of liability and proof. A willful refusal to abide by the terms of supervision might, perhaps, be defined as a new crime, as escape is now declared a crime. But then, the parolee would be entitled to demand a full trial, in which proof beyond a reasonable doubt and other procedural safeguards would apply. These safeguards are missing when a parolee is reimprisoned through a revocation hearing.[49]

Severity of the revocation penalty. Even were parole violations declared crimes, they would not deserve severe punishment unless they can be shown to be serious. Yet how reprehensible are technical parole violations? There is no immediate injury to others, such as occurs when the parolee commits most ordinary crimes. The parolee is not "getting away with" substantially less punishment than he deserves for his original crime—as occurs in prison escapes—since he has largely paid the price for that crime already, through his sojourn in prison before being released on parole. Of course, it is difficult to give a definitive rating to such conduct in the absence of a fuller theory of what constitutes seriousness.[50] But on

---

for technical violations—according to which the duration of reconfinement before release is to be 4-6 months, or 6-10 months, depending on the seriousness of the offender's original offense. The U.S. Parole Commission is somewhat more severe: its guidelines provide for reconfinement from 8 to 16 months in the event the parolee is found to have "a negative employment school record during supervision" or "lack of positive efforts to cooperate with parole plan," or if the violation occurred less than 8 months after release. The majority of States have no such guidelines, and there is little data available on their durations of reconfinement. Oregon Administrative Rules, Board of Parole, See 254-70-042 (1977). U.S. Parole Commission, *Regulations* §2.21, 42 *Federal Register* No. 151 (Friday, August 5, 1977).

49. See, discussion above entitled "Parole as a Separate Adjudicative System"; and, in more detail, see the Final Report, *supra* note 13, ch. 6.

50. See, note 13, *supra*.

these common-sense grounds alone, we would be skeptical of claims that a parole violation is so blameworthy in itself as to deserve the long durations of reconfinement that parole revocation potentially entails.

Try To Reform Supervision? If the severity of the revocation sanction creates the problem, could supervision be salvaged by scaling down that sanction?[51]   Would supervision, thus reformed, meet the desert requirements? And could it be effective, with such limited sanctions? The answers depend on which of the two models—Desert or Modified Desert—one chooses.

On a Modified Desert Model: Here, modest backup sanctions would be permissible. Even if such sanctions are viewed as deviations from the amount of the deserved punishment for the original offense, this model expressly allows such deviations, provided their extent is limited.

Effectiveness could, however, become more difficult to achieve. Through the revocation sanction, parole can now operate as a method of incapacitation: parolees who seem headed for new crimes can be taken out of circulation. Using parole supervision in this manner requires only that one identify empirically which kinds of behavior after release are indicative of enhanced risk of recidivism. If one limits the power to reconfine parole violators, however, supervision will have to change from an incapacitative to a rehabilitative technique: it will have to be capable of rendering parolees more law-abiding while they remain in the community. The task becomes the harder one of changing behavior, not just forecasting it.

We are, therefore, not optimistic about the prospects of success. The question of effectiveness can only be resolved, however, by empirical research. The research should examine not only the effect of supervision on recidivism rates, but also a second factor: cost. Parole supervision is unquestionably an expensive process, but little is known about how expensive it is, where the greatest costs lie, and how much money could be saved through elimination of needless procedures. Even if supervision were shown to have some effect on recidivism, it is important to consider whether those effects are sufficiently great to warrant the expense.

On a Desert Model. By requiring strict adherence to the commensurate deserts principle, this model would, in our opinion, rule out parole supervision, even with modest sanctions for parole violations.

Such sanctions could not be justified as part of the deserved punishment for the original offense, since they would impose on violators an added

---

51.   The new California law, in the form originally enacted in 1976, moved in this direction by limiting reimprisonment for revoked parolees to 6 months. Some proposals go even further: the Hart-Javits bill dealing with the Federal sentencing system, limits reimprisonment to 15 days.

  California Statutes, 1976, ch. 1139, §3057; S. 204, proposed "Federal Sentencing Standards Act of 1977" introduced by Senators Hart and Javits, 95th Congress, 1st Session (January 12, 1977), §11(a)(2)(B).

amount of punishment not suffered by nonviolators whose original crimes were of equal seriousness. Treating the violation itself as deserving of punishment is likewise problematic—since ordinarily, only *crimes* are punishable acts.[52]

Keep Supervision Under Other Models? Were someone to reject our desert-oriented models of justice, how would the conclusions differ?

One could no longer object to the potentially severe revocation sanction as undeserved. A more utilitarian sentencing philosophy might permit the added severity of parole revocation, if useful in reducing recidivism.*

But there remains the question of the effectiveness of conventional parole supervision. For the past 75 years, supervision has been routinely imposed, with negligible efforts to ascertain its effectiveness and cost. At least, this institution should be forced to undergo a period of rigorous testing, and should be discontinued if its utility is not demonstrated. One way this could be accomplished would be by setting a "sunset" date: existing authority to supervise would be made to expire in (say) 5 years. During that period, parole

---

52. For citation in footnote: Concerning the necessity of imprisonment, see, *Doing Justice*, *supra* note 1, ch. 13. One could create a new crime of infringing conditions of parole. But requiring violators to be prosecuted would make the supervision system so cumbersome and costly as, in our view, to reduce the likelihood of its being effective to near-zero.

Alternatively, one could retain an administrative proceeding to determine guilt for the violation—on the theory that the rigorousness of the fact-finding procedure may properly vary with the severity of the penalties. When the authorized sanctions are modest, as they would be in "reformed" parole, a less formal procedure arguably might suffice. The analogy that might be drawn is that of prison discipline discussed in the Final Report; briefly extending an inmate's stay in prison through an administrative proceeding, if he commits a disciplinary infraction.

But the analogy to prison discipline is a doubtful one. Even when potential penalties are small, why should there be fact-finding procedures less stringent than a criminal trial unless there clearly are no practical alternatives? Administratively imposed penalties for prison infractions are, arguably, a necessity in this sense. The Desert Model requires severe punishment for serious offenses; imprisonment is the only available severe punishment; and in prisons, maintaining order requires some significant penalties that can be administratively imposed, given the difficulties of prosecuting prison infractions. Parole sanctions do not fit this logic—for the measure they enforce, the supervision itself, is not a necessity under the Desert Model. There is an alternative that would dispense with the need for such sanctions: abolish the supervision.

* There could, however, be another ground for objection. In the section on "Parole as a Separate Adjudicative System" (pages 114-119), we argued against revoking and reimprisoning parolees charged with new crimes. The argument was not based on desert constraints, but on a broader principle of procedural fairness: that someone should not be punished for an alleged new crime without the state being required (if the charge is contested) to prove his guilt beyond a reasonable doubt. Someone who did not hold a desert-oriented sentencing theory might still accept this principle, since it relates not to the amount of punishment for the guilty, but to the criteria for deciding guilt. If so, he might wish to eliminate potentially severe penalties for technical violations of parole, because these can be misused so readily for the purpose of penalizing parolees thought guilty of new crimes. It is too easy, when a parolee is believed guilty of a new crime, to charge him with violating one of the numerous (and often vaguely worded) technical conditions and to use that violation as pretext for imprisoning him for the unproven crime.

agencies would be expected to devote much of their resources to the empirical testing of supervision methods (both as to effectiveness and cost). At the end of the period, the results would be evaluated, and unless substantial positive results emerged, the authority to supervise should be terminated.

Were supervision so tested, we venture to guess that if it survives at all, it will emerge with much smaller dimensions than it has today. Conceivably, supervision could be found effective (and worth its expense) for certain carefully selected categories of offenders. But we would be surprised if this elaborate and costly process needs to be imposed on all released offenders.

During the period of testing (and afterward, to the extent supervision survives), guidelines would also be needed. They should specify such matters as the type and intensity of supervision, the types of violations warranting reimprisonment rather than lesser sanctions, and the duration of imprisonment upon revocation. This could help somewhat in reducing disparities in the handling of similarly situated parole violators.[53]

Services to Parolees

Even if parole supervision is abolished or restricted, there remains the question of providing services to ex-prisoners. Imprisonment severs many of the prisoner's links to the outside world. When released, he will have to reestablish these links, and that will be made harder by the stigma of his criminal record. Furlough and work-release programs may ease this process somewhat, by providing the prisoner a "halfway out" status for a time before he leaves prison. But it will still be a difficult transition. The problems encountered by recently released prisoners have been cataloged by a number of researchers.[54] Not suprisingly, most report that the most pressing needs are material: financial aid, housing, employment, and obtaining credentials.

Provision of services has been one of the supposed functions of parole supervision. However, the services tend to be rudimentary, since the parole agent seldom has any resources for assistance at his disposal. Moreover, the helping and policing functions tend to conflict.[55] It has thus been suggested that services could better be performed were they made the sole focus of the state's involvement after the prisoner's release.[56] This would, it is said, allow

---

53. The Oregon parole board has implemented guidelines for duration of "active" parole supervision, and for duration of reimprisonment upon revocation. See, Oregon Administrative Rules, Board of Parole, §§254-90-005, 254-70-042; and note 48, *supra*.

54. See, e.g., Citizen's Inquiry, *supra* note 19; Studt, *supra* note 38; Rosemary J. Erickson, Wayman J. Crow, Louis A. Zurcher and Archie V. Connett, *Paroled But Not Free: Ex-Offenders Look at What They Need to Make It Outside* (New York: Behavioral Publications, 1973); John Irwin, *The Felon* (Englewood Cliffs, N.J.: Prentice-Hall, 1970); Daniel Glaser, *The Effectiveness of A Prison and Parole System* (New York: Bobbs-Merrill, 1969); and see, Robert Horowitz, *Back on the Street—From Prison to Poverty* (Washington, D.C.: American Bar Association, Transitional Aid Research Project for Ex-Offenders, Commission on Correctional Facilities and Services, June 1976.)

55. See, Elliot Studt, *supra* note 38.

56. See, e.g., Stanley, *supra* note 21, at 190-91.

more resources to be put into the provision of services, by freeing those now devoted to trying to control supervisees. And it could make ex-prisoners less reluctant to accept the help offered, because assistance would be separated from enforcement.

Which Objective: Crime Control or Help? In speaking earlier of programs for offenders, we were referring to those that were rehabilitative in the conventional sense: that is, those whose objective was to reduce participants' rate of return to crime. The criterion for success was whether individuals enrolled in the program recidivated less often than similar samples of non-participants.

It is sometimes claimed that voluntary services would succeed better in this rehabilitative task. This claim would have to be tested empirically, but hopes for much success may be disappointing. Those volunteering for treatment programs may well be the best risks: those who might not recidivate even without programs. Moreover, it is not merely compulsion that tends to interfere with treatment, but more fundamental problems such as the lack of understanding of the causes of criminal behavior.[57]

We think service programs should, instead, seek a different goal: helping ex-prisoners reestablish a tolerable life for themselves in the community. The criterion of success would not be recidivism control, but the programs' ability to alleviate suffering and disorientation among ex-inmates. Programs for ex-prisoners would thus be judged as social service.[58]

Meeting the Needs. The services for releasees should include provision of financial support during the difficult first weeks after the offender leaves prison; job placement and job training services; aid in locating housing; and "status clearance" services such as assistance in obtaining credentials, and psychological counseling.[59]

When should assistance be provided? Many authorities report that the period of greatest stress for releasees is the weeks and months immediately following release.[60] Priority should be given to providing assistance during this difficult early period. More specific answers about timing depend on the particular needs involved. A few are quite short term and could be met

---

57. *Doing Justice, supra* note 1, at 16.

58. This social service aim, rather than crime control, is also urged in the Citizen's Inquiry report, *supra* note 19, at 179.

59. For "status clearance," see, Studt, *supra* note 38; for services generally, see, *supra* note 54.

60. See, e.g., Studt, *supra* note 38; Irwin, *supra* note 54, at ch. 5; American Bar Association, *supra* note 20. Commentary to §9.6; A. Verne McArthur, *Coming Out Cold: Community Reentry from a State Reformatory* (Lexington, Mass.: D.C. Heath, 1974), at ch. 6; but see, Marc Rensema, "Success and Failure Among Parolees as a Function of Perceived Stress and Coping Styles," where he reports that the parolees in his study had problems "in abundance" but apparently little psychological stress, in Hans Toch, *Interventions for Inmate Survival*, Final Report submitted to LEAA, August 1976.

through furlough or other prerelease programs[61]—status clearance being an example. Most services, however, may have to continue for a time after release.

Parole systems now have a staff of parole agents working to carry out the traditional supervision function. If the recommendations of the last section were adopted, these agents may have little or no supervision left to do. Could the agents assume the service-providing function?

At present, the parole agency has few services at its disposal. However, the services could be obtained by having the parole agency contract for them with specialized community agencies. Then the individual agent could act as a broker or "resource manager."[62] He would inform his clients of the available resources, channel them to the program of choice, and followup to insure that the parolee receives the service. The agent could also act as a conduit to any programs offered to members of the community generally, such as welfare or adult education programs.

What remains to be seen is how well the parole agency and its agents would be suited to this new function. Parole agents have not been trained in locating and arranging social services and many tend to view their role as chiefly law enforcement.[63] Whether this change of mission could successfully be accomplished, and what retraining programs and other steps would be needed for the change, can be determined only by experimenting.

Voluntary or Compulsory Services? If the ex-prisoner does not wish to accept the services, should there be any penalty for refusal? We think not, for both pragmatic and moral reasons.

One objection concerns how participation could be policed if it were made obligatory. Because offenders would be living in the community rather than in the controlled environment of a prison, procedures would have to be developed for monitoring participation, reasserting control over nonparticipants, and imposing penalties—in short, something akin to a miniature

61. These programs are already in existence in many jurisdictions. For example, California has a furlough program which is restricted to inmates who are within 90 days of release. A description of that program as implemented in one correctional facility found that inmates leave on furlough with a few fairly specific objectives (e.g., finding housing). See, Norman Holt, "Temporary Prison Release," in Carter, Glaser and Wilkins, eds., *Correctional Institutions*, 2nd ed. (New York: J.B. Lippincott, 1977).

62. This role for parole agents was recommended by the National Advisory Commission, at 410-11. There is evidence that the service of locating sources of assistance might be useful, since the ex-prisoners tend to be unaware of the available helping resources. A study of county jail releasees found both awareness and use of "the more prominent aftercare agencies" fairly low. See, Peter C. Buffam, "The Philadelphia Aftercare Survey: A Summary Report," 56 *The Prison Journal* 3, 12-15 (1976). Furthermore, Studt reports that community social service agencies are reluctant to accept parolees as clients. Studt, *supra* note 38, at 131-32.

63. See, Studt, *supra* note 38; and the Citizen's Inquiry on Parole and Criminal Justice, *Prison Without Walls: Report on New York State Parole*, (New York: Praeger, 1975); but see, Robert C. Prus, *Revocation, Related Decision Making: A Labeling Approach*, (Ann Arbor, Mich.: University Microfilms, 1974; dissertation, University of Iowa, 1973).

system of supervision. As such a system of enforcement expands, the agency offering the services is likely to find its energies increasingly absorbed by administering the policing system, rather than providing services.

Compulsory services are questionable on moral grounds as well. In the second section, "Assumptions," (pages ____), we assigned a high value to preserving the liberty of the individual. Given this goal, we think that forcing the exoffender to accept services thought beneficial only (or primarily) to himself cannot be justified.[64]

Our view, therefore, is that the services should be voluntary. They should be offered to any offender who needs them, but he should be free to reject them. Participation should not be made a condition of release, nor should there be penalties (even mild ones) for refusal.

---

64. See, Gerald Dworkin, "Paternalism," in Joel Feinberg and Hyman Gross, *The Philosophy of Law*, (Encino, Ca.: Dickenson, 1975), at 123. For further discussion, see full Final Report, *supra* note 13, at 118-20.

Probation:
Call It Control—And Mean It*

Walter L. Barkdull
Assistant Director,
California Department of Corrections, Sacramento

Paradoxically public exasperation at rising crime is being channeled into more prison commitments at the expense of community dispositions at a time when prisons and prison construction are under attack. Prison populations are rising nationwide. It is more than a coincidence this is occurring at a time when correctional leadership is confused, discouraged and uncertain as to its aims. If California's experience is representative, the trend toward a higher proportion of prison commitments is certain to accelerate unless positive, practical steps are taken to counter it.

The Evidence

The first mandatory prison sentencing laws in more than 15 years were enacted last year by overwhelming legislative majorities and more mandatory sentencing bills are moving through the California Legislature this year. The effect is already being felt at Department of Corrections reception centers. Juvenile court "reform" bills that insist upon, or at least facilitate, the sending of 16- and 17-year-olds to prison for specified offenses are receiving serious consideration. Other legislation would remove the requirement that prison commitments be reduced from California's existing probation subsidy, purposely encouraging more prison commitments. The same measure would split the subsidy funds that now go solely for probation supervision with the police and others.

Judges are being required to state their reasons for granting probation and pending legislation would require an index of their decisions to make it easier for "court-watchers." Two metropolitan California newspapers are publishing sentencing box scores of local jurists.

Less well received legislation, sponsored by both liberal and conservative elements, proposes to eliminate probation and parole altogether.

The bills requiring prison commitment of persons convicted of using a firearm in the commission of specified serious offenses and for the sale of a half-ounce or more of heroin were not even referred to the fiscal committee of either house of the legislature despite their obvious potential for high costs. Basing its estimates on existing sentencing practices, the Department

---

* Reprinted, with permission, from *Federal Probation*, vol. 40 (1976), pp. 3-8.

of Corrections calculated an additional 850 persons or more would be sent to prison each year by the gun bill alone.

Significantly, legislators who were staunch friends of diversion, community dispositions, and rehabilitation have been quick to suggest or agree that mandatory sentences are the answer to the high crime rate. And these actions come at a time when the most recent figures show the probation violation index at its lowest point in a dozen years.

There has been no evident opposition from the courts to this implicit criticism of their judgment or the curtailment of their discretion. Despite the evidence that probation is a highly cost-effective and humane correctional method there has been no effective opposition from the probation leadership, the advocates of community correction, nor even from the hard-eyed taxpayers' associations who are otherwise quick to vent citizen concern with the high cost of government.

Advocates of mandatory prison sentences equate the "certainty of punishment" and its presumed deterrent effect with commitment to prison. This is inaccurate on at least two counts. First, it assumes that criminals are caught and convicted. A preliminary report of a special four-county study by the California Bureau of Criminal Statistics issued this year showed that out of more than 94,000 felony arrests, less than 14,000 were convicted in Superior Court. Had all of those convicted been sent to prison the odds would have been almost seven to one in favor of the criminal. If the statistics were based on crimes reported—or actual crimes committed—the chance of conviction would have been an even greater long shot.

With these odds operating, few criminals will be deterred by the remote possibility of a mandatory prison sentence *if* they get caught and *if* they get convicted. On a cost-effectiveness basis it would provide greater payoff to invest more resources in apprehending criminals rather than socking the relative few that are caught with long prison terms. Certainty of apprehension is by far the more effective deterrent. Certainty of conviction probably ranks next.

Second, equating punishment solely with prison ignores the reality that probation sentences or other available sanctions are or can be punishment. Furthermore unless mandatory sentencing legislation carries with it a clear commitment to allocate necessary resources to prisons, it can only make prison conditions worse. Present plants, many of them already overcrowded, will become home to even higher populations. With such overcrowding it is easy to anticipate more idleness, more frustration, more tension, greater dehumanization, violence, and loss of effectiveness both as to treatment and control.

Trend Reflects Public View

The trend to more prison sentences, however, does accurately reflect the public view that the present alternatives to prison simply do not meet public needs. Probation, as it is understood by the public, does not seem to *do* anything to the offender or for the public. It does not even serve a positive symbolic function.

The victim wants satisfaction. He wants his property restored or replaced, his injuries compensated, the likelihood of any future repetition reduced and some retributive penalty assessed on the offender. But what does he generally get? Too often, from the time he reports the crime, the police treat him as though he were the criminal. (Partly this is because they simply cannot become emotionally involved with case after case and a "professional" brusqueness masks their concern.) Offenders are seldom caught and police make what appears to be little effort to do so. If the victim's property is recovered, it's seized for evidence. If not, he's out the cost unless it's insured and that's another hassle. If the criminal is hurt, he gets free medical treatment but the victim is generally on his own.

When it's his turn to be a witness, his problems are compounded. Witnesses are expected to become involved, but when they do they become the object of suspicion, of repeated interrogation and finally of demands they appear for trial at a court sadly lacking a decent place to wait where hours later they are told the trial has been postponed. Witnesses lose time from work, make expensive trips, suffer personal inconvenience, defense harassment and even risk of retaliation. Is it surprising that they want enough to happen to the offender to at least crudely offset the trouble and risk they have taken?

Jurors are taken from jobs and sometimes families for months at a time for a task regarded as so unpleasant that numerous persons give up their vital right to vote just so they won't be identified for jury duty. Jurors ofttimes may correctly feel that they were punished more severely than the offender they convicted.

Police see the victims while the blood is wet. They may have tracked down and apprehended the offender at real risk to themselves and frequently have good grounds to believe he was the perpetrator of numerous other unprovable offenses. They are understandably displeased to see him on the streets again *apparently* free to resume his criminal activity.

The victim, witnesses, jurors, police—all of them want something to happen to the offender. This tends to accentuate demands for harsh sentences. Conversely changes in the criminal justice system could reduce such needs for retribution.

The criminal justice system has finally recognized the need for a more compassionate relationship with rape victims. It is time for a more sympathetic approach to *all* victims—starting at the point where the crime is reported to police. A little effort to explain police—and later court—processes, the practical problems, and the limitations under which they must work, would, in the long run, greatly facilitate the justice system's relationships with the people it serves.

Recovered property should be restored quickly to the victim rather than be kept for months as evidence. Unless he brought it on himself, the victim ought to be compensated for his injuries and losses.

Any subsequent presentence report should describe the impact of the crime on the victim, at the very least to the degree that it describes the impact of the sentence on the offender. Further, the victim should be consulted as to his views on the appropriate sentence. When the victim confronts the problem of sentencing a live human offender we might all be surprised as to what he would think is proper. The very fact he was consulted might lead to the victim's acceptance of reasonable terms and conditions though there would, no doubt, be some demands for a pound of flesh.

Better scheduling and communication by the courts could eliminate needless, expensive, and exasperating trips to court and cut down on unnecessary waiting time once there. Improved facilities could make such waiting time as absolutely needed more bearable.

Increased, realistic compensation is even more important to both witnesses and jurors. While service as either is the duty of a citizen, neither witnesses nor jurors should be called upon to financially subsidize the criminal justice system. (Incidentally, compensation of persons who report or prevent crimes or apprehend criminals could also be money well spent. In view of studies of those who currently become involved, this approach requires caution since there is some evidence such persons are overly confident, more opposed to criminals than sympathetic to victims, and could ignore the victim in pursuit of the offender.) The better communication, more considerate treatment, and improved compensation for the victim, witnesses, and jurors would permit greater flexibility and rationality in the choice of sentence.

More Sentencing Options Needed

But there also needs to be more actual sentence choices available and greater use made of those that are. Far more use could be made of economic sanctions and their returns could be better directed. Instead of bragging that this or that unit of the district attorney's office or probation office is self-supporting because of the money it collects, we would all be better off if we were able to say that a high percentage of crime victims were compensated for their losses.

Fines are one of the oldest criminal penalties in use and they may have greater application today than ever. They are particularly appropriate in commercial or other crimes committed mainly for economic gain. A penalty substantially offsetting the economic gain not only punishes, but tends to inhibit repetition and deters others. Confiscation and sale of expensive equipment used in the crime—such as aircraft used for transport of narcotics—serves the same purposes. A major portion of the fines could be used to compensate the victim instead of substituting for general tax dollars support of units of government. Actual restitution could more frequently be ordered. There is no reason the victim's losses should be ignored, especially for administrative conveniences or the presumed difficulty of collection.

In this day of easy credit let the offender use his Master Charge or other credit card to pay his fine or restitution if he's got one. Let him pay it in installments the way he pays most of his expenses. The indigent offender who has wrecked the car or spent the loot can be required to work on some public project with most of his wages going to the victim. Care must be taken, of course, in days of widespread unemployment that the offender does not gain benefits denied the honest man.

The direct offender-victim contract may have benefits for both that are lacking under impersonal systems where offender payments eventually reach the victim through some intermediate fund.

Certain funds to which the employable or even affluent offender can contribute have a real place since they can make up for the lack of contributions by the truly indigent, unemployable or even unapprehended offender. Yet there are many counties in California that have never assessed an offender a dime to go to the State's fund for the victims of violent crimes.

The institution we know of as probation is or can be an effective means of collecting fines and restitution. And it can do much more. Rehabilitation may be an elusive or even impossible goal. But we do know more than just how to punish—and probation can do that: We know how to control and we know how to help.

A probation sentence entails a much greater loss of liberty than we have led the public to realize. It is punishing. It is, to a degree, isolating and incapacitating. It can enforce an enormous range of sanctions and controls, beside the economic sanctions already discussed.

Probation conditions can govern the residence of the offender, inhibit his movements, require him to report regularly, avoid improper companions, persons or areas; forbid him from drinking or drinking to excess; require his participation in antialcohol treatments; compel participation in antinarcotic testing; regulate his installment purchases; require psychiatric treatment and even—in California, at least—can include a period in jail as a condition of probation.

Call It Control and Mean It

But even so, the public image of getting probation means getting off. That view now seems so firmly held that it probably cannot be corrected. While it may seem more semantic than real, it is time that we abandoned use of the present terminology of "granting probation." Instead we should be sentencing persons to a period of "community control" or some other phrase that connotes the realities of probation.

If we order a period of community control it must be more than a slogan. Community control conditions must be realistic, tailored to the individual and enforced. Successful control, successful enforcement, depends, in part at least, on the ability of the probation department to prescribe the appropriate conditions, provide the needed resources and then impose such supervision as to know whether the probationer—the prisoner in the community—is indeed living up to the terms of the sentence.

Realistically this means the identification of a broad range of suitable and accessible programs in the community or the development of them. Such development may take a systemwide reallocation of resources, but much more can be achieved in the community without necessarily increasing the total financial outlay because prison costs substantially more than most, if not all, of its alternatives.

The California probation subsidy was based on the concept that if the counties were given the money the State would have spent for keeping prisoners, the counties could provide community programming not only for the person who was not sent to prison but for several others as well, thus strengthening probation supervision over a broad front. The State saved as well since it was able to at least postpone the operation of some institutions and, up to now, eliminate the need for construction of others.

Development of such resources may require that the probation officer identify the needs and work with community groups, news media and others positively and constructively to encourage formation of the needed programs. Equally, successful community control means small enough caseloads so that the responsible officer can acutally keep tabs on his clients. The community control officer has got to know what his charges are doing. That means he's got to know what he's doing.

The officer that carries 200 or 300 cases doesn't have to know what he's doing because he doesn't have time to do it anyway. The officer with a 20- or 30-man caseload better know what he's doing or he may make matters worse rather than better. This means proper training and because of the complexities involved, it may also be an argument for the team concept of supervision. One officer or aide may specialize in surveillance. Working closely with local law enforcement units, he can determine whether the probationer is living where he says he does, working where he is supposed to (and regularly), how he spends his leisure hours and with whom, whether he's out at odd hours, if he's drinking, and in some circumstances whether he's taking a prescribed alcohol antagonist or other required medicine. This officer can also administer antinarcotic examinations and tests in appropriate cases. He also ought to have a pretty good idea where to find his client if he goes AWOL. Non-peace officer aides are often better at this latter assignment than are regular officers.

Another team officer may specialize in finding employment or other placement, continuing education or job training, helping the client get necessary licenses, credit and other bona fides, locating housing, and providing any necessary temporary assistance. Studies have shown that provision of temporary cash assistance by the (in this case parole) officer along with counseling and some expectations significantly reduced recidivism by some kinds of offenders.

Still a third officer may provide help with marital or family problems, counseling to help the client deal with everyday adversities, and other highly professional casework services. One thing to keep in mind is that one officer has got to be in charge or no one will be responsible for the probationer's behavior.

Again the community control officer should not have to supply this myriad of services independently, but he must know how to gain access to existing community resources for his client.

No single one of these programs is a panacea, but each has its specific utility, and sometimes only for a particular period. There is a time limit, for example, that one can expect an offender to serve on work furlough before temptation overpowers him or the stress such programs create causes him to fail by escape, withdrawal, or misconduct.

An important element of community control must be a realistic appraisal of the offender's performance and a readiness to act if he fails to perform properly. There is nothing so exasperating, indeed alarming, to the public than to have the officials charged with protecting it appear to overlook repetitive criminal conduct or ignore commonsense signs that the offender is prepared to strike again. Violation need not take the extreme of prison commitment. Rather it could be the imposition of additional conditions, closer supervision, residential placement in some midway facility or commitment to jail.

Substitute Jail for Prison

Commitment to jail is now extensively used—probably overused—as a condition of probation in California. It could be used instead as a substitute for commitments now made to prison. We will continue to need prisons. It should be apparent that there are offenders whose crimes are so serious, so repetitious, so dangerous or which so outrage the public that they must be committed to prison. There will be those that consistently fail every program short of prison until there is left no alternative to commitment. California's experience would seem to indicate this is something less than 15 percent of all felony convictions. It is no favor to society or the offender to prevent the replacement of obviously antiquated prison facilities nor to restrict capacity with the result of double-celling, program denial, idleness, improper classification, or other evils that result in escapes, or threaten the safety of inmates or staff.

The person normally considered a candidate for prison could be placed in jail. Mandatory incarceration and community corrections are not necessarily contradictory. If the offender must do mandatory time at least he could do it locally. There is no reason the jail cannot be one end of the continuum of local treatment that may also include other forms of residential and nonresidential treatment.

Jail sentences as substitutes for prison would have the advantage of keeping the offender close to home, facilitating visits by family and friends, and making it easier for the offender to keep in touch with his employer or prospective employer. More significant, this approach would keep him part of the community. Once the person is sent to prison he acquires the status of a state responsibility which tends to block his reintegration into the community. If he remains part of the community, the doors of community resources are open to him.

Jail sentences could not conscientiously be substituted for prison sentences—bad as prisons may be— without substantial improvement in the jails. Virtually all currently lack the physical facilities for the most basic prisoner needs even for brief stays. Involving the community would not only assist in making such improvement, but also provide important treatment and reentry resources. There is no need for the jailer to duplicate community services or to do without them.

The city or county recreation department can help develop recreational opportunities for those in jail that will have an important carryover value once the offender is released. Local libraries can extend their services to the incarcerated—and a good library service does lots more than just make books available. The county health department can conduct mental health programs including those concerned with drug abuse and alcoholism. The county welfare department can provide a variety of assistance and casework services to the offender and his family.

The public schools and community colleges can provide worthwhile literacy, academic, and vocational training in jail even when terms are short. More important their integration into the correctional system will facilitate the continuing education of the offender once he is restored to the community.

Most private self-help organizations such as Alcoholics Anonymous, Synanon, ethnic groups, churches and service clubs will be pleased to provide their specific services or to take the leadership in sponsoring particular events or programs if they are asked and guided. They will remain involved only so long as they feel they are being allowed to make a worthwhile contribution. Administrators must give them a real role and let them fill it—even if this becomes at times awkward.

These groups especially can provide a valuable carryover into the community that helps reduce the alienation of the offender and increase his self-esteem. The offender may continue as a member of the same group or at least be directed—with references—to a comparable community group. Though citizens can be very helpful, the probation or community control officer can no more abandon his responsibility for correctional activities to them than a doctor or lawyer could the practice of medicine or law.

There may also be opportunities to purchase services, providing them more flexibly and less expensively than government can. There are often advantages in having nongovernment personnel involved. The probation department that should have cultivated these resources anyway for nonresidential programs can work closely and tactfully with the jail management to marshal the programs and direct their use on a case by case basis to those incarcerated. One of the big failures of probation departments in California was to use any of their subsidy funds to provide jail services even though half the people on felony probation were serving some jail time as a condition.

An equally significant deficiency was the failure to develop any sort of reentry plan for the offender, despite the more than ample opportunity to do so. That kind of fractionalism cannot be tolerated. Employment, residence, family relationships, and admission to treatment facilities should have been arranged. If community control is to work effectively, community resources must not only be mobilized, they must be cooperatively integrated into an intelligent plan to serve the victim of crime, the criminal, and to protect the public.

Community Acceptance Vital

Even though effective, community control cannot succeed without public acceptance. As we have every reason to know by now, public acceptance will not come easily. There must be positive efforts made to gain the understanding of the various publics. The legislature is a vital public that must not be neglected. Though direct approaches are needed, the most effective may prove to be those made through others to whom the legislature is particularly responsive. Obviously leadership in such educational efforts must be taken by the probation professionals and the courts. Every opportunity should be seized and others developed to inform the public. Constructive relationships with the news media seem generally lacking as though this was somehow unprofessional.

Probation, community correction, must be identified with public protection, with sanctions, with the safety of citizens. Then its advantages of lower cost and greater humanity will take on meaning. This must not be mere sloganeering. Success can be based only on solid performance. Goals must be realistic. Overextension of the program is even more dangerous than overselling it. There is a small percentage of offenders who must be placed in prison for the protection of the public and to place them elsewhere is to risk not only individual failure, but condemnation of the entire concept of community control.

Community control affords a broad range of sanctions short of prison. Community control provides a degree of offender isolation. Community control can be incapacitating. Community control punishes. Not only is there nothing wrong in thinking of probation or community corrections in these terms—it is absolutely essential that we do so. Moreover, we must assist the public to view community control in these terms. Punitive terms.

But we do know how to do more than punish or simply isolate. We know how to control and, more important, we know how to help. Help may, in the long run, prove to be the most effective control.

Community control does require a broad range of adequately supported, professionally operated, intelligently interpreted and publicly accepted alternatives to prison commitment. With modest changes in the criminal justice system to make it more victim centered, procedurally sensitive, and oriented to public protection, both the sentiment for prison commitment and the actual need can be greatly reduced. Community corrections can then, and only then, play the role it has in the past and go forward to develop its full potential.

Advocacy, Brokerage, Community: The ABC's of Probation and Parole*

Frank Dell'Apa, Ed.D., W. Tom Adams,
James D. Jorgensen, and Herbert R. Sigurdson*

Probation, parole, and related community corrections programs have been subjected to extensive searching inquiry during the past decade. Demands for accountability by Federal, State, and local legislators and the community at large have had the positive if threatening effect of making correctional agencies reexamine premises upon which probation and parole have based their entire practice. While many administrators successfully defend current practices and effectiveness, many others are uncomfortable in the glare of damning revocation/recidivism rates and the range of treatment panaceas proposed to cope with this matter. Though many solutions are voiced, corrections practitioners are unable to rejoice about what really will work. The spectrum of judgment ranges from the pessimistic "nothing works" point of view to a more cautious position that holds that while some things work, we do not know why and with whom.

For almost a century, scholars and corrections practitioners have struggled to formulate predictive theories of crime and to design responsive models of intervention. Two polar positions have occupied much of the time and space allotted this troublesome arena of social problems. There are those who believe that crime is equivalent to sin and that swift and severe punishment represents an appropriate corrective response, as well as a deterrent for those who might otherwise contemplate criminal activity. However, there are also those who believe that crime is a social disease requiring therapeutic intervention. The sin/punishment model has a lengthy history of failure, just as has the social disease/therapeutic model.

There are serious theoretical and operational problems associated with both of these polar positions. The sin/punishment model has little implication for most offenders who enter the corrections component of the justice system. This is largely because this population tends to be composed of low-status losers from a highly stratified and complex society. The punishment administered by assignment to corrections is not too different from the

*Frank Dell'Apa is director of the Western Interstate Commission for Higher Education (WICHE) Corrections Program and project director of the Community Resources Management Team (CRMT). Consultants to the CRMT project are W. Tom Adams, associate, Pacific Institute for Research and Evaluation, Walnut Creek, Calif.; James D. Jorgensen, associate professor, Graduate School of Social Work, University of Denver; Herbert R. Sigurdson, senior associate, Training Associates, Inc., Boulder Colo.

* Reprinted, with permission, from *Federal Probation*, vol. 40 (1976).

punishment they routinely receive on the streets from an indifferent society. Thus, punishment as a consequence of criminal or deviant behavior is of little significance, as most of them live terrifying life styles of daily crises in which survival is tenuous at best.

The social disease/therapeutic model of corrections has never been tried on a large-scale basis and this may very well be a blessing in disguise. Corrections in general and those who proliferate this theory have been fraudulent regarding at least two fundamental assumptions. First, they assert that people who violate the law are psychologically (pathologically) ill. Yet a number of studies of undetected and unreported crime persuade us that most members of society have committed crimes that could result in assignment to corrections.[1] We do not impute illness to those offenders who do not enter the system, nor does it appear that therapy is needed. Somehow they reach a socially acceptable plateau of behavior without the benefit of our correctional interventions.

Second, corrections programs insisting upon therapeutic intervention generally hire staff having a bachelor's degree or less. These personnel are variously called by such titles as caseworkers, agents, counselors, and group workers. The bachelor level of study, however, is a long way from the training required of a "qualified therapist." Indeed, one might even argue that Malcolm X had a greater understanding of people's problems in Harlem than most corrections personnel have of their respective client populations. So it appears that most offenders in the corrections system are not ill, and if they were, corrections personnel by and large are not equipped to "treat" them.

Once again, corrections is at a crossroads. Unless promising alternatives are invented and tested, there is every reason to believe that conventional corrections methods will be abandoned for a simplistic policy in which the punishment is tailored to fit the crime. We believe that such a trend would be retrogressive; thus, in this article we present a plan for community corrections (probation and parole) that represents a radical departure from contemporary practices, a literal restructuring of field services.[2]

Basic Community Resources Management Team Assumptions

Every program or project rests upon assumptions, generalizations, and hypotheses about the motivation and control of human behavior. Frequently these are implicit, sometimes intuitive, often conflicting, but always serving as a basis for predicting that if we do A, B will follow.

1. J.S. Wallerstein and C.J. Wyle, "Our Law-Abiding Law Breakers," *Probation*, April 1947, pp. 107-112.

2. The authors of this article, all of whom have been involved in the design, implementation, and assessment of a program concept known as the Community Resources Management Team (CRMT), are grateful to the National Institute of Corrections for funding the demonstration and testing of a "field services" approach that appears to be a promising alternative for the future. Admittedly, the components of the CRMT design are not new. Rather, the integration of the components into this model is new, and, in particular, is new to the field of probation and parole.

We have tried to be thoughtful, logical, and systematic in formulating the basic assumptions that undergird the Community Resources Management Team approach to probation and parole services. They are as follows:

(1) Probation and parole services are in need of improved delivery system models.

(2) Most offenders are not pathologically ill; therefore, the medical (casework) model is inappropriate.

(3) Most probation and parole officers are not equipped by education and experience to provide professional casework counseling even if it is needed.

(4) Existing probation/parole manpower is not likely to be expanded. Consequently, these people must come to view their roles in different and perhaps radically new terms if they are to deal with the increasing numbers of offenders under supervision.

(5) Services needed by the offender to "make it" in society are available in the community social service network rather than in the criminal justice system.

(6) Probation and parole staff must assume advocacy roles in negotiating appropriate community-based services for offenders. They must assume a community organization and resource development role for needed services that do not exist.

(7) A team approach represents a powerful and viable alternative to the autonomous and isolated individual officer and "case" relationship.

History of CRMT

Multiple forces have provided the impetus for conceiving of CRMT as an alternative to present field service practice. First, there is widespread disillusionment with the clinical one-to-one counseling process. Although well-intended and presented as a humane intervention, the idea that one person can cause a client to change or adjust to society through a therapeutic casework relationship is losing support. This skepticism has been felt not only in corrections but in other areas of human service as well. Mounting evidence points to the conclusion that, at best, casework has not worked any better than nonintervention. More sobering, however, is the finding from many studies that, in fact, actual deterioration is associated with casework.[3]

In addition, there has been fully as strong a concern about the potential of casework to deliver services. The problem is that the caseworker attempts to be "all things" to everyone on the caseload. One's ability breaks down at the point where the offender's needs are not matched by the worker's skill. To give an example: If Offender X needs a job and Caseworker Y can offer counseling, Offender X is likely to get counseling. Conversely, if he needs counseling and the caseworker's chief skill is surveillance, the probationer or parolee will be watched a lot. In short, the caseload approach as a service delivery system precludes the possibility of a client's receiving maximum benefits from either the assigned officer or the services that are available in the community.

---

3. Joel Fischer, "Is Casework Effective: A Review," *Social Work*, January 1973, pp. 5-20.

In the *Corrections* volume of the National Advisory Commission on Criminal Justice Standards and Goals, the following statement was made:

> The caseload—the assignment of individual offenders—is the almost universal device for organizing the work of parole officers. This concept is being modified importantly in a number of offices through development of team supervision. A group of parole officers, sometimes augmented with volunteers and paraprofessionals, takes collective responsibility for a parolee group as large as their combined caseloads. The group's resources are used differentially, depending upon individual case needs. Decisions are group decisions and generally involve parolees, including the parolees affected by the decisions. Tasks are assigned by group assessment of workers' skills and parolees' objectives.[4]

Modification of the caseload approach and the initiation of team approaches have created some interesting spinoffs in probation and parole. The *Corrections* volume on Standards and Goals continued:

> Differentiating work activities permits staff assignments to be organized around a workload rather than a caseload. Tasks directed toward achieving specific objectives should be identified and assigned to staff to be carried out in a specified time. (This activity should be coordinated by a manager who makes an assessment of the staff members but is able to carry out given tasks.)
> A trend in modern organizational theory is to use teams of staff members with different backgrounds and responsibilities. Teams of individuals from ranging disciplines and with differing skills may be assembled for a given task or project and disbanded when the project is completed.[5]

Offenders generally have common needs regardless of geographical jurisdiction. They need jobs, job training, educational opportunities, legal aid, health services, and assistance to overcome drug and alcohol abuse, housing, and family assistance, among others. When the offender is placed on probation or parole, he is assigned to an agent/caseworker who attempts to secure these needs. Often these are of an emergency nature, constituting a life-crisis situation. The agent/caseworker often feels overwhelmed by the challenge, and the offender feels frustrated by the inadequacy of the response. The situation is compounded by large caseloads that promise to grow larger every year. This dilemma cannot be easily resolved under current traditional operation. In some agencies, the heavy emphasis on casework, counseling, and the clinical relationship is fast giving way. Increasingly, agencies are beginning to stress community resource development. To actually do this, however, a carefully thought-out strategy must be involved, one that emphasizes training of currently employed staff.

Supporting this position, the Commission document stated:

4. National Advisory Commission on Criminal Justice Standards and Goals, *Corrections*, Washington, D.C., Department of Justice, 1973, p. 311.
5. *Ibid.*, p. 322.

To obtain these resources, parole staffs must gear their attention to other community service agencies and develop greater competence in acting as resource managers as well as counselors. A parole staff has a specific task: to assist parolees in availing themselves of community resources and to counsel them regarding their parole obligation. Parole staff also must take responsibility for finding needed resources for parolees in the community.[6]

The foregoing considerations were of such significant importance in shaping and developing the CRMT concept, that in 1973, the National Institute of Corrections was not only open to, but gave active encouragement for, the concept to be developed, demonstrated, and evaluated. A training proposal provided the means whereby the Western Interstate Commission for Higher Education (WICHE), through its Corrections Program, could train selected probation and parole departments to function using basic CRMT concepts.

Ten probation and parole agencies from states west of the Mississippi River were selected for training in the CRMT approach. From these 10 agencies, "vertical slices" of staff (administrative, middle management, direct service, and auxiliary staff working in a common geographic area) were recruited for the actual training, the plan being that this mix of staff would insure diffusion of the innovation taking place when teams returned to their respective organizations. In March 1975, 2 weeks of training were initiated with 10 potential CRMT's.[7] Since that time, followup consultation, technical assistance, team building, interagency training, and other related forms of assistance have been provided by WICHE staff and consultants.

Planning for Change to CRMT

Training was considered the primary vehicle for the transition to a CRMT operation in an agency. The training design was based on many considerations, the primary one being that movement toward a Community Resources Management Team requires thorough planning and thoughtful implementation. It was recognized that, as an innovation, CRMT would be met with resistance, and that in order to properly tool up for change, several considerations needed to be addressed directly or indirectly through the training process.

Issues having to do with traditional organization and structure were of utmost concern in contemplating program change. The concept of team development and participative management is novel in public service and was considered an issue to be dealt with; the universal phenomenon that man naturally resists change was a predictable problem to overcome; the concept of social agency collaboration and the notion of the probation or parole agent acting as a broker of service was a complete reversal of tradi-

---

6. *Ibid.*, p. 431.

7. The teams were: Tucson, Arizona; Oakland, California; Salinas, California; Kansas City, Missouri; Topeka, Kansas; St. Louis, Missouri; North Dakota; Oklahoma City, Oklahoma; El Paso, Texas; and Portland, Oregon.

tional roles; the idea of a probation or parole officer assuming change agent responsibility in the area of community development was considered a major issue regarding job enlargement; and finally it became apparent that if these changes were to occur and the innovations were to "take hold," something extraordinary would have to occur in the training.

Special attention was paid to each of these issues under the following headings: (1) Organization Structure and Function of the Agency, (2) Procedures Within the Organization, (3) Staff Resistance and Organization Support, (4) The Relationship Between the Correctional Agency and the Community Social Service Agencies, (5) The Relationship Between the Worker and the Clients, and (6) Training and Staff Development.

(1) Organization Structure and Function of the Agency.—Most probation and parole agencies in the United States have a hierarchical organization with autocratic management styles that typically emerge from such organizations. Teams, if present at all, are given little autonomy. Caution and protection of the agency are often the order of the day. Decisionmakers in such agencies are naturally wary of a team approach, thinking that this is only a preliminary action to the manager's loss of control.

It was mentioned earlier that "vertical slices" were engaged from each organization for training in CRMT. The rationale for this was to insure that all key decision levels would be represented, and to provide positive sanctions for organizational change. These slices then became not only the targets for change, but ultimately became change agents in their own right when they returned to their organizations to implement the CRMT concept.

In hierarchical organizations it is vital that the top decisionmaker be a part of the team. The absence of personnel from this level reduces team strength, particularly when an attempt is made to introduce CRMT in agencies that are resistive, if not hostile to this new approach. In a number of cases we violated our own values regarding "what constitutes a vertical slice of an organization." Subsequently, we were required to repair damages that had resulted from these oversights.

(2) Procedures Within the Organization.—The determination of organizational procedures in the fully developed CRMT rests with the team itself. CRMT is based on participatory management, and participatory management requires that those who carry out the organizational mission should share in formulating the design of that mission. Ultimately, this means that decisions are made at the level of expertise rather than at the highest level of organizational authority.

Such a vital shift in power does not happen without creating stress in the organization. The giving up as well as the assumption of power is uncomfortable. Managers who have previously given orders must now consult. Workers who have taken orders must now make decisions and live with those decisions. When equilibrium is reestablished in the agency, it will look and behave very differently from what it did before the incorporation of these participative approaches.

(3) Staff Resistance and Organization Support.—Staff members often believe that what they do in the organization is significant in and of itself on behalf of the client as well as the organization. Thus, when a new way of operation is proposed, questions are asked such as, "We are operating well under our present system, why change?" This resistance is often based on the honest feeling that the organization is doing well since individual staff members believe they are doing well. Unfortunately, the sentiment has no basis in fact.

Another not uncommon reaction is, "If we change, what will happen to me?" or, "Who will do [   ] if we change?" These questions usually reflect fear of change.

To soften this resistance, the staff may need to consider the open-ended question, "If we were to start from scratch in our organization, how could we assign tasks to best serve our clientele?" This question tends to surface discontents that exist with existing organizational patterns and leads to staff-initiated change. Imposed changes or outside suggestions only solidify resistance to the unknown.

(4) The Relationship Between the Correctional Agency and the Community Social Service Agencies.—Not uncommonly where the caseload is the model for practice, each worker brokers for the individuals in the caseload on an agency-by-agency basis. The result of this is that every staff member potentially must deal with every social service agency in the community.

A concept inherent in CRMT is that one staff person can become the liaison to an agency or set of agencies that are providing common or related services. For example, one staff member could become the conduit for dealing with alcohol problems, while another staff person would broker employment services. The argument for this, besides the labor-saving features, is simply that a more coherent picture of supply and demand for services can be developed if there is a systematic process of referral and followup. The potential for strengthened relationships between the correctional agency and other social agencies is also present through such an arrangement.

(5) The Relationship Between the Worker and the Clients.—Whether the worker's self-image is that of a control agent, advocate, or counselor, the CRMT will have to assume an additional role—that of manager of community services. This managerial role is one that requires workers to view themselves as community developers who are capable of relationships not only with clients, but with other targets of change as well, namely, the principal social service institutions that exist in the community.

This new view transforms the way workers assess their clients. The client is now a person whose future depends not only on how well he adjusts and adapts to the environment, but additionally, on how well he is linked to social institutions. The CRMT worker views his responsibility to change the community as being at least as important as changing the client. In so doing, a new balance is struck between the traditional role of counseling and controlling the client and community development.

(6) Training and Staff Development.—CRMT embraces a number of concepts currently foreign to probation and parole practice. Many of these have been discussed in previous sections of this article. Common sense along with our personal experience convinces us that extensive training and collaboration is required, not only for practitioners to discover the potential of CRMT innovations, but also to overcome the persistent tendency in people to resist change.

A brief description of CRMT training follows.

First Level of CRMT Training

Community-Organization-Agency Analysis.—This phase of the training included: (1) A pretraining photographic essay where, through the development of a slide show and narrative, the teams told the story of crime and correction in their communities. These presentations depicted the ecology of each community as a generator of crime as well as forces for the socialization of offenders. More importantly, this exercise was a first step in functioning as a team. (2) An experiential "on the street" training experience. Trainees acted out scenarios individually and in teams as they attempted to secure various community resources. (3) A behavior-oriented caseload analysis (rather than psychological) completed by the team prior to training to provide data about the nature and severity of various problems on their caseloads. The caseload analysis was based on a Needs Scale on which each offender in the caseload was ranked in terms of priority need. *The data showed conclusively that employment ranked overwhelmingly as the top priority need, followed by vocational training, and to a significantly lesser extent, academic training.* Other areas of concern—health, mental health, legal, drug and alcohol, and housing—appeared to be of considerably less concern. A ranking of offender needs from highest to lowest as reflected in this analysis is as follows: (1) employment, (2) vocational training, (3) academic, (4) housing, (5) legal, (6) drug and alcohol, (7) health, and (8) mental health.

Team Building.—The elements provided in this segment of training were geared to provide skills in cooperation, conducting meetings, decisionmaking, conflict resolution, developing trust, communicating, and understanding managerial styles. Followup team building was provided later onsite as the CRMT developed and expanded in the community.

Sensitizing.—This component was an experiential live-in *con la familia* ("with the family"). Developed from a highly successful training program used initially with VISTA volunteers, trainees spent a weekend with families with a history of high exposure to the social service system as clients. The rationale for this training was to provide indepth experience with the consumer of the services and to sharply impress upon trainees the real needs of those under supervision.

Conceptual Breakthrough.—An attempt was made in this segment of training to stretch the world view of the trainees in relation to: (1) their overview of criminal justice, (2) fathoming the future direction of corrections, and (3) conceptualizing new models of service delivery. This was done by means of "futures planning" using a simulated situation based on the real life operation of corrections. Self-generated agency data was the basis upon which each team planned for restructured field services in its own organization.

Resource Management.—Trainees were introduced in this segment to the "how to's" of (1) the politics of social action; (2) utilizing the media; (3) grant writing and proposal development for demonstration projects; (4) working with boards, commissions, and councils; and (5) community organization and social action.

Practicum.—The final training component was concluded with the actual designing of a tailored CRMT model by each team with a concomitant plan for action to implement the model at home.

Second Level of CRMT Training

In November 1975, after 7 months of reality testing in the home agencies, the teams were reconvened for 6 days of followup training. This session, in addition to providing more indepth treatment of certain segments of the first level training, was also used to introduce new content in such areas as crisis intervention, surveillance and monitoring, organization development, evaluation, planning, mobilizing the social service network, and social action.

CRMT in Practice

What does the CRMT look like in operation? There are several models that can be adapted to various settings, depending upon the size, geographic area, or complexity of the organization. One model might work for Los Angeles while another might be best suited for Los Alamos, New Mexico. In any event, the four models described below are meant to be suggestive and not inclusive. More importantly, they are points of departure rather than final designs.

Model A: The Basic Agency Team.—A team is composed of a middle manager, no fewer than two line (field) staff, a clerical staff person, and a staff specialist.

Function: The combined caseload of these field staff is assigned to this team. The team has responsibility to serve all needs of the caseload. Decisions are made at team meetings and the middle manager leads the team. Tasks are determined through team consensus. The team has responsibility for a specific geographic area.

Note: The agency can assemble as many of these teams as it desires, depending upon the manpower. The teams are components of the parent agency.

Model B: The Agency-Community Extended Team.—A team is composed of a middle manager, no fewer than two line (field) staff, a trainee, one or more ex-offenders, a clerical staff person, with support from interested community social service agents from legal aid, welfare, employment security, mental health, minority group organizations, health, and education agencies. In addition, community persons such as successful ex-offenders and citizens' group leaders serve as resources to the team.

Function: The caseload is composed of a fixed number of clients, usually a cross section of the target population, who have distinct needs for supervision and assistance. They may come largely from one geographical area, be designated as drug- and alcohol-related offenders, represent distinct minority groups, and fall within definite age groupings.

The team is analyzed to determine the skills of each member, and the workload is the determinant of who does what. The parent agency staff serve as brokers of the services and coordinators among the attached support specialists. The team meets regularly to assess community resources and needs, as well as workload needs upon which the division of labor is based. The clients may be served by all members of the team or only one or any combination.

Note: This team model is dependent on actual cooperation between parent staff and those from support community agencies.

Model C: The Specialist Resource Team.—A team is composed of two or more line (field) staff who are supervised by a middle manager. Support community staff may be used where possible.

Function: The team has a specialized caseload; all of those clients who are distinguishable by one central concern, perhaps drug addiction, violence-prone behavior, chronic unemployment, or serious family crises. The team works only with these persons. The team also marshals all resources within the community that provide services to such clients.

Note: This team maintains autonomy but relies on good community relations.

Model D: The Total Department as a Community Resource Management Team.—The team may encompass the entire field agency. A task analysis is made of the agency workload. Specific assignments are made to individual staff members depending upon their capabilities. Attached community agency staff are recruited to serve as support personnel to the entire parent agency, rather than to a specific team within the agency.

Function: The agency sets the team into operation after a careful task analysis based on the workload needs of the agency. Some staff will function as court and liaison specialists, others will prepare presentence or preparole reports, and others will supervise those who require supervision by court order or in the judgment of the agency. In some instances, a single staff person may have the assignment for a specific need area such as employment, legal aid services, health, or education. A team will have no caseload but will serve as community resources identifiers and develop advocacy plans to link these resources to all clients.

Note: This complex organizational model requires careful task analysis and staff skills assessment as well as effective collaboration with significant community agencies. It is a total organizational approach. Its success will depend upon continuous revision of the structure and deployment of staff resources.

These models or variations of them are being field tested in probation and parole agencies today under the guidance and direction of the WICHE Corrections Program, Project CRMT.

Conclusion

Whether the CRMT concept is the direction community corrections should take has yet to be assessed. Field testing of CRMT, incorporating an evaluation design, seeks answers to specific questions in eight operating agencies. These questions are concerned with: (1) The degree to which the team approach is utilized in relation to the traditional approach of the agency, in terms of caseload analysis, addressing the community social service network, and processing the caseload as required by the court and the agency; (2) the degree of organizational change that results in order to accommodate this new approach—physical rearrangements, reassignment of duties, and changed work schedules; (3) the degree to which offender behavior is changed as a direct result of linkage to community services, e.g., those employed, attending school, etc.

Although a CRMT actually functions in this new modality and the organization accommodates the team functioning, which leads to increased services for the offender, there is no guarantee that revocation rates will be positively affected. This ultimate measure of effectiveness—revocation rates—will be dealt with in a subsequent phase of the evaluation, along with quality of life and cost benefit/cost efficiency measures.

For now, the best that can be accomplished is to measure client needs and determine the degree to which these are being alleviated. Implicitly, this assumes that behavior will change toward crime-free, socially acceptable behavior. A case analysis profile is maintained on each offender that charts the changes in his degree of need for various services. A sample case analysis profile is shown on page 151.

At the first iteration we are dealing with an offender whose employment record is spotty, not because he lacks vocational skills or education, but because of a high level of substance abuse which is directly related to his legal problems, i.e., arrests.

CASE ANALYSIS PROFILE

CRMT Case Number 001

First Iteration ──────

Second Iteration ── ── ──

CATEGORY OF NEED

High

DEGREE OF NEED

EMPLOY-MENT	VOCATIONAL TRAINING	ACADEMIC TRAINING	PHYSICAL HEALTH	MENTAL HEALTH	LEGAL	SUBSTANCE ABUSE	HOUSING
Without work. No prospects.	No marketable skills.	Functional illiterate.	Incapacitated. Needs medical services.	Unstable. Lashes out or retreats in to self.	Habitual civil & criminal problems.	Needs detoxification & treatment.	Constant transient.
Work unstable. Casual labor.	Laborer minimal skills.	Backward but able to function at basic level.	Chronically ill. Needs medical care.	Confused, anxious and/or self-deprecating.		Extensive substance abuse.	Moves often.
Work part-time. Little promise for future.			Occasional incapacitation.	Rational but occasional confusion.			
		G.E.D. and functions well.					
Working near potential.	Achieved full potential for work.		In sound health. Seldom ill.				

Low

At the second iteration services in the community were made available to him, primarily employment and alcoholic treatment services, with the result that the man is working and not drinking. He has stabilized his living pattern, his deficits as measured in the profile have been significantly alleviated, and he is able to function adequately in society.

The effectiveness of the linkage of community services to the offender is measured by the degree to which the individual's profile moves toward the lowest level of need. This is a direct measure of team efficiency, i.e., the competence of CRMT team members to insure linkage of community services to offender needs. Effectiveness, as measured by individuals who "make it" on probation or parole versus the number who are revoked, is the ultimate criterion of effectiveness of CRMT.

The results are not yet in regarding the effectiveness of CRMT, but the assumptions that undergird the approach possess face validity. A number of the teams participating in the WICHE training speak enthusiastically of the efficiency and effectiveness of the approach. Not only are probation and parole agents, as members of CRMT, able to provide specialized service to more offenders, but in addition, because of specialization, they are able to know about and have access to more appropriate community services than have otherwise been available in the traditional medical model (casework) or community corrections. These reasons alone provide logic for the diffusion of CRMT as a model for restructuring community corrections.

As members of the helping professions, we have special responsibilities for the delivery of urgently needed services to our clients. Often what they need least is counseling. Some obscure authorities have defined counseling as that which occurs when two anxious people face each other and the most anxious one gets help. Is it possible that we have been using traditional casework methods to feed and nurture our own needs? For too long now, we may have been playing games on our clients, which is evil enough; but more striking is the shocking possibility that for all these years we have been playing games on ourselves.

SOME OTHER ISSUES

Ever since John Augustus, the famous Boston shoemaker, "stood bail" for the first "probationers" in the 1880s[1] there has been a general interest in the reformative potential of giving the offender a "second chance." The slow and ponderous movement toward community-based forms of corrections accelerated in the early 1970s, and the types of community alternatives to imprisonment became so diversified that the National Advisory Commission stated that no new prisons needed to be built in the United States, and, indeed, that some could quite easily be phased out.[2] The community corrections movement, it seemed, had taken control.

Abruptly, however, in the mid-1970s, prison populations dramatically increased and soon reached or exceeded prison capacities. New prison fortresses were on the planning boards on both the federal and state levels.

Thus, in order to assess the contemporary status of community supervision of offenders, one must begin with a discussion of both of the above trends.

Three reasons for the trend toward community supervision were suggested by the President's Commission on Law Enforcement and the Administration of Justice in 1967.[3] First, the commission pointed out that community supervision is immensely cheaper than imprisonment. Figures vary widely from jurisdiction to jurisdiction, and also between adult and juvenile supervision, but these figures always indicate a substantially higher cost for imprisonment than for community corrections. The general range of these figures shows that imprisonment is from three to ten times as expensive. When one realizes that the savings are always in terms of thousands of dollars per offender per year, it comes as no surprise that several state governments began to pay their counties subsidies for each offender that county courts sentenced to probation instead of prison.[4]

Second, the commission stated that community supervision is *at least as effective* as incarceration as a rehabilitative device. In this area, where one of the primary goals is the rehabilitation of the offender, a powerful supporting argument can be found by looking at the evidence, which—though research has been scanty—shows that there is no reason to believe that a prison

---

1. *Probation and Related Measures*, (New York: United Nations, 1951).
2. National Advisory Commission on Criminal Justice Standards and Goals, *Corrections*, (Washington, D.C.: U.S. Department of Justice, 1973).
3. President's Commission on Law Enforcement and The Administration of Justice, *Task Force Report: Corrections*, (Washington, D.C.: U.S. Government Printing Office, 1967).
4. Center for the Administration of Criminal Justice, *An Evaluation of the California Probation Subsidy Program*, (Davis, Cal. 1977). (Mimeographed.)

sentence produces a lower recidivism rate than does community supervision. In fact, there is some evidence to the contrary.[5]

Third, the commission indicated that the prison system is generally more destructive, both to the offender and to society. It removes the offender from his or her community and family, creating stress in both relationships. Very often, families of male offenders are forced to become welfare clients during the man's prison tenure. (This is an additional "cost of incarceration" rarely figured in when comparing the costs of imprisonment to the costs of community supervision.) When a woman is incarcerated, the family unit may suffer even more. In both situations, great stress is placed on familial and social relationships that may later be crucial to the inmate's successful return to society. Most directly, however, prisons are destructive because they are purposefully designed as unhappy places to be, in every respect—from the people one is housed with to the things one is made to do.[6]

As a result of this reasoning, the major components of community corrections—probation, parole, halfway houses—received an increased proportion of the correctional load during the last decade. In fact, it was at one time argued that the days of community corrections were already here: fully two-thirds of all persons under correctional supervision lived in the community, not in institutions.[7]

There are those who viewed this movement as not altogether a wholesome thing. Some scholars argued that contrary to the usual analysis the flourishing of community corrections led to an *increase* in the level of state intervention.[8] The position taken was that the relatively inexpensive probation, parole and diversion programs allowed the state to exert social control in areas where its influence could not otherwise extend.

At the other end of the spectrum, some analysts argued that the use of lenient sentences had become too extreme, leaving us with a lax criminal justice system; one that allowed serious criminals to continue their interaction in society relatively unchecked.[9]

In the mid-1970s, the call came for a decreased scope of community supervision, with mandatory prison terms for selected felonies. The very idea of a determinate sentencing system, (where each criminal act automatically carried a set determined penalty), was an implicit denigration of community-based supervision, for one could not reduce or eliminate the parole board's power to grant early release, or the judge's power to grant probation,

5. Don Gottfredson et al., *Four Thousand Lifetimes: A Study of Time-Served and Parole Outcomes*, (Davis, Cal.: National Council on Crime & Delinquency Research Center, 1973).

6. See James B. Jacobs, *Stateville, The Penitentiary in Mass Society*, (Chicago: University of Chicago Press, 1977).

7. President's Commission, *Task Force Report: Corrections*.

8. See Franklin Zimring, "Measuring the Impact of Pre-Trial Diversion from the Criminal Justice System," *University of Chicago Law Review*, vol. 3 (1974), p. 241.

9. See James Q. Wilson, *Thinking About Crime*, (New York: Basic Books, 1975).

without also drastically reducing the number of offenders on community supervision.

The seemingly rapid move toward community corrections in the late 1960s and the early 1970s has slowed down considerably in the late 1970s. Critics, though, have not abated in their attack on the utility of community supervision. Ernest van den Haag,[10] John Conrad,[11] and James Q. Wilson,[12] all well-respected scholars, have seriously questioned the deterrent and control capacities of community supervision agencies. Robert Martinson has bluntly labeled community supervision as "kind of a standing joke."[13]

SOME CONTEMPORARY ISSUES IN COMMUNITY SUPERVISION

A complete catalog of the issues in present day community corrections would be impossible here, but an overview of the major areas of concern can be made.

A. *The Establishment of Operational Standards and Rules*

In the early days of community supervision, the granting of clemency was seen as purely a matter of discretion. As the use of community supervision became a more common—indeed, the preferred—mode of supervision, the need to standardize procodure inevitably followed. This standardization raised legal issues which can be divided into three main categories:

First, there are a series of issues concerning the community supervision selection process. Because the decision is largely discretionary, within the constraints of law, serious questions arise regarding discrimination in decision-making. For instance, since the decision to parole a prison inmate is made on a case-by-case basis, it is subject to arbitrariness and the personal biases of parole board members. Indeed, there may be *no* set operating policy to guide members in choosing those inmates who would be the best candidates for release. For example, an inmate may be given the impression at a parole board hearing that he is being denied parole because he is not religious. After a year of faithfully joining church groups and working with the chaplain, he may return to the board only to confront a different board member who has little concern for religion, but wants to know why the inmate has not been learning a trade or participating in group therapy. Obviously, paroling policy, or the lack of it, can be a source of great distress to inmates.

As a result of criticisms of such unguided decision-making, parole boards are developing innovative approaches to decision control. Among these are

---

10. Ernest van den Haag, *Punishing Criminals: Concerning a Very Old and Painful Question*, (New York: Basic Books, 1975).

11. John Conrad, "Why Do We Need Doorbell Pushers?", presentation to the New Jersey Seminar on Parole Supervision, Trenton, New Jersey, 30 November 1978.

12. Wilson, *Thinking About Crime*.

13. Robert Martinson "California Research at the Crossroads," *Crime and Delinquency*, vol. 22 (1976), p. 191.

"contracting," (in which an inmate is required to complete a legally-binding treatment contract in order to qualify for parole), the establishment of written reasons for denial or granting of parole, and the establishment of empirically based policy guidelines for parole decision-making.[14] Empirical methods for standardizing the decision-making process have also been developed for judges who must decide whether or not to place an offender on probation. Such empirical methods might, for example, enable a judge or parole board to look at a table or computer readout to see what decisions have beeen made about previous offenders with the same age, background, crime or other variables. Other groups, such as the American Bar Association,[15] have addressed the standardization of this selection process, recommending that probation be made the standard or normal sentence, with judges given the option to rule in favor of incarceration if, and only if, they submit, in writing, their specific reasons for this decision.

A second area of legal concern involves the conditions of community supervision. Usually, this issue relates to the *formal conditions* of probation or parole, which are the written behavioral restrictions of probation or parole supervision held binding against the offender. Often, these restrictions prohibit such activities as out of state travel, excessive drinking, use of illegal drugs, association with other convicted felons, and so forth. Other conditions may require certain behavior, such as obeying the probation officer, continuing in a marriage relationship, staying in a certain apartment unless given permission to move, or attending church services. Most probation and parole agencies have standard conditions which are applicable to all offenders under their supervision.

There have been legal challenges to such conditions. For example, the complaint that these conditions are vague and ambiguous ("cooperate with the directives of the probation officer"), inappropriate ("regular attendance at church of own choice"), or of questionable merit ("no out of state travel" when the offender lives on a state border and the nearest city is in another state), provides the basis for legal challenges regarding the fairness and practicality of their use in supervision of offenders. In fact, the indiscriminate application of "general" conditions has been attacked as a denial of due process, since most conditions are not necessarily related to the unique circumstances of each offender. The ideal, it is argued, is to have individualized conditions for each offender.

However, individualized (or "special") conditions have also been challenged on legal grounds because they have sometimes taken the form of rather bizarre, or even shocking behavioral requirements; sterilization, marital separation, and compulsory medication have all been ordered in the past as "special" conditions of community supervision. A widespread and popular special condition—restitution to the victim of the crime—is also

14. See David T. Stanley, *Prisoners Among Us: The Problem of Parole*, (Washington, D.C.: Brookings Institution, 1976), for a discussion of these approaches.

15. American Bar Association, *Standards Relating to Probation*, (New York: Institute for Judicial Administration, 1970).

open to abuse when the judge leaves the determination of the amount of restitution to the untrained probation officer. Financial disputes which are thorny issues for trained civil court judges are often resolved in spot decisions by probation officers.

Though the fundamental issue of due process is present in such cases, new questions involving equal protection, not to mention cruel and unusual punishment, are raised. For the most part, however, conditions commonly justified on an individual case basis have been acceptable to courts of review.[16]

Another area of concern, which raises even more delicate legal questions, relates to what might be called the *informal conditions* of community supervision. These conditions deal with the rights of both the offender on probation and his or her supervising agent. Serious questions exist regarding the enforcement of the offender's first amendment rights, the right to resist unreasonable searches, the right to refuse to answer inquiries, and so on. Does a probationer, for example, share the rights of other citizens living in society, or is he or she living in what has been termed a "prison without walls," subject to all of the restrictions of a prison inmate, though technically allowed to live outside of the prison? Can a probation officer search the pockets or even the apartment of a probationer with as few restrictions as a prison guard has when deciding to search a prison cell? Or must a probation officer fulfill the constitutional requirements of obtaining a search warrant before instigating a search?

Generally, courts are reluctant to support the claims of offenders who demand substantial rights while they are serving sentences in the community.[17] In the future, it will most likely be the informal conditions of community supervision that will be responsible for establishing legal and policy guidelines for both offenders and justice agencies.

The revocation of community supervision status is the third area involving legal and policy-oriented issues. Courts have been most active in this area, recognizing the legitimate interests of the offender in resisting unwarranted revocation of probation or parole.[18] In many ways, this is a similar issue to the one discussed above. If the probationer is simply a prison inmate who by the grace of the authorities is allowed to live in the community, then according to some prison officials, revoking that offender's probation and committing him or her to prison should be no more difficult than a decision to move a prison inmate from A Wing to B Wing of a prison. On the other hand, if the probationer or parolee gains some of the rights of an ordinary citizen, then transfer to the prison should be considered a drastic step; one which

---

16. Frank J. Remington et al., *Criminal Justice Administration: Materials and Cases*, (Indianapolis: Bobbs-Merrill, 1969).

17. Citizen's Inquiry on Parole and Criminal Justice, *Summary: Report on New York Parole*, (New York: Citizen's Inquiry, 1974).

18. See *Morrissey v. Brewer*, 408 U.S. 471 (1972); and *Gagnon v. Scarpelli*, 411 U.S. 778 (1973).

should only be undertaken after a full hearing (with presentation of powerful reasons, subject to rebuttal) has occurred.

As a result of debates over these kinds of questions, basic due process rights have been held to apply to probation and parole procedures.[19] A full trial is not required for removal from the community, but a full hearing is now mandatory. However, this control of discretion affects only one avenue of the revocation process. Research indicates, for example, that parole revocation may be more closely linked to organizational variables (involving management) than to the offender's behavior.[20] As a result, such legal controls as the granting of due process rights often occur too late in the process, usually well after the key decision has been made to initiate revocation procedures. A more fruitful means of control might be developed through the establishment of operational standards that would more properly outline the grounds for initiating revocation proceedings.

At each of these levels of decision-making—selection, supervision through formal and informal conditions, and revocation—the wide scope of discretion involved has traditionally been a major source of conflict. However, the use of empirical and administrative controls over selection and revocation discretion are slowly becoming more common. Supervisory discretion, unfortunately, has received a great deal less attention from reformers. This neglect may have serious ramifications, for the future of community supervision depends largely upon the development of useful discretion control mechanisms.

B. Formality vs. Informality in Community Supervision

Some scholars argue that the more deeply corrections intervenes in the offender's life, the less likely are the chances for successful reintegration of that offender.[21] The recent emphasis on diverting offenders away from the criminal justice system has resulted from just such a theory. The diversion argument essentially states that many criminals do not require formal correctional supervision; indeed it is said they would benefit most by receiving services directly from non-correctional agencies that would be willing to help them stay out of the criminal justice system. These agencies would provide such services as job training, family counseling, medical assistance, education and other similar help. For these individuals, a formal conviction carrying the stigma of "criminality" would be counter-productive, since it would close off opportunities, (such as certain types of employment), to the individual and increase the probability of that individual developing a criminal self-identification. The best alternative, it is argued, is for informal supervision and referral to community services without formal processing by

---

19. *Ibid.*

20. James Robison and Paul Takagi, "The Parole Violator as an Organization Reject," quoted in Robert Carter and Leslie T. Wilkins, eds., *Probation, Parole and Community Corrections,* 2nd ed., (New York: Wiley & Sons, 1976).

21. Edwin M. Schur, *Radical Non-Intervention: Re-Thinking the Delinquency Problem,* (Englewood Cliffs, N.J.: Prentice-Hall, 1973).

the criminal justice system. This is *diversion*. Diversion is being increasingly stressed as a positive alternative at each successive stage of the criminal justice process, from arrest to sentencing.

However, critics of diversion fear the informality of the procedure. They argue that key decisions, relating to the selection of offenders for diversion and the coercion of those "diverted" offenders, are made essentially without any formal controls. Thus, large numbers of offenders, diverted from formal processes, are having their rights violated and are being coerced into disagreeable actions by the government without any recourse or appeal. The critics argue that this is particularly true for juvenile offenders, who can be made to pay restitution, attend therapy sessions, restrict activities, or follow other rules, without any formal adjudication of guilt or exercise of constitutional rights.[22]

In some ways, this argument is difficult to understand, since this is exactly what diversion is supposed to do. Offenders who are guilty, but who would be harmed if processed through the formal criminal justice system, can be sent directly to treatment or control systems by waiving their rights to formal adjudication. In return, they do not develop a possibly harmful criminal record, and society is allowed to place them in a treatment or control situation. However, as in similar arguments over plea bargaining, there is a fear that the tremendous benefits of the process for defendants (a guarantee of no conviction) will coerce some defendants to allow themselves to be herded in this direction even though they are innocent or at least wish to retain their constitutional right to claim their innocence and force the government to prove a case against them.

The benefits of informality and the control of its potential and actual abuses, without the creation of an undesirable informality, are the key issues in the future of community supervision.

C. *The Role of Community Supervision*

One cannot evaluate the role of community supervision without first placing it in proper perspective; that is, determining its particular function in relation to the functions of the overall correctional system. For instance, should imprisonment be considered the basic correctional process, with community-based activities used as a frequent sentencing alternative, or should a variety of community supervision methods comprise the basic correctional process, with imprisonment used only as an occasional and drastic alternative? Public opinion, and to a lesser extent, professional judgment, are mixed on this issue. Clearly the public wants protection, and the problem of crime has become an increasingly volatile political issue. The fact that prisons ultimately provide no greater public protection at such tremendous cost often has little impact on the public's emotion-charged feelings toward crime.

In the late 1960s and early 1970s, scholars were largely in agreement,

---

22. Zimring, "Measuring the Impact of Pre-Trial Diversion."

however, that prisons should be phased into some lesser role in the correctional system. While a majority of scholars still support this position, a vocal minority has arisen which questions the goals of "treatment" and calls for a return to imprisonment as at least the central, if not the most common, form of penal response to conviction. This group, composed of liberal and conservative reformers, points to the failure of treatment programs as proof that the corrections system must shift back to the security of incarcerative punishment.

The discussion of the role of community supervision is certainly not now resolved. The future importance of community corrections rests largely in the clarification of the role of imprisonment and the control of the abuses of discretion and treatment. The debate is heated and will involve a great deal of study and tug-of-warring. Already, however, some scholars discern a rather ominous result of the dilemma: the creation of "dual" criminal justice systems. One, for less serious offenders, would be lenient, informal, community-based and largely devoid of due process. The other, for serious and violent offenders, would be based on due process, quite harsh, and have imprisonment for long periods as its central punishment.[23] Whether this duality is the only future likely for community supervision remains to be seen.

---

23. Donald J. Newman, *Introduction to Criminal Justice*, 2d ed. (Philadelphia: J.B. Lippincott, 1978).

SELECTED BIBLIOGRAPHY

Allen, H.E.; Carlson, E.W.; Parks, E.C.; and Seiter, R.P. *Halfway Houses*. Washington, D.C.: National Institute of Law Enforcement and Criminal Justice, 1978.

Amos, William E., and Newman, Charles, eds. *Parole: Legal Issues, Decision-Making and Research*. New York: Aberdeen Press, 1976.

Bennett, Lawrence A., and Ziegler, Max. "Early Discharge: A Suggested Approach to Increased Efficiency in Parole." *Federal Probation*, vol. 39 (1975), p. 27.

Boorkman, David; Fazio, Jr. Ernest J.; Day, Noel; and Weinstein, David. *An Exemplary Project: Community Based Corrections in Des Moines*. Washington, D.C.: U.S. Government Printing Office, 1976.

Czajkoski, Eugene H. "Exposing the Quasi-Judicial Role of the Probation Officer." *Federal Probation*, vol. 37 (1973), pp. 9-13.

Dawson, Robert O. "The Decision to Grant or Deny Parole; A Study of Parole Criteria in Law and Practice." *Washington University Law Quarterly*, vol. 3 (June 1966), pp. 243-303.

Dodge, Calbert R., ed. *A Nation Without Prisons: Alternatives to Incarceration*. Lexington, Mass.: Lexington Books, 1975.

Doleschal, Eugene. *Graduated Release*. Rockville, Md.: National Institute of Mental Health, 1971.

Dressler, David. *Practice and Theory of Probation and Parole*. 2d ed. New York: Columbia University Press, 1969.

"The Exclusionary Rule in Probation and Parole Revocation: A Policy Appraisal." *Texas Law Review*, vol. 55 (1976), p. 1115.

Greenberg, David. "Problems in Community Corrections." *Issues in Criminology*, vol. 10 (1975), p. 1.

Hahn, Paul H. *Community Based Corrections and the Criminal Justice System*. Santa Cruz, Calif.: Davis, 1975.

Kassebaum, Gene; Seldin, J.; Nelligan, P.; Takeuchi, D.; Wayson, B.; and Monkman, G. *Contracting for Correctional Services in the Community, Vol. 1, Draft Summary*. Washington, D.C.: National Institute of Law Enforcement and Criminal Justice, 1976.

Klapmuts, Nora. *Community Alternatives to Prison*. Hackensack, N.J.: National Council on Crime and Delinquency, 1973.

Neithercutt, Mark G., and Gottfredson, Don M. *Case Load Size Variation and Difference in Probation and Parole Performance.* Washington, D.C.: National Center for Juvenile Justice, 1975.

Newman, Donald J.; O'Leary, Vincent; and Christianson, Scott. *Community Alternatives to Maximum Security Institutionalization for Selected Offenders.* Albany, N.Y.: Institute for Public Policy Alternatives, 1975.

Ohlin, Lloyd E. *Selection for Parole.* New York: Russell Sage, 1951.

O'Leary, Vincent, and Hanrahan, Kathleen J. *Parole Systems in the United States.* 3d ed. Hackensack, N.J.: National Parole Institutes and Parole Policy Seminars, 1976.

"Parole: A Critique of Its Legal Foundations and Conditions." *New York University Law Review,* vol. 38 (June 1963), pp. 702-739.

Petersen, David M., and Friday, Paul C. "Early Release from Incarceration: Race as a Factor in the Use of 'Shock Probation.'" *The Journal of Criminal Law and Criminology,* vol. 66 (March 1975), pp. 79-87.

Prison Without Walls: Report on New York Parole. New York: Praeger Publishers, 1975.

Probation and Parole Activities Need to be Better Managed: Report to the Congress. Washington, D.C.: U.S. General Accounting Office, 1977.

"Procedural Due Process in Parole Release Proceedings—Existing Rules, Recent Court Decisions, and Experience in Prison." *Minnesota Law Review,* vol. 60 (1976), p. 341.

Prus, Robert C., and Stratton, John R. "Parole Revocation Decision Making: Private Typings and Official Designations." *Federal Probation,* vol. 40 (1976), p. 48.

Skolnick, Jerome K. "Toward a Developmental Theory of Parole." *American Sociological Review,* vol. 25 (August 1960), pp. 542-549.

Smith, Alexander B., and Berlin, Louis. *Introduction to Probation and Parole.* St. Paul, Minn.: West, 1976.

Stanley, David T. *Prisoners Among Us: The Problem of Parole.* Washington, D.C.: Brookings Institution, 1976.

State and Local Probation and Parole Systems. Washington, D.C.: National Criminal Justice Information and Statistics Service, 1978.

Thalheimer, Donald J. *Cost Analysis of Correctional Standards: Halfway Houses.* 2 vols. Washington, D.C.: U.S. Department of Justice, 1975.

von Hirsch, Andrew. "Prediction of Criminal Conduct and Preventive Confinement of Convicted Persons." *Buffalo Law Review*, vol. 21 (1972), pp. 717-758.

Waldron, Joseph, and Angelino, Henry R. "Shock Probation: A Natural Experiment on the Effect of a Short Period of Incarceration." *Prison Journal*, vol. 57 (Spring/Summer 1977).

Part Four

Treatment for the Offender

Warren F. Spalding, Secretary, Massachusetts Prison Association, "Indeterminate Sentences," Proceedings of the National Conference of Charities and Correction at the 24th Annual Session Held in Toronto, Canada, July 7-14, 1897, pp. 46-47.

The definite sentence had its origin in the theory regarding crime which prevailed centuries ago. A crime was then an act for which the State must retaliate upon the offender....

The theory upon which the indeterminate sentence is based differs from the old theory at every point. It denies that a crime is an act for which the State must retaliate upon the offender. If the individual who is harmed cannot and should not retaliate, it is not easy to see how the State can do so on his behalf. The State is not an avenger, with a mission to right the wrong which the criminal has done, but is to try to right the criminal, that he may cease to do wrong....

Nor should crime be dealt with as a past act merely. The State has a greater interest in the criminal's future than it has in his past. It has great interests bound up in his development, mentally, morally, physically, and spiritually. The relations between the criminal and the State are perpetual. They should change as he changes. They should not change until he changes. They are not those of debtor and creditor, which will cease when the penalty is "paid."

Leonard J. Hippchen, Ph.D., Virginia Commonwealth University, "An Overview for Standards Development in Correctional Classification and Treatment," Proceedings of the One Hundred and Fifth Annual Congress of Correction of the American Correctional Association, Louisville, Ky, August 17-21, 1975, p. 314. *

Principle #2—The punishment model of the criminal justice system should be replaced by a clinical model. The punishment model for delinquents and criminals was appropriate at an earlier time when our knowledge of many of the specifics of offender behavior was lacking. Our present-day knowledge, however, makes punishment inappropriate. The primary purpose of apprehension today should be for control and treatment purposes, not for punishment. Control and treatment also best serve the need to protect society, since they offer better opportunity for both short-term and long-term resolution of the offender problem.

With the clinical model approach to delinquents and criminals, the courts will need to have less concern with the problems of establishing guilt, plea bargaining, trials, and sentencing, and to have more concern with the questions of the degree and length of time needed for successful treatment. This not only will cut down on the great amount of time needed by the system, but allow more swift movement into a more just handling of offenders.

_____

*Principle 2 is only one of several principles which are interrelated and interdependent. This selection is used for illustrative purposes only and is not necessarily indicative of the author's stand on criminal corrections or penalties. Reprinted by permission.

DOES TREATMENT WORK?

THE DEFINITION OF TREATMENT

Before one can begin a discussion of treatment in corrections, one must first define just what treatment is. Unfortunately, as in much of corrections, what seems to be a simple preliminary task winds up not being simple at all. Despite the many attempts by scholars, we are sadly lacking a wholly satisfactory, well-turned-out definition of "correctional treatment." As might be guessed, there are a few theoretical obstacles that must be "hurdled" in order to develop such a definition.

The most important problem to deal with is the relationship of treatment to punishment. Usually people make the mistake of assuming that treatment is the opposite of punishment. It is thought that if one's goals are punitive, then one should mete out punishment. Or, if one's goals are non-punitive, then one should provide treatment. While this formula seems practical—even logical—on paper, it is never so clean-cut in practice.

There is little problem in the definition of punishment. It is the purposeful imposition of pain, or undesirable consequences by a properly constituted authority in response to a particular behavior on the part of the person being punished.[1] In corrections, the proper authority administers punishment (such as placing a person in prison) because of an act which that person has committed in the past (the offense for which the offender was convicted). As pointed out earlier, this punishment or pain may be imposed for several different reasons, including retaliation or deterrence. Thus, if a person has committed a specific illegal act, and has been convicted, then he or she will have to receive the painful consequence.

Treatment, on the other hand, is the response by the state to a condition or behavior observed in the offender. Its purpose is not to "get even" or to allow the offender to "pay his debt to society." Rather, treatment's purpose assumes that there is something wrong with the offender, and enlists the proper authorities to take steps to control, reduce or eliminate that problem or behavior. Thus, one can see that the opposite of punishment is not treatment. The opposite of punishment is reward.[2]

Oftentimes what punishment and treatment share in common is the utilization of pain. Only the goals are dissimilar. For example, a parent might spank a child because the parent is annoyed at the child, and wants to

1. Anthony Flew, "The Justification of Punishment," *Philosophy*, vol. 29 (1954), p. 291.
2. James Robison and Gerald Smith, "The Effectiveness of Correctional Programs," *Crime and Delinquency*, vol. 17 (1971), p. 67.

punish it for misbehavior—or, the parent might have deeply considered some form of learning theory, and reluctantly come to the conclusion that the best method of teaching the child proper behavior is to impose some pain (spanking) immediately after misbehavior, so that the child would eventually be conditioned, through this kind of treatment, to behave properly.

It should be obvious that there is a thin line between the two goals at times. Quite frequently, all that is apparent to the child is that he is being made to feel pain. There is, of course, always the problem that the child will interpret the spanking as the cruel act of an unloving parent, rather than as treatment administered to help the child lead a more responsible life.

In corrections, the same problem often exists. While officials may take actions which they believe are good and proper treatments, the offenders involved may instead feel that they are receiving punishment. In fact, this problem is often made worse by the fact that correctional treatments are usually administered in a punishment setting. The offender knows full well that he is in a prison, and has been sent there by society for punishment. Once there, he is forced to take part in a program which he finds personally painful, and does not wish to be a part of. It is not hard to see how the offender may come to see this treatment program as one more pain or punishment he must bear in prison.

Another problem is that the kinds of treatments which the correctional authorities are able to offer are often limited by society's demands for painful prison conditions. For example, one might argue that for a poor offender who has been convicted of numerous small thefts, the best way to end that illegal behavior might be to provide him with a good job with a $20,000 per year guaranteed income. This "treatment" might be the best way to achieve the goal of ending the illegal behavior. However, such a treatment would certainly run counter to the unwritten rules of correctional treatment: that such "treatment" must involve a sufficient amount of imposed pain. Programs that attempt to create an environment where a useful treatment atmosphere can be developed are commonly attacked as "country club prisons" that do not provide enough pain.

An argument close to the one above has also come up when offenders are given useful treatments or programs which are not commonly available to everyone in society. Quite understandably, a person who cannot afford to go to college, for example, might be upset to find out that college courses are available inside a local jail or prison at no cost to the offender. The argument that such a program is a "treatment" which offers the hope of reducing criminal behavior is not sufficient to counter the claim that those who maintain a law-abiding life-style are sometimes unable to receive benefits that society grants to those who are convicted of a crime.

Those who defend the current system sometimes argue that the combination of pain and treatment at the same time is not a problem, because the imposition of pain can sometimes be therapeutic. Witness, for example, the experience discussed above of the child being spanked. Certainly, pain is imposed, but it can be good for the child in the long-run. Similarly, the argument goes, a period of time in prison may seem painful, but it can have equally good results.

This argument can be extremely confusing and difficult to deal with, because it confuses two separate situations. "Criminal" is a legal term, given to those who are convicted of an illegal behavior, but "treatment" requires a more or less organic description of the person's condition or behavior to determine what the best therapy would be for that condition.

This confusion becomes a problem when officials decide that all burglars will receive "treatment number two." The criminal law involves breaking up illegal behavior into categories useful for prosecution and conviction. Thus, all persons who commit a certain defined type of act are considered "burglars." The legal process which leads to the application of such a label is quite different from the treatment process, which is based on an evaluation of the situation and needs of the particular individual. Some people who commit burglary may be in need of treatment, while some other persons who commit the same act may not be in need of treatment at all. It is a great and unjust leap of logic to assume that the application of a legal label (such as "burglar") also automatically implies the existence of a medical problem requiring treatment.

To summarize then, there are serious problems with the argument that all persons should be treated rather than punished. Though the two concepts are not opposites, they may work towards conflicting goals[3] and may be derived from different conceptual bases. The common confusion between punishment and treatment leads to misapprehensions regarding the goals of the two concepts. Punishments, we find, are all too often justified on the basis of treatment rationale ("some of that will do him some good"), and treatments are all too often evaluated on the basis of punishment criteria ("country club prisons").

Another area of difficulty related to the use of treatment in corrections has been discussed by Leslie Wilkins.[4] Wilkins deals with the problem that in modern corrections the treatments we use virtually always involve the imposition of some pain. If this is true, how then can we tell the "punishment activities" from the "treatment activities?" It is certainly not enough to rely on the intentions of the correctional administrators to differentiate the two: to do so is to say that "treatment exists whenever the prison warden says it exists." Certainly the potential abuses of such an approach are obvious. In another section of this book we discussed the problem of label-switching. The question might arise: what would you do if you were under some pressure to institute programs which had the look of modern scientific treatment, but did not want to give up your traditional punishment orientation? One response might be to keep your old prison program, but change the

---

3. See the appendix by Alan Dershowitz to 20th Century Fund Task Force on Criminal Sentencing, *Fair and Certain Punishment*, (New York: McGraw-Hill, 1976).

4. Leslie T. Wilkins, *Evaluation of Penal Measures*, (New York: Random House, 1969).

name and reasoning behind it. One is not, then, sent to your prison in order to receive painful punishment; one is sent to your "institution" in order to receive "environmental milieu therapy," (translate these florid euphemisms and you still have an offender being sent to prison in order to sit in a cell). Persons who misbehave after arriving in your prison are not sent to maximum security punishment cells, but rather are brought into an "operant conditioning sensory deprivation behavior adjustment therapy center" (otherwise known as the old maximum security punishment cells).

A final potential answer to the question of how to differentiate punishment from treatment might be to look at the *result* of the activity. If it resulted in a "cure," then it was treatment. However, there are serious shortcomings to this "after-the-fact" definition system. The exact same program can be considered treatment to those it "helped," but punishment to those it "failed." If beating a prisoner to the point of death convinces him to stop violating the law, does that mean it is a therapeutic treatment? If not, is it then a cruel punishment?

SHOULD WE TREAT AT ALL?

Even though we have had serious problems in dealing with the definition of treatment, a fundamental question still remains: *should* we treat criminals? The answer to this question has often been assumed to be yes, but in the past decade there has been a growing questioning of whether treatment can be considered to be a good goal.

Treatment as a goal has been criticized for a wide variety of reasons. One of the more common attacks in recent years has come from those who argue against treatment primarily on ideological and moral grounds.[5] Often, the point is made that the criminal law should be concerned only with criminal acts and not with the condition or mental health status of the offender.[6] Such critics argue that the purpose of the criminal law is to identify those members of society who have broken the law, and then to punish them. If that is the purpose of the law, forcing treatment on convicted offenders would constitute an overstepping of proper boundaries. The state may have the power to punish offenders, but it is debatable whether the state has the power to force offenders into treatment programs, and deal with problems it is not adequately equipped to handle.

Other critics, however, have argued that the problem goes further. Even if we should finally decide that the state has the power to force offenders into treatment programs, the ineffectiveness of the programs we now have, and the potential for abuses of treatment powers, would strongly argue against its use.[7] The growing body of literature, which analyzes treatment programs

---

5. See Andrew von Hirsch, *Doing Justice*, (New York: Hill and Wang, 1976).

6. See Herbert L. Packer, *The Limits of the Criminal Sanction*, (Stanford, Cal.: Stanford University Press, 1968).

7. See American Friends Service Committee, *Struggle For Justice*, (New York: Hill and Wang, 1971).

used in the past, has generally found very little of value to report.[8] The authors of such literature claim that, though treatment might be an acceptable goal, we just do not have the scientific technology to implement it. Bluntly, we would not know how to cure offenders even if we were given permission to do so.

In an earlier section, the problems of discretion and treatment powers were discussed. Many people who argue against treatment also cite the fact that in order to choose the proper treatment for each offender, the therapist must be given a great deal of choice and power. In the wrong hands, this power can be easily abused, and some writers have spent considerable time documenting how widespread abuses of this power in treatment have, in fact, occurred.[9] Those who hold this point of view suggest that in order to end these abuses, we must end the "treatment regime."

Because of the frequency of the types of attacks described above, there are fewer and fewer treatment enthusiasts left to defend this goal (at least publicly). Those who do speak out, however, argue that very little has really been tried in the area of correctional rehabilitation. There are two major shortcomings of correctional institutions, the defenders argue. First, what has been attempted in the way of treatment has been based on very inadequate knowledge about crime, and only the most neanderthal research has thus far been done.[10] So, while they agree that we may not know much about how to treat offenders, they argue that this is because we have not done very much to increase our knowledge. Very few prisons or corrections systems have put any significant amount of money into research.[11]

Second, those who have tried to develop new programs have been severely limited by both the treatment setting (which is usually the prison), and by some of the assumptions that they have made about the nature of offenders.[12] Some recent innovations, which have been based on more open approaches toward the offenders as well as the prison setting, have shown much more promise for success.[13]

Finally, those who favor treatment in corrections[14] argue that the concept

---

8. Robert Martinson, "What Works? Questions and Answers About Prison Reform," *The Public Interest*, vol. 35 (Spring 1974), p. 22.

9. Jessica Mitford, *Kind and Usual Punishment—The Prison Business*, (New York: Alfred A. Knopf, 1973).

10. Don M. Gottfredson et al., *Probation on Trial*, (Newark: Rutgers University School of Criminal Justice, 1978). (Mimeographed.)

11. W.S. Chaneles, "Prisoners Can Be Rehabilitated Now," *Psychology Today*, vol. 10 (1976), pp. 129-133.

12. Ted Palmer, "Martinson Revisited," *Journal of Research in Crime and Delinquency*, vol. 12 (1975), p. 133; Robert R. Ross and H.B. McKay, "Treatment in Corrections: Requiem for a Panacea," *Canadian Journal of Criminology*, vol. 20 (1978), pp. 279-295.

13. See Lloyd E. Ohlin et al., *Juvenile Correctional Reform in Massachusetts*, (Washington, D.C.: U.S. Government Printing Office, 1977).

14. See Karl Menninger, *The Crime of Punishment*, (New York: The Viking Press, 1966).

of utilitarian goals—in which punishment or corrections serves some useful purpose rather than, or in addition to, simple retaliation—has always been associated with the criminal justice system. A system which seeks only to gain revenge upon offenders merely returns to the streets angry people who have been made bitter by their confinement. Literally, it is possible that over a long period of time, this process of making offenders angry and bitter might make the crime problem worse than it initially was, by releasing back into society worse criminals than were taken off the streets originally. Defenders of treatment programs insist that while a treatment goal is being pursued, every attempt should be made to control the abuses made possible by treatment, so that correctional policy makers will not feel forced to abandon the potentially high benefits of a treatment goal.[15]

HOW SHOULD WE TREAT?

This brief overview of issues should give the reader some idea of the controversy which encumbers the notion of "correctional treatment." However, even if we can come to an acceptable definition of what treatment is, and even if we can come to the conclusion that treatment is a goal which we would like to attempt, then we must still deal with the question that most people seem to ask first—how can criminals best be rehabilitated?

Historically, this question was answered by the development of programs which viewed the criminal alone as the source of all crime. The assumption was that the criminal was somehow socially, emotionally or psychologically "disadvantaged" or "immature." This so-called "medical model" of criminality, which views crime as a disease, led to correctional treatment programs which focused primarily on changing the individual offender. Attempts were made to make the offender socially and emotionally "whole," with a primary emphasis on psychotherapy and clinical social work.[16] Recently, however, this focus has changed. One of the reasons for the change has been an extensive examination of prior programs of treatment, based on the assumptions of the medical model, which has shown these programs to be of rather limited effectiveness.[17] In addition, recent criminological theory has begun to emphasize the importance of environmental social systems in influencing, and even producing, criminality.[18] As a result, recent correctional programs are more likely to emphasize changing the community as well as the offender, a concept which began to gain wide acceptance after it

15. Robert G. Culbertson, "Corrections: The State of the Art," *Journal of Criminal Justice*, vol. 5 (1977), p. 39.

16. David Duffee, *Correctional Policy and Prison Organization*, (New York: Sage Publications, 1975).

17. See Martinson, "What Works?"; Robison and Smith, "The Effectiveness of Correctional Programs"; Douglas Lipton, Robert Martinson, and Judith Wilks, *The Effectiveness of Correctional Treatment: A Survey of Treatment Evaluation Studies*, (New York: Praeger, 1975).

18. Richard Cloward and Lloyd Ohlin, *Delinquency and Opportunity*, (New York: The Free Press, 1960).

was proposed by the 1967 President's Commission on Law Enforcement and the Administration of Justice.[19] Some of the ideas that were fundamental to this new move suggested that while one could reject the notion that society was *entirely* to blame for producing a criminal, one could not ignore the impact of environment and assume that all of the blame rested on factors totally unique to the offender. A combination of forces, both in society, and within the offender, had to share the blame, and had to be the target of efforts to produce crime-free behavior.

The more recent National Advisory Commission[20] reiterated the importance of this newer thrust, which has been termed the "reintegrative" approach. Because of the need to work with the offender within the community, (where, after all, he or she is going to have to live eventually), the reintegrative approach relies primarily on community-based corrections agencies such as probation, parole and half-way houses. For those incarcerated in institutions such as prisons, the reintegrative approach implies that the focus of correctional programs should be on the eventual release of the offender back into the community.

As a treatment technique, reintegration calls for multi-skilled correctional workers who can act as consultants to professional community agencies and services that will be dealing with the offender. The goal is to improve the offender's relationship with the community by involving him or her with normal and productive community institutions. As a result, the "treatment" may encompass a variety of activities such as job training, use of furloughs (to allow the offender to return home from prison, much as one leaves a military base "on leave"), correctional activities or institutions which include both sexes (the offender will have to learn to deal with the opposite sex, so why not begin under supervision?), the extensive use of volunteers or paraprofessionals (such as ex-convicts), and the development of programs which divert the offender away from the criminal justice system at an early date, or which develop alternative educational systems for offenders. The attempt of all of these programs is to "normalize" the situation of the offender within the community in such a way as to reduce the probability of future criminal behavior.

These new programs have not as yet shown themselves to be so successful that they can be immediately acclaimed. In fact, Nora Klapmuts, in an extensive review of community-based programs, notes that all new efforts in reintegrationist philosophy will have to "be viewed in the light of current thinking in correction (less-not more-intervention, the inutility of coercive programs, offender participation in the selection of services, etc.) and the

---

19. President's Commission on Law Enforcement and the Administration of Justice, *Task Force Report: Corrections*, (Washington, D.C.: U.S. Government Printing Office, 1967).

20. National Advisory Commission on Criminal Justice Standards and Goals, *Corrections*, (Washington, D.C.: U.S. Department of Justice, 1973).

evidence that no treatment effort has yet been unambiguously successful."[21]

Ultimately, the entire "how to treat" question rests on the future availability of research results which show effectiveness. So far, the findings are rather slim, and even those experiments which show positive results can often be questioned on the basis of problems in their experimental design.[22]

As a result, one is left in a familiar position in this field of study—the questions outnumber the answers both quantitatively and qualitatively: What is treatment? Should we do it? If so, how?

---

21. Nora Klapmuts, "Community Alternatives to Prison," *Crime and Delinquency Literature*, vol. 5 (June 1973), p. 320.
22. Klapmuts, "Community Alternatives to Prison," p. 316; Lipton, Martinson, and Wilks, *Effectiveness of Correctional Treatment*.

The Medical Model in Corrections*

Requiescat in Pace

Donal E.J. MacNamara
John Jay College of Criminal Justice
City University of New York

Of all the many correctional shibboleths religiously communicated to their students by professors of sociology, social work, criminology, and corrections, the "medical model" has proved most durable, and strangely so since there has been little, if any, empirical demonstration of its validity. The concept is at once so humane, so modern, so professional, and seemingly so scientific as to commend it to men of good will; and the process of follow-up evaluation so neglected and so fraught with methodological pitfalls as to permit widely disseminated claims of rehabilitative success based on little more than an overly optimistic belief in the ultimate perfectability of even the most dangerous and recidivistic offenders coupled with a statistical innocence more appropriate to an adolescent interest in batting and fielding averages. Its enduring quality, too, owes not a little to the neanderthal opposition: those who, however valid their overall negative evaluations of the model in practice, couch their countervailing arguments in such discriminatory, punitive, retributive, and unscientific language as to offend the sensibilities and reinforce the basic premises of the reformers and rehabilitators.

In its simplest (perhaps oversimplified) terms, the medical model as applied to corrections assumed the offender to be "sick" (physically, mentally, and/or socially); his offense to be a manifestation or symptom of his illness, a cry for help. Obviously, then, early and accurate diagnosis, followed by prompt and effective therapeutic intervention, assured an affirmative prognosis—rehabilitation. Diagnosis was the function of the presentence investigation (confirmed, expanded, or perhaps corrected during institutional classification); therapeutic intervention was decreed in the sentence and made more specific in the treatment plan devised by the classification committee; and the parole board decided (within certain legal constraints) when the patient was to be discharged back into the community as "cured." Basic to the medical model, although rather surprisingly denied by many of its proponents, is that the criminogenic factors are indigenous to the individual offender and that it is by doing "something" for, to, or with him that rehabilitation can be effected.

There are, to be sure, many illustrative cases to which this model applies:

---

* "The Medical Model in Corrections: Requiescat in Pace" by Donal E. J. MacNamara is reprinted from *Criminology*, vol. 14, no. 4 (February 1977), pp. 439-448, by permission of the publisher, Sage Publications, Inc.

the offender with a glandular imbalance correctable by chemotherapy; the cosmetic elimination of a disfiguring blemish with a consequent minimizing of social discrimination and reactive hostility; even the surgical removal of the testes of an habitual rapist. Somewhat more questionable are the claimed successes for psychiatric interventions; and it is difficult, indeed, since the more credulously religious days of past centuries, to find acceptable examples of moral regeneration. But the medical model school depended less on an affirmative showing that success crowned their programs than on aggressive excuses for failure: rehabilitation was underfunded; treatment was sabotaged by custodial staff; judges and parole boards responded to political and public pressures rather than to treatment imperatives; society had a lust for punishment; even rehabilitated offenders suffered socioeconomic discrimination which drove them back to criminal activity; the brutal, coercive, institutional atmosphere negated therapeutic interventions; "prisonization" (the resocialization of newly incarcerated offenders into the mores and folkways of the inmate community) was contra-rehabilitative; and, among those labelled "radical" criminologists, a retreat position inconsistent with the medical model that denounces the society which defines criminality rather than the offenders who violate society's laws.

The medical model has further implications for criminal justice. It entails wide discretion for the criminal court judiciary, permitting diversion of cases from the criminal justice system; sentencing alternatives ranging from probation to indeterminate sentences of polar dimensions (e.g., one day to life); paroling authorities within many cases equally liberal alternatives; and to some lesser degree an expanded use of the commutation and pardoning powers of the executive branch. Implicit in the model was the availability of a wide range of treatment alternatives, institutional and community; and anticipated too was an army of professional probation and parole officers, with a department store of social services awaiting referrals, who would not only supervise but service and support manageable caseloads, consisting of clients specially selected by judges and parole boards as being of minimal danger to the community and good prospects for societal readjustment. That judicial discretion has been abused and incompetently administered, that the arsenal of treatment alternatives has seldom been provided, that paroling authorities have proved incapable of either resisting pressures or distinguishing dangerous from nondangerous offenders, that probation and parole officers have for a variety of reasons failed either to supervise adequately or provide services and support, that the retributive forces in correction and in the public have inhibited certain rehabilitative approaches, and even that some humane and libertarian proponents of the medical model have, perhaps inconsistently, opposed the more draconian treatment interventions (e.g., behavior modification) may all be accepted as possible explanations for the failure of the rehabilitative ideal. But it is perhaps more likely than not that, even if these negatives could be corrected, the custodial-deterrent-retributive school would be vindicated. For the basic flaw of the medical model is its basic premise: that the offender is "sick" when in fact he is far more likely to be as "normal" as most nonoffenders but inadequately, negatively, or contraculturally socialized, at war with a world he never made, a world in which he has been subjected to abuse, brutalization, discrimination, and exploitation. No program of education, vocational training, medical or psychiatric therapy is relevant to his "cure" and none is likely to reverse his twenty or thirty years of antisocial conditioning. What alternative remains? Incapacitation by custodial control with perhaps some rather speculative deterrent impact on either the offender or on prospective offenders, or both.

Now these views would have earned an academic criminologist naught but contumely less than a decade ago, but correctional fads, fallacies, and fashions change. A proliferating literature, bearing the names of such respectable academicians as Norval Morris, James Q. Wilson, Andrew von Hirsch, Robert Martinson, David Fogel, and Ernest van den Haag, now rejects equally the "tear down the walls" war cry of those who would abolish prisons (in favor of a just society which would eliminate criminogenic factors) and the prison reform movement which campaigns and litigates for smaller, treatment-oriented institutions, court-mandated inmate rights, expansion of community corrections, decriminalization of victimless offenses, and diversion from the criminal justice system for many now subject to its sanctions. The new penologists, if one can so label a quite disparate group, accept prisons as a societal necessity, advocate a narrowing or elimination of judicial discretion in sentencing (flat or definite sentences imposed uniformly and consistently on those convicted of identical crimes), an end to coerced institutional treatment (although they favor voluntary participation by inmates in a variety of educational, vocational, and therapeutic programs), abolition or severe constraints on parole, and acceptance of a deterrent-retributive-punitive rationalization for dealing with offenders. Some implicitly, others more explicitly, justify imprisonment in terms of societal protection by incapacitating for at least the definite period of their confinement those dangerous and habitual offenders who are responsible for the almost paranoid fear of criminals widespread among certain segments of our population and reflected in the increasingly punitive orientation of courts and legislatures.

My colleague, Robert Martinson (and his co-authors Douglas Lipton and Judith Wilks) has perhaps received a less cordial reception for the highly significant monograph, *The Effectiveness of Correctional Treatment* (1975), than has been accorded Morris, Wilson et al.; yet he has furnished us with a more massive and convincing documentation of the irrelevancy and ineffectiveness of therapeutic interventions than have the authors of the more readable polemics. Certainly his book, articles, and lectures have stimulated much of the new and highly controversial correctional dialogue; yet he is actually anti-prison and to a limited extent pro-probation and parole (advocating a transfer of funding which would permit highly intensified, almost one-for-one, supervision or surveillance in the community), thus eliminating the negative impact of imprisonment and at the same time enhancing societal protection against recidivistic crimes by convicted offenders. Martinson advocates the removal of the criminal justice system from the "treatment business," abolishing the indeterminate sentence and parole boards, developing three categories of offenders (suspendees, restrainees, and isolates). *Suspendees* are first offenders to be returned to the community under neither supervision nor coerced treatment, but who are eligible for voluntary services arranged through broker-advocates (not too different from an idealized version of a probation officer) and under the sole injunction that they not be convicted again of a criminal offense. *Restrainees*, either suspendees who recidivate or offenders classified as nondeterrable by mere threat of punishment, would be placed under intensive surveillance within the community ("each *restrainee* will be assigned his own private policeman") by an agent who is unknown to him, with whom he is not to have interpersonal contact, and whose sole function would be to report to the police whenever he observes the restrainee committing a criminal offense. *Isolates*, either suspendees or restrainees who commit new and serious offenses or a small class of first offenders who are convicted of heinous, violent crimes and are too dangerous to be supervised in the community, would be imprisoned in one of a greatly reduced number of existing prisons, with neither treatment, reform, nor rehabilitation as the aim.

Norval Morris, prestigious dean of the University of Chicago Law School, in *The Future of Imprisonment* (1974), argues that prisons are necessary; that they can be made less brutal, corrupt, and dehumanizing; that all rehabilitative and treatment programs be entirely voluntary; that the range of judicial discretion in sentencing be severely constrained; that mandated programs of graduated community release precede parole; that terms of imprisonment be uniform and related to the seriousness of the offense rather than to speculative evaluation of "dangerousness" or potential for recidivism; and that model prisons, not unlike the Danish institution at Herstedvester, be provided for the custody and treatment of such habitually aggressive offenders as recidivistic rapists and murderers.

Ernest van den Haag, prolific polemicist on the faculty of the New School, advocates in *Punishing Criminals: Concerning a Very Old and Painful Question* (1975) a return to the pleasure-pain calculus, balancing temptation with swift and certain punishments, albeit somewhat less harsh than those advocated by many, e.g., day fines (related to the offender's income) for minor crimes; one- or two-year sentences for more serious offenders; longer, indeterminate imprisonment for incorrigibles; and perhaps "exile" for some (i.e., banishment with their families either to special penal communities or to small, isolated villages in which they might be more intensively supervised). This is in fact a feature of Italian penal law, used rather inconsistently as a means of controlling members of the Mafia, and was for centuries a basic penalty in China with the banishment distance in miles correlated to the offense but with the rigors of the climate and type of work available also inputs into the calculus. Van den Haag, probably the essential pragmatist of the new penologists, subordinates even charity and justice to the preservation of social order.

Andrew von Hirsch, of the Rutgers University School of Criminal Justice, in *Doing Justice: The Choice of Punishments* (1976), rejects the medical-rehabilitative model, advocates elimination of both the indeterminate sentence and parole, accepts punishment as the basic rationalization of society's response to criminality, opts for somewhat harsher sentences than does van den Haag (a five-year maximum, for all crimes except murder, which—although von Hirsch does not mention it—has been established by psychological research as the outer parameter of the human ability to project into the future), and emphasizes that offenders "deserve" to be punished in proportion to the gravity of their crime(s) against society.

James Q. Wilson, Harvard political scientist, has unlike the great majority of his disciplinary colleagues devoted much of his attention to the criminal justice system, forcefully dissenting from *The Challenge of Crime in a Free Society* (Ruth et al., 1971) and publishing an insightful study, *Varieties of Police Behavior* (1968). In a collection of essays, *Thinking About Crime* (1975), Wilson comes down hard on the side of prisons and punishments as mechanisms to reduce crime incidence substantially. Seeing the habitual, career criminal as responsible for a high proportion of serious criminality, he calls for incarceration, and holds out hope that imprisonment might additionally have some deterrent impact on others not yet committed to a life of crime. He, too, feels that swift and certain short terms of imprisonment (up to two years) can be effective, perhaps more effective than the much harsher maximum penalties provided for in the statutes but rarely imposed and even more rarely served. Wilson strongly implies that the failure of the prison population to increase proportionately to the significantly higher crime incidence after World War II was itself a cause of the increased criminality. And finally, he has short shrift for rehabilitation ("whatever it means") which he avers has no role in the prison sanction.

David Fogel's name has become synonymous with the rehabilitation of the "flat" or definite sentence and the "justice model" for corrections. While commissioner of corrections in Minnesota and later as director of the Illinois Law Enforcement Commission, he expressed very clearly his belief that rehabilitation and therapists have nothing to do with justice and safety, that rehabilitation should have nothing to do with whether an offender is sentenced to prison or when an offender should be released, and that the justice model must include justice for the victim (which led to his establishing the Minnesota restitution program). Fogel's sentencing recommendations divided crimes into categories based on degree of seriousness and provided limited judicial discretion (sentences could vary by as much as 20% if there were mitigating or aggravating factors); and, importantly, only offenders who were clearly dangerous to society would go to prison (e.g., he believes that all or most property offenders, many of whom now get committed to penal institutions, can be safely supervised within the community). Fogel's ineptly titled *We Are the Living Proof: The Justice Model for Corrections* (1975) is a clear and forceful presentation of his views and an especially convincing argument in favor of limiting the sentencing discretion of America's criminal court judges.

Finally, mention must be made of *Prison Without Walls* (1975), the report on parole in New York State by the Citizens' Inquiry on Parole and Criminal Justice (of which the author was a member and a consultant). Ramsey Clark and Herman Schwartz, both of whom might well be classified as prison abolitionists, headed the inquiry, and Jack Himmelstein, David Rothman, Richard Cloward, David Fogel, Michael Meltsner, Tom Wicker, Edward Bennet Williams, and William vanden Heuvel were among the better known students and practitioners of criminal justice lending their expertise. *Prison Without Walls* recommends that parole be abolished (as has Attorney General Edward Levi) because it is an adjunct of a sentencing process that attempts to reconcile elements of law, justice, and societal protection with considerations of rehabilitation and treatment. The result is an uneasy amalgam, as unfair to the offender as it is ineffective in the achievement of society's goals. Prisons do not "treat" offenders; they do not rehabilitate. Parole boards have little demonstrated competence in distinguishing dangerous from nondangerous inmates. Predictions of postinstitutional behavior, based largely on adjustment to the abnormal routines of institutional life, have proved disastrously inaccurate (in a California study, almost 90 % so). The parole decision-making process is itself inequitable, if not unconstitutional (arbitrary and without empirically derived guidelines, subject to whim and pressure). In addition to concluding that the parole board be abolished, the report made both long-term and transitional recommendations, including elimination of compulsory community supervision, shorter sentences within a much narrower range of judicial discretion, development of rational criteria for early release, development of new alternatives to incarceration, public scrutiny of correctional decision-making, a wide range of voluntary programs to be offered to offenders before, during, and after incarceration, a specific code of inmate rights in parole board proceedings, shifting the burden of proof to parole boards in denying parole, open hearings, one year maximum on parole supervision in the community, simplification of the parole contract, abolition of the law enforcement function of parole agents (revocation to be based only on a new crime), financial assistance for parolees, extensive social services, and crediting of time on conditional release toward maximum sentence. *Prison Without Walls*, though somewhat different in its genesis and orientation, fits comfortably into the matrix of justice model studies; and better than many documents its far-reaching and quite controversial conclusions are fortified with persuasive data from the official archives but, even more importantly, from the client population.

The new penologists posit a basic conflict between a medical model maintaining that crime is the product of individual defects and disorders that can be corrected in a program of medical, psychiatric, and social rehabilitation and a readjusted or reformed offender returned to his rightful place in society *versus* a justice model based on the more classic doctrine of the free moral agent and of individual responsibility for one's criminal behavior. The controversy is somewhat complicated by reform and pragmatic considerations—reformers who want not to abolish prisons but rather to make them more humane and their rehabilitation programs more effective, and realists who insist that society has a right to protect itself from predatory elements by confining them in prisons, whether or not this leads to their rehabilitation and in fact irrespective of whether it contributes to their further criminality after release. The battle lines involve power dynamics as well as ideological conflicts. Judges wish to retain the tremendous discretion with which the medical model has invested them over the past half-century, and parole board members fight valiantly to retain their posts of power and prestige; both probation and parole officers are defending their jobs and their careers; program staff members in institutions (educators, vocational training specialists, therapists) see themselves threatened by making inmate participation voluntary; custodial elements scent victory over the hated head-shrinkers; law and order politicians and some punitive-retributive legislators and pressure groups misread Morris, Wilson, Martinson, Fogel, von Hirsch and van den Haag as "lock 'em up and throw the key away" neanderthals; and the general public, ill-served by the communications media, is confused and unhappy. Perhaps least perturbed is the target population, offenders in or out of prisons. To a man they see this conflict as a charade...they *know* from past experience that nothing good ever happens to them. They have every expectation that no matter how things change, justice for them will remain very much the same.

References

Citizens' Inquiry on Parole and Criminal Justice (1975) *Prison Without Walls*. New York: Praeger.

Fogel, D. (1975) *We Are the Living Proof: The Justice Model for Corrections*. Cincinnati: W.H. Anderson.

Lipton, D., R. Martinson, and J. Wilks (1975) *The Effectiveness of Correctional Treatment*. New York: Praeger.

Morris, N. (1974) *The Future of Imprisonment*. Chicago: Univ. of Chicago Press.

Ruth, H. et al (1971) *The Challenge of Crime in a Free Society*. New York: Da Capo.

van den Haag, E. (1975) *Punishing Criminals: Concerning a Very Old Painful Question*. New York: Basic Books.

von Hirsch, A. (1976) *Doing Justice: The Choice of Punishments*. New York: Hill & Wang.

Wilson, J.Q. (1975) *Thinking About Crime*. New York: Basic Books.

_____(1968) *Varieties of Police Behavior: The Management of Law and Order in Eight Communities*. Cambridge: Harvard Univ. Press.

Is Rehabilitation Dead?*

Seymour L. Halleck
Professor of Psychiatry, School of Medicine,
University of North Carolina at Chapel Hill

Ann D. Witte
Assistant Professor of Economics,
University of North Carolina at Chapel Hill

Society sentences persons to prison for four basic reasons: to rehabilitate them, to deter them and others, to incapacitate them, and to make them "pay for their crime." Throughout most of this century and particularly during the 1960's, rehabilitation was considered the most important of these goals. However, because of three major trends during the last ten or twelve years, many now say that the major goals of imprisonment are deterrence and retribution.

The most important of these trends was the dramatic rise in crime rates. From 1960 to 1972 the crime rate went up 3.5 per cent per annum. The most rapidly increasing crimes during this period were robbery, which rose 6 per cent per annum, and larceny of $50 or more, which rose 6.5 per cent per annum. The increase in these largely economically motivated crimes has affected the lives of a large number of the well-to-do. Unaccustomed to the continual presence of the threat of crime, this group has developed a sense of powerlessness as its support of rehabilitative programs has failed to stem or even slow the rise in crime rates. This feeling of powerlessness has led to desperate searches for solutions, perhaps best illustrated by the recent film, *Death Wish.*

The misgiving about the efficacy of rehabilitation and the cry for retribution have received intellectual support from two streams of academic research that combine to form the second important trend in this period. The first stream consists of "evaluations of evaluations," publications that cast serious doubt on the efficacy of rehabilitation. The most comprehensive and in many ways the best of these assessments appeared as an article by Robert Martinson, who reported the results of his review of 231 studies of prison rehabilitative programs as follows: "With few and isolated exceptions, the rehabilitative efforts that have been reported so far have had no appreciable effect on recidivism."[1] Although only recently published, Pro-

---

1. Robert Martinson, "What Works?—Questions and Answers about Prison Reform," *The Public Interest*, Spring 1974, p. 25.

---

* Reprinted, with permission of the National Council on Crime and Delinquency, from "Is Rehabilitation Dead?" by Seymour L. Halleck and Ann D. Witte, *Crime and Delinquency*, October 1977, pp. 372-382.

fessor Martinson's scholarly and comprehensive work has had a powerful effect on criminal justice administrators. Many correctional officials who have viewed themselves as reformers are changing their philosophies. The conversion is best illustrated in a recent speech by Norman Carlson, head of the Federal Bureau of Prisons, which announced that correction is relinquishing the notion, borrowed from the mental health model, that crime can be "cured" and is discarding the credo (based on that notion) that rehabilitation should be the main reason for incarceration[2]—a particularly significant proclamation since for years the Federal Bureau of Prisons had been one of the most fervent supporters of rehabilitation and its underlying mental health model. This change in the criminal justice administrators' attitude has made it difficult—sometimes impossible—to obtain support for rehabilitative projects.

The second stream of academic research is made up of extensive empirical evidence that punishment does deter crime[3] and an economic model of crime that explains deterrence by punishment.[4] The empirical evidence, gathered from statistical techniques in economics, criminology, and sociology, has shown fairly consistently that crime is deterred by both a higher probability of punishment (certainty) and longer sentences (severity) and that the former is more potent than the latter. Severe punishment appears to be deterrent only with certain crimes, such as homicide. Research in deterrence theory has been used to justify the adoption of mandatory sentences for certain crimes in a few states.[5]

According to the economic model of crime, which provides a neat and plausible explanation of these findings, an individual weighs the relative gains available to him in criminal and in noncriminal activities and chooses a life of crime only if the anticipated gains exceed those he expects from a legitimate career. An increase in expected punishment decreases the gains expected from criminal activity, influences the individual to shift from a criminal to a noncriminal career, and thus reduces the amount of crime. These twin messages—that rehabilitation does not work and that punishment prevents crime—are the scientific justification for "getting tough" with the criminal.

The final trend working against rehabilitation has been generated by civil liberties workers,[6] who maintain that the rationale of the indeterminate sentence is the belief that the offender must be deprived of liberty until he

2. "Giving up the Medical Model?" *Behavior Today*, Nov. 10, 1975, p. 1.

3. For example, W.C. Bailey, J.D. Martin, and L.N. Gray, "Crime and Deterrence: A Correctional Analysis," *Journal of Research in Crime and Delinquency*, July 1974, pp. 124-43; and I. Ehrlich, "Participation in Illegitimate Activities: A Theoretical and Empirical Investigation," *Journal of Political Economy*, May-June 1973, pp. 521-65.

4. See G.S. Becker, "Crime and Punishment: An Economic Approach," *Journal of Political Economy*, March-April 1968, pp. 169-217; and I. Ehrlich, *supra* note 3.

5. Examples are the drug statutes in New York and the gun control law in Massachusetts.

6. For example, see Norval Morris, *The Future of Imprisonment* (Chicago: University of Chicago Press, 1974).

has been rehabilitated. Since several types of rehabilitation are known to be ineffective and there is no objective way to determine when an offender has been rehabilitated, his freedom depends on the highly arbitrary judgments of correctional officials and parole boards. Civil liberties workers have concluded that offenders can, in effect, be kept behind bars without due process. There is considerable evidence that indeterminate sentencing has been abused in some states to keep politically troublesome prisoners incarcerated for long periods even when their crimes have been minimal.

Civil libertarians have also been concerned about the use of drug therapy and behavior modification for the political repression of incarcerated offenders under the guise of rehabilitation. When a prisoner faces prolonged incarceration if he does not cooperate in rehabilitative efforts, does he really have the option to refuse the treatments? Some civil liberties attorneys have argued that the offender, much like the hero in *A Clockwork Orange,* is under such duress to accede to the rehabilitative intentions of his captors that he cannot exercise free will in giving consent. The prisoner's right *not* to be rehabilitated is an unresolved issue. A number of class action suits designed to restrict use of certain rehabilitative models and treatments have been instituted. Some have been won; others are pending.

The forces aligned against rehabilitation are formidable. They include not only traditional law-and-order groups but also prominent academicians, militants of the new left, zealous right-wing proponents of libertarianism, and prisoners themselves. But a careful assessment of the evidence and the reality of dealing with the convicted criminal suggest that supporting a shift in emphasis from rehabilitation to retribution and deterrence is a major error.

The Evidence

People adhering to the medical-model philosophy of rehabilitation see offenders as sick, deviant, or deficient and seek to influence their criminal behavior by changing their personality through group and individual therapy. Those adhering to the economic-model philosophy of rehabilitation see offenders as lacking desirable legitimate opportunities and seek to divert them from crime by providing money and jobs.

The vast majority of all evaluations that have questioned the efficacy of rehabilitation have pertained to personality-changing programs. Of the eleven categories in Martinson's review of rehabilitation studies, only one—skill development—could be regarded as opportunity-changing, and his concluding comment on his findings for studies in this category casts doubt on whether they should be so classified: "It is possible, then, that skill development programs fail because what they teach bears so little relationship to an offender's subsequent life outside the prison."[7] Two of the fifteen programs in the skill-development category can be considered successful as a

---

7. Robert Martinson, *supra* note 1, p. 28.

whole,[8] and two can be considered successful at least for those whose opportunities were changed by the program.[9]

To be successful by Martinson's extremely rigorous criteria, a program had to show significant differences between the recidivism rates of its control and experimental groups in most situations in which it had been evaluated. For these differences to be shown, a significant number of individuals in the experimental group would have to refrain from criminal activity (at least that activity for which they had been convicted) during the follow-up period. Considering the types of programs evaluated, the failure to achieve dramatic alterations is certainly not surprising. Correctional rehabilitation programs have generally been perfunctory, underfunded, understaffed, and carried out in settings certainly not ideal. In general they have affected offenders for only a portion of their period of supervision, ranging, in the case of skill development, from 150 hours to two years.

With programs so limited in duration and quality, limited rather than dramatic changes in lifestyles would seem likely. Indeed, in a number of cases where Martinson reports no significant differences in recidivism rates, he does find significant differences in more limited measures of recidivism, such as a decline in the seriousness of offenses committed.[10] Expectations for the outcomes of limited programs should be more realistic than those posited by Martinson. Recidivism should be evaluated as complex, in the light of frequency and seriousness of offense, not treated simplistically as reconviction v. no reconviction.

To be successful by Martinson's criteria, a program must have no—or very few—negative results. Considering the variety of programs evaluated, finding some variants that yield negative results should not be surprising. What is surprising in this context, says Palmer, is that 48 per cent of the studies reviewed by Martinson in his *Public Interest* article had positive or partly positive results.[11]

Martinson's response to this finding is that it is "essential to *weigh* the evidence and not merely count the findings as if the studies were peanuts in a

---

8. C.E. Sullivan and W. Mandell, "Restoration of Youth Training: A Final Report," Staten Island, N.Y., Wakoff Research Center, April 1967 (processed); and F.W. Kovacs, "Evaluation and Final Report of the New Start Demonstration Project," Colorado Department of Employment, October 1967 (processed).

9. W.J. Gearhart, H.L. Keith, and G. Clemmons, "An Analysis of the Vocational Training Program in the Washington State Adult Correctional Institutions," *Research Review*, No. 23, Washington Department of Institutions, May 1967 (processed); and D. Glaser, *The Effectiveness of a Prison and Parole System* (Indianapolis: Bobbs-Merrill, 1964).

10. See, for example, A.J.W. Taylor, "An Evaluation of Group Therapy in a Girls' Borstal," *International Journal of Group Psychotherapy*, April 1967, pp. 168-77; C.F. Jesness, "The Fricot Ranch Study: Outcomes with Small versus Large Living Groups in the Rehabilitation of Delinquents," Research Report No. 27, California Youth Authority, Oct. 1, 1965; and R.B. Levinson and H.L. Kitchenet, "Demonstration Counseling Project," 2 vols. (Washington, D.C.: National Training School for Boys, 1962-64) (mimeo.).

11. Ted Palmer, "Martinson Revisited," *Journal of Research in Crime and Delinquency*, July 1975, p. 142.

sack."[12] True, but Martinson's method of weighing studies is largely subjective and hence impossible to replicate.[13]

Martinson is looking for a cure-all, a program that works for everyone all or almost all of the time. If one subscribes to the medical model, a search for a cure-all certainly seems inappropriate. Rather, this model suggests that we should tailor the treatment to fit the disease. It should not be surprising that programs designed to deal with personality problems are not effective for people who do not have these problems. Indeed, one of the great contributions of Martinson's work is that it points to a number of programs which seem to work consistently for certain types of individuals or in certain treatment situations. Martinson scorns such limited successes because programs with such limited success do not reduce the crime rate.[14] But perhaps the correct matching of programs and offenders can at least help to achieve this goal.

Note the period covered by Martinson's review—1945-67, when evaluation as a discipline was in its infancy. Evaluations since 1967 have, in general, been more thorough and more reliable statistically than those before that date. Positive findings discovered by Martinson are often questioned because findings after 1967 would be less subject to this criticism.

Evaluations of a number of opportunity-changing programs since 1967 have shown reason for optimism. Two evaluations of work-release programs in California have shown that men who participate in these programs have significantly lower recidivism rates than do comparable control groups.[15] While showing no differences in overall recidivism rates, an evaluation of the work-release program in North Carolina showed significantly less serious criminal activity for those who participated in the program.[16] Two pretrial intervention projects which provide employment-oriented assistance mainly to first offenders appear to reduce recidivism in the short but not the long run.[17] Researchers on a recent opportunity-change project in Baltimore

12. *Criminal Justice Newsletter*, Jan. 19, 1976, p. 2.

13. "When the studies are grouped in categories . . . , the survey team must make judgments as to whether one study should be given more weight than another within a given category. In this survey such judgments were based in part on the rating system described above and in part on the sizes of the sample population involved, evaluation of the methodology used . . . , and all of the other factors that enter into an inductive process of arriving at conclusions." Douglas Lipton, Robert Martinson, and Judith Wilks, *The Effectiveness of Correctional Treatment: A Survey of Treatment Evaluation Studies* (New York: Praeger, 1975), pp. 20-21.

14. *Supra* note 12.

15. R. Jeffrey and Stephen Woolpert, "Work Furlough as an Alternative to Incarceration: An Assessment of Its Effects on Recidivism and Social Cost," *Journal of Criminal Law and Criminology*, September 1974, pp. 405-15; and A. Rudoff and T.C. Esselstyn, "Evaluating Work Furlough: A Followup," *Federal Probation*, June 1973, pp. 48-53.

16. A.D. Witte, *Work Release in North Carolina: An Evaluation of Its Post-Release Effects* (Chapel Hill, N.C.: Institute for Research in Social Science, 1975).

17. R. Taggart III, *The Prison of Unemployment: Manpower Programs for Offenders* (Baltimore, Md.: Johns Hopkins University Press, 1972).

found that job-placement services had no effect on recidivism but that financial aid significantly reduced the percentage of men convicted of theft, robbery, burglary, or larceny.[18] The evidence is preliminary but it does seem to point to the effectiveness of opportunity-changing programs, particularly for individuals who committed economic crimes. Since these crimes are increasing the most rapidly, such programs seem at least to be worth a try. While opportunity-changing programs appear to be most effective for adults, Martinson found that the programs he reviewed were more successful with juveniles. Again, successful rehabilitation appears to be possible only when offenders who can be helped are matched with programs that fit their needs. The "who can be helped" proviso is important, since between 15 and 25 per cent of convicted offenders may be incapable of change through any intervention.

The major methodological grounds on which research on deterrence can be criticized is its use of aggregate data to test a theory of individual motivation. The efficacy of *rehabilitation* has always been evaluated by looking at *individual behavior;* in contrast, the efficacy of *deterrence* has almost always been tested on *aggregate data*. The greater ease of finding statistical significance in aggregate data should moderate our acceptance of the effectiveness of deterrence. Before accepting the conclusion that deterrence works, we should require that individual data be used to show that it works.

This criticism aside, recall that the major finding of deterrence research is that certainty of punishment seems to be a more effective deterrent than severity of sentence. The logical inference is that we ought then to adopt administrative policies that would make punishment more certain, not necessarily more severe. We can do this only by apprehending and convicting more offenders through greater police effectiveness, by strengthening the efforts of prosecuting attorneys, and by increasing the overall efficiency of our court system. Finally, we might take the drastic step of abridging the constitutional rights of offenders, thereby eliminating many of the legal options for avoiding punishment.

All of the above measures have been advocated by the new apostles of retribution. But most public officials, aware that such steps would be costly, only moderately effective, or politically unpopular, have taken a simpler and more drastic approach to the question of deterrence. They are now calling for longer sentences and the elimination of judicial discretion to shorten a sentence. In effect, the new outlook would increase the severity, not the certainty, of punishment—it is *not* a logical derivative of the findings of deterrence theory. A policy that increases the severity of punishment may actually decrease the certainty of punishment. A case in point is the crime of rape. One of the reasons for relatively few convictions for rape is that juries and judges are reluctant to come up with a finding of guilt because the punishment for the crime is so extreme.

---

18. K.J. Lenihan, "The Life Project: Some Preliminary Results, Design Questions and Policy Issues," report prepared for the Manpower Administration, U.S. Dept. of Labor by Bureau of Social Science Research, February 1975.

The Civil Liberties Issue

Many minor offenders, men who have not committed dangerous crimes, have been kept in prison indeterminately because they have failed to meet some nebulous criterion of rehabilitation. It is obviously desirable to protect offenders against such abuses, but it is simplistic to assume that the only way they can be protected is to do away with rehabilitative programs. Norval Morris, an eminent criminologist and dean of the University of Chicago School of Law, has offered a succinct principle as a solution to the problem: "Power over a criminal's life should not be taken in excess of that which would be taken were his reform not considered as one of our purposes."[19] Morris is arguing that the restriction of liberty of offenders is justifiable only for purposes of deterrence, incapacitation, or retribution. Any restriction of liberty should be governed by due process of law. Rehabilitative efforts would not infringe upon the civil rights of offenders if they were conducted within a framework of fixed sentencing. They can be safely continued even within a framework of indeterminate sentencing if they are used as a way to achieve earlier release, but the absence of rehabilitation ought not be used as a reason for restricting liberty indefinitely. With changes in laws in a few states and with careful monitoring of rehabilitative programs, most of the apprehensions of civil liberties advocates regarding restrictions of liberty can be relieved.

The ethical issue of experimenting with the minds and bodies of offenders is more complex. Given the current primitive state of the technology of mind control, this issue can, in the short run, be resolved by vigorously enforcing the offender's right to refuse rehabilitation. If an offender is given a fixed maximum sentence and has a reasonably good idea of his probable release date, he can make a rational choice between submitting to a rehabilitative technique which may or may not help him gain an early release and simply "doing time." His decision is intelligent and voluntary to the extent of his having full information on the possible adverse effects of any treatment for which he might volunteer. Increasingly, criminals are demanding and receiving such information. Recently the courts have prevented prison officials from depriving nonvolunteering prisoners of commonly available privileges.

In summary, the civil rights issue reminds us that we must monitor and curb overzealous attempts at rehabilitation. It is not, given the current state of our science of behavior modification, an injunction to abandon rehabilitation.

The Irrationality of Abandoning Rehabilitation

The force recommending punishment rather than reform is made up of two camps. One recommends not only greater use of imprisonment but also deliberate creation of harsh prison conditions superimposed on restriction of

19. Norval Morris, "The Future of Imprisonment: Toward a Punitive Philosophy," *Michigan Law Review*, May 1974, pp. 1161-80.

liberty. The other camp argues that life in the prison should be made as comfortable as possible and that deprivation of liberty is sufficient punishment in itself. The latter group is, in effect, advocating benign warehousing.

Is it possible to create a benign prison environment without trying to rehabilitate offenders? Probably not. It is not easy to control the daily activities of large groups of people. A society of captives will usually make demands that will require the captors to become more repressive to retain control. Though crimes of excessive punishment are sometimes committed in its name, rehabilitation is usually based on a humane concern for the needs of the individual offender, and, in turn, belief in it exerts a powerful moderating effect upon inmates, their captors, and the public.

To survive the ordeal of captivity, an offender must hope that he will emerge from it capable of enjoying life in a free world, and he must be assured that the portion of his life that is spent in prison was not entirely wasted. Without hope and a sense of significance, he is more likely to become embittered and to view himself as a victim of society's arbitrary vengeance. The offender who feels society is trying to help him may accept some of the restrictions imposed on him. The offender who feels that society has no goal other than to punish him will feel justified in attacking his captors. The behavior stemming from his feeling that he has been victimized triggers harsher retaliation and repression by the prison authorities. A prison that houses long-term offenders who have little hope of early release and no sense of usefulness to sustain their future visions cannot be anything but a jungle. Even prisons that are dedicated to rehabilitative goals are vicious and brutal.

What kind of person would want to work in an institution devoted primarily to benign warehousing? Correctional workers, too, must have hope and a sense of usefulness. No one wants to be his brother's keeper unless he is convinced that the process of keeping will be helpful. Our correctional system already has too many lethargic, bureaucratically insensitive, and even sadistic employees. A warehousing philosophy attracts more of them and reduces the possibility of creating a benign environment.

Finally, we must consider the expense of adherence to a strictly deterrent philosophy. The cost of incarceration today is already very high—in fiscal 1972, it was almost $2.5 billion. Even with this level of expenditure, the increasing crime rate coupled with longer sentences and less liberal parole decisions has led in many correctional systems to dangerous overcrowding, a condition not likely to be long tolerated by the federal judiciary, as evidenced by the recent federal court order dealing with the Alabama prison system. Even with minimum warehousing, the average inmate cost cannot be pushed much below $5,000 per annum. This figure assumes no increase in security cost, which seems doubtful in such a prison system. Indeed, the *direct* correctional expenditure per inmate in fiscal 1972 averaged more than $8,000 a year, even with extensive overcrowding. If benign warehousing is desired or court ordered, the average cost per inmate per year would fall in the $10,000-$15,000 range. It seems unlikely that the public will be willing to pay these kinds of prices for deterrence. Whether such a program would be cost effective—whether the benefits of deterrence would outweigh the cost of incarceration—is questionable. Rehabilitative programs such as work release can substantially reduce the cost of incarceration and would seem to merit serious consideration for inclusion even in a program of strict deterrence.

Imprisonment is more than merely punishment; it is immersion in a different kind of life. It is unlikely that anyone can leave a prison with exactly the same attitudes, emotions, and responses that characterized him before he went in. At least some of what the offender learned in prison is likely to affect his subsequent behavior. To the extent that we seek control of the contingencies that influence learning in prison, we are knowingly or unknowingly involved in efforts to change the offender. We can change him in a way that we think is good or bad for him and good or bad for the rest of us. Whenever we do anything to an offender that we believe will result in behavior that is favorable to his own needs or the needs of society, we are involved in rehabilitation.

Unless offenders are simply locked in solitary confinement for the duration of their sentence, the prison must find something for them to do. It must provide work, study, and recreation. If it is to be a relatively benign prison, it must take care of the health needs of its inmates and provide medical and psychiatric care as well as counseling. How can any of these activities fail to influence the offender? None of them might be critical in teaching the offender to abandon crime, but each of them would change him in some way.

Some Critical Questions

Posing the question as *whether* we can or should throw out the concept of rehabilitation is simplistic. It would be more helpful to formulate it as "To what extent should we invest our resources in attempting to rehabilitate criminals?" and "What limits should be placed on society's right to rehabilitate criminals?" The first question must be decided by weighing possible gains from rehabilitative programs, including adherence to the moral standards generally upheld by our society, against the likely gains of an approach based more on deterrence. At least some forms of rehabilitation provide more general social benefit than a strict deterrence philosophy and justify a large budget. In the short run it might help to rehabilitate a few offenders and would create a more benign climate for all offenders; in the long run, it might substantially decrease recidivism. A subsidiary justification for some types of rehabilitative programs is that they simply cost less than warehousing.

Given the relatively modest goals of rehabilitation, our ultimate decisions on the amount we will invest in them will depend upon our values. We must weigh individual needs and suffering against economic considerations, and we must weigh the values of repentance and forgiveness against the values of retribution and vengeance. In a sense, we must continue the 2,000-year-old dialogue on the desirability of New Testament versus Old Testament values. At the moment we have no scientific dicta to guide this dialogue. Just as there is no evidence that reform works, there is no evidence that the kind of retribution now being advocated works.

What limits should be placed on society's right to rehabilitate criminals? The question will become more excruciating as our technologies for altering human behavior—new drugs, psychosurgery, and behavior modification—become more efficient. Coercive or questionably voluntary rehabilitative techniques are not now abused but they probably will be as the technology of behavior control improves.

To place the application of behavior control to criminal offenders in proper perspective, we must acknowledge the complexity of the concept of rehabilitation. If we are concerned only with the protection of society, we define rehabilitation as merely the prevention of recidivism. However, if we are concerned with the individual offender as well as society, we define it as an absence of recidivism without damage to the individual (usually the most lofty goal we seek) or, more ambitiously, as law-abiding behavior accompanied by the offender's becoming a better and happier citizen (obviously the most difficult goal to achieve).

If we are not concerned with the individual and are occupied merely with stopping him from repetitive commitment of a given crime, many rehabilitative alternatives are open to us. We can rehabilitate the pickpockets by chopping off their hands, rehabilitate the rapists and child molesters by castrating them, rehabilitate many violent offenders and perhaps many property offenders by lobotomizing them. As a society committed to respecting the rights of even its criminal citizens, we have rejected such drastic forms of treatment.

But what will happen if the crime problem becomes more burdensome and our technologies become more sophisticated? What will happen when we develop technologies that only minimally disrupt the individual's potentialities while constricting his capacity to perform criminal acts? The temptation to use them will be irresistible and perhaps justified. It will not always be necessary for treatment to be coercive. Many offenders would volunteer for treatment that can alter their minds or bodies if they knew it would spare them years of incarceration. A number of sex offenders in our prisons have already volunteered for castration.

Research in behavior control based on altering the individual's biological state is well funded, is conducted by persons not particularly sophisticated in criminology, and will continue irrespective of public policies that deemphasize rehabilitation. At some time in the future, public officials will become aware of the possibility of combining drugs and psychosurgery with sophisticated behavior modification techniques to change criminal behavior. Defined simply as a cessation of criminal behavior without concern for the needs of the individual, rehabilitation would then become an effective force in criminology. At that point the concerns of civil rights advocates will be far more relevant than they are now.

The new preoccupation with the protocols of vengeance will not stop crime. It will distract us from studying and seeking to change those social, economic, and psychological forces that create criminality. It will discourage research that is designed to discover benign ways of changing criminals who really want to change. Finally, it will distract us from dealing with the critical ethical issue of how to utilize the powerful mind-altering technologies that will assuredly be developed.

None of this means that we should repeat the mistakes of the past and unreflectively endorse a correctional philosophy that is wholly or largely based on the concept of rehabilitation. Our plea is that rehabilitation be viewed as one of several potentially useful approaches to the crime problem. Contrary to much current belief, Martinson has not proven that rehabilitation does not work. Contrary to the belief of many humanists, there is no reason why rehabilitation programs must inevitably compromise the offender's liberties. And, contrary to the sanguine beliefs of so many of those who make policy decisions in criminal justice, there is good reason to fear that a correctional program that does not include rehabilitation will be extremely difficult to implement, will be absurdly expensive, and will encourage us to ignore critical ethical issues.

SOME OTHER ISSUES

Perhaps the most significant problem facing treatment in corrections today is a current crisis in confidence. Both practitioners and the general public have begun to lose faith in the ability of treatment professionals to change offenders.

The suspicion that treatment might not be a correctional panacea began in the late 1960s as part of that era's trend of questioning the effectiveness of various treatment programs. By the early 1970s, it had advanced beyond a series of questions to a liberal dogma: treatment in a correctional setting does not, and cannot work. This perspective is perhaps most clearly articulated by Robert Martinson in his highly influential summary of research results published in *The Public Interest.* After reviewing over 200 studies of treatment programs, Martinson concluded that there is

> "very little reason to hope that we have in fact found a sure way of reducing recidivism through rehabilitation. This is not to say that we have found no instances of success; it is only to say that these instances have been isolated, producing no clear pattern to indicate the efficacy of any particular method of treatment."[1]

Martinson's conclusions were timely, but they were hardly novel. Other researchers had taken similar overviews of treatment schemes with similar conclusions. Among the best known are those by Robison and Smith,[2] and Bailey.[3]

With an unsettling consistency, evaluations of most treatment projects have failed to show that the treatment involved has had any impact on success rates of offenders. However, the popular conclusion—that treatment "doesn't work"—may not be entirely justified by the data.

COUNSELING AND THE MEDICAL MODEL

Before summary statements can be made about the effectiveness of treatment, the general assumptions underlying both treatment and the kinds of programs commonly attempted must be understood. For the past two decades, innovative treatment in corrections has been dominated by assump-

---

1. Robert Martinson, "What Works—Questions and Answers About Prison Reform," *The Public Interest*, (Spring 1974), pp. 22-54.
2. James Robison and Gerald Smith, "The Effectiveness of Correctional Programs," *Crime and Delinquency*, vol. 42 (1971), p. 67.
3. Walter C. Bailey, "Correctional Treatment: An Analysis of One Hundred Outcome Studies," *Journal of Criminal Law, Criminology and Police Science*, vol. 62 (1966), p. 153.

tions regarding the effectiveness of "the medical model." In most programs, the offender's criminality was seen as a manifestation of deep-seated disorders in personality. Given this view, the thrust of corrections was primarily to repair the disorder.

One consequence of the medical model was that the focus of correctional intervention became the individual offender. The idea was that treatment programs should be designed to "deal with" those shortcomings in personality which "caused" the offender to commit a criminal act. The strategy central to this kind of treatment always included some variant of "counseling." Direct tangible services, such as job training, financial assistance and so forth were seen as "support services" which were secondary to the main job facing correctional professionals.

Though counseling may not have been equally effective with all offenders, it *was* seen as a "need" of all "clients." It was therefore not unusual that the generalist counselor was considered to be the most appropriate staff member for treatment.

It is this strategy of counseling-for-everyone which has proven consistently unsuccessful. One of the reasons this approach so often fails is that there is a common-sense feeling prevalent among counselors and supervisors that the act of counseling is, at worst, a neutral act. In those cases where the offender's behavior does not improve with counseling, it is usually assumed that the counseling has had no impact, either positive or negative, on the offender. Like many other common-sense beliefs about crime and justice, there is a good deal of evidence available to suggest that the exact opposite of this assumption holds true.

A famous experiment reported by Stuart Adams, called the PICO Project,[4] illustrates this point. In this case, the offenders were given intensive counseling while they were incarcerated. However, unbeknownst to the counselors, trained clinicians had already evaluated all of the subjects in advance to see if they were likely to benefit from counseling. Only a partial group of those amenable to therapy and a partial group of those not amenable to therapy were given counseling. The rest were just left alone and not given any sort of treatment.

The results of this experiment are important. As might be expected, the persons designated in advance as "amenables" did indeed fare better after receiving intensive counseling. However, those who were designated as "non-amenable" and were given counseling fared worse than that group of non-amenables who were not given counseling. In other words, counseling persons who were not amenable to therapy *decreased* their chances of success following treatment. As a group, they would have fared better if no treatment at all had been given.

---

4. Stuart Adams, "Effectiveness of Interview Therapy With Older Youth Authority Wards. An Interim Evaluation of the PICO Project," Research Report no. 20 (Sacramento, California Youth Authority, 1961). (Mimeographed.)

One can speculate as to the causes of such a finding. For example, it has long been known that people take their self-images in part from their understanding of how others are responding to them. Verbal interaction is never neutral.[5] By taking part in intensive therapy, the offender will hear the therapist relate to him in a particular way, and it is possible that this may have a negative effect upon his or her self-image, which in turn may negatively affect his or her behavior.

Therefore, it should be clear that counseling as a *standard* treatment may fail because it actually damages the chances of successful performance of some people. However, this damage may hide the fact that counseling has a positive effect on other groups of people.

For example, based on past experience, we might take a group of 200 offenders and make the prediction that 25% of them will be unsuccessful after release. If all 200 offenders are then given intensive counseling, and we later find that 25% of them did in fact fail, it would be a logical conclusion that the treatment did not work. Just as many did fail after treatment as we would have expected to have failed without any treatment at all.

Yet, while this is the logical conclusion, it may not be the correct one. It is possible that, say, 10% of the group of offenders expected to fail were actually helped by the counseling, while 10% of the group expected to benefit from counseling were, in fact, hurt by it. These groups balanced each other out, with the end result that the same expected 25% of the total group failed. If this is the correct conclusion, then the proper step would be to make a clinical evaluation of which individuals are amenable to counseling, and only treat that group. If we are correct, then this group would improve, while the non-amenables who are not treated would not be hurt, and the overall percentage of successes in the total group of 200 would rise above the expected 25% mark. In isolation, this might not sound like a very radical conclusion to make, but it is important because in corrections, it has frequently been assumed that counseling is the proper and needed treatment for *all* offenders *all* of the time. Those who have looked at the research results of this approach have tended to conclude that counseling as treatment does not work at all.

Another reason that counseling so often fails relates to the *quality* of counseling in corrections. Quay has argued:[6]

> "Before we can legitimately conclude that a method of correctional treatment has been shown not to work, there is a great deal we need to know beyond the experimental design and the outcome criteria. This third face of evaluation involves an assessment of the integrity of the treatment program itself."

5. Edwin M. Schur, *Radical Non-Intervention Re-Thinking the Delinquency Problem*, (Englewood Cliffs, N.J.: Prentice Hall, 1973).

6. Herbert C. Quay, "The Three Faces of Evaluation: What Can Be Expected to Work," paper presented at the National Conference on Criminal Justice Evaluation, Washington, D.C., 22-24 February 1977.

By "integrity" Quay means not just the theoretical soundness of the treatment model, but also the practical implementation of the treatment—did skilled persons actually provide services of high quality? If so, and the program has no effect on the success rate, then it can truly be said to have failed.

Too often, however, the treatment being evaluated—particularly in the case of counseling—is a sham, lacking integrity. Rather than a quality treatment program, poorly trained officials engage in limited and counterproductive low quality interaction with offenders, and then call it "counseling." In some states, a single undergraduate psychology course qualifies an employee as a "counselor" without additional training. Quay illustrates the effect of such quality limitations by discussing problems related to the implementation of a group counseling experiment as reported by Kassebaum, Ward and Wilner,[7] and demonstrates that the failure of group counseling, in this instance, may have been more a result of poor treatment "integrity" than the inappropriateness of counseling as a treatment technique.

Even with the current deficiencies in counseling, it is likely that counseling will continue to be the most common treatment technique in corrections. After all, any penological treatment method will of necessity involve some human interaction. This interaction should be handled as therapeutically as possible. On the other hand, it is high time that the nature and the focus of therapeutic counseling underwent change.

In order to improve the system's present handling of therapeutic counseling, it is first essential that those individuals for whom intensive counseling is a necessary aspect of treatment are appropriately identified. Second, the parameters of counseling in corrections, including who does it, how, and under what conditions, must change to insure a high integrity of treatment. Third, a full panoply of methods that goes beyond the assumptions of the "counseling-for-everyone" medical model needs to be developed.

A CHANGE IN FOCUS: SERVICES, COMMUNITY STRUCTURES AND OFFENDER BEHAVIOR

In recent years, there has been an upsurge of interest in other correctional methods besides counseling; methods which manage to successfully avoid the limiting assumptions of the medical model. Perhaps the most widely promoted alternative to counseling treatment is the provision of direct services. This emphasis on services stems from the growing professional literature in criminal justice on research and theory.

The theoretical arguments have been presented before,[8] and will only be summarized here. Perhaps the most famous statement in this area was made by Cloward and Ohlin, when they argued that the kinds of opportunities for achievement in a community heavily influence the amount and the type of

---

7. Gene Kassebaum, David Ward, and Ed Wilner, *Prison Treatment and Parole Survival: An Empirical Assessment*, (New York: John Wiley & Sons, 1971).

8. The Presidents Commission on Law Enforcement and the Administration of Justice, *Task Force Report: Corrections*, (Washington, D.C.: U.S. Government Printing Office, 1967).

delinquency within that community.[9] As a result of this epic work, correctional policy began to reflect a concern for creating legitimate work opportunities for citizens who lived in high-delinquency areas. The basic idea was the delinquency was highest in those places where the struggle for fundamental material needs was greatest. Therefore, corrections placed new emphasis on the provision of services: job placement, welfare services, medical services, emergency services, financial assistance, and so on. The concept behind the implementation of special delivery agencies was that if people could not meet basic social and personal needs through legitimate, legal avenues, they would have to resort to illegitimate, law-breaking actions. The existence of special service delivery agencies would eliminate the necessity for many people to use criminal force.

This point of view was supported by the research of Elliot Studt, who found that parolees, when asked what they had found most helpful about their parole supervision, mentioned concrete services most frequently. Generally, they failed to give a high priority to the counseling that was provided by the parole officer.[10] When further questioned about the counseling, parolees gave Studt the impression that counseling was important to the *officer's need* for an interactive relationship with the parolees, but had little influence on parole success, and certainly less impact than the provision of direct services.

The belief in service delivery as a means of improving the correctional system's success rate has led to the recent development of service-advocacy concepts, of which the most widely discussed is the Community Resource Management Team.[11] This approach involves no direct services from correctional agencies at all. Instead, correctional officials serve as referral agents, guiding offenders to relevant community programs or agencies that provide the kinds of services which the offender needs.

One argument for the community services approach suggests that before the community will really become a place where offenders can live crime-free, it must take at least some share of responsibility for the existence and control of crime. One formal way for the community to express this interest is to make its own service delivery systems responsive to the needs of those offenders in its midst. This is a way of accepting the duty of integrating ex-offenders into the mainstream of community life. For example, a local hospital may have developed an excellent treatment facility for alcoholics. All too often, however, these facilities are limited to middle-class drinkers, and the agency is not interested in having felons in its building, preferring instead to deal with housewives who pour a bit too much rum in their coffee.

9. Richard A. Cloward and Lloyd E. Ohlen, *Delinquency and Opportunity: A Theory of Delinquent Gangs,* (New York: Free Press, 1968).

10. Elliot Studt, *Surveillance and Service in Parole,* (Los Angeles: U.C.L.A., 1972).

11. Frank Dell'Apa, W. Tom Adams, James D. Jorgenson and Herbert R. Sigurdon, "Community Resources Management Team: An Innovation in Restructuring Probation and Parole," (Boulder, Colo.: Western Institute of Correctional Higher Education, 1977). (Mimeographed.)

Yet, many criminals have serious drinking problems, and often no agency is available to help them. The above argument requires that the local community take its share of responsibility in dealing with its members with problems, rather than asking correctional agencies to solve all problems related to crime.

Sometimes, of course, the needed services do not exist. Other times, although they exist, there is a reluctance to provide them in the ways that are uniquely relevant to offenders. School systems are a good example. Presumably, schools are a community institution designed to meet the educational needs of the citizenry. Sometimes though, school programs (such as remedial classes, night school, special tutoring, and similar programs), that might benefit certain kinds of offenders, do not exist. In addition, the school may actually be part of the criminogenic problem. Inconsistent overly strict (or lax) disciplinary practices, racist policies involving students, irrelevance to some classes of individuals, may all contribute to high delinquency rates. Some labeling theorists have argued that by tracking students (in college preparatory classes, general diploma classes, all-day woodshop or auto repair classes) or by labeling as slow learners otherwise intelligent enough students who merely have poor memorization skills (a skill rarely required outside of the classroom), schools tend to take some students and force them into a pattern which too often leads to delinquency. A student who has little chance of graduating has little to lose by being involved in delinquent behavior. However, if he stood to lose college admission or graduation because of an arrest, he might take the trouble to be more careful about his activities.[12]

In such cases, the problem facing corrections is to change community structures to make them more responsive to the needs of corrections clientele. For example, in the case of schooling, efforts would have to be made to meet with school officials, identify problems in school policy that block the acceptance of an offender as a student, and attempt to resolve these problems. This kind of situation, it is often argued, repeats itself in hiring practices, welfare eligibility, professional services, and similar areas.

The extensive use of community services, however, raises further issues that relate to treatment. For example, many of these services are designed primarily to enhance the quality of life of the clients. Yet, many critics argue that the offender's general quality of life is not the proper concern of corrections. Instead, it is argued:[13]

"...that corrections is forced to accept a very simple working hypothesis: offenders are offenders because of their present behavior. Then the task becomes that of asking what facet or facets of this person's behavior is critical for his having become an offender. ...We can evaluate correc-

---

12. Kenneth Polk and Walter E. Schafer, *Schools and Delinquency*, (Englewood Cliffs, N.J.: Prentice Hall, 1972).

13. Herbert C. Quay, "What Corrections Can Correct, and How," *Federal Probation*, vol. 37 (1973), pp. 3-4.

tions on the basis of the extent to which it succeeds, in the correctional setting, in changing those behaviors which it has set out to change."

According to this approach, the corrections mandate is limited to the reduction and control of law-breaking behavior. The offender's life-style, attitudes and beliefs, insofar as they are unrelated to criminal behavior, are not the proper concern of corrections. The only concern of corrections is only that an offender not violate the law; other individual choices regarding modes of life are for the offender to freely make, not correctional officials.

For those who would focus on behaviors, an array of behavior-based treatment strategies become available for adoption, many of which fall under the general title "behavior modification." The general process of behavior modification includes the identification of behaviors targeted for change, specification of the conditions under which those behaviors might be altered, and then the creation of the conditions in such a way as to achieve the planned alterations in behavior. In this process, one normally thinks of "conditions" as rewards and punishments, and certainly the policy of efficient use of rewards and punishments has a long history in corrections. Parole, for example, is a system that lets one go back to the community (reward) or stay longer in the prison (punishment) as the result at least theoretically, of the offender's behavior in the prison.

However, other "conditions" equally apply to this formula. Perhaps the most controversial conditions are those which involve chemical substances and other external means for the control of behavior. For example, in aversion therapy, the use of antabuse—a drug which creates a death-like physical reaction temporarily in its user—raises the deepest issues about the rights of the state to force behavioral compliance and leads to questions regarding the propriety of behavior-control methods. In a society where the U.S. Supreme Court has ruled that whipping or physically beating prisoners is "cruel and unusual punishment," it strikes many people as illogical to allow psychiatrists to use a drug which convinces many offenders that they are dying, simply because it has been called "treatment." Certainly the most brutal guard could testify that severely beating prisoners with huge sticks after they violate the rules is also aversion therapy treatment. By demonstrating to the prisoners that there is an external control of their behavior (being beaten) the hope is that prisoners would learn to internalize this control and avoid future rule-breaking behavior voluntarily. Why is this cruel and unusual when done by a guard but accepted scientific practice when done by a psychiatrist? (For a horrific vision of a treatment technology based on effective behavior alteration, read Anthony Burgess's futuristic novel, A Clockwork Orange.)

Defenders of this method respond by saying that the choice is not whether or not to engage in behavior change, but whether or not one wants an effective reduction in the recidivism rate. The point is well taken, since after all, the purpose of counseling, direct services and other non-behavioristic methods is ultimately to eliminate law-breaking behavior. It is safe to say that behavioral scientists will continue to develop new technologies for changing the behavior of offenders, and these will range from relatively non-threatening interactive therapies to the more inflexible chemical and contingency therapies. In light of this focus on change technology, the more crucial questions facing treatment in corrections may involve the need to control or eliminate coercion.

TREATMENT AND COERCION

To the degree that behavior change is a scientific technique, the operation of change-producing programs will tend to fall in the hands of scientists—whether they be psychologists, physicians, "behavioral engineers" or other "professionals." So long as professionals are charged with conducting the offender change effort, the problem facing corrections will be how to place controls on this discretion, and prevent abuses of its use.

The problem, as outlined in other sections of this book, is that discretion—the ability to make choices rather than follow a strict set of rules—is considered to be an important part of any treatment-based program. Since people are different, the professional change agent must have the ability to make different decisions about which types of treatment are best for each person. However, it has been documented that indefensible abuses of discretion have occurred in the handling of offenders.[14] The primary issue now is whether such abuses are a natural consequence of a coercive treatment model. If they are not a natural consequence, is it possible that such abuses can be controlled or eliminated through correctional policies which would maintain control over behavior-change treatment programs?

There are many different types of abuses, and indeed there is some debate on exactly what constitutes an abuse. For example, if the therapist is given the authority (discretion) to order any treatment that is needed to control the offender's behavior, what happens if, in the therapist's best professional judgment, the proper therapy called for would be to have the offender whipped and beaten every day, and then locked in a dark cell at night with only bread and water to live on? The U.S. Supreme Court has said that whipping is cruel and unusual punishment, but what if a psychiatrist has said that it isn't punishment at all, but rather a scientific attempt to strengthen a weak superego by demonstrating to an offender that there are external controls on his behavior? What if some scientist decides that the offender should be forced to have part of his brain severed, or should be medically castrated, or should be administered drugs which are more painful and psychologically harmful than a whipping could ever be? These are real suggestions made by correctional psychiatrists in recent years. If the corrections system decides to use scientific technology to completely alter a person's personality, is this a proper use of technology to achieve the result we all want—a person who no longer commits crimes—or is it the feared brainwashing and personality alteration predicted in the totalitarian state of George Orwell's *1984?*

---

14. Jessica Mitford, *Kind and Usual Punishment—The Prison Business*, (New York: Alfred A. Knopf, 1973).

On a slightly different level, some scientists have expressed the fear that while behavioral science has advanced greatly in recent years, there has not been an ethical philosophy which has advanced at an equal rate. In the physical sciences, some scientists have worked on such inventions as the atomic and hydrogen bomb, while claiming that the use of such weapons is a political decision, which is out of their hands. Other scientists have argued that science is not a value-free discipline, and that people should not invent techniques to destroy the world and then claim they are not responsible for the death and destruction that results from their work.

Similarly, there is the issue of whether behavioral scientists should invent methods of altering personalities, unless they are willing to accept responsibility for the results of their inventions. If we can invent a science which can easily change a person's beliefs and behaviors, what happens if an unscrupulous politician obtains the use of these techniques? Of course, at this date we are talking about making child molesters and muggers into crime-free citizens. But couldn't these same techniques be used to alter the personality of a citizen who found it difficult to live under an oppressive government? If a future Adloph Hitler gained control of these techniques, why couldn't he use them to "alter" those citizens who insisted that they wanted to live under democracy? If the politicians who engineered the Watergate affair were willing to wiretap, illegally break and enter offices, and use "dirty tricks" to sabotage an opponent's campaign, would they stall long in using technology to alter the personality of various opponents of their tactics? Already the Soviet Union has labeled those who oppose the government as "sick," and is utilizing mental hospitals to imprison many of them, with the active help of trained psychiatrists.

There is a school of thought that argues that the best course of action is to control discretion so as to prevent major abuses of this power. This point of view might be characterized as a conservative reformist approach to treatment, and has been discussed by several different authors. Nicholas Kittrie in his important book on the subject, *The Right to be Different: Deviance and Enforced Therapy*, recognizes the need for a limited *parens patriae* mental health system, where some persons might be forced to enter institutions against their will for treatment, but also advocates a "Bill of Rights" for these mental patients.[15] The most fundamental aspect of these rights follows a definite theme: the state must clearly demonstrate the basis for coercive treatment by showing that there is an existing threat of harm to other citizens, and the state must deomonstrate that it can provide a program which will reduce that threat. Further, the program must be the least intrusive needed to control that threat. Thus, the position taken is that, under extreme conditions, the state should have the ability to compel treatment. However, this ability is constrained by the requirement that the state adequately justify its actions, and take the least drastic actions available. The least drastic alternative model would, for instance, argue that no person

---

15. Nicholas Kittrie, *The Right to be Different: Deviance and Enforced Therapy*, (Baltimore: John Hopkins Press, 1971).

should be committed to an institution against his or her will for treatment, unless it can be demonstrated that a lesser measure, such as outpatient care, would not be sufficient to deal with the problem.

Recently, this limited intervention approach was adapted to the corrections field, with similar conditions for coercive correctional treatment.[16] First, it was argued that coercive treatment was permissible only for those offenders who represented a substantial risk of committing a new, serious offense, and that reliable procedures were to be used in determining that risk. Second, it was argued that coercive treatment could be applied only to factors in the offender's situation which contributed to the risk. This would mean, for example, that drug use or unemployment could be dealt with coercively, but not, say, marital discord. Third, the treatment applied should have a demonstrably strong chance of successfully reducing the risk (that is, the program must be "effective"). Fourth, the intervention used must be the least intrusive method of controlling the risk—in most cases, the offender should be able to select from a variety of methods, services or programs. Again, the thrust of this approach is to place limits on correctional discretion regarding the requirement of treatment, while at the same time allowing some discretion to exist.

There are abolitionists, however, who believe that discretion should be eliminated. Most frequently, these individuals call for a completely voluntary system of correctional programming.[17] While many of these abolitionists come from the field of law, some are themselves members of the behavioral science professions. Hans Toch, for example, has persuasively argued that effective institutional treatment is impeded by giving the treatment officer control over the offender's release date.[18] His argument is that the therapeutic task is unavoidably under cut because the client is put in the position of using his or her superficial compliance with the therapist to bargain for an early release. Since freedom depends upon the client showing signs of improvement, there is a great deal of pressure on the offender to put his energy toward showing the proper signs, rather than to take an active role in making changes. The logical conclusion of this argument is that treatment should not be one of the conditions responsible for determining the length of imprisonment. This argument is not hurt by the fact that many therapists, when developing their techniques, have suggested that these techniques will only work well when the client is a voluntary and willing patient.

Others have argued this same point, from a different perspective. Parole, when linked to a rationale of rehabilitation, leads to unfair disparities in sentences and the arbitrary use of power because, unfortunately the ability does not exist to accurately judge whether rehabilitation has in fact occur-

16. Todd R. Clear, *A Model for Supervising the Offender in the Community*, Report to the National Institute of Corrections, 1978. (Mimeographed.)

17. Norval Morris, *The Future of Imprisonment*, (Chicago: University of Chicago Press, 1975).

18. Hans Toch, "Rehabilitation in Corrections," presentation to the Colloquium on Criminality, Indianapolis, Indiana, 22 September 1978.

red.[19] Critics insist that since we do not really know when rehabilitation has occurred, it is quite unfair to use rehabilitation as the basis for setting a release date from prison. Sometimes it means that the better the offender is at acting, the faster he or she will be released from prison. The suggestion has even been made that professional criminals, wise to the rules of the prison game, are in a better position to act out these signs of change, and to obtain release earlier. For example, under the old California system, where the indeterminate sentence allowed the Adult Authority (parole board) to keep an inmate incarcerated until rehabilitated or changed, many inmates found that the easiest way to get out was to pick some fights and break some rules as soon as they entered prison. They could then enter therapy, reduce the number of fights per month, and finally stop fighting altogether, thereby showing that as a result of therapy they had been "changed," and no longer had a need for violence. The unsophisticated offender who does not pick fights early in the term of imprisonment has a much harder time showing major change in his or her behavior.

However, the most persuasive points in this argument have to do with the inhumane nature of compulsory treatment programs in prisons. The image is one of captive humans living in a punitive environment, subjected to the compulsory "treatments" of their captors. These treatments are designed and implemented according to the whims of the captors, with the degree of compliance to these whims determining the duration of the punitive captivity.[20] Expressed in this manner, compulsory treatment is hardly a humanitarian approach.

The answer, according to the reformers, is to remove these powers from the treaters, making the duration of the penalty unrelated to compliance with treatment. Instead of coercive treatment, corrections would provide programs only on a voluntary basis with no threat or promise of manipulating the conditions of punishment.

Coming full circle, the future of correctional treatment policy will reflect the system's struggles with these issues. The relative value given to counseling, direct services and community organization will depend on the continuing research in these areas. Simply put, the more effective each method is shown to be in reducing or controlling crime, the more pressure there will be to implement them.

However, the degree to which any form of treatment becomes compulsory will probably be more a reflection of how the philosophical issues discussed above are resolved rather than how the research findings turn out regarding the effectiveness of the programs. The decisions that determine whether certain programs are fair, ethical or humane will have more impact on the future than simple questions that ask whether these programs will, in fact,

19. See David T. Stanley, *Prisoners Among Us: The Problem of Parole*, (Washington, D.C.: Brookings Institution, 1976); The American Friends Service Committee, *Struggle for Justice*, (New York: Hill and Wang, 1971); Andrew von Hirsch, *Doing Justice*, (New York: Hill and Wang, 1976).

20. George Jackson, *Soledad Brother*, (New York: Bantam Books, 1971).

work. Simple effectiveness may be a false issue. The most effective form of specific deterrence is simple capital punishment. If we execute every violator of the criminal code, we can at least be sure that these programs are "effective" to the extent that those persons executed will not commit further crimes. However, we have already tried that approach once in our history, when in colonial days we had a great many capital offenses. No matter how many persons we executed, it seemed there was a problem in general deterrence, since our hangmen never had to be laid off for lack of future customers. This early approach, however, was discontinued as the settlers began to determine what kind of society they wanted to live in. A brutal society where thousands of persons were executed each year did not fit the humane, ethical, modern concepts of humanity that many persons had.

Of course, an argument against capital punishment for *many or all* offenders is not the same as an argument against capital punishment for *some* offenders. It simply points out that a "program" might be "effective" according to some set of criteria (such as the fact that no executed criminal will commit further offenses) but may still be a violation of the basic principles of humanity under which we wish to live.

SELECTED BIBLIOGRAPHY

Allen, Francis A. "Criminal Justice, Legal Values, and the Rehabilitative Ideal." *Journal of Criminal Law, Criminology, and Police Science*, vol. 50 (September/October 1959), pp. 226-232.

Almore, Mary G. "Rehabilitation: The 'Fudge Factor' of Corrections." *Criminology*, vol. 15 (1976), pp. 147-148.

Bailey, Walter. "Correctional Outcome: An Evaluation of 100 Reports." *Journal of Criminal Law, Criminology and Police Science*, vol. 57 (1966), pp. 153-160.

Conrad, John P. "We Should Never Have Promised a Hospital." *Federal Probation*, vol. 39 (1975), pp. 3-9.

Dershowitz, Alan M. "Indeterminate Confinement: Letting the Therapy Fit the Harm." *University of Pennsylvania Law Review*, vol. 123 (1974), p. 297.

DiGennaro, D., and Vetere, E. "The Crisis of the Concept of Correctional Treatment." *International Journal of Criminology and Penology*, vol. 2 (1974), pp. 295-314.

Eriksson, Torsten. *The Reformers: An Historical Survey of Pioneer Experiments in the Treatment of Criminals*. New York: Elsevier, 1976.

Gobert, James J. "Psychosurgery, Conditioning and the Prisoner's Right to Refuse 'Rehabilitation.'" *Virginia Law Review*, vol. 61 (1975), p. 155.

Hippchen, Leonard, ed. *Correctional Classification and Treatment*. Cincinnati, Ohio: W.H. Anderson, 1975.

Kassebaum, Gene; Ward, David; and Wilner, D. *Prison Treatment and Its Outcome*. New York: John Wiley and Sons, 1971.

Lipton, Douglas; Martinson, Robert; and Wilkes, Judith. *The Effectiveness of Correctional Treatment: A Survey of Treatment Evaluation Studies*. New York: Praeger, 1975.

Mangrum, Claude T. "Corrections Tarnished Halo." *Federal Probation*, vol. 40 (1976), p. 9.

Martinson, Robert; Palmer, Ted; and Adams, Stuart. *Rehabilitation, Recidivism, and Research*. Hackensack, N.J.: National Council on Crime and Delinquency, 1976.

Palmer, Ted. "Martinson Revisited." *Journal of Research in Crime and Delinquency*, vol. 12 (1975), p. 133.

Parker, Tony. *The Frying Pan: A Prison and its Prisoners*. New York: Basic Books, 1970.

Robison, J., and Smith, Gerald. "The Effectiveness of Correctional Programs." *Crime and Delinquency*, vol. 17 (1971), pp. 67-80.

Ross, Robert R., and McKay, H. Bryan. "A Study of Institutional Treatment Programs." *International Journal of Offender Therapy and Comparative Criminology*, vol. 20, no. 2 (1976), pp. 165-173.

Scott, Edward M. "Group Therapy With Convicts on Work Release in Oregon." *International Journal of Offender Therapy and Comparative Criminology*, vol. 20, no. 3 (1976), pp. 225-235.

Shover, Neal. " 'Experts' and Diagnosis in Correctional Agencies." *Crime and Delinquency*, vol. 20 (1974), pp. 347-358.

Smith, Alexander B., and Berlin, Louis. *Treating the Criminal Offender*. Dobbs Ferry, N.Y.: Oceana Publications, 1974.

Warren, Marguerite Q. "All Things Being Equal." *Criminal Law Bulletin*, vol. 9 (July/August 1973), pp. 473-490.

Wicks, Robert J. *Correctional Psychology: Themes and Problems in Correcting the Offender*. San Francisco: Canfield Press, 1974.

Wilkes, Judith, and Martinson, Robert. "Is the Treatment of Criminal Offenders Really Necessary?" *Federal Probation*, vol. 40 (March 1976), pp. 3-9.

Wolfgang, Marvin. "Corrections and the Violent Offender." *Annals of the American Academy of Political and Social Science*, vol. 381 (January 1969), pp. 119-124.

Ziegler, Ron; Costello, Robert; and Horvat, George. "Innovative Programming in a Penitentiary Setting: Report from a Functional Unit." *Federal Probation*, vol. 40 (June 1976), pp. 44-49.

Part Five

Emerging Issues and Change

John Locke, "The Second Treatise of Government: An Essay Concerning The True Original, Extent, and End of Civil Government," 1689.

10. Besides the Crime which consists in violating the Law, and varying from the right Rule of Reason, whereby a Man so far becomes degenerate, and declares himself to quit the Principles of Human Nature, and to be a noxious Creature, there is commonly *injury* done to some Person or other, and some other Man receives damage by his Transgression, in which Case he who hath received any damage, has besides the right of punishment common to him with other Men, a particular Right to seek *reparation* from him that has done it. And any other Person who finds it just, may also joyn with him that is injur'd, and assist him in recovering from the Offender, so much as may make satisfaction for the harm he has suffer'd.

11. From these *two distinct Rights,* the one of *Punishing* the Crime for *restraint,* and preventing the like Offense, which right of punishing is in every body; the other of taking *reparation,* which belongs only to the injured party, comes it to pass that the Magistrate, who by being Magistrate, hath the common right of punishing put into his hands, can often, where the publick good demands not the execution of the Law, *remit* the punishment of Criminal Offences by his own Authority, but yet cannot *remit* the satisfaction due to any private Man, for the damage he has received. That, he who has suffered the damage has a Right to demand in his own name, and he alone can *remit.*

Whitney North Seymour Jr., "Major Surgery for the Criminal Courts," Brooklyn Law Review, vol. 38 (Winter 1972), pp. 572-3, 576-7. *

The present remedies available in the criminal courts are narrow and retrogressive—jail, fine, probation. Attention to other judicial remedies and how they might be used more constructively to produce better results offers the most promising key for unlocking the secret to the effective administration of justice.

Throughout recent legislative history, the persistent emphasis of new laws dealing with social problems and programs has been ultimate reliance on the criminal sanction. . . .How frequently have we convicted the wrongdoer who has preyed on large numbers of innocent victims and then punished him in a way which has done nothing to help the victims themselves and done little to deter others from following his course? Too often, in view of the limitations on criminal sanctions, there is painful truth in the inverted aphorism "crime pays."

. . .By establishing a punitive system embracing compensation as well as incarceration, the gross and egregious inequities presently existing between sentences meted out for white-collar crimes and those handed down for other serious infractions of the law could at least be mitigaged. In permitting perpetrators of white-collar crimes to retain their lucre without suffering any significant jail term, the legal system not only fails to ameliorate the plight of victims but also causes the criminal law to fail in its essential purpose—the discouragement of similar acts hostile to the public welfare and the rehabilitation of the transgressor. Compelling restitution and damages within the scheme of criminal justice can serve to readjust the present imbalance of the system achieving the purposes for which it was designed.

---

* Reprinted, with permission.

EMERGING ISSUES

It should be apparent by now that the central theme of this text is that American corrections is characterized by confusion, conflict and paradox. In earlier sections, some of the basic technologies of corrections, such as incarceration and community supervision, were targets of major debate. As the excerpts which open each section show, there is often little difference between the reform proposals made over a hundred years ago and the reform proposals of today.

It is thus difficult to think in terms of "emerging" issues. After reading the introductory excerpts, one finds this phrase rather ironic—it would seem much more appropriate to say that most issues nowadays are merely "re-emerging." Nevertheless, there are several problem areas which have attracted the lion's share of attention from scholars and practitioners in the past few years, and which promise to be the focus of debates in the near future. This section will examine some of these issues.

Recently, a number of correctional issues have gained attention as key political issues. There are proposals and actions in several states which have significant implications for correctional agencies. For example, as was already mentioned, parole supervision has been abolished in Maine, and parole release has been eliminated in several other states, with similar legislation pending in still more states.

The death penalty is back in many states, after the U.S. Supreme Court ruled that capital punishment is not, or at least need not be, cruel and unusual punishment, and is thus not unconstitutional.[1] Another field of expanding concern is prisoners' rights. As a branch of law, prisoners' rights is really less than fifteen years old, and more court intervention in the correctional process can be expected in the coming years. Yet, at the same time that society is beginning to recognize that some important complaints of inmates and other persons under correctional control are valid, there appears to be a growing "get tough" philosophy emerging across the country regarding the proper method of dealing with criminals.

This is not the only area where there is a seeming paradox, with trends that seem to be opposites taking hold at the same time, and often in the same place. Just as legislatures are making prison sentences mandatory for certain offenders, and generally stiffening criminal penalties, one can find work release, furlough and halfway house programs springing up almost

---

1. *Gregg* v. *Georgia*, 428 U.S. 153, 49 L.Ed.2d 859, 96 S.Ct. 2909 (1976), and companion cases.

everywhere.[2] And, at the same time that the criminal justice system has made the victim of a crime an almost negligible figure, (except when he or she is called upon as a witness for the prosecution), a growing interest in the plight of the victim has engendered a matching development in restitution and victim compensation programs.[3]

If there is one constant in American corrections, it is that everything changes. Yet, one can make a serious argument that at the same time, nothing of consequence changes.

UNANSWERED QUESTIONS

Today, as in the past, correctional programs and agencies are faced with sharp criticism, while important questions remain unanswered. In fact, one major trend that is true more often than not is that concern is diverted from broad, important questions concerning purpose and goals to a lower level of questions dealing with techniques and programs. In brief, three basic questions have remained since people first wondered how to deal with those persons who violated the law: 1) Who should be subjected to correctional intervention? 2) How should those persons be treated at the hands of the state? 3) What is, or what should be, the rationale for criminal penalties?

Unfortunately, all three of these questions are so interrelated that they can only be artificially separated. Who you punish, and how you deal with those persons, depends first of all upon why you punish. If you punish to deter, then a second set of questions arises involving who can be deterred and how. If you punish to treat, then another set of questions arises concerning treatment techniques to be used. Though the three basic questions above refer to separate and unique problems, the thread that ties them all together is the principle that punishment need not be barbaric in order to be effective. This principle, in many ways, was responsible for the original development of the American correctional system. It must be remembered that 200 years ago, there was no such thing as a correctional system—there was no need for one; all violators of the law were subjected to either capital or corporal punishment. Our entire system of corrections was founded on the idea that executing hordes of citizens was not the hallmark of a civilized society—it was, rather, the sign of a brutal, perhaps even primitive society.

People assumed it was possible to achieve the same effect by less brutal means. They argued that it was only necessary to punish an offender with as much punishment as was needed to stop future offenses, or perhaps to deter others. This argument has been held by most people to be part of the proscription against cruel and unusual punishment in the Eighth Amendment. It may be possible that the framers of the Bill of Rights had it in mind to ban only such punishments as slow drowning, mutilation, or boiling in oil, but it

---

2. See Donald J. Newman, *Introduction to Criminal Justice*, 2nd Edition, (Philadelphia: J.B. Lippincott, 1978), pp. 413-14.

3. See T.W. Condit, S. Greenbaum, G. Nicholson, *Forgotten Victims—An Advocate's Anthology*, (Sacramento, Cal.: California District Attorney's Associations, 1977).

has generally been recognized that it is just as cruel and unusual to allow a punishment to far exceed the severity of the crime. Imprisonment for jaywalking would be cruel and unusual punishment because the penalty is so much more drastic than the misconduct. Although this is the accepted principle, in practice the courts have usually let the legislatures determine proper penalties, and have rarely stepped in to overturn those penalties.

Today, a modern refinement of this idea is the "least drastic alternative."[4] This principle dictates that the penalty imposed on an offender be no more severe than that required to achieve the desired result. Those who support this principle seek a realistic assessment of our policies to see if we are over-punishing our offenders.

Application of the least drastic alternative would mean that if a convicted offender posed no threat to society and suffered greatly from guilt, then he or she would not be given any additional penalty. Likewise, the offender who did pose a serious threat to society, but who could be effectively controlled in the community, would not be subject to incarceration. Capital punishment would only be considered as a last resort, when incarceration could not adequately serve to both punish the offender and protect society.

Of course, those in favor of this system argue that the concept of societal revenge should be used as little as possible. They ask: if the goal of the corrections system is to protect society, and a particular offender does not pose a threat to society, what is accomplished by incarcerating that offender at great cost?

This principle is applicable not only to protection, but to punishment as well. There is no need to impose added conditions above those which are absolutely required, on offenders already under parole or probation supervision. It would be unjustifiable, for instance, to impose a "no drinking" condition on someone who has never been drunk, and for whom alcohol consumption is not related to criminality.[5]

Often this principle is not explicitly laid out by those who are arguing for a change in correctional policy, but it is nevertheless related. A case in point can be seen in the contemporary arguments regarding prison industries.[6] Prisoners are often assigned to work in prison-run factories which produce goods used by the state or federal government, such as license plates, office furniture and prison uniforms. These inmates would be considered drastically underpaid on any scale, let alone in comparison with those free citizens working at the same types of jobs outside the prison.[7] An argument can be

4. Richard Singer, "Sending Men to Prison: Constitutional Aspects of the Burden of Proof and the Doctrine of the Least Drastic Alternative as Applied to Sentencing Determinations," *Cornell Law Review*, vol. 50 (1972), p. 51.

5. Todd R. Clear, *A Model for Supervising the Offender in the Community*, (Washington, D.C.: National Institute of Corrections, 1978), pp. 80-85.

6. Econ, Inc., *Study of the Economic and Rehabilitative Aspects of Prison Industry, Analysis of Prison Industries*, (Washington, D.C.: U.S. Government Printing Office, 1977).

7. Robert Mintz, "Federal Prison Industry—The 'Green Monster'," *Crime and Social Justice*, (Fall/Winter 1976), pp. 43-44.

made that enforced labor at low wages is an unnecessary burden on the prisoner, particularly when added to those hardships which naturally accompany incarceration. The related issue of how persons should be treated will be dealt with later, in the section on electronic surveillance.

For now the crucial question we must ask ourselves is what purpose does punishment serve? The corrections system can gear its goals toward only one of two main purposes: either we are to prevent future criminality, or else we are responding to past law violations.

The primary issue is whether we ought to be concerned with future offenses when dealing with those convicted of a past offense. If we are dealing with punishing past offenses, rather than trying to stop future offenses, then there is no justification for forced rehabilitation. In fact, taken to the extreme, corrections need not be concerned with the future at all. If we only want to redress past injuries, if the offender owes a debt to society which he pays through punishment, then we would have no need at all for rehabilitation programs. In fact, such a philosophy could justify the scrapping of work release, furlough, and other programs designed to help the incarcerated offender adjust to a new kind of life in the free community.[8]

On the other hand, if the goal of criminal corrections is the prevention of future crimes, then rehabilitation becomes a logical activity. Taken to its extreme, the prevention of future crimes could be used as the rationale for identifying and prospectively "correcting" those individuals who simply appear likely to commit crimes.

One sobering thought is that any easy resolution to these issues and problems is out of the question. The extreme fragmentation of authority for making these decisions, with federal, state and local officials all caught up in the highly volatile and political world of decision-making in our system, militates against a simple solution.

As in the past, these decisions will be made politically. The fragmentation of authority means that there is no central power base from which correctional administrators and staff can operate. If the current debate on these issues lasts long enough, however, just such a base may yet be created, as correctional personnel form alliances to influence the policy decisions which will restrict them in the future.[9] Perhaps corrections as a political force is one emerging issue which has only just begun to be recognized.

---

8. Eugene Doleschal, *Graduated Release*, (Washington, D.C.: National Institute of Mental Health, 1975).

9. David Fogel, "The Politics of Corrections," *Federal Probation*, vol. 41, p. 29.

LOCATING DISCRETION

For the past 150 years, correctional interventions have been aimed at reducing the future criminality of convicted offenders. Whether through the policies of reform, rehabilitation or reintegration, as discussed in Part I, the overriding concern was with future crimes and how to prevent them. There is currently a movement away from such future-oriented policies, towards a punishment rationale which is "backwards looking." Its emphasis is on punishing for the past act rather than worrying about the possibility of future crimes. Supporters of this movement point out that our own criminal justice system is based on the principle that a person is innocent until proven guilty of a *past* criminal act. Thus, the prosecutor's only responsibility is to prove that the offender *has already* committed a criminal act, not that he or she *might* commit one in the future.

One of the major problems with the future-oriented policies we have had is that they have led to the development of a very broad discretionary power vested in correctional offices and agencies. As pointed out earlier, this power is considered necessary in order to individualize justice, and to ensure the successful prevention of future crimes. The trained intervention agent must have the power to take whatever steps are necessary to make proper changes in the behavior of the offender.

However, as was noted in Part IV, the ability of the corrections system to change the probability of future crimes is rather questionable. Furthermore, critics have identified many undesirable consequences of the broad discretionary power used in sentencing and corrections. Quite simply, the discretionary power officials now possess can be abused. These abuses and their consequences can be lumped together under the single heading of "disparity."

In short, disparity refers to differences in the treatment of similar offenders convicted of similar crimes. The major complaint is that under a rationale of individualized justice, inequitable treatment of offenders can take place unseen. Those proposing reforms disagree on exactly what form the sentencing structure and the correctional system should take, but all seem to agree that the final result should be a reduction in, or an elimination of, the current areas of broad discretion.

Reform proposals suggest that the elimination of judicial sentencing discretion and the near abolition of discretionary parole release could be accomplished by legislatively fixing criminal penalties.[1] If a prime worry is

---

1. Twentieth Century Fund Task Force on Criminal Sentencing, *Fair and Certain Punishment*, (New York: McGraw-Hill, 1976).

that two equal offenders may receive either extremely different sentences, or else the same sentence, but with one let out by an arbitrary parole board and the other kept in, then the simple solution seems to be to just require that all offenders of a certain type and certain crime receive exactly the same sentence to the day.

A less drastic method of dealing with the same problem is to retain the discretionary power of both judges and parole boards, but to structure that power through the adoption of specific guidelines.[2] There are almost innumerable variations on these themes, but nearly all call for a diminution of discretion.

While it is difficult to oppose proposals which, at least theoretically, would result in more equitable treatment of offenders, some observers are reluctant to support these recommendations for change. In Part I we argued that corrections is only one part of a larger justice system, and that this entire system is characterized by the broad discretion granted to decision-makers. Those who oppose the new reform efforts often do so on the basis that current reform proposals fail to consider the systemic nature of the justice process. These persons argue that it makes little sense to limit discretion at only one point in the system, especially if some of that discretion is used to correct faulty decisions made at earlier points in the justice process.

The following two essays illustrate these two positions in the current debate over sentencing and correctional discretion. Very often those seeking to reform the system find themselves opposed by others who, though concurring with their evaluation of present conditions, and agreeing that change is needed, disagree over the likely effects of contemporary reform proposals.

---

2. See Peter B. Hoffman and Barbara Stone-Meierhoefer, "Application of Guidelines to Sentencing," *Law and Psychology Review*, vol. 3 (1977), pp. 53-70; and Leslie T. Wilkins et al., *Sentencing Guidelines: Structuring Judicial Discretion*, (Washington, D.C.: U.S. Government Printing Office, 1978).

Lawlessness in Sentencing*

Marvin E. Frankel
Former United States District Judge for the Southern District of New York

Indeterminate Sentences

Among the changes in the law of punishments over the last 100 years or so has been the movement toward what may be loosely referred to as "indeterminate sentences."[1] The quoted term is widely used. But it has somewhat indeterminate meaning.[2] As I use it here, it refers generally to any sentence of confinement in which the actual term to be served is not known on the day of judgment but will be subject, within a substantial range, to the later decision of a board of parole or some comparable agency.[3] In this sense there are varying degrees of indeterminacy, ranging from places like California, where the Adult Authority is empowered to set a maximum term of anywhere from a year to life,[4] to, say, our federal system where, as a general matter, the Board of Parole has discretion to grant parole at any point between completion of one-third and two-thirds of the stated sentence.[5]

The basic premise of the indeterminate sentence is the modern conception that rehabilitation is the paramount goal in sentencing. The idea is to avoid the Procrustean mold of uniform sentences to fit crimes in the abstract and to focus upon the progress over time of the unique individual in order to determine when it may be safe for society and good for him to set him free, at least

---

1. P. Tappan, *Crime, Justice, and Correction* at 432-37. (1960). The first statute providing for indeterminate sentences was passed for the Elmira Reformatory in New York in 1877. N.Y. Laws 1877, ch. 173.

2. See *ABA Sentencing Standards* 38.

3. For a different, probably more orthodox usage, see S. Rubin, *Crime and Juvenile Delinquency* 175-76 (2d ed. 1961).

4. Under California law, the judge may not "fix the term or duration of the period of imprisonment"; he merely imposes the sentence of imprisonment "prescribed by law." *Cal. Penal Code* § 1168 (West 1970). After service of the prison sentence has begun, the Adult Authority may then "determine and redetermine...what length of time, if any, such person shall be imprisoned." *Id.* § 3020. This power to set a term of imprisonment and "redetermine" it is subject to any maximum or minimum prescribed by statute for the particular offense. *Id.* § 3023. If the statute prescribes only a minimum term of imprisonment, as is frequently the case, *e.g., Id.* §§ 213 (robbery), 461 (burglary), the "maximum" is life imprisonment. *Id.* § 871.

5. 18 U.S.C. § 4202 (1964); see also *Id.* §§ 4161-64.

---

within the limits of parole supervision. At the same time, the power given to a single parole agency may be expected to mitigate the disparities in sentencing caused by the unregulated vagaries of individual judges. While it has not been advanced as a primary justification for the indeterminate sentence, this seeming power of equalization appears to be at least one among the conceptions of their functions entertained by parole boards.[6]

The goals of flexibility and even-handedness seem compellingly worthy. While they do not state the whole case, they go far to explain why the movement toward indeterminacy in sentencing is a powerful and continuing one. Recognizing that the shift means a transfer of much power and responsibility from the sentencing judge to the parole board, many judges have warmly endorsed this development.[7] Troubled by the weight of the burden, authoritatively aware of their limited qualifications, and committed to the principle that sentencing is for rehabilitation, concerned judges are often eager to hand the task on to the supposedly more expert and full-time attention of parole officials. The principle of at least substantial indeterminacy has acquired potent support through adoption in such august products as the Model Penal Code,[8] the proposed Federal Criminal Code of the National Commission on Reform of Federal Criminal Laws,[9] and the Model Sentencing Act proposed in 1963 by the National Council on Crime and Delinquency.[10] The impact of these models in State revisions of their criminal codes has been, and continues to be, substantial.[11]

In short, the trend toward indeterminate sentences seems irresistible at the moment. I think, however, that it should be resisted.

6. *United States Board of Parole, Biennial Report* 13, 22 (1971). See Johnson, *Multiple Punishment and Consecutive Sentences: Reflections on the Neal Doctrine*, 58 *Calif. L. Rev.* 357, 381-82 (1970); Wechsler, *Sentencing, Correction, and the Model Penal Code*, 109 *U. Pa. L. Rev.* 465, 477 (1901); *Note, Individual Treatment of Criminal Offenders*, 33 *Neb. L. Rev.* 467, 471 (1954). But *cf.* H.L.A. Hart, *Punishment and Responsibility* at 440 (1968).

7. *E.g.,* Devitt, *Setting the Maximum and Minimum Term of Imprisonment*, 26 F.R.D. at 317-18; (1959). *Seminar and Institute on Disparity of Sentences for Sixth, Seventh and Eighth Judicial Circuits*, 30 F.R.D. at 459 (1961).

8. *Model Penal Code* § 6.06 (Proposed Official Draft 1962). Under section 6.06, all sentences of imprisonment for felony are indeterminate. The sentencing court sets a minimum term, ranging from one to ten years for a felony of the first degree to one to two years for a felony of the third degree. But the maximum, ranging from possible life imprisonment for a felony of the first degree to five years for a felony of the third degree, is fixed by the statute. The actual length of the sentence is determined by the Board of Parole. *Id.* § 402.2(1)(a). See also *id.* §§ 6.05(2) (special term for young adult offenders), 6.07 (sentence of imprisonment for extended terms). Alternate section 6.06 would authorize the sentencing court to fix both the minimum and maximum.

9. See *Proposed Federal Criminal Code* 284-86 (proposed 18 U.S.C. § 3201), which largely follows the *Model Penal Code* scheme described at note 17 *supra*, except that it would authorize the sentencing judge to fix a maximum below the outside limit set by statute and would not require him to impose a minimum term.

10. Under sections 5, 8, and 9 of the Model Sentencing Act, a defendant sentenced to imprisonment is eligible immediately for parole. The judge is empowered to set only a maximum term of confinement.

11. See *e.g.,* Conn. Gen. Stat. Ann. § 53a-35 (Special Pamphlet 1972); Kan. Stat. Ann. §§ 21-4501 to -4504, 21-4603 (Supp. 1970); N.Y. Penal Law § 70.00 (McKinney 1967).

Before seeking to justify this reactionary stance, let me state it a bit more precisely: I do not argue that the indeterminate sentence is always and everywhere inappropriate. I believe, however, that its unqualified use rests upon undemonstrated premises; that the premises, even if sound, should not have the sweeping application they are given; and that the excessive extension of indeterminacy has probably resulted in much cruelty and injustice, rather than the great goods its proponents envisage.

1. The case for the indeterminate sentence rests upon what a perceptive scholar has called, and skeptically appraised as, the "rehabilitative ideal."[12] The offender is "sick," runs the humanitarian thought, and/or dangerous. He needs to be treated and cured. Nobody, certainly not the sentencing judge, can know when he will be well or safe. Hence, those charged with treating and observing him must be left to decide the time for release.

The theory is flawed in the vagueness and overbreadth of its first premise, the idea of "sickness" calling for medical or quasi-medical "treatment." Many convicted people are not in need of any known form of therapy or rehabilitation. We sentence large numbers of people who probably fall within the class tagged in a lively, psychoanalytically oriented book as "normal criminals" (in contrast with those driven to crime by neurotic or psychotic drives)—that is, people who have coldly and deliberately appraised the risks and rewards, taken their stand against received morality, but then had the misfortune to be caught.[13] Whatever else such defendants may need or deserve, they are not promising candidates for any sort of useful "treatment" available in either our prisons or our hospitals.

Many defendants, especially among those passing through the federal courts, are clearly outside the reach of the indeterminate sentence theory; they are, that is, neither in need of nor amenable to any known form of rehabilitation. One thinks, for example, of the doctor who evaded taxes, the corrupt public official, the antitrust violator. The sentences of at least many such defendants may be thought to serve the ends of deterrence, of "denunciation,"[14] or, if we face what many judges are openly doing, of retribution. Again, however, only a somewhat thoughtless lack of discrimination would subject them to the horror of indeterminacy—to wait while a parole board, with no pertinent criteria for judgment, decides that release should be ordered.[15]

---

12. F. Allen, *The Borderland of Criminal Justice* 25-41 (1964).

13. See generally F. Alexander & H. Staub, *The Criminal, the Judge, and the Public* 79, 179, 222-23 (1956); N. Walker, *Sentencing in a Rational Society* 11-12 (1971).

14. See generally 2 J. Stephen, *A History of the Criminal Law of England* 75-93 (1883); Hart, *The Aims of the Criminal Law*, 23 *Law & Contemp. Prob.* 401, 404-05, 436-37 (1958). But *cf.* H.L.A. Hart, *Punishment and Responsibility* 169-73 (1968); N. Walker.

15. To take an example from an area of current anguish, there is evidence and a firm belief among responsible observers that Selective Service violators motivated by the hostility to the war in Vietnam are most unlikely to make early parole. See Solomon, *Sentences in Selective Service and Income Tax Cases*, 52 F.R.D. 481, 483 (1970). They are at the same time not subjects for any of the available forms of therapy or training in the prison system. See W. Gaylin, *supra* note 23, at 26. The cited passage in Judge Solomon's article does not report

Yet notable advocates of indeterminacy and parole board discretion make no distinctions. The Model Penal Code makes *all* sentences indeterminate,[16] leaving to the parole board in all cases a broad range of discretion to determine the eventual length of the sentence. The distinguished National Commission that has lately proposed a new (and in many respects admirable) Federal Criminal Code[17] and the National Council on Crime and Delinquency, in its Model Sentencing Act,[18] do the same. A number of the States have similar provisions.[19] None of these several codes says what the parole board is supposed to do—what standards it is to follow, what kinds of judgments it is to make—in deciding when to release those who are neither sick nor dangerous.

2. The essentially medical model is employed crudely and simplemindedly by the proponents of indeterminate sentences—ignoring how little is known about rehabilitation and misconceiving the medical analogy in the process. I have started this attack by taking the burden, by arguing that there are many defendants positively identifiable as not suitable subjects for rehabilitation. But the shoe ought really to be on the other foot. The question has to do with locking people up. That is a fierce, tangible step—and a palpable evil, as the utilitarians highlighted for us long ago. The burden of justification, for the confinement and its duration, is upon the jailers. If we say that the prisoner must stay until the experts declare him "cured"—or cured enough—we ought to start with a theory of the illness and a definition of what the experts are good at. But, with some exceptions, that does not happen. The drug addict, the assaultive sex offender, the youth, the juvenile—some kinds of defendants, in substantial numbers, we may have some hopes of trying to "treat." Even as to these the hopes are modest, not only because knowledge is thin but because our human and material resources are exiguous. Yet the well-intentioned pressure for treatment and confinement of uncertain duration is scarcely abated, and is not limited to special categories of defendants.

Because we commonly do not know for sure what we mean by treatment, it is a corollary that we cannot know how long it will take. It follows for the indeterminate sentencers, on beneficient grounds, that the prisoner must live with the torture of "one year to life" or some similar atrocity.[20] It seems to be

---

detailed documentation. His statement has been disputed by parole officials. I have checked with him, and he has graciously supplied substantial evidence for what he says. My observations, if not systematic, corroborate his. The refutation by the Board of Parole—that it has no parole "policy" for draft resisters, any more than for others—is neither persuasive nor comforting.

16. See note 8 *supra*.

17. See note 9 *supra*.

18. See note 10 *supra*.

19. *E.g., Cal. Penal Code* §§ 1168, 3020, 3023 (West 1970); *Ill. Ann. Stat.* ch. 38, § 1-7(d) (Smith-Hurd Supp. 1970); *Ohio Rev. Code Ann.* §§ 5145.01-.02 (Page 1970).

20. Under the Federal Youth Corrections Act, a young offender may be sent for study and a report within 60 days when the judge believes this will help him to sentence intelligently. 18 U.S.C.A. § 5010(c) (1969). Thereafter (or without requiring such a report), confinement may be ordered until any date when the Youth Correction Division orders the offender

assumed that the indeterminancy inheres in the treatment, and there is no doubt some analogous experience from fields like phsychotherapy where a precise estimate of total time for treatment is not feasible. But the logic employs bizarre premises. The unthinking use of the medical analogy overlooks that many kinds of medical treatment have reasonably precise timetables. As to chronic ailments, discriminating estimates are possible: some are expected confidently to endure for the patient's life; some are known to require intensive care indefinitely; some may be manageable with only occasional interventions by the physician. Varying with the illness, varying prospects may be predicted for the patient and for those around him. Analogous judgments do not appear even to be contemplated, let alone required, by the proponents of indeterminate sentencing.

The naive faith in the presumed expertise of penologists and parole officials effectively blots out some of the stark and familiar realities of prisons as they actually function. The notion that the unrehabilitated prisoner should be denied parole because he needs more treatment is not merely unsupported; it runs counter to considerable evidence and opinion concerning the effects of confinement. Taking prisons as they are, and as they are likely to be for some time, it is powerfully arguable that their net achievement is to make their inhabitants worse, not better.[21] It may be bracing doctrine to insist that the prisons must be improved to make rehabilitation a reality.[22] Passing now the question whether we know how to do this, the ideal is worthy beyond question. And I hope nothing said here suggests any cavil about that. My central point, however, entails a firm view about the proper order of things: we have no right to keep people confined ostensibly to rehabilitate them when we lack the means of rehabilitation. Until or unless we have some reasonable hope of effective treatment, it is a cruel fraud to have parole boards solemnly order men back to their cages because cures that do not exist are found not to have been achieved.

This view does not demand certainty or preclude a degree of experimentation conducted with candor and self-awareness. It would allow, for example, for confinements under the Federal Narcotic Addict Rehabilitation Act, despite the frank understanding that our ability to treat addiction is highly doubtful and that treatment may mean the trial-and-error testing of varying hypotheses.[23] But this, after all, is not unlike other kinds of strictly medical

---

released "conditionally," except that the youth must be so released after four years. However, the youth may later be confined again until he is discharged "unconditionally" six years after conviction. See *id.* §§ 5017-20 (Supp. 1972). It is not taught officially, but the young people facing such treatment, and commonly dreading it, have come to call it a sentence of "60 to 6" or "zip-six."

21. See, *e.g.*, *ABA Sentencing Standards* 63, 72-73; *Law of Criminal Correction* 268-72.

22. See, *e.g.*, R. Clark, *Crime in America* 192-218 (paperbound ed. 1971), reviewed in *Radzinowicz, The Vision of Ramsey Clark*, 47 *Va. Q. Rev.* 459 (1971).

23. Under title II of the Act, a court may send an "eligible offender" it suspects of being a narcotics addict to the Attorney General for an examination to determine whether he is an addict and whether he is likely to be rehabilitated through treatment. 18 U.S.C.A. § 4252 (1969). Following the examination, if the court finds that the offender satisfies the two criteria, "it shall commit him to the custody of the Attorney General for treatment" for an

problems. It differs from the vague credo of "rehabilitation" as a general aim in that it (a) centers upon a defined species of malady, (b) entails rationally limited and prescribed forms of attempted treatment, (c) is subject to reasonably objective measures of achievement, and (d) is an enterprise in which the inmate, like a patient, may be (and, in my own experience, normally is as a condition to applying the Act) enlisted as a willing participant seeking an objective he understands and desires for himself.

Moving to a related but separate category, the "dangerous offender" may perhaps be confined for indeterminate periods upon acceptably principled and defined, if desperately risky, grounds. Existing and proposed measures of this nature[24] raise difficult questions—for example, as to the kinds of dangers warranting such treatment, the availability of reliable tests for dangerousness, the soundness of the hypothesis that a man found "safe" by testing in prison is thereby established as a good risk,[25] and the large prospect that parole officials will play it safe by erring regularly on the side of continued custody for cases of doubt.[26] But these perplexities are suitable for separate handling and discrete judgments, free from foggy pieties about rehabilitation. The dangerous offender, if he can fairly be identified, is a just subject for *incapacitation*. If we are able to "treat" him, usually a dubious hope, so much the better. We may have to hold him for an uncertain and long time, but we ought to be willing to forego certainty and absolute security, remembering that freedom and risk are inseparable. However we handle this distinct and limited category, neither it nor others similarly identifiable justify all-embracing provisions for indeterminate sentencing.

3. The allure of indeterminate sentences, including the prospect of leaning more heavily upon such experts as parole board members, leads to uncritical transfer of concerns on which the boards have no claim to either expertise or legitimate authority. The therapeutic or penological considerations presumably underlying parole decisions have nothing to do with the sentencing aims of deterrence or denunciation. Nor is the form or timing of the parole decision suited to the service of such ends. Yet the Model Penal Code, followed by the new Federal Code lately proposed by a distinguished National Com-

---

indeterminate period not to exceed 10 years or the maximum that could otherwise have been imposed. *Id.* § 4253(a). After receiving six months of treatment, the offender may then be "conditionally released" at the discretion of the Board of Parole, *Id.* § 4254.

24. *E.g.,* Organized Crime Control Act of 1970, § 1001(a), 18 U.S.C.A. §§ 3575-76 (Supp. 1971); *Conn. Gen. Stat. Ann.* § 53a-40 (Special Pamphlet 1972); *Model Penal Code* §§ 6.07, 6.09, 7.03, 7.04 (Proposed Official Draft 1962); *Model Sentencing Act* §§ 5, 6.

25. There is a considerable body of opinion, which I find persuasive, that a person, "adjusted" after a long term of confinement and minimal autonomy, is likely on that very basis to have become unfitted for effective functioning on the outside. See, *e.g.,* H. Griswold et al., *supra* note 53, at 252-53; Schreiber, *Indeterminate Therapeutic Incarceration of Dangerous Criminals: Perspectives and Problems,* 56 *Va. L. Rev.* 602, 604 (1970).

26. See R. Dawson, *Sentencing: The Decision as to Type, Length and Conditions of Sentence* 187-88 (1969).

There is a considerable body of opinion, which I find persuasive, that a person, "adjusted" after a long term of confinement and minimal autonomy, is likely on that very basis to have become unfitted for effective functioning on the outside.

mission, includes judgments upon such subjects among the things given over wholesale to the parole board.

To explain: for the sentencing court, probation is presumptively preferred to confinement under the Model Penal Code

unless, having regard to the nature and circumstances of the crime and the history, character and condition of the defendant, it is of the opinion that his imprisonment is necessary for protection of the public because:
(a) there is undue risk that during the period of a suspended sentence or probation the defendant will commit another crime; or
(b) the defendant is in need of correctional treatment that can be provided most effectively by his commitment to an institution; or
(c) *a lesser sentence will depreciate the seriousness of the defendant's crime.*[27]

The words I have italicized sound retributive, but it appears that their authors did not conceive of themselves as acting from any such disfavored motive.[28] Accepting without question that the need not to "depreciate the seriousness of the...crime" relates to the assessment of the sentence as a deterrent, this would seem to be peculiarly a matter affecting *the sentence*, when and as it is pronounced, and the court's authoritative voice as the agency for that purpose.[29] But when we turn in the Model Penal Code to the criteria for parole, we find that the identical worry about depreciated seriousness of the crime is included. The parole board is instructed that there is a presumption favoring parole, like that favoring probation in the sentencing court, unless one of four countervailing factors is present. The one of interest here is: "unless...release...would depreciate the seriousness of [the] crime or promote disrespect for law."[30] At this point, what started out as a device for rehabilitation and reform becomes a means for handing on to the parole board judgments quite outside the field of its supposed competence. The "seriousness of the crime" is a matter of law and policy within the province of judges, best known to the participants in the trial, and properly to be estimated for purposes of voicing the community's condemnation at the time of the pronouncement of sentence. It is, more importantly, not a subject on which there is need to "wait and see" whether the defendant is ready for release. On the contrary, the inclusion of such a criterion in the parole board's domain is, though all inadvertently, an invitation to the illicit, "political" judgments of public opinion of which parole boards are often suspected.[31]

---

27. *Model Penal Code* § 7.01(1) (Proposed Official Draft 1962) (emphasis added). See the similar 18 U.S.C. § 3101 in *Proposed Federal Criminal Code* 277-78.

28. See *Model Penal Code* § 7.01, comment 2, at 34 (Tent. Draft No. 2, 1954).

29. *Cf.* T. Szasz, *Law, Liberty, and Psychiatry* 97-98 (1963); Lewis, *The Humanitarian Theory of Punishment*, 6 Res Judicatae 224, 225 (1952); Wechsler, *Sentencing Innovations*, 46 F.R.D. 519, 522 (1968).

30. *Model Penal Code* § 305.9(1)(b) (Proposed Official Draft 1962).

31. See, *e.g.*, *Invisible Federal Parole*, N.Y. Times, Aug. 30, 1971, at 28, col. 2 (editorial).

4. What people "suspect" about parole boards obviously cannot be accepted as sufficient grounds for any sort of firm conclusion. But the suspicions are themselves facts, in prison and out. They are born, as suspicions commonly are, of the absence of clear information freely given. The point is worth noting here because parole boards, the powers of which increase with the degree of indeterminancy of sentences, have not been among our most admired and confidence-inspiring agencies.

The qualified esteem has been earned. Parole boards, as I have mentioned, commonly proceed secretly, without explanation, subject to no (or almost no) objective standards, in reaching unreviewable decisions.[32] The proponents of expanded power for parole boards tend to support improved procedures and the promulgation of at least some standards.[33] The Model Penal Code even goes to the extent of having the board make a record, though it is not clear whether the final board decision must be written down.[34] And, as noted earlier, the New Jersey Supreme Court has recently broken new ground and made explanations a requirement for its parole board.[35]

Apart from such developments, the poor performance record of parole boards is not in itself a decisive reason for opposing indeterminate sentences. The nature of the necessary improvements is known and manageable, given a decent measure of will and public support.[36] I note with concerned scepticism, however, the imposing consensus that would leave parole decisions still final and unreviewable.[37]

This arrangement is favored even by exponents of the growing opinion that the sentencing decision should be reviewable.[38] The contrast, even if logic is not the law's whole life, is striking for its essential illogicality as well as the absence of any clear basis in policy. The idea that the board's decision may not be appealed is not justifiable on grounds of trouble or expense, though both are involved. It may be explained, but it cannot be justified, by an awareness that the reasons for denials of parole have never been articulated so that they have not been subject to effective review. The material

---

32. See K. Davis, *Discretionary Justice* 126-33 (1969).

33. See *id.*, *Model Penal Code* §§ 305.6-.10 (Proposed Official Draft 1962).

34. See *Model Penal Code* §§ 305.6, 305.8, 305.10 (Proposed Official Draft 1962).

35. See *Monks* v. *New Jersey State Parole Bd.*, 58 N.J. 238, 277 A.2d 193 (1971).

36. See *President's Comm'n on Law Enforcement and Administration of Justice, Task Force Report: Corrections*, app. A, 184-90 (1967); E. Sutherland & D. Cressey, *Principles of Criminology* 586-87 (6th ed. 1960); D. Taft & R. England, *Criminology* 490-91 (4th ed. 1964).

37. See *Model Penal Code* § 305.19 (Proposed Official Draft 1962); *Proposed Federal Criminal Code* 303-04 (proposed 18 U.S.C. § 3406). But see K. Davis, *supra* note 52, at 132-33. The *Proposed Federal Criminal Code* does provide for review of denial by the Parole Board of "constitutional rights or procedural rights conferred by statute, regulation or rule." But this is of small moment. It may well be the law already, without a provision like the one thus proposed. See *Sobell* v. *Reed*, 327 F. Supp. 1294, 1302 (S.D.N.Y. 1971).

38. Compare *Proposed Federal Criminal Code* 317 (proposed 28 U.S.C. § 1291) (review of sentence) with *id.* 303-04 (proposed 18 U.S.C. § 3406) (unreviewable parole denial).

considerations affecting the parole decision, if there are valid ones, are not so numerous or mysterious that their statement is impossible.

In sum, to the extent we should maintain provisions for indeterminate sentence with discretionary parole, it should be where the decisions are capable of regulation under explicit standards and thus subject to an effective system of appeals. It may be that the scope of review will be narrow—perhaps a version of the "abuse of discretion" test[39] or the "rational basis" test[40]—but that is equally probable for review of the judicial sentence. At the very least, the case for judicial review of parole decisions stands on an equal footing with the case for review of sentences. The contrary opinion now abroad reflects the fundamental fallacy, widely extirpated lately in other areas, of worshipping Expertise without defining, understanding, or placing salutary limits upon it.

5. My final contention in this brief against indeterminancy is closer to first in importance: the rage and resentment probably bred by indeterminate sentences outweigh in most cases the supposed benefits. This proposition does not rest upon incontrovertible proof. But there is a fair amount of evidence—and introspection and conversation lead me to believe—that the prisoner experiences as cruel and degrading the decision that he must remain in custody for some uncertain period while his fellows study him, grade him, and decide if and when he may be let go. It is remarkable that the supporters of indeterminancy seem not to have consulted much, if at all, with those sentenced to indefinite terms. I have not seen evidence, for example, of such inquiries by the drafters of the Model Penal Code or the recently proposed Federal Criminal Code. The inquiries would be germane. Surely this is so if we mean our profession that we care about convicted persons for themselves. It is true likewise when we consider that the efficacy of any "treatment" is likely to be affected in part by the impact as felt by its beneficiary.

Proceeding first at a more or less *a priori* level, I wonder if, in dealing with convicted persons, we have been guilty of the familiar practice of keeping like things hermetically sealed off from one another as a way of living with flat inconsistencies.[41] In much of our law we quest after predictability as a basic need. The need springs from powerful demands for fairness, equality, and security. We want to be able to gauge in advance the taxes on the deal, the duration of an employment contract, the length of a lease. For the defendant under an indeterminate sentence, however, the need is thought to be less pressing than other supposed values. It has been suggested, in fact, that the possibility of early release on parole is an attractive incentive, to be contrasted with the gray inexorability of a long, fixed term.[42]

39. See K. Davis, *supra* note 32, at 132-33.

40. See generally K. Davis, *Administrative Law Treatise* § 30.05 (Supp. 1970).

41. "If you think you can think about something which is attached to something else without thinking about what it is attached to, then you have what is called a legal mind." Thomas Reed Powell, in an unpublished manuscript, as quoted in Arnold, *Criminal Attempts—The Rise and Fall of an Abstraction*, 40 Yale L.J. 53, 58 (1930).

42. See *e.g.*, R. Clark, *supra* note 22, at 203.

However that may be, and whether or not that is the apt comparison, prisoners and students of their plight report no joy from the incentive. On the contrary, it appears recurrently in the literature that the uncertainty is a steadily galling affliction. At least in many existing institutions, and probably in any we can foresee for the service of indeterminate sentences by prisoners of all kinds, there is a sense of mystery and bewilderment about what the rules are, about what will "work" toward the tightly focused goal of release.[43] Though the captors, or some of them, perceive the ordeal as "treatment," their charges, closer to the mark, consider that they are being punished, experience the process as hostile, and react with hostility.[44] There is a widespread cynicism that teaches the unsuitability, arbitrariness, and essential corruption of those in power. At least very often, the immediately seen wielders of the power convey to the prisoner that his hope lies in proper "attitudes" and in his demonstration that he can "behave"—a message understood, probably not inaccurately, to counsel a cramped orthodoxy and docility as the stigmata of reformation. There is a sense of helplessness with its concomitants of frustration and rage.

Reactions of this sort seem expectable in a system under which sentences are routinely indefinite and subject to discretionary prolongation without some intelligible prescription of the grounds and goals of "treatment." If we were compelled to choose between such a system and one of rigidly definite sentences across the board, I would prefer the latter. Fortunately, the options are not that limited. Indeterminate sentences, employed with discrimination and under rational criteria, may achieve limited benefits without the monstrous and arbitrarily allocated costs of employing them wholesale.

43. D. Ward & G. Kassebaum, *Women's Prison: Sex and Social Structure* 18-29 (1965). McCleery, *Authoritarianism and the Belief Systems of Incorrigibles, in the Prison* 260, 268-69 (D. Cressey ed. 1961).

44. See *Law of Criminal Correction* 132; Kirby, *Doubts about the Indeterminate Sentence*, 53 *Judicature* 63 (1969).

Deceptive Determinate Sentencing*

Caleb Foote
Professor of Law, University of California, Berkeley.

If there is one implication which runs through [these discussions], it is that sentencing is not amenable to piecemeal reform, that we are dealing with a problem, or rather a series of tightly interrelated problems, in which tinkering or half-baked reform is the enemy of comprehensive reform.

I have found myself here thinking of the fable of Medusa, when, according to Greek mythology, Perseus sought to destroy her evil force by beheading her, only to find that the decapitated head retained its petrifying power and that Pegasus and Chrysaor sprang full grown from her blood.

That is likely to be the fate of reform movements under even the best of circumstances, and there is nothing favorable about the circumstances under which the current rash of mislabeled determinate sentencing bills are being enacted. I happen to be in favor of determinate sentencing by rule; I was the principal author of the American Friends Service Committee's report, *Struggle for Justice*, which was one of the first statements advocating this policy. But present legislation, proposed or recently enacted, bears almost no resemblance to the position we advanced. Some of the legislation, like that of Maine, under no stretch of the imagination can be called determinate sentencing; all of it ignores or glosses over critical problems which must be faced before determinate sentencing can be fair or even feasible.

The one hint of significant change which runs through the current proposals is the elimination or downgrading of parole. But much of our discussion has confused the two quite separate functions allegedly served by parole: discretionary release and supervision of paroled inmates. I agree with Norval Morris and many others who regard the parole system's supervision of conditionally released inmates as ineffective and a waste of money. This aspect of parole, however, is not relevant to the subject matter of this conference. It is parole as a discretionary release mechanism which is being eliminated or severely restricted by the so-called determinate sentencing legislation.

To eliminate discretionary release without doing anything significant about discretionary intake is likely to produce more injustice, not less. I am no friend of parole, with its arbitrary and capricious decision-making masked by the myth of parole readiness, and the slow Chinese torture of indeterminacy which is its concomitant. In 1971-72 I observed hundreds of

* Reprinted, with author's permission, from *Determinate Sentencing: Reform or Regression*, Law Enforcement Assistance Administration, Washington, D.C., 1978, pp. 133-140.

hearings of the California Adult Authority and for weeks at a time virtually lived with its decision-makers. It was an appalling experience in many ways, but the Authority had at least some redeeming virtues.

The Authority's more obvious abuses, moreover, and the only ones that California's S.B. 42 may partially correct, could have been easily corrected by simple legislation. The Authority had the power, which it exercised in a small percentage of the cases coming before it, to hold prisoners almost indefinitely; this could have been cured by the simple expedient of establishing reasonable maximum terms. Another source of much discontent with the Authority was its habit of indefinite postponement in making the decision of when to release; this could have been eliminated by a one paragraph directive requiring prompt hearing and determination of the inmate's release date.

It became obvious during my study that if disparity, capriciousness and arbitrariness were the enemies, the paroling function was only one cog in the machinery that produced them. Moreover, what has been overlooked in the decisions to eliminate discretionary release is that parole boards, for all their shortcomings, are able to mitigate some of the abuses of discretionary sentencing. The Authority was at least dimly aware of the gross disparities which characterized the initial sentencing decisions made by judges and prosecutors. They knew, for example, that in some counties less than five percent of convicted felons were sent to state prison, while in others that figure was six times larger. These figures understate the disparity, for they are simply county averages and the range of disparity between individual judges is probably greater. When, for example, an Authority member noticed that a particular case came from Stanislaus or some other county known for its high rate of commitment, or from a judge whose disproportionate severity was known to him, he would tend to cushion the disparity, recognizing that it was highly probable that the inmate would not have been sent to state prison at all had his case been processed in Los Angeles or Alameda counties. Not infrequently one would hear a member of a decision-making panel say things like, "This case doesn't belong in state prison," or, "What could have possessed Judge X to send this guy to San Quentin?" The members also probed behind the curtain of plea bargaining, where there is likewise great disparity between counties, and made some attempt to equalize treatment on the basis of actual facts of each case rather than the fiction of the offense category to which a plea had been entered.

I don't want to exaggerate. This process of rectification of abuse was itself capricious and uncertain. Whether a particular inmate who was a victim of a grossly disparate commitment would obtain any relief depended on a host of other variables: e.g., the identity of the particular decision-maker drawn by lot to hear his case; the factors that a particular panel happened to be emphasizing at the moment it heard his case; the state of the political climate at the time; or whether the panel members had recently been burned by a release decision that backfired. But many corrections to reduce disparity were made; moreover, an inmate passed over one year could hope for better luck in next year's lottery when his case would almost certainly be heard under different circumstances by a different panel.

The problem of initial disparity is not only of importance to academic purists who are old fashioned enough to believe that equal treatment of similar offenders is an important value in a system allegedly concerned about equal justice under law. It has more immediate practical impact for penal administrators, who find their inmates sometimes strangely restive when a man serving ten years finds that his cellmate with a similar record but from a different judge or jurisdiction is carrying only two years. The autobiographical reminiscences of ex-wardens are full of discussions of this problem, and it was a persistent theme in the speeches of James V. Bennett and in the reports of the Bureau of Prisons under his direction. It is said that Bennett had two collections of judicial sentencing horror stories, those perpetrated by Eastern judges, which he used to illustrate his speeches on the West Coast, and vice versa. It is clear that he viewed parole as at least one means of dealing with the problem.

Restriction or abolition of parole discretionary release, therefore, removes this avenue for redress from initial sentencing disparity, and the new [California] legislation does not provide any viable substitute remedy. The methods which the new legislation utilizes to control this initial disparity are certain to be ineffective. As we have already seen earlier in the conference, the disparity abuses associated with plea bargaining are going to be aggravated. The new legislation would channel and equalize judicial discretion by the promulgation of administrative standards which the judge is supposed to apply. But the standards are vague and unworkable; in both the California and proposed federal legislation the underlying theory behind many of the standards is the same rehabilitative and incapacitative rationale which a hundred years of parole board experience has proved to be unworkable. Parole release has been discredited because the standards of rehabilitation and prediction of future dangerousness required determinations which are impossible to make with present or forseeable knowledge. The new legislation does not abolish reliance upon these treacherous uncertainties; it merely transfers their administration from parole boards to prosecutors and judges. There is every reason to believe that disparity abuse will be still greater with decentralized discretionary sentencing than it was under parole administration, and by the restriction or elimination of parole the possibility of post-sentence correction has been virtually eliminated.

Given the state of current sentencing law, with its grossly inflated penalty schedule, population control is another essential function performed by a releasing agency with broad discretionary power. I was amazed to hear Norval Morris downgrade this function as not a significant factor in deciding whether or not to retain parole. All the historical evidence is to the contrary. Concern over prison overcrowding dominates Nineteenth Century American penal literature and provided major impetus for the development and rapid expansion of parole. As for current practice, the only firsthand data I have is for California, which I cannot believe is wholly atypical. The Adult Authority seldom talked directly about prison population but the question dominated much of their thinking. They were cajoled, manipulated, begged by the Department of Corrections, one of whose central concerns, of course, is to have enough prisoners but not too many. Told to cut prison population by the governor's office; the Authority complied. Told to reverse the process, they complied again. The members eagerly perused the monthly statistical projections with which they were provided, which extrapolated from their current practice what the prison population was predicted to be one, three, or five years hence. They spent most of their working hours in penal institutions, absorbing the values of the correctional world—and those values center on population control. Indeed, it could be argued that they had been effectively captured by Corrections, for 13 of the 18 decision-makers whom I observed when I was doing my research were former correctional officials.

As a release mechanism parole is absolutely critical if one despairs of reforming and regularizing the work of prosecutors and judges. It is parole release discretion that makes tolerable from a management standpoint, if not from a moral or principled perspective, the uncontrolled discretion of prosecutors and judges. If this safety-valve is abolished or severely restricted, I would predict rocky times ahead until the system develops new devices which can regulate supply to demand or, much more likely, until discretionary release is reestablished in another swing of the policy pendulum.

The concern over prison population is one facet of underlying economic realities affecting sentencing policy which is almost entirely masked in current discussions of sentencing. These economic constraints are products of an imbalance between supply and demand. Institutional capacity to impose punishment is severely limited, but legislative proscription of conduct that is punishable is prodigal. Legislatures constantly tend to meet public crisis or private complaint by enacting new criminal laws or by increasing the severity of punishment for existing ones. This typical legislative response to any social malaise has built-in attractions for politicians. The enactment of criminal legislation creates the illusion of decisive political action at minimal risk of provoking organized or effective opposition and, as implementation by budget appropriation is not required, with no political cost in higher taxes.

Contrasting sharply with this flexible expansionism are police and court structures which can only process so many cases and penal establishments whose inelasticity is literally defined by concrete and steel. While there is some flexibility in prison capacity, it is strictly limited. Of course the number of prisoners in cells can be doubled up, or corridors, workshops or day rooms can be converted into dormitories—until at some point a series of Attica-like riots remind us that even human degradation has its limits. In many states, although not yet in California, these limits are being approached. Typically all sectors of the enforcement and correctional machinery operate at full capacity, with crowded jails, courts that are perpetually understaffed and behind in their dockets, and professional workers crushed under heavy case loads.

Any significant increase in the number of available punishment slots in a correctional system is likely to take a minimum of ten years in politicking, planning and construction and, for each new inmate bed, to cost at least $30,000 in capital outlay and thereafter $2,000 or up in annual upkeep. To talk, therefore, about substantial increases in both the proportion of criminals sent to prison and in the severity of terms is to engage in fantasy. One could do one or the other; one could send more felons to prison for shorter terms, or fewer felons for longer terms, but one cannot do both.

In California, only ten to 15 percent, varying somewhat from year to year, of felons convicted in Superior Courts are sentenced to state prison. Only about 20 percent of robbery convictions end up with a prison sentence. Both figures understate the actual disparity, for many felons, including many robbers, are plea-bargained to lesser offenses. If these proportions were increased by more than a few percentage points, and there was no discretionary release mechanism, over a period of a few years seomething approaching chaos would be occurring in the correctional world. Unless accompanied by massive increases in the correctional budget, political measures which would have the effect of sharply increasing prison populations are divorced from reality.

If the masks of individualization and rehabilitation are stripped away, the basic function of discretion in paroling and sentencing practice is revealed: to adjust an impossible penal code to the reality of severe limitations in punishment resources. By an impossible penal code I refer to the fact that, given economic constraints, full or equal enforcement is totally out of the question. By necessity, from the masses of convicted persons legislatively declared to be eligible for imprisonment, most must be diverted and only a small proportion winnowed out for actual imprisonment. What we have evolved is a system of symbolic punishment in which each San Quentin inmate stands for half a dozen or a dozen other convicted felons who are by any standards equally eligible to be there but for whom there are no beds. This system is efficient in court administration, for the threat of being the symbol keeps the guilty pleas flowing smoothly. It is economical by cost-benefit standards, for it probably maximizes the return in general deterrence for dollars expended. It is politically expedient, at least in the short run, because it dupes and pacifies an otherwise potentially rebellious public. It is also, in my opinion, profoundly immoral, violates the spirit of due process and equal protection, turns our criminal courts into sausage factories and breeds disrespect for law in most of those whom it touches. But I'm not going to pursue these factors, both because I don't have the time and because I think the points are obvious.

Faced with these economic realities we have three alternative courses of action. The first is to multiply by five or ten times the size of correctional budgets to make possible implementation of the draconion thirst for punishment which characterizes the majority of the public and which is so popular in the legislatures. However, once the public got a taste of what this alternative would do to their tax bills, I assume it would not be pursued.

Second would be a comprehensive attempt to introduce equal justice to sentencing by adjusting penalties to the limited supply of punishment resources. This would involve control of prosecutors, perhaps using German criminal procedure as a model to start from; sentencing by rule and precedent; massive decriminalization spurred by a recognition that imprisonment was a costly resource to be used only in extreme circumstances; and extensive and imaginative use of non-incarcerative punishments. The key factor would be rules which sharply limited the criteria which could be taken into account in determining the seriousness of an offender's punishment. The seriousness of the offense category, the seriousness of the circumstances of the particular offense, and the extent of the offender's prior conviction record are criteria that are both relevant to the offender's just deserts and that, being objective, could be administered fairly and evenly. The myriad of other criteria which dominate past and present practice are relevant only to improper or unachievable goals, e.g., the discredited concept of rehabilitation, discriminatory class or race bias, or the capricious game of guessing about an offender's future dangerousness in the absence of any scientific or validated basis for such predictions.

Such an approach could achieve determinate sentencing in reality rather than only in fiction. It would require, however, a substantial reduction of our present level of severity in order to bring punishment resources into line with the output of the criminal courts. The fact that real determinate sentencing consistent with the principle of equal justice has zero political chance of adoption or serious attention gives emphasis to the principal obstacles to meaningful reform of criminal law and its administration: (1) the unrealizable expectations and ignorance of the public, aggravated by (2) the biased and deliberately misleading reporting of a media concerned with reaping profits from sensationalism; (3) the entrenched power of self-interested pressure groups able to block almost any change (a problem by no means unique to criminal law but one for which a democratic polity appears to have no solution); (4) irresponsible legislators who exploit public fear of crime for narrow political benefits and whose cheap tricks (e.g., creating new crimes or increasing penalties for existing crimes without budgeting funds necessary for any implementation) merely aggravate our sorry state of affairs; and (5) a society not unlike ancient Rome which uses the politics of crime as its Colosseum spectacle to divert attention from more fundamental and pressing problems.

Given the political impossibility of treating all like offenders with either equal severity or equal moderation, this leaves the third alternative as the likely outcome: to continue as at present with symbolic punishment, combining excessively severe prison sentences for the few with excessively lenient dispositions for the many, using broad grants of discretionary power at all levels as the mechanism to keep the system in balance. Given this direction, one would not be far off the mark by predicting that, from an historical perspective, the current flurry of so-called determinate sentiment will turn out to have been a fad, a minor and temporary irritant to a system whose politics irrevocably wed it to discretion.

WHAT IS 'DANGEROUSNESS'?

Cross v. *Harris*, **418 F.2d 1095 (D.C. Cir., 1969)**

To determine "dangerousness" is one of the most difficult decisions to make in the criminal justice system. Unfortunately, the system is forced to make determinations of exactly this question at virtually every stage of the justice process.[1]

For example, there is intense pressure on judges to make some assessment of dangerousness in setting bail, with the direct implication that those who are indeed dangerous should be given a higher bail than would normally be called for simply to guarantee the arrestee's presence in furture court proceedings. Similar considerations come up in sentencing, where pressures exist to "incapacitate" or "warehouse" dangerous offenders with lengthy sentences so that they are not free to commit new crimes.

After sentencing, the corrections system must again make these determinations. Intensive supervision projects are popular in probation offices, with the more "dangerous" offender assigned to smaller or more control-oriented caseloads. Prison officials have to decide whether to use maximum or minimum security prisons, or even, in some states, "maxi-maxi" prisons for the very dangerous.

There is no place in the social control system, however, where this question is so "up front" or obvious as in the civil commitment process. The laws of many states allow for a sentence of indeterminate length for persons found to be "mentally ill, and dangerous to himself or others." While there is some evidence that this legislative restrictive criteria is ignored in many cases in

---

1. See John Monahan and Lesley Cummings, "Social Policy Implications of the Inability to Predict Violence," *Journal of Social Issues* 31(2) (1975), pp. 153-164; Milton G. Rector, "Who Are the Dangerous," *Bulletin of the American Academy of Psychiatry and the Law*, 1 (1973), pp. 186-188; G. Gulevich and Peter Bourne, "Mental Illness and Violence," in D. Daniels, M. Gilula, and F. Ochberg, eds., *Violence and the Struggle for Existence*, (Boston: Little, Brown, 1970); Edwin I Megaree, "The Prediction of Dangerous Behavior," *Criminal Justice and Behavior*, 3(1) (1976), pp. 3-22; Beverly Koerin, "Violent Crime: Prediction and Control," *Crime and Delinquency*, (1978). pp. 49-58; Michael A. Peszke, "Is Dangerousness an Issue for Physicians in Emergency Commitments?" *American Journal of Psychiatry*, (August 1975); Murray L. Cohen, A. Nicholas Groth, Richard Siegel, "The Clinical Prediction of Dangerousness," *Crime and Delinquency*, (January 1978), pp. 28-39; Nicholas N. Kittrie, *The Right to Be Different*, (Baltimore: Johns Hopkins Press, 1971); Henry J. Steadman, "Some Evidence on the Inadequacy of the Concept and Determination of Dangerousness in Law and Psychiatry," *Journal of Psychiatry and Law*, (Winter 1973), pp. 409-461; B. Rubin, "The Prediction of Dangerousness in Mentally Ill Criminals," *Archives of General Psychiatry*, (September 1972), pp. 397-407.

favor of a simple finding of mental illness,[2] the issue becomes more difficult in those states which retain sexual psychopath statutes. Designed for the most part in the 1940s, these statutes were supposed to allow for the civil commitment of those offenders who were not "insane" under strictly defined laws, but were indeed mentally disturbed and additionally dangerous.

These laws have fallen into some disrepute in recent years, as the definition of "mentally ill" has taken the place of legal "insanity" in civil commitment statutes, and more and more psychiatrists have argued that the term sexual psychopath no longer has any important meaning.

The case below deals with this specific problem, that of whether a man who would be classified a sexual psychopath under the old definition but not under the new definition, can continue to be held as a "sexual psychopath." The underlying issue—determining the definition of "dangerousness," especially when many years of confinement hang in the balance—is the same issue that has to be considered throughout the criminal justice system.

In the case below, a classic debate on the definition of dangerousness which occurred between District of Columbia Court of Appeals Chief Judge David Bazelon and Circuit Judge Warren Burger (who has since been "promoted" to Chief Justice of the U.S. Supreme Court) is presented. The entire court agreed on the disposition of the case (to send it back to the District Court for a new hearing) but Burger dissented from the majority views on the nature of dangerousness.

Bazelon felt there must be both a likelihood of "substantial injury," and that the word "likely" should be carefully examined to be sure that the dangerous behavior had at least a high probability of manifesting itself. Burger argued for a much broader definition of "danger," and a much weaker definition of "likely."

In this case, Thomas B. Cross was first committed to St. Elizabeth's Hospital in Washington, D.C. at the age of 18. His problem was that he had a tendency to indecently expose himself in public. While this crime is only punishable in that jurisdiction by a jail sentence of not more than 90 days, Cross was held at St. Elizabeth's for 15 years. He was released in 1967, got married to a former fellow patient, and they had a child. However, he was soon arrested and charged with six counts of indecent exposure. Once again, he was determined to be a sexual psychopath and returned to St. Elizabeth's Hospital, to be held there until he was considered cured, or else for life.

The case became complicated when at his commitment hearing, both of the examining psychiatrists from D.C. General Hospital told the court that while Cross may indeed be a sexual psychopath, they could not recommend hospitalization. Confinement would "increase his emotional tensions" and

2. See G.E. Dix, "Acute Psychiatric Hospitalization of the Mentally Ill in the Metropolis: An Empirical Study," *Washington University Law Quarterly*, pp. 485-558; Thomas J. Scheff, "The Societal Reaction to Deviance: Ascriptive Elements in the Psychiatric Screening of Mental Patients in a Midwestern State," *Social Problems*, (1964), pp. 401-413.

"would remove him for many years from self-support of his family" without "benefit (to) anyone." They recommended a program of outpatient care, which they felt did offer some hope of preventing further acts of exposure, while inpatient care did not.

The lower court held that while this may indeed be true, the law [22 D.C. Code #3508 (1968)] simply provided that a sexual psychopath shall be committed to St. Elizabeth's Hospital "to be confined there." In this case, he had petitioned for habeas corpus, arguing that the regular law covering civil commitment [The Mentally Ill Act of 1964, 21 D.C. Code #501-91 (1967)] required the court to consider less restrictive treatment alternatives before ordering this total confinement. Cross argued that since sex offenders are not more dangerous as a class than mentally ill persons who were committed, both must be given equal rights under the law. The court rejected this argument, and it was appealed to the D.C. Court of Appeals.

While all of this was going on, the D.C. Court of Appeals issued another opinion, *Millard* v. *Harris*, 406 F.2d 964 (1968), which is referred to extensively in this decision. The Millard decision restricted the sexual psychopath law under which Cross was sentenced, and included a ruling that the finding of dangerousness must be based on a high probability of substantial injury.

The case has been edited, and re-arranged into more of a debate format, with most footnotes removed.

BAZELON, Chief Judge:

We attempted in *Millard* to provide an analytical framework to guide lower courts in applying the conclusory term "dangerous to others." Without some such framework, "dangerous" could readily become a term of art describing anyone whom we would, all things considered, prefer not to encounter on the streets. We did not suppose that Congress had used "dangerous" in any such Pickwickian sense. Rather, we supposed that Congress intended the courts to refine the unavoidably vague concept of "dangerousness" on a case-by-case basis, in the traditional common-law fashion.

This does not mean, however, that the statutory language may be disregarded. To be "dangerous" for the purposes of the Sexual Psychopath Act, one must be

likely to attack or otherwise *inflict injury*, loss, pain, or other evil on the objects of his desire.

The focus of the statute is not on expected conduct, but on the harm that may flow from that conduct. Commitment cannot be based simply on the determination that a person is likely to engage in particular acts. The court must also determine the harm, if any, that is likely to flow from these acts. A mere possibility of injury is not enough; the statute requires that the harm be *likely*. For no matter how certain one can be that a person will engage in particular acts, it cannot be said that he is "likely to * * * inflict injury" unless it can also be said that the acts, if engaged in, are likely to result in injury.

These determinations must be made on the basis of the record in the particular case before the court. The expert testimony will therefore be relevant to three questions of fact: (1) the likelihood of recurrence of sexual misconduct; (2) the likely frequency of any such behavior; and (3) the magnitude of harm to other persons that is likely to result.

Having found the facts, the court must then determine as a matter of law—in this case, as a matter of statutory construction—whether those facts provide a legal basis for commitment. Two questions must be answered in making this determination. The first is what *magnitude of harm* will justify commitment. It is clear that Congress did not intend to authorize indefinite preventive detention for those who have a propensity to behave in a way that is merely offensive or obnoxious to others; the threatened harm must be substantial. Thus, commitment under the Sexual Psychopath Act requires that a person be found likely to engage in sexual misconduct in circumstances where that misconduct will inflict substantial injury upon others.

The second question is what *likelihood of harm* will justify commitment. It may well be impossible to provide a precise definition of "likely" as the term is used in the statute. The degree of likelihood necessary to support commitment may depend on many factors. Among the particularly relevant considerations are the seriousness of the expected harm, the availability of inpatient and outpatient treatment for the individual concerned, and the expected length of confinement required for inpatient treatment.

It is particularly important that courts not allow this second question to devolve, by default, upon the expert witnesses. Psychiatrists should not be asked to testify, without more, simply whether future behavior or threatened harm is "likely" to occur. For the psychiatrist "may—in his own mind—be defining 'likely' to mean anything from virtual certainty to slightly above chance. And his definition will not be a reflection of any expertise, but * * * of his own personal preference for safety or liberty."[3] Of course, psychiatrists may be unable or unwilling to provide a precise numerical estimate of probabilities, and we are not attempting to so limit their testimony. But questioning can and should bring out the expert witness's meaning when he testifies that expected harm is or is not "likely." Only when this has been done can the court properly separate the factual question—what degree of likelihood exists in a particular case—from the legal one—whether the degree of likelihood that has been found to exist provides a justification for commitment.

Millard had been committed because of exhibitionism and masturbation in public, but he had performed no such acts during six years of hospitalization. Extensive expert testimony was presented at his habeas corpus hearing

---

3. Dershowitz, "Psychiatry in the Legal Process: 'A Knife that Cuts Both Ways,'" Address Delivered at the Harvard Law School Sesquicentennial Celebration, September 22, 1967.

to show that he was likely to engage in such conduct only on infrequent occasions. The experts testified that *isolated* exposures to acts of this nature were likely to cause psychological harm only to a small group of uniquely sensitive women. If Millard would but rarely expose himself at all, he was prima facie unlikely to do so in the presence of a member of this small group. Consequently, the record showed that he was not *likely* to inflict substantial harm on others—at least in the absence of evidence as to the vulnerability to injury of any likely viewers of his occasional self-exposures.

Appellant is, like Millard, a potential exhibitionist, though the record does not disclose that he is also a public masturbator. There is no indication in the record that he has ever been violent or assaultive. On the other hand, unlike Millard, he has apparently engaged in numerous recent acts of indecent exposure. Thus, one of the predicates of our holding that Millard was not dangerous under the Act is not present in this case.

Appellant may, however, be able to demonstrate that he will not be a frequent offender. His doctors offer an explanation for his recent spate of lapses which suggests that a repetition may be avoidable. The likelihood that appellant will voluntarily accept a course of outpatient treatment which will prevent frequent lapses is a factor to be considered in determining whether he is likely to inflict substantial injury on others. And even if appellant cannot show that his future acts of exhibitionism will be infrequent, he may nevertheless be able to show that they will be harmless. In light of evidence as to the character and size of the likely viewing audience and the harm it may suffer, the District Court will have to consider whether appellant's potential exhibitionism can be deemed a sufficiently grave danger to warrant an indeterminate commitment.

. . . .

We have not, either here or in *Millard*, decided any constitutional questions. But when a determination of "dangerousness" will result in a deprivation of liberty, no court can afford to ignore the very real constitutional problems surrounding incarceration predicated only upon a supposed propensity to commit criminal acts. Incarceration may not seem "punishment" to the jailers, but it is punishment to the jailed. Incarceration for a mere propensity is punishment not for acts, but for status, and punishment for status is hardly favored in our society. In essence, detention for status is preventive detention.

Only a "blind court" could ignore the intense debate, in and out of Congress, over the extent to which the Constitution can tolerate preventive detention. Similar questions have been raised sporadically for years, but the problem has rarely been analyzed. It may be that in some circumstances preventive detention is in fact permissible. If so, such detention would have to be based on a record that clearly documented a high probability of serious harm, and circumscribed by procedural protections as comprehensive as those afforded criminal suspects. Detention for any significant period of time would have to be attended by periodic review as well as continuing assurance of bona fide efforts at treatment suited to the particular individual detained.

Unquestionably, Congress may prohibit acts of exhibitionism even if such acts are unlikely to do serious harm; and Congress may punish willful violations of laws forbidding indecent behavior. But the test of what anticipated conduct may justify preventive detention cannot be simply whether the legislature has power to prohibit such conduct or to attack the evil it portends. Congress may legislate to protect many different interests—psychic and esthetic as well as physical and economic. But while it may prohibit ugly billboards because they give offense, it may not lock up ugly people for the same reason. The power to control an evil does not remove all restrictions on the means that may be employed for that purpose. This principle is fundamental to the constitutional order.

On the present record, confinement of appellant under the Sexual Psychopath Act would deprive him of his liberty indefinitely—and perhaps permanently—for a propensity to commit acts punishable by a fixed jail sentence. Moreover, confinement would ignore, and apparently frustrate, his treatment needs. Confinement for a mere propensity is preventive detention. Particularly when the act in question is commonly punishable only by a short jail sentence, indefinite confinement, even though labeled "civil," is preventive detention with a vengeance. If required by the Sexual Psychopath Act, it would raise not only one but many difficult constitutional issues:

. . . Is the harm threatened by a potential exhibitionist sufficiently serious to provide a constitutional justification for indefinite deprivation of liberty?

. . . Is the possibility that no harm will in fact result from appellant's future conduct sufficiently large to make incarceration based on possible harm arbitrary and capricious and therefore in violation of the due process clause?

. . . If less restrictive alternatives would in fact adequately protect the public while best promoting appellant's rehabilitation, is confinement a deprivation of his liberty without the justification required by the due process clause?

. . . If appellant's need for treatment requires that he not be confined, is indefinite confinement because of his condition cruel and unusual punishment?

BURGER, Circuit Judge (concurring and dissenting in part):

I must . . . dissent from those portions of the majority opinion relating to "dangerousness."

In *Millard* the majority discounted Appellant's demonstrated inclination for exhibitionism which "most women would find * * * repulsive" even though, depending upon their sensitivity, they might be "quite upset" but for *only* 'two or three days' " 132 U.S.App.D.C. 146, 158, 406 F.2d 964, 976 (1968) (emphasis added). Judicial concern ought to be fairly apportioned between the delinquent offender and the victims whose traumatic injury may be very grave.

The *Millard* court also noted the possibility of serious psychological harm which might result to small children from witnessing Millard's "expected exhibitionism," but concluded that none of these factors warranted the delinquent offender's commitment. Both in *Millard* and in the instant case the majority has placed an undue emphasis on the subject's lack of a physically assaultive or violent nature, denigrating the hazard of psychic trauma which is so much the subject of psychiatric inquiry. Such an approach seems to equate "dangerousness" with conduct involving only physical impact; it tends to ignore the potential for psychic damage to the young. There is simply no basis whatever, either in common law or common sense, for so limiting the range of public values and interests which a legislature may legitimately protect. The law properly shelters psychological as well as purely physical interests. No reasons have been advanced in this case which justify substitution by the majority of its own theories of psychiatry or public policy for those of the legislative branch.

This is not a case where an individual is being committed solely because of an imagined propensity to engage in *anticipated* conduct obnoxious or offensive to others; thus, contrary to the majority, I do not think we are confronted with a situation involving strictly preventive detention. Appellant's record stipulation that he recently engaged in various acts of indecent exposure supplies the basis for commitment to one of the institutions designated by Congress. A civil commitment statute is not rendered constitutionally suspect as a form of preventive detention simply because in a given case the civil confinement may exceed the sentence which could be imposed under a criminal statute for the same acts. The possible disparity of confinement, which is by no means inevitable, may reasonably be justified by the social desirability and public necessity of providing the patient with therapy.

Admittedly there are a multitude of problems involved in determining psychological trauma to the victims and then in balancing the gravity of the harm to the public with the necessity for involuntary commitment of a delinquent or emotionally disabled offender. But these are essentially legislative policy determinations, not primarily judicial questions. Indeed, Congress, being sensitive to the fact that psychiatry is at best an infant and developing discipline which employs imprecise and changing standards and definitions,[4] has experimented with a variety of statutes to provide a rehabilitative system for individuals prone to aberrant sexual conduct. Since we are not here dealing with *penal* legislation we should be especially cautious of substituting our own predilections concerning psychiatry for those of a fact-finding body entrusted with formulating our legal and social policies; courts have neither the authority nor the facilities nor the competence for marshalling the data necessary to displace the policy judgments

4.   An illustration of this is found in the many state statutes addressed as the "sex psychopath," a term now rejected by many psychiatrists as without meaning; yet this term is embalmed in codes in many jurisdictions.

of the legislature. The approach of each of us is all too likely to be shaped by what books we read on the subjects outside our own discipline.

Aside from the undesirability of engaging in legislative-type speculation, the views expressed by my colleagues, both here and in *Millard*, are at odds with the recent obscenity cases. The *Millard* opinion discussed at great length the questionable impact on various groups which might result from public exposure of a given course of sexual misconduct. I think it significant that in discussing virtually the same problem in the context of upholding a state law precluding the sale of obscene literature to minors under 17 years of age, the Supreme Court employed a sensibly fluid standard of causality between the condemned material and the danger sought to be avoided. The court stated that it was "require[d] only * * * to say that it was not *irrational* for the legislature to find that exposure to material condemned by the statute is harmful to minors." Ginsberg v. New York, 390 U.S. 629, 641, 88 S.Ct. 1274, 1281, 20 L.Ed.2d 195 (1968) (emphasis added). And even though it was "very doubtful" that the legislative findings "express[d] an accepted scientific fact," the fact that a " 'causal link has not been disproved' " precluded the Supreme Court from concluding that the statute had "no rational relation to the objective of safeguarding * * * minors from harm." Likewise, in the present case, there is no assertion by Appellant, or determination by the majority, that it was irrational for Congress to conclude that exposure to Appellant's conduct may cause harm. And regardless of whether this Congressional finding represents an "accepted scientific fact," since a "causal link has not been disproved" this court is precluded from substituting its own preferences for the views of Congress. *Id.* at 641-643. The standard set forth in *Ginsberg* also governs the instant case, and its use would result *a fortiori* in affirmance since we are dealing with action rather than mere words. We would do well to exercise the restraint demonstrated by the Supreme Court in *Ginsberg*.

Moreover, it is well established that the state may legitimately shelter specific groups of individuals from exposure to obscene materials. *See, e.g.,* Ginsberg v. New York, supra; Prince v. Com. of Massachusetts, 321 U.S. 158, 64 S.Ct. 438, 88 L.Ed. 645 (1944). Yet the *Millard* Court relied heavily on the conclusion that "only a small proportion of the population" would be injured by Appellant's misconduct. This not only contravenes the controlling principles, most recently stated by the Supreme Court, that the State may properly guard against the "danger that obscene material might fall into the hands of children * * * *or that it might intrude upon the sensibilities or privacy of the general public;*" it also flies in the face of common human experience. Stanley v. Georgia, 394 U.S. 557, 567, 89 S.Ct. 1243, 1249, 22 L.Ed.2d 319 (1969) (citations and footnote omitted) (emphasis added). However grievous the instrusive potential of the written word, it seems clear that overt public misconduct has an even more devastating impact, an impact destructive of the "privacy and sensibilities of the general public." We need not assess "fault" on the lewd actor; but we must be able to remove him from public areas—gently but firmly—in order to protect the public and to carry out corrective treatment.

BAZELON, Chief Judge:

The dissenting opinion is in large part an attack on Millard v. Harris, which controls our decision today. But although it misreads the holdings and rationales of both decisions,[5] it raises issues of such importance that with all due respect, we are constrained to address ourselves to some of the dissent's statements....

...The dissent apparently would construe the statute so as either to read out of it the word "likely" or to read into it an unascertainable congressional intent to confine all exhibitionists as "dangerous."[6]

. . . .

...The dissent apparently considers the constitutional questions we have sought to avoid deciding so insubstantial that their very mention occasions rebuke. "This is not," we are told, "a situation involving strictly preventive detention." By our construction of the statute we have done our best to make this statement true. But the dissent would read the statute to bring this issue into the clearest possible focus. Appellant has been "treated" in Saint Elizabeth's Hospital for fifteen years—his entire adult life. Both of the examining psychiatrists testified that further hospitalization will not improve—and may aggravate—his condition, while outpatient treatment offers some hope of a cure. Perhaps the consequences of his exhibitionism could be shown to present such a grave risk to the public that he may legally be confined indefinitely solely for their protection. But if this is to be done, we should *at least* acknowledge what we are doing. We are not confining an unfortunate man in order to provide him with treatment that will lead to his rehabilitation; we are locking him up for our own "protection," in direct op-

---

5. To avoid confusion, we emphasize: (1) that Congress has never indicated any intention to detain all exhibitionists indefinitely as "dangerous"; (2) that we did not question congressional power to punish acts of exhibitionism; (3) that we did not in any way restrict the kinds of ends and interests that Congress may, by appropriate means, seek to promote; (4) that we did not say that harm to only a small segment of the population could not be sufficient to support a commitment under the Sexual Psychopath Act, so long as that harm was, in the language of the Act, *likely* to occur; (5) that we did not exclude any lasting harm of any sort to children, women, or anyone else from the category of "substantial injury" which may justify commitment under the Act, provided there is evidence that such harm is *likely* to occur; and (6) that far from relying on any psychiatric theories of our own, we simply accepted in *Millard* the testimony of the psychiatrists concerning the likely consequences of Mr. Millard's exhibitionism, as in this case we must rely on the expert testimony concerning Mr. Cross. Nor is this list exhaustive.

6. Our decision in *Millard* turned upon the record, which showed that no harm was likely to flow from Mr. Millard's expected future conduct. In taking issue with *Millard*, the dissent speaks of "traumatic injury" and "psychic trauma" to bystanders without any discussion of the likelihood that such trauma will in fact occur. Although it may be true that in certain circumstances frequent exhibitionism is necessarily "dangerous" within the meaning of the Sexual Psychopath Act, there is certainly no evidence on the record either here or in *Millard* to support such a conclusion; we consequently left the issue open on remand. It would therefore appear that the dissent is either (1) relying upon unmentioned extra-record psychiatric theories in order to conclude the exhibitionism is dangerous *per se*, or else (2) giving no effect to the word "likely" in the statute.

position to his treatment needs. Awareness of this fact might impel us to approach the problem with greater humility and caution.

. . . The dissent takes us to task for giving insufficient weight to "the *possibility* of serious psychological harm which might result to small children" (emphasis added). We are not unaware of this possibility. But the statute says that commitment is justified only if the person to be committed is "*likely* to * * * inflict injury" on other persons. Whatever may be the requisite standard of likelihood, there is surely no warrant for reading "likely" as synonymous with "might possibly."

. . . One premise lies at the core of the dissenting opinion: that exhibitionism is necessarily dangerous, no matter what the circumstances. This assumption so pervades the dissent that it can flatly state, with no citation of authority whatsoever, that Congress has decided that exhibitionism is dangerous; consequently, the dissent strenuously objects to what it conceives to be our disregard of Congressional intent. But the House Report on the bill, the Senate Report, and the Congressional Record are empty of any indication that Congress even considered the question, let alone answered it. Determination of the legislative intent is often difficult, and even careful examination of the legislative history may leave grounds for disagreement. At the very least, however, courts should determine the intent of Congress from the legislative record, and not simply infer it from general notions of proper policy.

. . . The dissent, in successive paragraphs, first attempts to remove this case from the sphere of "preventive detention" by focusing on appellant's past conduct, and next resurrects the tired cliche that "we are not here dealing with *penal* legislation." The first of these paragraphs of course ignores both the language and operation of the Sexual Psychopath Act, which requires neither a criminal conviction nor any showing, attended by the procedural safeguards constitutionally required in criminal cases, that the person to be committed has engaged in specified proscribed conduct. And the two paragraphs taken together well illustrate the willingness with which many of us deny the reality of preventive detention. All too often courts justify a punitive disposition by looking to past conduct, while simultaneously ignoring the procedural requirements of criminal cases by invoking the false promise of "nonpenal" treatment and rehabilitation. "Non-criminal" commitments of so-called dangerous persons have long served as preventive detention, but this function has been either excused or obscured by the promise that, while detained, the potential offender will be rehabilitated by treatment. Notoriously, this promise of treatment has served only to bring an illusion of benevolence to what is essentially a warehousing operation for social misfits.

Predicting future behavior and evaluating its consequences is a uniquely difficult, if not impossible task.[7] It must be forthrightly confronted, not

---

7. See Dershowitz, "On Preventive Detention," *New York Review of Books*, Mar. 13, 1969, at 22.

avoided by sugar-coating reality. There is no way on this record that we can escape the reality that a "penal" incarceration would set appellant free in 90 days, while the dissent's "non-penal" solution would likely confine him for years, if not for the rest of his life. The record here contains uncontradicted expert testimony that appellant's continued confinement would not "benefit anyone," while out-patient treatment offers the best chance for improvement of his condition. Judicial speculation is no substitute for record evidence.

ELECTRONIC SURVEILLANCE

Related to the question of who should be assigned which penalties is the issue of how these persons should be treated. The kind of treatment given is oftentimes subject to specific limitations on the state's power to punish or coerce offenders.

Sensitive issues, revolving around the powers and rights of the state, are surfacing as the science of behavior control becomes more and more sophisticated. Today psychobiology and sociobiology are important fields of study which promise an increased understanding of the causes of human behavior. In late 1978, the American Society of Criminology decided to make this new field the theme of its annual meeting. Literally dozens of researchers presented papers pointing out the value of this new field of study.

The society's president, C. Ray Jeffery, in his own paper, pointed out the limitations of studying punishment through traditional methodology:

> People do not learn to behave in a lawful way by being punished; they learn to avoid and escape punishment. The whole criminal justice system is the most beautiful example of escape and avoidance conditioning that one can imagine. We do not punish people into obeying the law; we condition them to avoid the police, to avoid arrest and prosecution, to plea bargain if arrested, to tell the judge and probation officer a fairy tale if convicted, and to make maximum use of the inmate subculture if sent to prison. A major industry called criminal justice is supported by the psychobiological principle that avoiding pain is reinforcing.[1]

Where this new emphasis will lead us is not hard to imagine. Medical and behavioral science technology are rapidly advancing to the point where human behavior may actually be controllable in the near future. Once the causes of criminal behavior are known, a technology of control is not far behind.

When prisons were first built, one of the main issues centered on the use of capital and corporal punishment. The issue today may well be whether psychosurgery and chemotherapy can be considered corporal punishment,[2]

---

1. C. Ray Jeffery, "Punishment and Deterrence: A Psychobiological Statement," paper presented at the annual meeting of the American Society of Criminology, Dallas, Texas, 1978.
2. James Gobert, "Psychosurgery, Conditioning and the Prisoner's Right to Refuse 'Rehabilitation,'" *Virginia Law Review* vol. 61 (1975), p. 155.

and, even if they are not necessarily "cruel and unusual" forms of punishment, the question remains: is it proper for the state to employ such mind control devices and practices?

This is not an insignificant debate. While some argue that democracy is based on free will, and that any physical or chemical coercion by the state to alter or modify socially deviant behavior is the hallmark of a totalitarian society rather than of a free society, one commentator has generally argued that this entire notion is hogwash. Psychologist B.F. Skinner has attacked the general notion behind American criminal law, which states that man has free will. Skinner suggests that if man is free to act in any way he chooses, then those who choose to break the law are bad people, and proper subjects for state imposed punishment. According to Skinner, this freedom of action is superficial and illusory—man is only free to avoid punishment. Man is no less free if he is conditioned by society to act in the correct manner without punishment. Thus, the best "corrections" system is one which uses scientific technology to change a person who breaks the law so that this person *wants* to act in the manner best suited to the survival of the culture.[3]

The upcoming articles provide a pro/con look at the uses of behavior modification, both within the prison walls and in the "civilization" outside.

---

3. B.F. Skinner, *Beyond Freedom and Dignity*, (New York: Alfred A. Knopf, 1971).

Electronic Surveillance and Control of Behavior and Its Possible Use in Rehabilitation and Parole*

Barton L. Ingraham
Gerald W. Smith

In the very near future, a computer technology will make possible alternatives to imprisonment. The development of systems for telemetering information from sensors implanted in or on the body will soon make possible the observation and control of human behavior without actual physical contact. Through such telemetric devices, it will be possible to maintain twenty-four hour-a-day surveillance over the subject and to intervene electronically or physically to influence and control selected behavior. It will thus be possible to exercise control over human behavior and from a distance without physical contact. The possible implications for criminology and corrections of such telemetric systems is tremendously significant.

The purpose of this paper is: (1) to describe developments during the last decade in the field of telemetry and electrophysiology as they relate to the control of human behavior; (2) to dispel, if possible, some of the exaggerated notions prevalent amongst legal and philosophical Cassandras as to the extent of the power and range of these techniques in controlling human behavior and thought; (3) to discuss some applications of these techniques to problem areas in penology and to show how they can make a useful contribution, with a net gain, to the values of individual freedom and privacy; and (4) to examine critically "ethical reservations" which might impede both valuable research in these areas and the application of their results to solving the problem of crime control.

Electronic Techniques for Observing and Controlling

Behavior in Humans

A telemetric system consists of small electronic devices attached to a subject that transmit via radio waves information regarding the location and physiological state of the wearer. A telemetry system provides a method whereby phenomena may be measured or controlled at a distance from where they occur—i.e., remotely (Grisamore, 1965). The great benefit derived from the use of such systems in studying animals (including man) lies in the ability to get data from a heretofore inaccessible environment, thus avoiding the experimental artifacts which arise in a laboratory setting (Slater, 1965; Schwitzgebel, 1967b). It also provides long-range, day-to-day, continuous observation and control of the monitored subject, since the data

* Reprinted, with permission, from *Issues in Criminology*, vol. 7 (1972), pp. 35-52.

can be fed into a computer which can act as both an observer and a controller (Konecci, 1965a).

Telemetry has been put to many and diverse uses. In aerospace biology, both man and animal have been telemetered for respiration, body temperature, blood pressure, heart rate (ECG's), brain waves (EEG's) and other physiological data (Konecci, 1965b; Slater, 1965; Barr, 1960). Telemetric devices have been placed on and in birds, animals and fish of all kinds to learn about such things as migration patterns, hibernation and spawning locations, respiration rates, brain wave activity, body temperatures, etc. (Slater, 1965; Lord, 1962; Sperry, 1961; Mackay, 1961; Young, 1964; Epstein, 1968). Telemetry has also been used in medicine to obtain the EEG patterns of epileptics during seizures, and to monitor heart rhythms and respiration rates in humans, for purposes of diagnosis and rescue in times of emergency (Slater, 1965; Caceres, 1965). The technology has proceeded so far that one expert in the field remarked (Mackay, 1965):

"It appears that almost any signal for which there is a sensor can be transmitted from almost any species. Problems of size, life, and accuracy have been overcome in most cases. Thus, the future possibilities are limited only by the imagination."

Telemetric systems can be classified into two types of devices—"external devices" and "internal devices."

External Devices

For the past several years, Schwitzgebel (1967a, b; Note: *Harvard Law Review*, 1966) at Harvard has been experimenting with a small, portable transmitter, called a Behavior Transmitter-Reinforcer (BT-R), which is small enough to be carried on a belt and which permits tracking of the wearer's location, transmitting information about his activities and communicating with him (by tone signals). The tracking device consists of two containers, each about the size of a thick paperback book, one of which contains batteries and the other, a transmitter that automatically emits radio signals, coded differently for each transmitter so that many of them may be used on one frequency band. With a transmitting range of approximately a quarter of a mile under adverse city conditions and a receiving range of two miles, the BT-R signals are picked up by receivers at a laboratory base station and fed into a modified missile-tracking device which graphs the wearer's location and displays it on a screen. The device can also be connected with a sensor resembling a wristwatch which transmits the wearer's pulse rate. In addition, the wearer can send signals to the receiving station by pressing a button, and the receiver can send a return signal to the wearer.

At present, the primary purpose of the device is to facilitate medical and therapeutic aid to patients, i.e., to effectuate the quick location and rescue of persons subject to emergency medical conditions that preclude their calling for help, such as cases of acute cardiac infarction, epilepsy or diabetes (Schwitzgebel, 1967a). Also, so far, the use of the device has been limited to volunteers, and they are free to remove the device whenever they wish (Schwitzgebel, 1967b). Schwitzgebel has expressed an interest in applying his device to monitoring and rehabilitating chronic recidivists on parole.

At the University of California, Los Angeles, Ralph Schwitzgebel's brother, Robert Schwitzgebel, has perfected a somewhat similar device in which a miniature two-way radio unit, encased in a wide leather belt containing its own antenna and rechargeable batteries, is worn by volunteer experimental subjects (R. Schwitzgebel, 1969). Non-voice communication is maintained between a central communications station and the wearer by means of a radio signal which, when sent, activates a small coil in the wearer's receiver unit that makes itself felt as a tap in the abdominal region, accompanied by a barely audible tone and a small light. Information is conveyed to the subject by a coded sequence of taps. In turn, the wearer can send simple coded signal messages back to the central station, indicating his receipt of the signal, his general state of well being, or the lack of it, and many other matters as well. So far, this device and its use depend entirely upon a relationship of cooperation and trust between experimenter and subject.

Another use of radiotelemetry on humans which has reached a high level of sophistication is the long-distance monitoring of ECG (electrocardiogram) waves by Caceres (1965) and his associates (Cooper, 1965; Hagan, 1965). They have developed a telemetry system by which an ambulatory heart patient can be monitored continuously by a central computer in another city. The patient has the usual electrocardiograph leads taped to his chest, which are connected to a small battery powered FM radio transmitter on the patient's belt. The ECG waves are transmitted, as modulated radio frequencies, to a transceiver in the vicinity which relays them via an ordinary telephone (encased in an automated dialing device called a Dataphone). The encoded signals of the ECG can then be transmitted to any place in the world which can be reached by telephone. On the receiving end, there is an automatic answering device that accepts the call and turns on the appropriate receiving equipment. In the usual case this will be an analog-to-digital converter, which quantizes the electrical waves and changes them to a series of numbers, representing amplitudes at certain precise times. The computer then analyzes the numerical amplitude values and, when an abnormal pattern appears, it not only warns the patient's physician (with a bell or light) but will produce, on request, some or all of the previous readings it has stored. The computer can monitor hundreds of patients simultaneously by sharing computer time among hundreds of input signals, and produce an "analysis" of ECG activity for each in as little as 2.5 minutes—the time required for the signal to get into the computer's analytical circuits. Although this "analysis" does not yet amount to a diagnosis of heart disease or the onset of an attack, there is no reason why computers could not be taught to read ECG patterns as well as any heart specialist, and with their ability to make stochastic analyses, in time they should become better at it than most doctors.

The third area where external telemetry has been used to advantage is also in the medical field. For several years, Vreeland and Yeager (1965) have been using a subminiature radiotelemeter for taking EEG's of epileptic children. The device is glued to the child's scalp with a special preparation and electrodes extend from it to various places on the child's scalp. A receiver is positioned in an adjoining room of the hospital and sound motion pictures record the child's behavior, his voice and his EEG on the same film. Some of the benefits derived from the use of this equipment are: (1) that it permits readings to be taken of an epileptic seizure as it occurs; and (2) it allows studies to be made of EEG patterns of disturbed children without encumbering them in trailing wires. At present however, the device is "external" in the sense that the electrodes do not penetrate into the brain, and only surface cortical brain wave patterns are picked up by the transmitter. It is believed, however, that many epileptic seizures originate in areas deep in the subcortical regions of the brain (Walker, 1961), and to obtain EEG readings for these areas, it would be necessary to implant the electrodes in these areas stereotaxically. The significance of such modification would be that if the transmitter were transformed into a transceiver (a minor modification), it would then be possible to stimulate the same subcortical areas telemetrically. This would, then, convert the telemetry system into an "internal" device, such as the ones we are now about to describe.

Internal Devices

One of the leaders in the field of internal radiotelemetry devices is Mackay (1961). He has developed devices which he calls "endoraidosondes." These are tiny transmitters that can be swallowed or implanted internally in man or animal. They have been designed in order to measure and transmit such physiological variables as gastrointestinal pressure, blood pressure, body temperature, bioelectrical potentials (voltage accompanying the functioning of the brain, the heart and other muscles), oxygen levels, acidity and radiation intensity (Mackay, 1965). In fact, in many cases for the purposes of biomedical and physiological research, internal telemetry is the only way of obtaining the desired data. In the case where the body functions do not emit electrical energy (as the brain, heart and other neuromuscular structures do), these devices have been ingeniously modified in order to measure changes in pressure, acidity, etc., and to transmit electrical signals reflecting these changes to receivers outside the body. In this case the transmitters are called "transducers." Both "active" and "passive" transmitters containing a battery powering an oscillator, and "passive" transmitters not containing an internal power source, but having instead tuned circuits modulated from an outside power source. Although "passive" systems enjoy the advantage of not being concerned with power failure or battery replacement, they do not put out as good a signal as an "active" system. Both transmitter systems, at present, have ranges of a few feet to a dozen—just enough to bring out the signal from inside the body (Mackay, 1965). Thus, it is generally necessary for the subject to carry a small booster transmitter in order to receive the weak signal from inside the body and increase its strength for rebroadcasting to a remote laboratory or data collection point. However, with the development of integrated circuits, both transmitters and boosters can be miniaturized to a fantastic degree.

Electrical Stimulation of the Brain

The technique employed in electrophysiology in studying the brain of animals and man by stimulating its different areas electrically is nothing new. This technique was being used by two European physiologists, Fritsch and Hitzig, on dogs in the latter half of the 19th Century (Sheer, 1961; Krech, 1966). In fact, much of the early work in experimental psychology was devoted to physiological studies of the human nervous system. During the last twenty years, however—perhaps as a result of equipment which allows the implantation of electrodes deep in the subcortical regions of the brain and the brain stem by stereotaxic instruments—the science of electrophysiology has received new impetus, and our understanding of neural activity within the brain and its behavioral and experiential correlates has been greatly expanded.

The electrical stimulation of various areas of the brain has produced a wide range of phenomena in animals and humans. An examination of published research in electrical stimulation of the brain suggests two crude methods of controlling human behavior: (1) by "blocking" of the response, through the production of fear, anxiety, disorientation, loss of memory and purpose, and even, if need be, by loss of consciousness; and (2) through conditioning behavior by the manipulation of rewarding and aversive stimuli (Jones, 1965). In this regard, the experiments of James Olds (1962; 1967) on animals and Robert G. Heath (1960) and his associates at Tulane on humans are particularly interesting. Both have shown the existence in animals and humans of brain areas of or near the hypothalamus which have what may be very loosely described as "rewarding" and "aversive" effects. The interesting thing about their experiments is that both animals and man will self-stimulate themselves at a tremendous rate in order to receive stimulation "rewards" regardless of, and sometimes in spite of, the existence of drives such as hunger and thirst. Moreover, their experiments have put a serious dent in the "drive-reduction" theory of operant conditioning under which a response eliciting a reward ceases or declines when a point of satiation is reached, since in their experiments no satiation point seems ever to be reached (the subject losing consciousness from physical exhaustion unless the stimulus is terminated beforehand by the experimenter). Thus their experiments indicate that there may be "pleasure centers" in the brain which are capable of producing hedonistic responses which are independent of drive reduction. In humans, however, the results of hypothalamus stimulation have not always been as clear as those with animals, and some experimenters have produced confusing and inconsistent results (King, 1961; Sem-Jacobsen, 1960).

Current research in the field of electrophysiology seems to hold out the possibility of exerting a limited amount of external control over the emotions, consciousness, memory and behavior of man by electrical stimulation of the brain. Krech (1966) quotes a leading electrophysiologist, Delgado of the Yale School of Medicine, as stating that current researches "support the distasteful conclusion that motion, emotion and behavior can be directed by electrical forces and that humans can be controlled like robots by push buttons." Although the authors have the greatest respect for Delgado's expertise in his field, they believe he overstates the case in this instance. None of the research indicates that man's every action can be directed by a puppeteer at an electrical keyboard; none indicates that thoughts can be placed into the heads of men electrically; none indicates that man can be directed like a mechanical robot. *At most*, they indicate that some of man's activities can possibly be deterred by such methods, that certain emotional states might be induced (with very uncertain consequences in different individuals), and that man might be conditioned along certain approved paths by "rewards" and "punishments" carefully administered at appropriate times. Techniques of direct brain stimulation developed in electrophysiology thus hold out the possibility of influencing and controlling selected human behavior within limited parameters.

The use, then, of telemetric systems as a method of monitoring man, of obtaining physiological data from his body and nervous system, and of stimulating his brain electrically from a distance, seems in the light of present research entirely feasible and possible as a method of control. There is, however, a gap in our knowledge which must be filled before telemetry and electrical stimulation of the brain could be applied to any control system. This gap is in the area of interpretation of incoming data. Before crime can be prevented, the monitor must know what the subject is doing or is about to do. It would not be practical to attach microphones to the monitored subjects, nor to have them in visual communication by television, and it would probably be illegal (Note: *Harvard Law Review*, 1966). Moreover, since the incoming data will eventually be fed into a computer,[1] it will be necessary to confine the information transmitted to the computer to such non-verbal, non-visual data as location, EEG patterns, ECG patterns and other physiological data. At the present time, EEG's tell us very little about what a person is doing or even about his emotional state (Konecci, 1965a). ECG's tell us little more than heart rhythms. Certain other physiological data, however, such as respiration, muscle tension, the presence of adrenalin in the blood stream, combined with knowledge of the subject's location, may be particularly revealing—e.g., a parolee with a past record of burglaries is tracked to a downtown shopping district (in fact, is exactly placed in a store known to be locked up for the night) and the physiological data reveals an increased respiration rate, a tension in the musculature and an increased flow of adrenalin. It would be a safe guess, certainly, that he was up to no good. The computer in this case, *weighing the probabilities*, would come to a decision and alert the police or parole officer so that they could hasten to the scene; or, if the subject were equipped with an implanted radiotelemeter, it could transmit an electrical signal which could block fur-

1. Obviously, no system monitoring thousands of parolees would be practical if there had to be a human monitor for every monitored subject on a 24 hour-a-day, seven-day-a-week basis. Therefore, computers would be absolutely necessary.

ther action by the subject by causing him to forget or abandon his project. However, before computers can be designed to perform such functions, a greater knowledge derived from experience in the use of these devices on human subjects, as to the correlates between the data received from them and their actual behavior, must be acquired.

Conditions Under Which Telemetry Techniques Might Initially be Applied In Correctional Programming

The development of sophisticated techniques of electronic surveillance and control could radically alter the conventional wisdom regarding the merits of imprisonment. It has been the opinion of many thoughtful penologists for sometime that prison life is not particularly conducive to rehabilitation (Sutherland, 1966; Sykes, 1966; Vold, 1954; Morris, 1963). Some correctional authorities, such as the Youth and Adult Corrections Agency of the State of California, have been exploring the possibilities of alternatives to incarceration, believing that the offender can best be taught "to deal lawfully with the given elements of the society while he functions, at least partially, in that society and not when he is withdrawn from it" (Geis, 1964). Parole is one way of accomplishing that objective, but parole is denied to many inmates of the prison system, not always for reasons to do with their ability to be reformed or the risk of allowing them release on parole. The development telemetric control systems could help increase the number of offenders who could safely and effectively be supervised within the community.

Schwitzgebel suggests (1967b) that it would be safe to allow the release of many poor-risk or nonparolable convicts into the community provided that their activities were continuously monitored by some sort of telemetric device. He states:

"A parolee thus released would probably be less likely than usual to commit offenses if a record of his location were kept at the base station. If two-way tone communication were included in this system, a therapeutic relationship might be established in which the parolee could be rewarded, warned, or otherwise signalled in accordance with the plan for therapy."

He also states:

"Security equipment has been designed, but not constructed that could insure the wearing of the transmitting equipment or indicate attempts to compromise or disable the system."

He further states that it has been the consistent opinion of inmates and parolees interviewed about the matter that they would rather put up with the constraints, inconveniences and annoyances of an electronic monitoring system, while enjoying the freedom outside an institution, than to suffer the much greater loss of privacy, restrictions on freedom, annoyance and inconveniences of prison life.

The envisioned system of telemetric control while offering many possible advantages to offenders over present penal measures also has several possible benefits for society. Society, through such systems, exercises control over behavior it defines as deviant, thus insuring its own protection. The offender, by returning to the community, can help support his dependents and share in the overall tax burden. The offender is also in a better position to make meaningful restitution. Because the control system works on conditioning principles, the offender is habituated into non-deviant behavior patterns—thus perhaps decreasing the probability of recidivism and, once the initial cost of development is absorbed, a telemetric control system might provide substantial economic advantage compared to rather costly correctional programs. All in all, the development of such a system could prove tremendously beneficial for society.

The adequate development of telemetric control systems is in part dependent upon their possible application. In order to ensure the beneficial use of such a system, certain minimal conditions ought to be imposed in order to forestall possible ethical and legal objections:

1. The consent of the inmate should be obtained, after a full explanation is given to him of the nature of the equipment, the limitations involved in its usage, the risks and constraints that will be placed upon his freedom, and the option he has of returning to prison if its use becomes too burdensome.

2. The equipment should not be used for purposes of gathering evidence for the prosecution of crimes, but rather should be employed as a crime prevention device. A law should be passed giving the users of this equipment an absolute privilege of keeping confidential all information obtained therefrom regardless of to whom it pertains, and all data should be declared as in-admissible in court. The parole authorities, if they be the users of this equipment, should have the discretionary power to revoke parole whenever they see fit without the burden of furnishing an explanation, thus relieving them of the necessity of using data obtained in this fashion as justification for their actions. The data should be destroyed after a certain period of time, and, if the system is hooked up with a computer, the computer should be programmed to erase its tapes after a similar period of time.

By employing the above safeguards, the use of a telemetric system should be entirely satisfactory to the community and to the convicts who choose to take advantage of it. Nevertheless there are a number of ethical objections which are bound to arise when such a system is initially employed that deserve special discussion.

Ethical Objections

The two principal objections raised against the use of modern technology for surveillance and control of persons deemed to be deviant in their behavior in such a degree as to warrant close supervision revolve around two issues: privacy and freedom (Note: *Harvard Law Review*, 1966; King, 1964; Miller, 1964; Fried, 1968; Ruebhausen, 1965).

Privacy

It has often been said that privacy, in essence, consists of the "right to be let alone" (Warren, 1890; Ernst, 1962). This is a difficult right to apply to criminals because it is precisely their inability to leave their fellow members of society alone that justifies not leaving them alone. This statement, however, might be interpreted to mean that there is a certain limited area where each man should be free from the scrutiny of his neighbors or his government and from interference in his affairs. While most people would accept this as a general proposition, in point of fact it is not recognized in prison administration, where surveillance and control are well-nigh absolute and total (Sykes, 1966; Clemmer, 1958). Therefore, it is difficult to see how the convict would lose in the enjoyment of whatever rights of privacy he has by electronic surveillance in the open community. If the watcher was a computer, this would be truer still, as most people do not object to being "watched" by electric eyes that open doors for them. It is the scrutiny of humans by humans that causes embarrassment—the knowledge that one is being judged by a fellow human.

Another definition of privacy is given by Ruebhausen (1965).

"The essence of privacy is no more, and certainly no less, than the freedom of the individual to pick and choose for himself the time and the circumstances under which, and most importantly, the extent to which, his attitudes, beliefs, behavior and opinions are to be shared with or withheld from others."

To this statement the preliminary question might be raised as to the extent to which we honor this value when we are dealing with convicts undergoing rehabilitation, mental patients undergoing psychiatric treatment, or even minors in our schools. Certainly it is not a statement that can be generally applied, especially in those cases where every society deems itself to have the right to shape and change the attitudes, beliefs, behavior and opinions of others when they are seriously out of step with the rest of society. But a more fundamental objection can be raised, in that the statement has little or no relevance to what we propose. Not only does the envisioned equipment lack the power to affect or modify directly the "attitudes," "beliefs" and "opinions" of the subject, but it definitely does not force him to share those mental processes with others. The subject is only limited in selected areas of his behavior—i.e., those areas in which society has a genuine interest in control. The subject is consequently "free" to hold any set of attitudes he desires. Of course, on the basis of behavioral psychology, one would expect attitudes, beliefs and opinions to change to conform with the subject's present behavior (Smith, 1968).

Still a third definition of privacy has been proposed by Fried (1968) in a recent article in the Yale Law Journal, an article which specifically discusses Schwitzgebel's device. He advances the argument that privacy is a necessary context for the existence of love, friendship and trust between people, and that the parolee under telemetric supervision who never feels himself loved or trusted will never be rehabilitated. While this argument might have some validity where the device is used as a therapeutic tool—a point that Schwitzgebel (1967b) recognizes since he would use it partly for that purpose—it is not particularly relevant where no personal relationship is established between the monitors and the subject and where the emphasis is placed upon the device's ability to control and deter behavior, rather than to "rehabilitate." Rehabilitation, hopefully, will follow once law-abiding behavior becomes habitual.

As far as privacy is concerned, most of the arguments are squarely met by the conditions and safeguards previously proposed. However, when one begins to implant endoradiosondes subcutaneously or to control actions through electrical stimulation of the brain, one runs into a particularly troublesome objection, which is often included within the scope of "privacy," although perhaps it should be separately named as the "human dignity" or "sacred vessel of the spirit" argument. This is the argument that was raised when compulsory vaccination was proposed, and which is still being raised as to such things as birth control, heart transplants, and proposals for the improvement of man through eugenics. The argument seems to stem from an ancient, well-entrenched belief that man, in whatever condition he finds himself, even in a state of decrepitude, is as Nature or God intended him to be and inviolable. Even when a man consents to have his physical organism changed, some people feel uneasy at the prospect, and raise objections.

Perhaps the only way to answer such an argument is to rudely disabuse people of the notion that there is any dignity involved in being a sick person, or a mentally disturbed person, or a criminal person whose acts constantly bring him into the degrading circumstances, which the very persons praising human dignity so willingly inflict upon him. Perhaps the only way to explode the notion of man as a perfect, or perfectible, being, made in God's image (the Bible), a little lower than the angels (Disraeli), or as naturally good but corrupted by civilization (Rousseau), is to review the unedifying career of man down through the ages and to point to some rather interesting facets of his biological make-up, animal-like-behavior, and evolutionary career which have been observed by leading biologists and zoologists (Lorenz, 1966; Morris, 1967; Rostand, 1959). Unfortunately, there is not time here to perform such a task or to rip away the veil of human vanity that so enshrouds these arguments.

Freedom

The first thing that should be said with regard to the issue of human freedom is that there is none to be found in most of our prisons. As Sykes (1966) remarks:

> "...the maximum security prison represents a social system in which an attempt is made to create and maintain total or almost total social control."

This point is so well recognized that it need not be belabored, but it does serve to highlight the irrelevancy of the freedom objection as far as the prison inmate is concerned. Any system which allows him the freedom of the open community, which maintains an unobtrusive surveillance and which intervenes only rarely to block or frustrate his activities can surely appear to him only as a vast improvement in his situation.

Most discussions of freedom discuss it as if man were the inhabitant of a natural world, rather than a social world. They fail to take into account the high degree of subtle regulation which social life necessarily entails. As Hebb (1961) put very well:

"What I am saying implies that civilization depends on an all-pervasive thought control established in infancy, which both maintains and is maintained by the social environment, consisting of the behavior of the members of society.... What we are really talking about in this symposium is mind in an accustomed social environment, and more particularly a social environment that we consider to be the normal one. It is easy to forget this, and the means by which it is achieved. The thought control that we object to, the 'tyranny over the mind of man' to which Jefferson swore 'eternal hostility,' is only the one that is imposed by some autocratic agency, and does not include the rigorous and doctrinaire control that society itself exercises, by common consent, in moral and political values. I do not suggest that this is undesirable. Quite the contrary, I argue that a sound society must have such a control, but let us at least see what we are doing. We do not bring up our children with open minds and then, when they can reason, let them reason and make up their minds as they will concerning the acceptability of incest, the value of courtesy in social relations, or the desirability of democratic government. Instead we tell them what's what, and to the extent that we are successful as parents and teachers, we see that they take it and make it part of their mental processes, with no further need of policing."

"The problem of thought control, or control of the mind, then, is not how to avoid it, considering it only as a malign influence exerted over the innocent by foreigners, Communists, and other evil fellows. We all exert it; only, on the whole, we are more efficient at it. From this point of view the course of developing civilization is, on the one hand, an increasing uniformity of aims and values, and thus also of social behavior, or on the other, an increasing emotional tolerance of the stranger, the one who differs from me in looks, beliefs, or action—a tolerance, however that still has narrow limits."

Discussions of freedom that one customarily finds in law journals also fail to take into account the distinction between objective and subjective freedom. Objective freedom for each man is a product of power, wealth or authority, since it is only through the achievement of one or more of these that one can control so as not to be controlled—i.e., it is only through these that one can, on one hand, guard against the abuses, infringements, and overreaching of one's fellow man which limit one, and, on the other hand, commit those very offenses against one's neighbor and, by doing so, obtain all one's heart desires. This is not to neglect the role of the law in preventing a war of all against all, in providing the freedom that goes with peace, and with ensuring that all share to a certain extent in the protections and benefits of a well-ordered society. But laws are themselves limitations imposed upon objective freedom. Radical objective freedom is inconsistent with social life, since in order for some to have it, others must be denied it. Such a radical freedom may also be intolerable psychologically; one may actually feel "constrained" by an excess of options (Fromm, 1963).

Subjective freedom, on the other hand, is a sense of not being pressed by the demands of authority and nagged by unfulfilled desires. It is totally dependent on *awareness*. Such a concept of freedom is easily realizable within the context of an ordered society, whereas radical objective freedom is not. Since society cannot allow men too much objective freedom, the least it can do (and the wise thing to do) is to so order its affairs that men are not aware or concerned about any lack of it. The technique of telemetric control of human beings offers the possibility of regulating behavior with precision on a subconscious level, and avoiding the cruelty of depriving man of his subjective sense of freedom.

Conclusion

Two noted psychologists, C.R. Rogers and B.F. Skinner, carried on a debate in the pages of *Science* magazine (1956) over the issue of the moral responsibility of behavioral scientists in view of the everwidening techniques of behavior control. Skinner said:

"The dangers inherent in the control of human behavior are very real. The possibility of misuse of scientific knowledge must always be faced. We cannot escape by denying the power of a science of behavior or arresting its development. It is no help to cling to familiar philosophies of human behavior simply because they are more reassuring. As I have pointed out elsewhere, the new techniques emerging from a science of behavior must be subject to the explicit counter control which has already been applied to earlier and cruder forms."

Skinner's point was that the scientific age had arrived; there was no hope of halting its advance; and that scientist could better spend their time explaining the nature of their discoveries so that proper controls might be applied (not to stop the advance, but to direct it into the proper channels), rather than in establishing their own set of goals and their own *ne plus ultra* to "proper research." This is a valid point. Victor Hugo once said: "Nothing is as powerful as an idea whose time has arrived." The same holds true for a technology whose time is upon us. Those countries whose social life advances to keep pace with their advancing technology will survive in the world of tomorrow; those that look backward and cling to long-outmoded values will fall into the same state of degradation that China suffered in the 19th and early 20th Centuries because she cherished too much the past. These are not inappropriate remarks to make here, because the nations that can so control behavior as to control the crime problem will enjoy an immense advantage over those that do not. Whether we like it or not, changes in technology require changes in political and social life and in values most adaptable to those changes. It would be ironic indeed if science, which was granted, and is granted, the freedom to invent weapons of total destruction, were not granted a similar freedom to invent methods of controlling the humans who wield them.

Rogers agreed with Skinner that human control of humans is practiced everywhere in social and political life, but framed the issues differently. He said (1956):

"...They can be stated very briefly: Who will be controlled? Who will exercise control? What type of control will be exercised? Most important of all, toward what end or what purpose, in pursuit of what values, will control be exercised?"

These are very basic questions. They need to be answered, and they should be answered.

Jean Rostand (1959), a contemporary French biologist of note, asks: can man be modified? He points to the fact that, since the emergence of *homo sapiens* over 100,000 years ago, man has not evolved physically in the slightest degree. He has the same brain now that he had then, except that now it is filled up with the accumulated knowledge of 5,000 years of civilization—knowledge that has not seemed to be adequate to the task of erasing certain primitive humanoid traits, such as intraspecific aggression, which is a disgusting trait not even common to most animals. Seeing that man now possesses the capabilities of effecting certain changes in his biological structure, he asks whether it isn't a reasonable proposal for man to hasten evolution along by modifying himself into something better than what he has been for the last 100,000 years. We believe that this is a reasonable proposal, and ask: What better place to start than with those individuals most in need of a change for the better?

References

Barr, N.L.
   1960 "Telemetering Physiological Responses During Experimental Flight." *American Journal of Cardiology* 6:54.
Caceres, C.A. and James K. Cooper
   1965 "Radiotelemetry: A Clinical Perspective." *Biomedical Telemetry*. Edited by C.A. Caceres. New York: Academic Press.
Clemmer, Donal
   1958 *The Prison Community*. New York: Holt, Rinehart and Winston.
Cooper, James K. and C. A. Caceres
   1965 "Telemetry by Telephone." *Biomedical Telemetry*. Edited by C.A. Caceres. New York: Academic Press.
Ernst, Morris L. and Alan U. Schwartz
   1962 *Privacy: The Right to Be Let Alone*. New York: Macmillan.

Epstein, R.J., J.R. Haumann and R.B. Keener
    V1968 "An Implantable Telemetry Unit for Accurate Body Temperature Measurements." *Journal of Applied Physiology* 24(3):439.
Fried, Charles
    1968 "Privacy." *Yale Law Journal* 77:475.
Fromm, Erich
    1963 *Escape From Freedom*. New York: Holt, Rinehart and Winston.
Geis, Gilbert
    1964 "The Community-Centered Correctional Residence." Correction in the Community: Alternatives to Incarceration. Sacramento, California: Youth and Adult Corrections Agency, State of California.
Grisamore, N.T., James K. Cooper and C.A. Caceres
    1965 "Evaluating Telemetry." *Biomedical Telemetry*. Edited by C.A. Caceres. New York: Academic Press.
Hagan, William K.
    1965 "Telephone Applications." *Biomedical Telemetry*. Edited by C.A. Caceres. New York: Academic Press.
Heath, R.G. and W. A. Mickle
    1960 "Evaluation of Seven Years' Experience with Depth Electrode Studies in Human Patients." *Electrical Studies of the Unanesthetized Brain*. Edited by E.R. Ramey and D.S. O'Doherty. New York: Paul B. Hoeber, Inc.
Hebb, D.O.
    1961 "The Role of Experience." *Man and Civilization: Control of the Mind; A Symposium*. Edited by Seymour M. Farber and R.H.L. Wilson. New York: McGraw-Hill.
Jones, H.G., Michael Gelder and H.M. Holden
    1965 "Behavior and Aversion Therapy in the Treatment of Delinquency." *British Journal of Criminology* 5(4):355-387.
King, D.B.
    1964 "Electronic Surveillance and Constitutional Rights: Some Current Developments and Observations." *George Washington Law Review* 33:240.
King, H.E.
    1961 "Psychological Effects of Excitation in the Limbic System." *Electrical Stimulation of the Brain*. Edited by Daniel E. Sheer. Austin: University of Texas Press.
Konecci, E.B. and A. James Shiner
    1965a "The Developing Challenge of Biosensor and Bioinstrumentation Research." *Biomedical Telemetry*. Edited by C.A. Caceres. New York: Academic Press.
    1965b "Uses of Telemetry in Space." *Biomedical Telemetry*. Edited by C.A. Caceres. New York: Academic Press.
Krech, David
    1966 "Controlling the Mind-Controllers." *Think* 32(July-August):2.

Lord, R.D., F.C. Bellrose and W.W. Cochran
1962 "Radiotelemetry of the Respiration of a Flying Duck." *Science* 137:39.

Lorenz, Konrad
1966 *On Aggression*. New York: Harcourt, Brace and World, Inc.

Mackay, R.S.
1961 "Radiotelemetering from Within the Body." *Science* 134:1196.
1965 "Telemetry from Within the Body of Animals and Man: End-oradiosondes." *Biomedical Telemetry*. Edited by C.A. Caceres. New York: Academic Press.

Miller, A.S.
1964 "Technology, Social Change and the Constitution." *George Washington Law Review* 33:17.

Morris, Desmond
1967 *The Naked Ape*. New York: McGraw-Hill.

Morris, Terrence and Paulene Morris
1963 *Pentonville: A Sociological Study of an English Prison*. London: Routledge and Kegan Paul.

Note
1966 "Anthropotelemetry: Dr. Schwitzgebel's Machine." *Harvard Law Review* 80:403.

Olds, James
1962 "Hypothalamic Substrates of Reward." *Physiological Reviews* 42:554.
1967 "Emotional Centers in the Brain." *Science Journal* 3(5):87.

Reubhausen, O.M. and O.G. Brim
1965 "Privacy and Behavior Research." *Columbia Law Review* 65:1184.

Rogers, C.R. and B.F. Skinner
1956 "Some Issues Concerning the Control of Human Behavior." *Science* 124:1057.

Rostand, Jean
1959 *Can Man Be Modified?*. London: Secker and Warburg.

Schwitzgebel, Ralph, Robert Schwitzgebel, W.N. Pahnke and W.S. Hurd
1964 "A Program of Research in Behavioral Electronics." *Behavioral Science* 9:233.

Schwitzgebel, Ralph
1967a "Electronic Innovation in the Behavioral Sciences: A Call to Responsibility." *American Psychologist* 22(5):364.
1967b "Issues in the Use of an Electronic Rehabilitation System and Chronic Recidivists." (unpublished paper).

Schwitzgebel, Robert L.
1969 "A Belt from Big Brother." *Psychology Today* 2(11):45-47, 65.

Sem-Jacobsen, C.W. and Arne Torkildsen
1960 "Depth Recording and Electrical Stimulation in the Human

Brain." *Electrical Studies of the Unanesthetized Brain*. Edited by E.R. Ramey and D.S. O'Doherty. New York: Paul B. Hoeber, Inc.

Sheer, Daniel
1961 "Brain and Behavior: The Background of Interdisciplinary Research," *Electrical Stimulation of the Brain*. Edited by Daniel Sheer. Austin: University of Texas Press.

Slater, Lloyd E.
1965 "A Broad-Brush Survey of Biomedical Telemetric Progress." *Biomedical Telemetry*. Edited by C.A. Caceres. New York: Academic Press.

Smith, Gerald W.
1968 "Electronic Rehabilitation and Control: An Alternative to Prison." Paper read at the American Correctional Association Meeting, San Francisco.

Sperry, C.J., C.P. Gadsden, C. Rodriguez and L.N.N. Bach
1961 "Miniature Subcutaneous Frequency-Modulated Transmitter for Brain Potentials." *Science* 134:1423.

Sutherland, Edwin and Donald R. Cressey
1966 *Principles of Criminology*. Seventh Edition. Philadelphia: Lippincott.

Sykes, Gresham
1966 *The Society of Captives*. New York: Atheneum.

Vold, George B.
1954 "Does Prison Reform?" *Annals of the American Academy of Political and Social Science* 293:42-50.

Vreeland, Robert and C.L. Yeager
1965 "Application of Subminiature Radio Telemetry Equipment to EEG Analysis from Active Subjects." Paper delivered at Sixth International Congress of Electroencephalography and Clinical Neurophysiology, Vienna.

Walker, A.E. and Curtis Marshall
1961 "Stimulation and Depth Recording in Man." *Electrical Stimulation of the Brain*. Edited by Daniel Sheer. Austin: University of Texas Press.

Warren, Samuel D. and Louis D. Brandeis
1890 "The Right to Privacy." *Harvard Law Review* 4:193.

Young, I.J. and W.S. Naylor
1964 "Implanted Two-Way Telemetry in Laboratory Animals." *American Journal of Medical Electronics* 3:28.

The Control of Conduct: Authority vs. Autonomy*

Thomas S. Szasz
Professor of Psychiatry, State University of New York, Upstate Medical Center, Syracuse

There is only one political sin: independence; and only one political virtue: obedience. To put it differently, there is only one offense against authority: self-control; and only one obeisance to it: submission to control by authority.

Why is self-control, autonomy, such a threat to authority? Because the person who controls himself, who is his own master, has no need for an authority to be his master. This, then, renders authority unemployed. What is he to do if he cannot control others? To be sure, he could mind his own business. But this is a fatuous answer, for those who are satisfied to mind their own business do not aspire to become authorities. In short, authority needs subjects, persons not in command of themselves—just as parents need children and physicians need patients. Hence, too, the paradox that self-control may be defined as precisely that capacity which, the less of it a person possesses, the more of it the authorities want him to have, and the more of it he possesses, the less of it they want him to have.

Autonomy is the death knell of authority, and authority knows it: hence, the ceaseless warfare of authority against the exercise, both real and symbolic, of autonomy—that is, against suicide, against masturbation, against self-medication, against the proper use of language itself.[1]

Control

The parable of the Fall illustrates this fight to the death between control and self-control. Did Eve, tempted by the Serpent, seduce Adam, who then lost control of himself and succumbed to evil? Or did Adam, facing a choice between obedience to the authority of God and his own destiny, choose self-control?

How, then, shall we view the situation of all those countless persons who are now considered to be "mentally ill" and are called "mental patients"? For example, how shall we view the so-called neurotic, who may be fearful, depressed, obsessive, compulsive, and so forth; or the so-called psychotic, who may feel too important or not important enough, may refuse to eat or

---

1. See Szasz, *The Second Sin* (Doubleday, Inc. 1973), and *Ceremonial Chemistry* (Doubleday, Inc. 1974).

---

* Reprinted, with the author's permission, from *Criminal Law Bulletin*, vol. 11 (1975).

speak or sleep, be depressed and suicidal, and so forth; or the so-called pervert, who may engage in sexual practices disapproved by ecclesiastic, legal, and psychiatric authorities; or the so-called drug abuser or drug addict, who may ingest chemicals forbidden by legal and medical authorities?

Should we think of these persons (the list is, of course, virtually inexhaustible) as stupid, sick, and helpless children—lured by forbidden impulses or unconscious drives, pressured by hormones or peers, tempted by the pleasures of caresses or chemicals—succumbing to "irrestible impulses" and thus losing control of themselves? Or should we think of them as persons in control of themselves, choosing, like Adam, the forbidden fruit as the elemental and elementary way of affirming their identity by pitting themselves against authority?

There is, as a rule, no empirical or scientific way of choosing between these two answers, of deciding which is right and which is wrong. The questions frame two different moral perspectives, and the answers define two different moral strategies.

If we side with authority and wish to repress the individual, we shall treat him *as if* he were helpless, the innocent victim of overwhelming temptation. We shall then "protect" him from further temptation by treating him as a child, a slave, or a madman. The so-called mental patient is thus typically viewed as someone who has, or is alleged to have, lost control of himself. Psychiatry and behavioral science supply the ideology and the justification, and the courts and the police supply the authority and the power, for controlling him.

If we side with the individual and wish to refute the legitimacy and reject the power of authority to infantilize him, we shall treat him *as if* he were in command of himself, the executor of responsible decisions. We shall then demand that he respect others as he respects himself by treating him as an adult, a free individual, or a "rational" person. However, the person securely in control of himself frustrates others from controlling him; hence, he is the object of both admiration and envy, awe and hate.

Either of these positions and policies makes sense. What makes less sense—what is confusing in principle and chaotic in practice—is to treat people as both adults and children, as both free and unfree, as both sane and insane.

Nevertheless, this is just what social authorities throughout history have done: In ancient Greece, in medieval Europe, in the contemporary world, we find various mixtures in the attitudes of the authorities toward the people. In some societies, the individual is treated as more free than unfree, and we call these societies "free"; in others, he is treated as more determined than self-determining, and we call these societies "totalitarian." In none is the individual treated as completely free. Perhaps this would be impossible: Many persons insist that no society could survive on such a premise consistently carried through. Perhaps this is something that lies in the future of mankind. In any case, we should take satisfaction in the evident impossibility of the opposite situation: No society has ever treated the individual, nor perhaps could it treat him, as completely determined. The apparent freedom of the authority, controlling both himself and subject, provides an irresistible model: If God can control, if pope and prince can control, if politician and psychiatrist can control—then perhaps the person can also control, at least himself.

Power

The conflicts between those who have power and those who want to take it away from them fall into three distinct categories. In moral, political, and social affairs (and I, of course, include psychiatric affairs among these), these categories must be clearly distinguished. If we do not distinguish among them, we are likely to mistake opposition to absolute or arbitrary power with what may, actually, be an attempt to gain such power for oneself or for the groups or leaders one admires.

First, there are those who want to take power away from the oppressor and give it to the oppressed as a class—as exemplified by Marx, Lenin, and the Communists. Revealingly, they dream of the "dictatorship" of the proletariat or some other group.

Second, there are those who want to take power away from the oppressor and give it to themselves as the protectors of the oppressed—as exemplified by Robespierre in politics; Rush in medicine; and by their liberal, radical, and medical followers. Revealingly, they dream of the incorruptibly honest or incontrovertibly sane ruler leading his happy or healthy flock.

And third, there are those who want to take power away from the oppressor and give it to the oppressed as individuals, for each to do with as he pleases, but hopefully for his own self-control—as exemplified by Mill, von Mises, the free-market economists, and their libertarian followers. Revealingly, they dream of people so self-governing that their need for and tolerance of rulers is minimal or nil.

While countless men say they love liberty, clearly only those who, by virtue of their actions, fall into the third category, mean it.[2] The others merely want to replace a hated oppressor by a loved one—having usually themselves in mind for the job.

Psychiatrists, psychologists, and other so-called mental health professionals have traditionally opted for "reforms" of the second type; that is, their opposition to existing powers, ecclesiastic or secular, has had as its conscious and avowed aim the paternalistic care of the citizen-patient, and not the freedom of the autonomous individual, Hence, medical methods of social control tended not only to replace religious methods, but sometimes to exceed them in stringency and severity. In short, the usual response of medical authority to the controls exercised by nonmedical authority has been to try to take over and then escalate the controls, rather than to endorse the principle

---

2. See especially von Mises, *Human Action* (Yale University Press 1949).

and promote the practice of removing the controls by which the oppressed are victimized.

As a result, until recently, most psychiatrists, psychologists, and other behavioral scientists had nothing but praise for the "behavior controls" of medicine and psychiatry. We are now beginning to witness, however, a seeming backlash against this position. Many behavioral scientists are jumping on what they evidently consider to be the next "correct" and "liberal" position, namely, a criticism of behavioral controls. But since most of these "scientists" remain as hostile as they have always been to individual freedom and responsibility, to choice and dignity, their criticism conforms to the pattern I have described earlier: They demand more "controls"—that is, professional and governmental controls—over "behavior controls." This is like first urging a person to drive over icy roads at breakneck speed to get over them as fast as possible, and then, when his car goes into a skid, advising him to apply his brakes. Whether because they are stupid or wicked or both, such persons invariably recommend fewer controls where more are needed, for example in relation to punishing offenders—and more controls where fewer are needed, for example in relation to contracts between consenting adults.

The supporters of the Therapeutic State are tireless: Now they are proposing more therapeutic controls in the name of "controlling behavior controls." Typical of this trend is the view, and the policy it engenders and justifies, that there is a class of human beings whose members although innocent of crime, may justly be deprived of liberty in psychiatric institutions, but who, while so deprived of liberty, are alleged to possess a "constitutional right to treatment." This position is now officially endorsed not only by the American Psychiatric Association and the United States Department of Justice, but, characteristically, also by the American Civil Liberties Union.[3]

Clearly, the seeds of this fundamental human propensity—to react to the loss of control, or to the threat of such loss, with an intensification of control, thus generating a spiraling symbiosis of escalating controls and countercontrols—have fallen on fertile soil in contemporary medicine and psychiatry and have yielded a luxuriant harvest of "therapeutic" coercions. Our attitude toward these practices—that is, whether we approach them with a favorable or unfavorable prejudice—will depend largely on our attitude toward the two fundamental methods of regulating social relations.

Principles for Regulating Social Relations

There are two basic principles and procedures for regulating social relations, and two only: contracts, or agreements reached willingly and voluntarily between consenting parties; and commands, or codes of conduct imposed by stronger parties on weaker ones.

3. See, for example, Szasz, "The ACLU's 'Mental Illness' Cop-Out," 5 Reason, 4-9 (Jan. 1974); Shapiro, "Legislating the Control of Behavior Control," So. 47 Cal.L.Rev., 237-356 (Feb. 1974); and Ballantine, Jr., "Who Should Control the Scalpel?" Prism 42-43, 50-51 (Jan. 1975).

Free societies are characterized by the fact that—or are free because—the scope for contracting in them is large, while the scope for being commanded is relatively small. That is, the relations between the rulers and the ruled are hedged in by contractual guarantees-constitutions, the common law, the "rule of law" itself; and relations among the ruled themselves are largely governed by contracts. Despotic or totalitarian societies, on the other hand, are characterized by the fact that—or perhaps are unfree because—the scope for being commanded in them is large, while the scope for contracting is negligible. The relations between the rulers and the ruled are here unfettered by constitutional or other enforceable limits; and the relations among the ruled themselves are almost wholly bureaucratic rather than contractual.

It has been well established—indeed, no one disagrees with the contention—that in the case of psychiatric sanctions, coercion flows from the judgment of authorities, not from the breaking of contracts. In the Therapeutic State toward which we are marching under the banner of Health and Medicine, law is replaced by psychiatry, crime by insanity, and justice by therapy.[4] Those, then, who want to preserve or enlarge our traditional liberties must view any reduction in the scope of contracting with caution; and must view any such reduction justified by psychiatric considerations and replaced by psychiatric methods of control with positive alarm.

---

4. See Szasz, *Law, Liberty, and Psychiatry* (Macmillan Co., Inc. 1963); *Psychiatric Justice* (Macmillan Co., Inc. 1965); and *Ideology and Insanity* (Doubleday Anchor 1970).

RESTITUTION: DEAD OR ALIVE?

One of the most popular proposals of the 1970s has been to incorporate restitution into the criminal justice system. Since under most circumstances, restitution to the crime victim occurs after conviction and sentencing, it would be proper to consider it part of the corrections segment of the system.

This is not a new concept, especially if one wishes to argue that personal reparation by the offender or his family was the basis of primitive and early Western law.[1] Early restitution provisions can be found in the Law of Moses, early English law, the Dooms of Alfred, and numerous other places.[2] There was an extensive airing of restitution proposals at the Sixth International Penal Conference of 1900[3] but very little was heard after that until English reformer Margery Fry took up the cause in the 1950s.[4] Kathleen Smith created a short stir in the 1960s, when she postulated an entire penal system based upon restitution.[5] The end result of these intermittent rallies was the development, throughout the American and Anglo world, of victim compensation plans in which the state footed the bill for programs which paid limited monies to limited numbers of victims of violent crimes.

In the past, most writers rejected the idea of restitution as impractical, given the massive problems involved in obtaining an offender who was willing and able to pay. Not only would the convicted offender have to be put into some type of community-based supervision, he would also have to be provided with both the skills and the opportunity to earn enough money to make significant payments.

But a number of things happened in the 1970s to bring back the idea of restitution. Perhaps most important was the announcement by the U.S. Department of Justice's Law Enforcement Assistance Administration that it

1. Marvin E. Wolfgang, "Victim Compensation in Crimes of Personal Violence," in Walter C. Reckless and Charles L. Newman, eds., *Interdisciplinary Problems in Criminology*, (1969), p. 169.

2. See E. Adamson Hoebel, *The Law of Primitive Man*, (1954), pp. 310-318; Egan Bittner and Anthony Platt, "The Meaning of Punishment," *Issues in Criminology*, vol. 2 (1966), pp. 83-84; Margery Fry, *Arms of the Law*, (London, 1951), p. 124; R.H. Hodgkin, *A History of the Anglo-Saxons*, (1935), p. 270; Stephen Schafer, *The Victim and His Criminal*, (New York: Random House, 1968), p. 16.

3. Samuel June Barrows, *The Sixth International Congress, Brussels, 1900, Report of Its Proceedings and Conclusions*, (1903).

4. Fry, *Arms of the Law*; Margery Fry, "Justice for Victims," *Journal of Public Law*, vol. 8 (1959), pp. 191-194.

5. Kathleen J. Smith, *A Cure for Crime: The Case of the Self-Determinate Sentence*, (London: Duckworth, 1965).

was interested in restitution by the offender, and that it was willing to fund a number of major restitution projects across the country. Needless to say, applications were quickly forthcoming and programs were set up.

The literature and programs coming out of Minnesota, especially those by Burt Galaway of the University of Minnesota at Duluth, have been particularly instrumental in promoting the current trend towards restitution. The publication of books and numerous articles on the subject as well as the organization of national conferences on restitution, and a parole restitution project in a halfway house also did much to stimulate interest.[6]

Restitution, of course, had been used more or less informally for many years across America, perhaps most commonly as a condition of probation. More than a decade ago, the President's Commission on Law Enforcement and the Administration of Justice Task Force on Corrections noted that "it is not uncommon for a large probation agency to supervise the collection of millions of dollars in restitution for crime victims each year."[7]

Thus, by being given the power to recommend to the court whether restitution should be paid, and the amount due, probation officers in some jurisdictions are placed in almost the same position as civil court judges. "Too often, victims, particularly corporate victims, seek to gain through restitution conditions that which they would have great difficulty in gaining in civil court. Civil courts are meticulous in restoring exactly what has been lost.... Since the criminal court judge rarely conducts a full-dress hearing on the question of restitution, preferring to assign resolution of the matter to the probation officer, the judicial effect of the probation officer's determination of restitution is significant indeed."[8]

There are, of course, many other more informal procedures for restitution. Insurance companies, for example, are often willing not to prosecute if they are given the opportunity to purchase or accept the return of a stolen item,[9] and, when arrested, professional thieves commonly offer to yield up

6. See Burt Galaway, "The Uses of Restitution," *Crime and Delinquency*, vol. 23 (January 1977), pp. 57-67; Joe Hudson and Burt Galaway, "Undoing the Wrong," *Social Work*, vol. 19 (May 1974), pp. 313-318; Joe Hudson, Burt Galaway, and Steve Chesney, "When Criminals Repay Their Victims," *Judicature*, vol. 60 (February 1977), pp. 312-321; Burt Galaway, "Restitution as an Integrative Punishment," in Randy E. Barnett and John Hegel III, eds., *Assessing the Criminal, Restitution, Retribution and the Legal Process*, (New York: Bellringer Press, 1977); Burt Galaway and Joe Hudson, eds., *Offender Restitution in Theory and Action*, (Lexington, Mass.: Lexington Books, 1978); Joe Hudson and Burt Galaway, eds., *Considering the Victim: Readings in Restitution and Victim Compensation*, (Springfield, Ill.: Charles C. Thomas, 1975).

7. President's Commission on Law Enforcement and the Administration of Justice, *Task Force Report: Corrections*, (Washington, D.C.: U.S. Government Printing Office, 1967), p. 35.

8. Eugene H. Czajkoski, "The Quasi-Judicial Role of the Probation Officer in the Operation of the Court," paper presented at the annual meeting of the Academy of Criminal Justice Sciences, Omaha, Nebraska, 24 March 1973; See also Irving E. Cohen, "Twilight Zones in Probation," *Journal of Criminal Law and Criminology*, vol. 37 (1946), p. 291.

9. "Note, Restitution and the Criminal Law," *Columbia Law Review*, vol. 39 (1939), p. 1202.

stolen property in exchange for a promise not to prosecute.[10] In many cases, before sentence is passed, judges will take into consideration the fact that restitution was made.[11] In some crimes, however, such as embezzlement, the case is never reported to authorities because some kind of restitution agreement has been worked out between the private parties.

Both of the authors of the articles which follow understand that there are many obstacles to implementing restitution schemes. Where they differ is in their optimism concerning the ability of the criminal justice system to incorporate restitution goals into its operating procedures.

Galaway, while recognizing that not all the LEAA-funded programs worked well in promoting restitution, ultimately concludes that "many of the practical issues which are frequently raised in regard to restitution can be resolved."

Klein, having operated a pilot restitution program, examines some of the objections to the issue and comes to a rather different conclusion. He looks at a particular set of recommendations and a particular set of laws—regarding the Canadian criminal justice system—and concludes that the problems may not be resolvable.

Though Klein centers in on the work and suggestions of the Law Reform Commission of Canada, the problems and laws he discusses are not very different from those in any American state, and his observations and conclusions are equally relevant to this country's criminal justice system.

---

10. Wolfgang, "Victim Compensation," p. 229.
11. Dan Robertson, "Payments of Compensation to Victims of Crimes of Violence," *Prison Service Journal*, vol. 3 (1964), p. 21.

Is Restitution Practical?*

Burt Galaway
School of Social Development, University of Minnesota, Duluth

The idea that wrongdoers should be required to make a payment of money or services to their victims is an ancient concept which may be on the verge of a renaissance in the American criminal justice system. Restitution by the offender to the victim of crime has likely been a part of probation practice since the probation services were developed in the mid- and latter 19th century. Restitution, however, has not been placed in a central role in the American criminal justice system; with the development of psychological and psychiatric approaches to dealing with the offender during the 20th century, restitution has been further discounted and relegated to a peripheral role. Mounting evidence discrediting the effectiveness of coerced therapy in the criminal justice system,[1] increasing costs of imposing traditional criminal justice sanctions, and the tendency of criminal justice officials to ignore the victim of crimes have all contributed during the past few years to a renewed interest in the ancient concept of restitution.

Beginning in the early 1970's a number of pilot restitution programs have been established in the United States and Canada.[2] During 1976 and 1977 the Law Enforcement Assistance Administration has systematically funded a series of pilot adult and juvenile restitution programs to further test the feasibility of using this concept in the criminal justice system. At present there is a critical need for a review and synthesis of the experiences of restitution programming initiated in the 1970's. Unfortunately no one is presently seriously considering such a review. Presently, considerable attention is being given to expanding restitution programming and conceptualizing restitution as a more central component in the criminal justice system. Arguments are being advanced to support the use of restitution as a punishment for crime,[3] a second line of argument has been advanced to define the purpose of the criminal justice processes as insuring that crime victims receive restitu-

1. Douglas Liton, Robert Martinson, and Judith Wilks, *The Effectiveness of Correctional Treatment—A Survey of Treatment Evaluation Studies*, Springfield: Praeger Publishers, 1975.

2. Burt Galaway, "The Use of Restitution." *Crime and Delinquency*, 23:1 (January 1977), 57-67; Joe Hudson, Burt Galaway, and Steve Chesney, "When Criminals Repay Their Victims: A Survey of Restitution Programs," *Judicature*, 60:7 (February 1977), 312-321.

3. Stephen Schafer, *Compensation and Restitution to Victims of Crime* (Montclair: Patterson Smith, 1970), 117-129; Burt Galaway, "Restitution as an Integrative Punishment," in Randy E. Barnett and John Hegel III (eds.), *Assessing the Criminal: Restitution, Retribution, and the Legal Process* (New York: Bellringer Press, 1977).

* Reprinted, with the author's permission, from *Federal Probation*, vol. 41 (1977), pp. 3-8.

tion from offenders.[4] Some practical problems at operationalizing the restitution concept must be conceptualized and resolved before either of these offender or victim oriented purposes for the use of restitution can be realized.

Determining the Amount of Restitution

A number of problems are associated with assessing the amount of restitution. These include the problems of victim overestimation of losses, whether the victim should receive restitution for nonmonetary losses such as pain and suffering, whether the offender should be required to make restitution in excess of victim losses, and the appropriate procedures for determining the amount of restitution. Many of the presently operating pilot restitution programs report some concerns that victims may inflate loss claims and, in effect, attempt to victimize the offender. No evidence exists as to the extent to which this occurs and an equally plausible and theoretically sound rival hypothesis is that in many cases offenders may underestimate the extent of damage done.[5] The neutralization strategies hypothesized by Sykes and Matza[6] as well as the justification strategies formulated by the social equity theorists[7] suggest that offenders may frequently deal with their own sense of guilt and distress by minimizing the extent of damages caused to the victim. Additionally, many offenders are unlikely to have an experience base from which to make realistic estimates of repair costs and damages done to property and thus may tend, from their own lack of knowledge and experience, to underestimate the damages resulting from their criminal behavior. Differences between victim and offender estimates of damages resulting from the criminal offenses may be as likely to result from offender underestimation as the victim overestimation of losses.

Most pilot restitution programs have developed workable procedures for resolving this problem. Two clear models, an arbitration and a negotiation process, are presently in use to arrive at the amount of the restitution obligation. In the arbitration model a neutral expert (usually a judge but frequently a probation officer) receives information from victims and offenders and arrives at a restitution amount which is then binding upon the offender (the amount is not necessarily binding upon the victim, however, who does have the resource of civil suit available). The negotiation model is operationalized by the Minnesota Restitution Center[8] and several other projects[9] which bring

---

4. Randy Barnett, "Restitution: A New Paradigm of Criminal Justice," *Ethics* 87:4 (July 1977), 279-301.

5. Burt Galaway and William Marsella, "An Exploratory Study of the Perceived Fairness of Restitution as a Sanction for Juvenile Offenders," paper presented Second International Symposium on Victimology, Boston, Massachusetts, September 1976.

6. David Matza and Gresham Sykes, "Techniques of Neutralization: A Theory of Delinquency," *American Sociology Review* 22 (1957), 664-669.

7. Elaine Walster, Ellen Berscheid, G. William Walster, "New Directions in Equity Research," *Journal of Personalty and Social Psychology*, 25 (1973), 151-176.

8. Joe Hudson and Burt Galaway, "Undoing the Wrong: The Minnesota Restitution Center," *Social Work*, 19 (May 1974), 313-318; Robert Mowatt, "The Minnesota Restitution Center:

the victim and offender together with a staff member of the restitution project to negotiate a restitution agreement. Both of these approaches appear to be workable procedures for arriving at a restitution amount. The arbitration model may have the advantage of efficiency and will involve minimal criminal justice staff time at arriving at a restitution decision. The mediation model is more likely to produce a restitution decision which is acceptable and perceived as just by the parties involved due to their own input into the decisionmaking process. This model further has the advantage of bringing the victim and offender into direct communication and should reduce stereotypes which they may have held of each other.

To what extent should victims receive reimbursement for nontangible losses such as pain, suffering, and emotional distress? The predominant pattern among present restitution programs is to limit restitution to out-of-pocket losses sustained by the victims. For the most part, restitution is used with property offenders; with property offenses nontangible losses are sufficiently rare and, if present, extremely difficult to quantify which may account for their omission from present restitution schemes. The future development of restitution programming should build on past experience and not attempt to include pain, suffering, and other nontangible losses in restitution agreements. If victims feel strongly that they should be reimbursed for these damages they should, of course, be free to pursue the matter in civil proceedings.

Another set of questions center around the issues of partial and excessive restitution. Partial and excessive are relative to the damages experienced by the victim. Partial restitution occurs when the offender is required to make less restitution than the damages experienced by the victim and excessive restitution occurs when the offender's restitution obligation exceeds the amount of damages experienced by the victim. The experience of restitution programs today indicates that full restitution can be made in most cases without creating an unjust hardship on the offender. This experience tends further to be confirmed by available data indicating that the losses sustained in most victimizations are sufficiently modest that offenders can reasonably be expected to make full restitution.[10] Unusual situations may, of course, occasionally occur when offenders' actions may result in inordinately high

Paying Off the Ripped Off," Joe Hudson (ed.), *Restitution in Criminal Justice* (St. Paul: Minnesota Department of Corrections, 1976), 190-215.

9. Restitution in Probation Experiment, Des Moines, Iowa; Pilot Alberta Restitution Center, Calgary, Alberta; Victim Offender Reconciliation Project, Kitchner, Ontario.

10. United States Department of Justice. *Crime in the United States*, 1974 (Washington: U.S. Government Printing Office, 1975), 29-31; Burt Galaway and Joe Hudson, "Issues in the Correctional Implementation of Restitution to Victims of Crime," in Joe Hudson and Burt Galaway (eds.) *Considering the Victim: Readings in Restitution and Victim Compensation* (Springfield: Charles C. Thomas Publisher, 1975), 351-360; Minnesota Department of Corrections, *Interim Evaluation Results: Minnesota Restitution Center* (St. Paul: Minnesota Department of Corrections, 1976); Roger O. Steggerda and Susan P. Dolphin, *Victim Restitution: Assessment of the Restitution in Probation Experiment* (Des Moines: Polk County, Iowa, Department of Program Evaluation, 1975).

losses to victims. In these rare cases questions may be raised about the appropriateness of requiring full restitution; when this occurs the decisionmaking process used to arrive at the restitution amount (either arbitration or negotiation) would involve a consideration of the extent of the loss in relation to the nature of the crime and might arrive at a less than full restitution obligation. This contingency reaffirms the desirability of using a negotiation rather than an arbitration process. Situations in which the victims have negotiated and accepted a less than full restitution agreement are much more likely to be accepted as fair and just situations than those in which the amount is determined by an arbitrator leaving the victim with only the resources of accepting the amount or attempting a civil suit. Further, laboratory research testing the equity theory formulations suggests that full restitution is more desirable than either partial or excessive restitution because full restitution is more likely to be voluntarily made by the wrongdoer.[11]

Questions around the issue of excessive restitution are much more complex. Obviously the community incurs considerable costs in solving a crime, apprehending the offender, and arriving at a determination of guilt. Should offenders be reasonably accepted to share in these costs? Unless attempts are made to attach restitution obligations to concepts such as pain, suffering, and mental anguish, many serious crimes may involve considerably minor damages in which restitution for out-of-pocket losses may be a very mild penalty. To a large extent, this problem could be controlled by limiting restitution to property crimes. Further, without the possibility of excessive restitution, major class injustices may occur in which wealthy offenders might easily make restitution whereas poor offenders would find the restitution obligation much more burdensome. This problem has led a number of restitution scholars to accept the notion of excessive restitution. Kathleen Smith proposes that offenders be sentenced to pay restitution as well as a discretionary fine set by the judge and based on the seriousness of the offense; in Smith's scheme all offenders would go to prison, would be provided with work opportunities at prevailing market wages, and would remain in prison until they had worked and earned sufficient money to complete both restitution and discretionary fine obligations.[12] Stephen Schafer, one of the most consistent modern advocates of restitution, thinks that restitution must be combined with other penalties to avoid class injustices.[13] Most presently operating restitution programs do, at least indirectly, require excessive restitution inasmuch as obligations in addition to restitution are imposed upon the offender. Frequently restitution is attached along with other

11. Walster, Berscheid, and Walster, op. cit., supra note 7; Ellen Berscheid and Elaine Walster, "When Does a Harm-Doer Compensate a Victim?", Journal of Personality and Social Psychology, 6 (1967), 435-441.

12. Kathleen Smith, A Cure for Crime: The Case for the Self-Determinate Sentence (London: Duckworth, 1965): Kathleen Smith, "Implementing Restitution Within a Penal Setting," in Joe Hudson and Burt Galaway (eds.), Restitution in Criminal Justice (Lexington: D.C. Heath/Lexington Books: 1977), 131-146.

13. Schafer, op. cit., supra note 3.

obligations of probation, required residence in a community correction center, mandatory counseling, or other correctional sanctions. Programs in Georgia[14] and Oklahoma,[15] however, are apparently moving away from this pattern and are attempting to demonstrate the use of restitution as a sole sanction. Offenders in these states are technically on probation status while making restitution; they appear, however, to have very few other obligations and will be discharged from probation upon the completion of the restitution requirement. The problem of excessive restitution might well be resolved by beginning to find types of crime (predominantly property crimes) in which restitution might be the sole sanction and identify other more serious crimes (predominantly crimes against person) in which restitution might reasonably be required but in which the offender would also be subject to other criminal justice sanctions. The concept of court costs might also be expanded by establishing a set fee based on the type of crime which all convicted offenders should be required to pay to partially reimburse the community for the costs of their apprehension and conviction. Parenthetically, the converse of this would also be reasonable. Persons who are subjected to criminal charges which are later dismissed or for which they are acquitted should receive compensation from the community for their legal costs and other losses.[16]

The questions of determining the amount of victim damages for which restitution is to be made, assessing whether or not restitution should be made for intangible damages such as pain, suffering, mental anguish, etc., and the issues of partial and excessive restitution are all practical problems which must be resolved; present experience clearly indicates that they are resolvable. Two procedures—arbitration and negotiation—are being employed to resolve these issues on a case-by-case basis. Generally the negotiation procedures hold greater promise for arriving at resolutions which will be accepted as fair by all parties to the victimization.

Enforcing the Obligation

A second set of issues centered around the question of how to enforce restitution requirements. There are two aspects to this problem. One aspect is that of the indigent offender (how-to-get-blood-out-of-a-turnip) and the other is enforcing a restitution sanction against the solvent offender who may be reluctant to give up resources. The problem of the indigent offender may be overstated. The experience to date is that the restitution amounts are quite modest; the vast majority of restitution contracts negotiated by the Minnesota Restitution Center, for example, have been under $200.[17] With

---

14. Bill Read, "How Restitution Works in Georgia," *Judicature* 60:7 (February 1977), 329-331.

15. Mark R. Arnold, "Making the Criminal Pay Back His Victim," *National Observer*, April 2, 1977, p. 1.

16. Richard Moran and Stephen Ziedman, "Victims Without Crimes: Compensation to the Not Guilty," in Israel Drapkin and Emilio Viano (eds.), *Victimology: A New Focus; Volume II Society's Reactions to Victimization* (Lexington: D.C. Heath/Lexington Press, 1974), 221-225.

17. Galaway and Hudson, *op. cit., supra* note 9; Minnesota Department of Corrections, *op. cit., supra* note 9.

the aid of installment payment plan, most offenders will be able to handle their restitution obligations. In some situations other resources may need to be made available to the low income offender. These resources could include assistance with job finding or the use of short-term public service employment by which the offender would be put to some useful public work in order to earn sufficient money to meet the restitution obligations.

One occasionally expressed fear is that indigent offenders will steal in order to make their restitution obligations. While this is certainly a possibility, there is no evidence from current restitution programs that it occurs except in isolated instances. This, admittedly undesirable contingency, could certainly be controlled with even minimal monitoring of the offenders' sources of income as they complete the restitution requirement.

Another alternative is personal service restitution in which the offender completes restitution by working for the victim rather than making a cash payment. Several restitution projects report examples of this type of restitution,[18] although to date there has been no systematic study of the use of personal service restitution. This does appear to be a viable option which might be explored and used with some indigent offenders. If restitution decisions are made through a negotiation process the possibility of personal service restitution could be discussed and considered as one of the alternatives under consideration.

There will be some offenders who will willingly agree to a restitution obligation to avoid harsh outcomes of the criminal process. Some will then attempt to avoid completing the obligation even when they have income and resources to do so. In view of these problems, the criminal justice system must maintain the possibility of imposing a more severe sanction if the offender fails or refuses to meet the restitution obligations. While many offenders will undoubtedly meet their obligation out of a sense of duty, some will be evasive and means must be available to coerce those who wish to evade their responsibility. This, of course, is a current practice when restitution is made a condition of probation; failure to make the restitution obligation can then become grounds for violation of probation or imposing the original penalty.

Securing compliance with the restitution obligation is not an insurmountable obstacle. Procedures must be developed to monitor the progress of completing the restitution obligations and to be aware of the sources of money being used by the offender to make restitution. Installment payments will undoubtedly be necessary in many circumstances. In a few cases, the offender may require assistance in finding employment or being provided with public service employment. Serious consideration should be given to exploration of the use of personal service restitution. Finally, the criminal justice system must maintain the capability of coercing the restitution re-

18.   Galaway, *op. cit., supra* note 2; Patricia Groves, "A Report on Community Service Treatment and Work Programs in British Columbia," *Community Participation in Sentencing* (Ottawa: Law Reform Commission of Canada, 1976), 121-177.

quirement through imposing an additional sanction when offenders do not complete their obligations.

The Costs of Restitution

Will the more systematic use of restitution in the criminal justice system increase the costs of administering criminal justice programs? This depends upon the role restitution is to pay vis-a-vis other criminal justice sanctions. If restitution is simply added to the present panoply of sanctioning and correctional programs then the cost is likely to increase. If, on the other hand, restitution can be used in lieu of existing criminal justice programs then the cost will be decreased. Less staff time will be necessary to establish a restitution agreement (even using negotiating procedures) and in monitoring the implementation of that agreement than is now being used in probation services to develop presentence evaluations and to carry out probation supervision. Substituting restitution for probation will lower cost; the cost savings will be even greater if restitution can be used as an alternative to incarceration which, of course, is an extremely expensive sanction and effectively penalizes the victim twice—once by the offender and secondly through taxes to support the incarcerated offender. Another alternative which would reduce costs is to use less restrictive incarceration and restitution in lieu of traditional imprisonment. The Minnesota Restitution Center retained offenders (who had previously been in a maximum security prison) in a community corrections center where they completed their restitution obligation at less per diem cost than that required to operate the prison.[19] Likewise the Georgia restitution shelters are providing a degree of incarceration and restitution at considerably less costs to the taxpayers in Georgia than would be incurred if the offenders in the shelters were placed in a more traditional prison.[20] If restitution can be substituted for the concept of coerced counseling and therapy, sanctioning will become a less labor-intensive—and thus less costly—undertaking. On the other hand, there is considerable danger that restitution will simply be added to the present range of criminal justice treatment-sanctioning activities and, thus, would increase the overall cost. Restitution, to save money, must result in a reduction in other types of correctional programming. This in turn requires an identification of types of offenses for which restitution would be a suitable sole penalty and a systematic exploration of the use of restitution alone without other types of sanctions.

Victim Culpability

An additional practical problem centers around the question of the victims' precipitation of their own victimization. There is an increasing body of evidence to suggest that in many situations crime victims, either actively or through carelessness, engage in behavior which partially precipitates their own victimization.[21] If the victim is partially at fault should the offender be

19. Mowatt, *op. cit., supra* note 8, 203.
20. Read, *op. cit., supra* note 14, 327.
21. Lynn A. Curtis, *Criminal Violence* (Lexington: D.C. Heath/Lexington Books, 1974), 81-100.

required to make full restitution for the victim's losses? This is an issue which has not been addressed explicitly in most present restitution programs. Most appear to operate on the assumption that the offender was fully responsible for the victim's losses and should, therefore, make full restitution.

There are two directions by which this issue might be resolved. One direction would be to develop a procedure by which the offender could request a reduction in the amount of agreed-upon restitution based on evidence that the victim was partially at fault. This may be similar to the concept of contributory negligence in civil suits. Such a procedure would, of course, involve additional legal costs. A similar process which might accomplish the same ends would be to permit the issue of victim culpability to be considered in either the arbitration or negotiation processes designed to arrive at a restitution amount. The offender might be permitted to try to negotiate a lesser restitution amount based on contentions that the victim contributed to the victimization or, perhaps, the arbitrator might award less than full restitution to the victim on the same bases.

A second approach is to assume that even in situations of high provocation, an individual has more than one alternative way of behaving. Persons who select an alternative which leads to damages to another person, even if provoked, should be held accountable for the damages which flow from their decision. This approach would suggest that so long as noncriminal alternatives are available, offenders should be held accountable for their acts even if provoked. This alternative response to the question of victim culpability has some distinct advantages. First, basic human dignity of the offender is protected because the offender is perceived as a responsible person who has the power and obligation to make decisions. Conversely, an offender is not perceived as a sick or helpless person who, in a deterministic manner, responds criminally in provocative situations. Secondly, the interests of the community are better protected by a policy stance which expects and demands responsible behavior from persons. To permit easy rationalizations is simply to encourage irresponsible behavior.

The problem of victim culpability is also not an insurmountable issue. One direction for resolution is to permit procedures which would result in a reduction in the restitution obligation based on some assessment of a culpability of the victim. A second and preferred alternative is to treat the offender as a responsible person who chooses alternative forms of behavior and who should be held responsible for the damages which flow from such a choice. This latter approach does not deny the reality of the victim precipitation but rather affirms the principle of holding people responsible for their behavior and rejects a policy which permits easy rationalizations for irresponsible behavior.

Conclusions

Restitution programming has been demonstrated in a number of pilot projects over the last few years. Unfortunately the experience of these projects has not yet been fully reported and synthesized. There is a crucial need for a careful review and summarization of the restitution project's experiences to guide further programming in this area. Sufficient experience is available, however, to suggest that many of the practical issues which are frequently raised in regard to restitution programming can be resolved. Fair restitution amounts can be determined. Differences in perceived damages between victims and offenders are resolvable and guidelines are available to deal with the issues of payment for intangible damages, partial restitution, and excessive restitution. There does not appear to be any particular reason to believe the major problems will be encountered in enforcing the restitution obligation so long as installment payments are authorized; implementation of the restitution agreement is monitored; judicious use is made of job finding services, public employment, and personal service restitution; and a more severe sanction can be imposed if the offender refuses to complete the restitution obligation. If restitution can be used as an alternative to present correctional programs, the overall sanctioning costs will be reduced. Attention should be given to defining types of offenses for which restitution might be a sole penalty. Finally, the issue of victim culpability should not deter from the imposition of a restitution requirement; an offender's dignity is much more protected when he is treated as a responsible person who can be held accountable for choosing a criminal alternative even when confronted with a provocative situation.

The practical issues can be resolved on a case-by-case basis using a negotiation procedure by which the victim and offender work with a public official to arrive at a restitution agreement. Once developed, this agreement should be enforced as the major sanction against the offender. Such a program should reduce the need for large correctional bureaucracies and should be actively pursued as a means for dealing with specified types of offenses, especially property crimes.

Revitalizing Restitution: Flogging a Horse that may have been Killed for Just Cause*

John F. Klein

Associate Professor, Simon Fraser University, British Columbia

Introduction

Before the state monopolized the institution of social control, the "criminal law" and its often barbaric retaliatory force was in the hands of the individual, clan or tribe. To attack another was to provoke attack; in the end result, it was often difficult to distinguish the offender from the victim. This remained true even with the diminuation of resort to bloodshed in dispute resolution. With the ascendence of monetary compensation as an offender-chosen alternative to outlawry or death, the choice was sometimes one of Hobson's. Victims and offenders were not always social or economic equals. For the impecunious tiller of the soil in the middle ages, restitution or compensation in the amount of 5 pounds could spell disaster for himself and his family and result in his being cast into bondage. If one is to believe Pollock and Maitland,[1] the state of affairs during what Schafer[2] has termed the "golden age of the victim" can only be described as brutal.

Purposefully or coincidentally, the alleviation of the situation was found in the monopolization by the State of criminal law and its administration and the consequent divestment of criminal and civil law. The occurrence should be recognized for what it was: a landmark in legal history. Some might suggest that this development was little more than a reflection of Royal greed in that the Crown could now arrogate fines and confiscate property. While this may be true to some unknowable extent, there is also reason to believe that the change also came about in response to popular distress about the often horrid ways in which perceived wrongs were being dealt with otherwise. In any case, the true significance of this change is to be found in the recognition of the need to sort out in law which wrongs violated public interests and which violated essentially private interests. The change recognized that there were some wrongs—those wrongs best exemplified by

*This is a revised and expanded version of a presentation given at a conference sponsored by the Solicitor General of Canada, Diversion: A Canadian Concept and Practice, Quebec City, October 24 to 26, 1977. While the views contained herein are those of the author, he would like to gratefully acknowledge the helpful suggestions and comments of Professors M.B. Brinkerhoff, M.M. Mackie, D.L. Mills and, in particular, J.C. Levy.

1. Pollock and Maitland, *The History of English Law*, 2nd ed. (London, Cambridge Univ. Press, 1968), vol 2 at pp. 448-62.
2. Schafer, *The Victim and His Criminal* (New York, Random House, 1968).

* Reprinted, with permission, from *Criminal Law Quarterly*, vol. 20 (1978), pp. 383-408.

the wrongs enumerated in the Criminal Code—which, if left unchecked, threatened to destroy the social fabric. As such, the apprehension, conviction and sanctioning of such wrongdoers should be pursued by the State.

In contrast, those wrongs which did not threaten the social fabric but were none the less wrongs, were to be pursued by the individual who was wronged against. However, such wrongs were to be within the contest of law—the civil law of torts.

One need only glance at the differences between our civil and criminal courts to see how profound were the implications of sorting out public and private interests: differences with respect to the burden of proof, procedures and penalties while still sharing in common a commitment to "doing justice". With respect to "doing justice", through contrasting the civil and criminal courts, we see a rather striking difference in focus.

In the civil arena, assuming that the court has found that there is a preponderance of evidence in favour of the plaintiff's position, the court will take a careful look at what and how much should be done *for the plaintiff* with respect to liquidated, unliquidated and punitive damages.

In contrast, assuming that a court of criminal jurisdiction finds beyond a reasonable doubt that an individual in question had committed the offence which was alleged by the State, the focus then shifts to what should be done *to the offender* in terms of sanctioning him for his behaviour, protecting the community and reaffirming core values to members of the community.

The importance of the preceding distinctions can perhaps be more fully appreciated as we turn our attention to the recent reemergence of the cry of "What about the victim of a criminal offence?" and consequent proposals for righting the plight of the victim through restitution and compensation schemes. These are proposals which, we believe, are laudable in terms of their common intent but are, at best, naive in terms of accomplishing what is being proposed and, at worst, capable of creating a greater sense of injustice—both real and imagined—in the eyes of both victims and offenders than is sometimes presently the case.

Doing Justice for the Victim in the Criminal Courts

In recent years, there has been considerable and renewed interest in the role of restitution—rehabilitative and otherwise—in the criminal justice process.[3] The popular appeal of restitution undoubtedly resides, at least in part, in the belief that it "makes sense" and in its seeming goodness and simplicity combined with the fact that it is something which, by and large, is not being done. This is seen in the words of the Law Reform Commission of Canada:

Doesn't it seem to be a rejection of common sense that a convicted of-

---

3. See, *e.g.*, Macaulay and Walster, "Legal Structures and Restoring Equity", 27 J. of Soc. Issues 173 (1971) and Galaway, "The Use of Restitution", 23 Crime and Delinquency 57 (1977).

fender is rarely made to pay for the damage he has done? Isn't it surprising that the victim generally gets nothing for his loss? Restitution—making the offender pay or work to restore the damage—or where this is not possible, compensation—payment from public funds to the victim for his loss—would seem to be a natural thing for sentencing policy and practice. Yet, under present law they are, more frequently than not, ignored.[4]

The Law Reform Commission further suggests that restitution should assume a central role in sentencing,[5] that, under certain circumstances, it should be used as a sentence in its own right,[6] and that, when the sanction of restitution is used by the court, those found to be in wilful default in the payment of restitution should be liable for a fine or jail term not to exceed six months.[7] Given the presumed logic and simplicity of such a proposal, combined with what has come to be regarded as the almost total bankruptcy of our current correctional approaches, one can understand the popular appeal of reviving restitution. However, it might be wise to recall the stricture of the Swiss historian, Jakob Burkhardt, that, "The worst form of tyranny is the denial of complexity."

In analyzing the practicality of the Law Reform Commission's proposals regarding restitution, two issues rise to the surface: (1) the proposals cannot deliver what they seem to promise to deliver; and (2) they may well constitute a legal nightmare—both philosophically and operationally. There are several problems which loom before us if restitution (and compensation) are to become more central issues in the sentencing of criminal offenders. Some of these are problems which can perhaps be resolved as case law emerges which sets standards for instances in which restitution or compensation are at issue in criminal cases;[8] others are problems which can be resolved only if we are willing to make rather substantial changes in our legal philosophy and subsequent changes in the law itself. (This, of course, begs the question of whether actors within the criminal justice system will change their attitudes so as to be in accord with other such changes.)

A. *Restitution and the Criminal Code*

At present, the provisions in the Canadian Criminal Code, R.S.C. 1970, c. C-34, are woefully inadequate if the Law Reform Commission's proposals are to be effected. Further, Chasse has described Canadian law with respect to restitution as being in a state of anarchy in that "there has not been any authoritative statement—case law or statute law—demonstrating or elucidating the link between restitution and the purposes of the criminal law."[9]

---

4. Law Reform Commission of Canada, Working Paper 5, *Restitution and Compensation* (1974), at p. 5.

5. *Ibid.*, at p. 8.

6. Law Reform Commission of Canada, Working Paper 7, *Diversion* (1975).

7. Law Reform Commission of Canada, *A Report on Dispositions and Sentences in the Criminal Process: Guidelines* (1976).

8. See, generally, Chasse, "Restitution in Canadian Criminal Law" (1977), 36 C.R.N.S. 201.

9. *Ibid.*, at p. 201.

The provisions for employing a restitutive sanction in the Criminal Code are generally inadequate if the courts are to begin to implement the proposals of the Law Reform Commission.[10] That this is so is most apparent in two respects: the restrictiveness of the provisions in terms of when and how restitution can be used as a sanction and the inability of the court to be able to enforce effectively restitution orders under the current provisions. The latter difficulty resides not only in the law itself but, and perhaps more significantly, in the day-to-day organizational and operational realities of the criminal justice system.

Sections 616, 654 and 655 of the Criminal Code have to do with the restoration of property which has been held by the police or the court for the purposes of trial and for the restoration of stolen property which has been unwittingly purchased by innocent third parties. As such, these provisions cannot properly be construed as enabling the court to employ a restitutive *sanction*. These provisions are essentially civil in nature and, in the view of the Law Reform Commission, "appear to be historical carryovers from English legislation that were grudgingly grafted onto the penal law in order to save victims the expense of a civil suit to regain stolen property or secure compensation."[11] These provisions come into operation upon the application of the party aggrieved.

Under s. 388 of the Code, the court may order restitution ("compensation") in cases of property damage. However, the amount may not exceed $50. While this provision may have enabled the court to grant some measure of relief to certain victims at the turn of the century, this is clearly not the case today. Given inflationary trends and the tendency to settle minor cases of property damage out of court, in most instances to order an offender to compensate a victim in the amount of $50 in a case involving property damage can only be regarded as a token gesture. And, as we shall see, there exists some psychological evidence which suggests that partial restitution has negative consequences if a sense of balance is to be restored and if the offender is to acknowledge and not rationalize away his wrongdoing.

A provision in the Criminal Code (s. 653(1)) which the Law Reform Commission describes as "little-used"[12] is one under which the victim may ask the court, at the time that sentence is imposed for an indictable offence, to "order the accused to pay to that person an amount by way of satisfaction or compensation for loss of or damage to property suffered by the applicant as a result of the commission of the offence of which the accused is convicted."

---

10. *Supra*, footnotes 4 and 7.

11. *Supra*, footnote 4, at p. 9.

12. *Supra*, footnote 4, at p. 9. S. 653(1) has been ruled *ultra vires* Parliament in *R. v. Zelensky* (1976), 33 C.C.C. (2d) 147, 36 C.R.N.S. 169, 73 D.L.R. (3d) 596, [1977] 1 W.W.R. 155 (Man. C.A.). While the Supreme Court of Canada granted leave to appeal this decision, 14 N.R. 450n, judgment was reserved (29 Nov., 1977). This aside, it should be noted that s. 653(2) provides a specifically civil enforcement mechanism.

Respecting the foregoing provisions in the Criminal Code, that these provisions are less than adequate is suggested by the claim that:

> In practice these provisions are used infrequently and even when they are, it is often a large company that appears as the victim to ask for compensation. More frequently losses by companies tend to be dealt with under insurance law, a mode of settlement that many lawyers and businessmen prefer to applications in the criminal courts.[13]

This is to say that even with the existence of these provisions, application to the civil courts is viewed by those whom it would be fair to consider the more knowledgeable in such matters, as a preferable means of obtaining redress. Why this is so is open to question: it may be because of the inadequacy of these provisions in the Criminal Code or, as a result of experience, certain victims or their counsel have learned that the civil courts are better equipped to render an equitable decision.

Finally, s. 663(2)(e) provides that restitution may be made a condition of a probation order. While this provision more directly addresses the avowed need for the courts to be able to use restitution creatively as a sanction for a criminal offence, experience indicates that it has not been used to any great extent. For example, the Law Reform Commission reports that, "In a survey of records covering over 4,294 convicted appearances from 1967 to 1972. . . restitution was recorded for only 6 convictions".[14] Frequency of use aside, a more salient issue is that of the enforceability of restitution orders when they are a condition of probation. If offenders can scoff at such orders, knowing that they either cannot or will not be enforced, whatever rehabilitative value such a sentence may have is surely lost. And, of course, the victim does not receive his just deserts and will, perhaps, become estranged or further estranged from the criminal justice process.

In the experience of this writer,[15] the enforcement of a restitution condition under a probation order is, indeed, problematic. This is so for a number of reasons:

(1) When probation orders are issued without a condition that the offender is to report to a probation officer, the monitoring of his behaviour with respect to his making restitution is, to say the least, ineffective.

(2) Even when such probation orders require reporting, there are instances where often overworked probation staff fail to determine whether the restitution condition is being fulfilled.

---

13. *Supra*, footnote 4, at p. 10.

14. *Supra*, footnote 4, at p. 10. This might be a function of s. 663(2)(h)—one might speculate as to whether or not a restitution or compensation order as a condition of probation could ever meet the requirements of this latter subsection.

15. The author was, from September, 1975 to April, 1977, Director of the Pilot Alberta Restitution Centre, a pilot project jointly funded by the Solicitor General of Canada and the Solicitor General of Alberta. The views reflected in this article are those of the author and do not in any way purport to be those of the sponsors of the P.A.R.C. project.

(3) There are times when it is found that a probationer has breached the conditions of his probation order; however, it is rare that a person is returned to court for a hearing with respect to the breach of his probation. This appears, in part, to be a result of heavy caseload pressures on the part of both probation officers and Crown prosecutors and a recognition of the generally ineffectual consequences of a hearing on a breach of probation under s. 666(1).

(4) Finally, the offender who has become somewhat wise to the ways of the law knows that he can avoid the payment of restitution as a condition of probation simply by absconding, preferably outside of the province in which the order was issued. While a warrant may be issued as a result of his behaviour, it will rarely be executed outside of the province in which it was issued. Why this is so may reside in the relatively minor nature of the offence for which probation was given, the expense of returning the offender to the jurisdiction where the warrant was issued, and the realization that the knowledge of the existence of an outstanding warrant may effectively serve to banish the offender from the jurisdiction where the offence took place.

While it can probably be agreed that the previously enumerated inadequacies in statute law (case law, if anything, is presently even more inadequate[16]) constitute a serious impediment if restitution is to become a viable sanction, such inadequacies are resolvable. There are also issues which should be bracketed until such time as much more fundamental issues related to the actual *merit* of the Law Reform Commission's proposal are adequately examined.

B. *Combining public and private interests*

As we have seen, historically, as the State came to monopolize much of the institution of punishment, the rights of the injured or aggreived person came to be separated from the criminal law. Now, the Law Reform Commission suggests that private interests should once again be considered in criminal cases which, of course, deal with public interests. The logic which the Commission apparently uses in making their case that such a state of affairs should come into existence once again is deceptively simplistic. Since the standard of proof in criminal cases is "beyond a reasonable doubt" as opposed to a "balance of probabilities" in civil cases, there appears to be nothing unreasonable about dealing with the question of restitution in criminal cases. However, if we can agree that the question of restitution or compensation is essentially civil in nature, then some problems emerge. An example may make this clear.

Let us assume that an individual has been charged with robbery involving violence in which it is alleged that he beat the victim and robbed him of $650. The accused elects trial by judge and jury and is convicted by the jury. At the time of sentencing, the victim, under the auspices of s. 653(1) of the

---

16.   Chasse, *supra*, footnote 8.

Criminal Code makes application for restitution in the amount of $650 plus $2,500 in unliquidated damages for pain and suffering. The offender contends that his proceeds from the crime were only $250. While the judge points out that s. 653(1) cannot be used for unliquidated damages, he does partially side with the victim: he sentences the offender—who to his knowledge is a first offender who engaged in what might more popularly be termed a mugging—to two years less a day in jail, with a delayed probation order of two years' duration which stipulates that restitution in the amount of $650 must be made to the victim. He also suggests to the offender that the threat of additional time in jail is a real one if he fails to comply with the restitution condition of the probation order. Neither party is happy but, of course, the criminal process was never intended to make people especially happy. The offender becomes even less happy when he considers that he now has to face twelve charges having to do with $950 in bad cheques as a result of his having refused to accept a deal whereby the cheque charges would be dropped in exchange for a plea of guilty to the robbery charge.

What are some of the problems in this example which the Law Reform Commission either ignored or did not see as being especially problematic? (1) The victim must still go to civil court (in which the system of pleading delineates the issues in a way that has no real parallel in criminal cases) if he is to effect his claim to unliquidated damages. (2) No examination for discovery, which is an important aspect in the process of settling claims for damages, was held nor was there the production of documents. (3) The offender was effectively denied his right to a civil trial by jury with respect to the issue of the liquidated damages. (4) The offender was threatened with jail in lieu of nonpayment of what is essentially a civil debt—imprisonment for debt, in the United States, is deemed unconstitutional and, in Canada, is a practice which is frowned upon. (5) Had the offender accepted the plea bargaining arrangement, the victims in the bad cheque cases would be denied the possibility of reaping the benefits of restitution which they might accrue as a result of the conviction of the offender.

The preceding example points to some of the problems which may evolve if we attempt to settle *at the same time* what are questions of public and private interests in a proceeding that is presently structured so as to deal adequately with only one set of values. What this example suggests is that the test of the viability and acceptability of the Law Reform Commission's suggestion that the issue of restitution should be dealt with as a matter of course in criminal cases should be the test of "what is good for the goose should be good for the gander"—if it is acceptable to deal with private interests through a vehicle which has been structured to deal with public interests, then the reverse should also be true. It is an issue which the Law Reform Commission has failed to address and, in failing to do so, made its restitution proposal seem to be more acceptable than it might otherwise appear to be.

Another example might make this point more clear. Following the line of thinking of the Law Reform Commission, we would find it acceptable, if not laudable, if in a case where an accused has been convicted of dangerous driving, he was ordered by the judge at time of sentencing to make restitution to the owner of a motor vehicle which he side-swiped when he was speeding through a residential area.

Now let us reverse the situation, but only somewhat: an individual side-swipes a motor vehicle while speeding through a residential area. While the investigating officer believes it to a moral certainty that dangerous driving was involved, he does not feel that there is sufficient evidence, due to the lack of witnesses, to warrant the laying of a charge. The victim, however, launches a civil suit. Prior to the hearing, he has gone door-to-door in his neighbourhood and has discovered that there were indeed witnesses who will testify that the driver of the vehicle which side-swiped his car was speeding and driving in an extremely reckless manner. After having heard the evidence, the judge is absolutely convinced that not only should the plaintiff's claim for damages be upheld but that, also, the defendant was, indeed, speeding and driving in a reckless manner. While we would agree that in such a situation damages should be awarded, most would react in horror should the judge also fine the individual because of his dangerous driving.

These examples are intended to suggest that the rather romantic posture which has been taken by the Law Reform Commission and others that restitution represents a criminal justice tradition of ancient times which was inopportunely abandoned, may be unwarranted. Rather, the current status of restitution in the criminal process may, in fact, reflect the accumulated wisdom derived from centuries of mistakes.

Restitution and Its Relation to Reality

Additional problems with making restitution a central issue in the criminal justice process surface when one considers some of the organizational and operational realities of the criminal justice system. It is suggested here that the Law Reform Commission[17] has erred in its restitution proposal in that it appears to choose to ignore certain organizational and operational realities which cast doubt on the viability of restitution as an important and beneficial criminal sanction. That this is so should become apparent as we consider the following issues.

A. *How amenable will the criminal courts be to considering restitution if they see themselves as acting as a collection agency?*

If the judges spoken to by this writer are representative of the majority of judges, the indication is that any move to make restitution a central consideration in sentencing will not be looked upon with favour. In a recent case in Alberta, Chief Justice William McGillivray, delivering orally the Appeal Court's judgment, took strong exception to having the criminal courts used to effect the collection of a debt. In this case, the Appeal Court overturned a probation order that called for paying back $7,200 in a fraud case in which a

---

17. Law Reform Commission of Canada, Working Paper 5, *Restitution and Compensation* (1974).

motor vehicle was sold and represented as having a clear title which, in fact, it did not.[18]

Some judges have perhaps rightfully expressed the fear that if restitution does become a central issue in sentencing, then some individuals will attempt to use the criminal courts as a cheap and ready means of attempting to collect a debt in lieu of turning to a collection agency or the civil courts.

Further, even if the law were to be changed so as to reflect the philosophy of the Law Reform Commission, that would not ensure that the philosophy would be carried out in practice. A precedent for this assertion is to be found in judicial practices regarding the granting of absolute or conditional discharges. While the philosophy behind amending the Criminal Code so as to allow for the granting of discharges, was that certain "minor" offenders should not be given the stigma of a criminal record and that, for some, simply having to appear in criminal court is a sufficient sanction, some judges have simply refused to consider this particular disposition. The often-stated reasoning behind this stance is that, "If a person has committed a criminal offence, he deserves a criminal record." (Some Crown Prosecutor's offices routinely file an appeal whenever such a sentence is given.)

So long as judges are granted discretion in sentencing, there is no assurance that restitution will be routinely considered, used and, more importantly, used with any degree of consistency. As such, this, of course, raises the issue of equal protection under law for victims as well as offenders.

B. *A salient issue with respect to having the criminal courts deal with the issue of restitution has to do with the competency of the courts in this area*

As McLean notes:

The criminal courts, busier now than they have ever been, have neither the time nor in many cases the expertise for assessing the measure of damages or complicated issues in respect of title, and the civil courts may be said to be the proper forum to claim reparation for civil wrongs.[19]

This position was reaffirmed in a recent and unanimous decision delivered by Mr. Justice William Morrow, in a case which came before a Northwest Territories Court of Appeal panel. The appellant, who had pleaded guilty to having set off an explosion in a gold mine shaft, was given a sentence of three years' imprisonment. Upon application of the party aggrieved under s.653(1), the court then ordered that the convicted make restitution in the amount of $65,000. Upon appeal, the court found, in part, that the amount of property loss was "too serious" a matter to be decided in such a summary manner in criminal court despite the convenience and efficiency of doing so.

---

18. "Fraud case decision overturned", *The Calgary Herald*, October 5, 1977, p. B2.
19. I. McLean, "Compensation and Restitution Orders", [1973] Crim. L. Rev. 3, at p. 3.

Rather, the court felt that matters such as this need to be examined closely by a civil court.[20]

The case cited above should not permit us, however, to lose sight of the more basic issue of the competency of the busy criminal courts to deal adequately with the question of restitution in generally all but very straightforward cases. Granted, we may have no quarrel with the court ordering restitution in the case of an individual who has been convicted of uttering a $150 N.S.F. cheque or in a case where both the victim and offender agree as to the amount of the loss. However, it can be argued that at present and in the foreseeable future, our criminal courts will be ill-equipped to deal with many of the instances which come before it where restitution is at issue. A few examples should suffice to make this clear:

(1) A young thief steals a battery from an automobile. The victim makes application for restitution in the amount of the cost of a new battery. Counsel for the defence argues that the court, in considering the amount of restitution, should take into account the age and condition of the battery and prorate the amount accordingly. Further, the offender states that, while he admits to having stolen the battery, he did so only to later discover that the battery was dead and would not hold a charge.

(2) On a crisp fall evening, a young housebreaker breaks the basement window of a widow's house in order to effect his entry. As he starts to go through the window, he discovers that there is a shelf beneath the window upon which the occupant has been growing her prized cacti. Viewing them as the functional equivalent of a barbed-wire fence, he removes them from the shelf and sets them outside. He steals her liquor and a portable radio and then departs by the back door, leaving the cacti outdoors where they freeze to death. The Crown asks that restitution be considered in passing sentence. The question then arises as to the value of the liquor (most of the bottles had already been opened) and the value of the cacti which the victim herself had cultivated.

While some might argue that since the amounts of loss in the above cases are relatively small, no great damage would be done if the court were to make some determination and order the offenders to make restitution, especially since the order, being a sentence of the court, could be appealed. However, one can also persuasively argue that the real issue is that of justice. Further, if the offender were to appeal his sentence on the basis of the restitution order, the costs for the offender (if he hires his own lawyer) and to the general public (court costs plus, possibly, tax-supported legal aid costs) would be greater than had the claim been dealt with in small claims court to

---

20. "Court cancels $65,000 gold mine restitution", *The Alberta*, November 29, 1977, p. 3. At the time of this writing, the decision was yet to be reported. However, similar concerns were raised in *R. v. Zelensky, supra*, footnote 12, *per* Matas, J.A., Hall and O'Sullivan, JJ.A., concurring, at p. 148 C.C.C., pp. 170 and 171-2 C.R.N.S., and Hall, J.A., concurring with Matas, J.A., at p. 170 C.C.C., pp. 198-9 C.R.N.S.

begin with—a court far better equipped for dealing with such minor matters.

C. *To the extent that willingness to make restitution will result in a measure of leniency, will there be instances where the practice smells of trading dollars for leniency or even liberty?*

As Schafer notes:

> In some legal systems to make restitution is regarded as an essential condition for the suspension of a sentence or the award of probation; and almost everywhere restitution, performed before sentence, is considered as a mitigating circumstance.[21]

Further, there exists a danger that the motivation of some offenders for *offering* to make restitution as a part of one's sentence is simply that of mitigation of sentence (*e.g.*, obtaining a sentence of probation with a condition that restitution be made as opposed to a sentence of incarceration while having no intention of actually making restitution). While offenders who consider participating in a restitution programme may be routinely warned that their entering into a restitution agreement with a victim prior to sentencing may not influence the sentence given, such a warning may not extinguish such an expectation.[22]

While some may argue that the motivation of the offender in expressing his willingness to make restitution is unimportant in that the victim will none the less benefit, the issue is more complex than that. If mitigation is the motivation and if it is not perceived that mitigation has been the outcome, then the likelihood increases that the offender will feel a sense of injustice which, in turn, may lead him to renege on the agreement. Indeed, the experience of the Pilot Alberta Restitution Centre (P.A.R.C.) project indicates that of 114 offenders referred to the project and interviewed by the project staff, 64% thought that entering into a restitution agreement would result in being treated more leniently by the court.[23] Yet, the impression of the project staff was that, in many instances, restitution ended up being a sanction *in addition* to the sanction which the offender would have normally received. This may be because some judges took the view (and perhaps correctly) that a restitution agreement presented at the time of sentencing (as opposed to a pronouncement at the time of sentencing that restitution had been made) smacked of being a rather blatant attempt at influencing, if not interfering with, judicial discretion. The presumed result of the judicial behaviour with respect to the sentence given may account for the fact that approximately one-third of the offenders who entered into restitution agreements later-reneged on these agreements.[24] And, what does this do to the attitudes of the

---

21. Schafer, *Compensation and Restitution to Victims of Crime,* 2nd ed. (Montclair, N.J., Patterson Smith, 1970), p. 108.

22. Pilot Alberta Restitution Centre, *Progress Report: September 1, 1975 - November 30, 1976* (1976), p. 22.

23. Data obtained from the Pilot Alberta Restitution Centre as of July 31, 1977.

24. P.A.R.C., *supra,* footnote 22, at pp. 53 and 57.

victims who became involved in such agreements? Yet, unless we wish to entrench a system of class justice, restitution on an installment plan is the only feasible means for some to make restitution, even if it involves a relatively small amount of money.

If dollars for leniency is a salient issue, then it should be clear that it is the poor who will be discriminated against (and perhaps their dependants who will also suffer the consequences). It also means that, in some instances, those who did not need what they stole (and who are presumably somewhat more culpable as a consequence) are dealt with more leniently than the poor. Moreover, if restitution does assume a more central role in sentencing, then it might suggest to the rational criminal that he would be better off to steal from ten poor victims rather than one wealthy one since it is unlikely that, if apprehended, he would be charged with, let alone be convicted of, all ten offences.

Associated with the issue of trading dollars for leniency or liberty is the question of what is the price of leniency or liberty. In this context, consider the following cases:

(1) It was reported that a restaurant cashier who was convicted of stealing nearly $50,000 from her employer chose to go to prison rather than to make restitution. As a result, she was sentenced to two years in prison and fined $3,000.[25]

(2) A travel agent was convicted of embezzling $50,000 and reportedly had the opportunity to have a conventional sentence of incarceration or a sentence of six months in jail followed by a delayed probation order with restitution as a condition. He chose the former and received a sentence of 18 months. In other words, one year in jail (less remission!) was equated with $50,000—probably more than the presiding judge was earning per year.[26]

(3) Two young men were charged with breaking and entering and public mischief involving two separate incidents. As a result of their behaviour, approximately $18,000 in damage resulted. They were tried separately with one of the co-accused being convicted and given a sentence of 18 months in jail. This sentence was later upheld on appeal. The second individual entered a plea of guilty and representations were made by his counsel regarding the consideration of restitution in sentencing. He was sentenced to 12 months in jail along with a delayed probation order of three years' duration which specified that restitution in the amount of $3,600 (representing the deductable amount on the insurance policies) be made.[27]

This last example simply begs another question which the Law Reform

---

25. *Calgary Herald, supra*, footnote 18, at p. B16.

26. "Supreme Court to decide if criminal can be ordered to repay his victim", *The Financial Post*, July 23, 1977, p. 32.

27. P.A.R.C., *supra*, footnote 22, at pp. 50-2.

Commission failed to deal with in its proposal on restitution—the issue of joint and several liability.[28] What do we do in those cases where there is more than one offender and the court orders restitution be made, only later to discover that not all of the offenders have conformed to the order? Should the principle of joint and several liability be invoked with those who have been conforming with the order being forced to assume the financial obligation of those who chose not to conform? That is, should it be that those who have demonstrated by their behaviour after sentence that they are more morally worthy end up suffering more dire consequences?

Finally, if leniency is a primary motivating factor in making restitution, then this may well draw into question some of the avowed reformative claims made by some of the proponents of restitution.[29] Encouragement of this attitude is seen in its extreme form in the practice of some criminal lawyers of holding the proceeds of their client's crime in trust until the outcome of the trial. If the client is found guilty, then restitution is made and submitted as a mitigating circumstance at the time of sentence; if the client is acquitted, restitution is not made and, presumably, the prospects of receiving one's fee are enhanced.[30]

D. Is the current popularity for restitution programmes which is grounded in their rehabilitative claims warranted?

As Galaway correctly notes, there is, at present, insufficient empirical evidence to buttress any of the claims which have been made respecting the rehabilitative claims of the advocates of correctional restitution.[31] Given our current state of knowledge with respect to the effectiveness of various correctional approaches, the safest conclusion which we can draw at present is that restitution, as a correctional measure, simply will not make any difference.[32] In fact, there are some theoretical reasons for suspecting that, under certain conditions, the correctional value of ordering an offender to make restitution to his victim may be negative.

As previously noted, restitution as a sanction is, under present law,

---

28. Law Reform Commission of Canada, Working Paper 5, *Restitution and Compensation* (1974).

29. See, *e.g.*, Schafer, *The Victim and His Criminal* (New York, Random House, 1968), p. 115; Law Reform Commission, *supra*, footnote 28, at pp. 7-8; Eglash, "Creative Restitution: Some Suggestions for Prison Rehabilitation Programs", 20 Am. J. Corrections 20 (1958); and Smith, *A Cure for Crime* (London, G. Duckworth, 1965).

30. This practice was openly discussed at a meeting of criminal lawyers attended by the author. Similar allegations were made to the author by offenders whom he interviewed in conjunction with, Klein, *Let's Make a Deal: Negotiating Justice* (Toronto, D.C. Heath; Lexington, Mass., Lexington Books, 1976). Further, as a speculation, how would legal aid react to an application from a person who is making restitution voluntarily? Would the assets being thus employed be taken into account in assessing eligibility? Also, how would this apply to court-ordered restitution?

31. Galaway, "The Use of Restitution", 23 Crime and Delinquency, 57 (1977).

32. See, generally, Lipton, Martinson and Wilks, *The Effectiveness of Correctional Treatment: A Survey of Treatment Evaluation Studies* (1975).

something which is generally "added on" to the sentence of the court—it is not a sentence in its own right. Wilkins notes that there is some evidence to suggest that the more complex a sentence becomes, the more likely it is that the recidivism rate will increase.[33] (Additionally, the more complex a probation order or parole agreement, the more likely that technical violations will occur in the absence of a new offence.) In other words, the rule of parsimony appears to apply to efficacious sentencing.

Sykes and Matza have noted that when one does harm to another, various "techniques of neutralization" come into play which enable a wrongdoer to justify his conduct.[34] Within this context, Macaulay and Walster draw our attention to the fact that, in the realm of social psychology, compensating one's victim for the harm done and justifying the harm done are alternative rather than complementary ways in which a wrongdoer reacts to his victim.[35] One of the main reasons that restitution is supposed to have a rehabilitative value is because it involves a tangible recognition on the part of the offender that he has done harm to another, thus disallowing him the opportunity to rationalize his behaviour by suggesting that the victim "had it coming" or that no real harm was inflicted.

In the abstract, this claim about the rehabilitative value of restitution does receive some theoretical support.[36] However, given the contingencies which develop in the real world of the criminal court, the rehabilitative claim becomes questionable. As Macaulay and Walster point out, the legal process in actuality is one which promotes bargaining and compromise at the expense of total compensation.[37] Further, when an agreed-upon amount of restitution comes about as a result of bargaining and compromise, true equity is not restored and this, in turn, promotes a rationalization of one's behaviour on the part of the wrongdoer. This is especially true when the victim is seen as being too demanding; as a consequence, the offender may have the justification which he needs for viewing the victim as one who "had it coming". Since victims often overestimate the amount of harm that was done (monetary loss, pain, suffering and inconvenience) and offenders tend to underestimate the amount of harm done (*e.g.*, the thief who believes that he should only have to compensate the retailer for the invoiced cost of what was stolen),[38] many offenders will still be able to rationalize their behaviour as a result of being required to make restitution; in fact, in many instances, the issue of restitution may actually foster and promote such rationalizations.

---

33. Wilkins, *Evaluation of Penal Measures* (New York, Random House, 1969), p. 83.

34. Sykes and Matza, "Techniques of Neutralization: A Theory of Delinquency", 22 Am. Soc. Rev. 65 (1957).

35. Macaulay and Walster, "Legal Structures and Restoring Equity", 27 J. of Soc. Issues 173 (1971), at p. 177.

36. Walster, Walster and Berscheid, *Equity: Theory and Research* (1978), pp. 6-20.

37. Macaulay and Walster, *supra*, footnote 35, at pp. 182-3.

38. See, generally, Brock and Buss, "Effects of Justification for Aggression in Communication with the Victim on Post-Aggression Dissonance", 68 J. Abnorm. Soc. Psych. 403 (1964).

E. *Who will benefit from restitution?*

While much of the rallying cry for revitalizing restitution centres around the presumably forgotten victim, promoting restitution on this basis is to do little more than to promote false hopes for most actual and potential victims. This resides in the fact that the majority of crimes go unsolved, not all crimes which are solved result in an arrest, not all arrests culminate in a conviction, and, finally, restitution is not an appropriate sanction for all convicted offenders. In the absence of data on who gets into the criminal justice system, how they got into the system and what happens to them once in the system, the assumption that correctional restitution will assist a significant proportion of victims of crime is probably unwarranted. This may be so for several reasons; reasons which are related to the naive assumption that we have operating a full enforcement model of criminal justice[39] and an absence of public and private agencies outside the scope of the criminal justice system which are designed in whole or in part to serve the needs of crime victims. Moreover, to generate in potential victims a false hope that the criminal justice system will come to their rescue with respect to restitution should they be victimized may partially serve to negate efforts aimed at encouraging citizens to secure and insure their property.

(1) Any student of the criminal justice system recognizes that the assumption of a full enforcement model is unwarranted. This assumption fails the moment one begins to analyze crime statistics. In the first instance, victimization surveys remind us that not all crimes are reported to the police.[40] In general, in the case of property offences, the greater the amount of loss, the more likely the crime is to be reported to the police.[41] In addition, the smaller the loss, the more likely it is that the offence will be handled informally.[42] In many instances (we do not know how many), the actual laying of a charge is related to the recovery of the property. For example, it is probably safe to assume that in nearly 100 % of the cases of shoplifting in which a charge has been laid, the merchandise has been recovered. Obviously, much the same holds true with respect to charges laid in respect to being in possession of stolen property. Even many juvenile break-and-enter artists have acquired the "street wisdom" which tells them to steal cash rather than merchandise since, if they steal only the former and are questioned by the police (and even confess to the offence), it is unlikely that a charge will be laid in that, in the absence of other evidence, the prospects of obtaining a conviction are far from bright. In such instances, the offences are simply "cleared otherwise".[43]

---

39. *Cf.* Skolnick, *Justice without Trial* (New York, Wiley, 1966).

40. See, generally, Nettler, *Explaining Crime*, 2nd ed. (1978), pp. 87-97.

41. Skogan, "Citizen Reporting of Crime", 13 Criminology 535 (1976).

42. Nettler, *supra*, footnote 40, at p. 98.

43. For the year 1976, the Calgary (Alberta) Police Service had 33,772 property offences reported to it. Of these, 9,983 (30%) were cleared with adults being found responsible in 77% (7,783) of the cases. With respect to those offences involving adults, 46% (3,560) were cleared by charge with remaining 54% (4,220) being cleared otherwise. Finally, of those

The foregoing suggests that legal and operational realities dictate that those charges ending up in court with respect to property offences are, in all likelihood, not representative of all such victimizations. While it may be true that the larger the amount of loss, the more likely the offender is to find himself in court, it is in such instances that a sentence of incarceration is seen as justified, thus diminishing the prospects for restitution.

(2) To what extent are the needs of victims not being met? Again, data to inform us are absent. What proportion of the victims of property crimes recover their property? To what extent is restitution carried out informally irrespective of whether or not a charge is laid? How many victims have their losses covered through private insurance schemes? (And, in fact, to what extent are losses inflated in making an insurance claim and are there instances where some victims attempt to recover their loss twice over, once through their insurance company and again through the offender?) Finally, in addition to private insurance there are other schemes which, on occasion, function to alleviate partially, if not totally, the plight of the victim: medicare, welfare, unemployment insurance, crime compensation boards, and the like.

The foregoing is not intended to be so callous as to suggest that the needs of all or even many victims are being met; it is, however, intended to suggest that we might do well to find out what these needs are before rushing headlong into a perhaps dubious and probably expensive process of law "reform". Moreover, it has yet to be established that the primary needs of victims are monetary in nature. Fogelman's research raises the possibility that the needs of many victims are more psychological than monetary; they are needs which require understanding and compassion.[44] To the extent that this is so, then dealing with an understanding police officer who appreciates the psychological trauma that comes with the realization that one can no longer view one's home as one's castle once it has been broken into; and appearing as a witness in a court which is organized so as not to require one to make several unproductive appearances, may do much to alleviate the plight of some victims.

(3) Is restitution feasible for many offenders? The Law Reform Commission went to some length to rebut what it claimed to be "the chief argument against the implementation of restitution as a major consideration in sentencing and dispositions"[45] (and, in doing so, gave further evidence as to the naiveté of its proposal)—the ability and the willingness of the offender to pay. In order to buttress their argument that many offenders can and will

---

property offences involving adults which were cleared by charge, property was recovered in 63% (2,252) of the cases. Pilot Alberta Restitution Centre, *Progress Report: Diversion Research* (1977).

44. Fogelman, "Compensation to Victims of Crimes of Violence—The Forgotten Program" (1971). Unpublished M.S.W. thesis, Univ. S. Calif., L.A.

45. Law Reform Commission of Canada, Working Paper 5, *Restitution and Compensation* (1974), pp. 12-13.

pay, the Commission noted that in Toronto, 79% of the fines which were imposed were paid and that 68% of the fines imposed were $75 or less. Further, the Commission noted that in 1970 in Toronto, "the average value of stolen goods as estimated in police reports was less than $25.00 in 27 percent of the cases. In another 36 percent the value of the goods was between $26.00 and $100.00."[46] Finally, the Commission cited "Studies in 1966 in Ontario and 1973 in Vancouver [which] indicated that the amount of the loss to victims, including both personal injury and property loss, on the average, approximated $300.00."[47]

For several reasons, these data do not convince: data from the Pilot Alberta Restitution Centre indicate that of 192 referrals which were made to the project (59 of which resulted in a restitution agreement), 21% of the cases involved amounts under $100 while 38% of the referrals involved amounts over $500.[48] Further, of the 59 agreements which had been made, 62% had either been paid in full or payments were being maintained; for the remainder of the agreements, they were either in default or arrears.[49]

The Commission's data on the amount of loss per victimization do not constitute a convincing argument that restitution will be within the means of many offenders. As noted, these data are from police victimization reports; as such, it is unlikely that they are representative of the cases which actually end up in court. More importantly, the data refer to individual victimizations rather than to offenders. The implication of this is obvious to anyone who has observed the mystification of a magistrate as the charges are labouriously read off against a cheque artist or the consternation of a constable as the Crown withdraws eight charges of breaking and entering and the accused then pleads guilty to three remaining charges.

While the Commission does not confront the weaknesses in its own data, it does hedge its bet by suggesting that, "If the offender does not have the money to make good a restitution order, he should be given an opportunity to do work either for the victim, some other person, or some agency" under the auspices of a Community Service Order.[50] While such a suggestion may have some merit, the experience of the Pilot Alberta Restitution Centre was that very few victims would even give serious consideration to having the offender work for them, let alone having any contact with the offender.[51] And, while the notion of community service "makes sense", one might well anticipate that in times of high unemployment, the community itself will not be all that receptive to the idea that the "bad guys" get jobs which might otherwise go to the "good guys".

---

46. *Ibid.*, at p. 13.
47. *Ibid.*
48. P.A.R.C., *Progress Report: September 1, 1975 - November 30, 1976* (1976), p. 44.
49. *Ibid.*, at p. 45.
50. Law Reform Commission, *supra*, footnote 45, at p. 14.
51. P.A.R.C., *supra*, footnote 48, at p. 65.

F. *What are the implications of plea bargaining with respect to giving primacy to restitution in sentencing?*

Plea bargaining is increasingly being recognized as a pervasive reality in the Canadian criminal justice system.[52] In common with restitution, there is a dearth of statute and case law governing its use.[53] This state of affairs further undermines the practicality and the value of the Law Reform Commission's restitution proposal.[54]

Simply stated, what is to be done for the victims in those cases that are "dealt away" as a result of pre-trial negotiations at the police or prosecutorial level? Are they somehow to be considered to be less worthy of restitution than those victims whose cases were dealt with by the court? Yet, most would react in shock should the court order restitution for offences for which an individual was neither charged nor convicted as happened in *People v. Miller.*[55]

To this some might respond that this is simply further evidence of the undesirability of plea bargaining; as such, it is a practice which should be abolished.[56] However, the simplicity of such a position is surpassed only by its *naivete'* with respect to the parameters and dynamics of "justice by negotiation".[57] The practice is such that it cannot be made to disappear by fiat; rather, such a decree will have the likely consequence of making the practice even more *sub rosa* than it is at present.

Plea bargaining aside, what is to be done for those victims in cases in which an offender may be known to be guilty to a moral certainty but for which there is insufficient evidence to warrant the laying of a charge? Or what do we do for victims in cases where the offender is acquitted on the basis of a legal technicality? It should be clear that in all of the foregoing situations alluded to, to do justice to the victim would mean doing an injustice to the offender which would simply not be countenanced by the courts. As such, the situation still remains that of "let him sue".

Furthermore, the existence of such situations serves to undermine the

---

52. See, generally, Klein, *Let's Make a Deal: Negotiating Justice* (Toronto, D.C. Heath, 1976); Grosman, *The Prosecutor* (1969); and Hartnagel, "Plea Negotiation in Canada", 17 Can. J. of Crim. and Corr. 45 (1975).

53. See Chasse, "Restitution in Canadian Criminal Law", 36 C.R.N.S. 201, and Ferguson and Roberts, "Plea Bargaining: Directions for Canadian Reform", 52 Can. Bar Rev. 497 (1974).

54. See Law Reform Commission, *supra*, footnote 45. Nowhere in this report is the issue of plea bargaining as it relates to restitution discussed.

55. See Jacobson, "Notes: Use of Restitution in the Criminal Process: *People v. Miller*", 16 U.C.L.A.L.R. 456 (1969).

56. See, *e.g.*, National Advisory Committee on Criminal Justice Standards and Goals, *Courts* (Wash. D.C., U.S. Govt. Print. Office, 1973) at pp. 42-9; Dean, "The Illegitimacy of Plea Bargaining", 38:3 Fed. Prob. 18 (1974); and Gallagher, "Judicial Participation in Plea Bargaining: A Search for New Standards", 9 Harvard Civil Rights-Civil Liberties L.Rev. 29 (1974).

57. Klein, *supra*, footnote 52, at pp. 126-8.

claim of some restitution advocates that making restitution an important consideration in sentencing and dispositions will result in greater citizen support for and confidence in the criminal justice system. If anything, in cases such as above, less support for the system may well be the outcome. Also undermined in such instances is the assumption that bringing restitution to the fore in sentencing and dispositions will have some deterrent value and will assist the offender in seeing that he is responsible for his behaviour.

G. *Will making restitution a central consideration in sentencing and dispositions encourage the abuse of the criminal process to aid debt collection?*

Given what some may view as the current inadequacies in statute law respecting restitution in criminal cases, many victims now find themselves in a situation where they perceive that they must choose between restitution and prosecution. This is often the case with respect to N.S.F. cheques[58] and in minor incidents involving theft and property damage where the investigating officer, in effect, informally negotiates a civil settlement between offender and victim in lieu of laying a charge.

The irony is that while the Law Reform Commission views the present law governing restitution as a *weakness* in terms of its restitution proposal, this same law can be seen as *strength* inasmuch as it lends encouragement to the type of behavioural response which is advocated in the Commission's Working Paper on *Diversion*.[59] In this light it seems reasonable to assume that if the Commission's restitution proposal is to be adopted and put into practice in the ways hoped for by the Commission, that as word of this practice spreads among victims, some of those victims who previously had to make a choice between informal restitution or prosecution (with little possibility of restitution) will opt for the best of both worlds, demanding prosecution with a good possibility of receiving restitution upon conviction. Such a state of affairs could encourage prosecutions which are essentially vexatious, constituting an abuse of the criminal process to aid in the collection of what would otherwise be viewed as a debt. In addition, as Barton has indicated, in such cases the defendant's position with respect to abuse of process as a plea in bar of trial is not strong.[60]

Conclusion

We find ourselves in agreement with Stenning and Ciano that:

Working Paper 5's most refreshing quality is its direct and pointed style. The Commission has first to be commended for avoiding the typical legal jangle of official reports, and stating its position in clear and eminently readable terms.[61]

---

58.   Klein and Montague, *Check-Forgers* (forthcoming, 1978).

59.   Law Reform Commission of Canada, Working Paper 7, *Diversion* (1975).

60.   Barton, "Abuse of Process as a Plea in Bar of Trial", 15 Crim.L.Q. 437 (1972-73), at pp. 455-7.

61.   Stenning and Ciano, "Restitution, Compensation and Fines", 7 Ottawa L. Rev. 316 (1975), at p. 316.

It is here, however, that our praise for the Working Paper by and large begins and ends. As such, it has been the purpose of this article to draw attention to a number of issues which should be afforded greater respect and consideration than is apparent in the Working Paper on *Restitution and Compensation*. While the Commission asserts that:

> In coming to the point of view that restitution be a central consideration in sentencing and dispositions, the Commission has drawn upon the social sciences and philosophy as well as history.[62]

Given the contents of the Working Paper, I am not convinced that this was done with the care and diligence which would justify the adoption of the Commission's recommendations. To adopt these recommendations without further deliberation might well result in creating more problems than are solved.

This should not be construed as demeaning the Commission's obvious concern with the plight of crime victims; that concern is, of course, laudable. However, as William James reminds us, "With mere good intentions, hell is proverbially paved."

---

62. Law Reform Commission of Canada, Working Paper 5, *Restitution and Compensation* (1974), p. 8.

SELECTED BIBLIOGRAPHY

Annals of the American Academy of Political and Social Science. *The Future of Corrections.* Philadelphia, January 1969.

Arthur, Lindsay G., and Karsh, Katherine H. "Release Hearings: To Protect the Public." *Federal Probation,* vol. 40 (1976), pp. 55-59.

"Aversion Therapy: Its Limited Potential for Use in the Correctional Setting." *Stanford Law Review,* vol. 26 (1974), p. 1327.

Berk, Richard A., and Rossi, Peter H. *Prison Reform and State Elites.* Cambridge, Mass.: Ballinger, 1977.

"Conditioning and Other Technologies Used to 'Treat?' 'Rehabilitate?' 'Demolish?' Prisoners and Mental Patients." *Southern California Law Review,* vol. 45 (1973), p. 616.

Dawson, Robert O. "The Decision to Grant or Deny Parole: A Study of Parole Criteria in Law & Practice." *Washington University Law Quarterly,* vol. 1966 (June 1966), pp. 243-303.

Deming, R.R. *Divergent Corrections.* San Francisco: R & E Research Association, 1977.

Dershowitz, Alan. "The Law of Dangerousness: Some Fictions About Predictions." *Journal of Legal Education,* vol. 23 (1970), p. 24.

Determinate Sentencing: Reform and Regression? Washington, D.C.: U.S. Government Printing Office, 1978.

Dodge, Calvert R., ed. *A Nation Without Prisons: Alternatives to Incarceration.* Lexington, Mass.: D.C. Heath, 1975.

Galaway, Burt, and Hudson, Joe, eds. *Considering the Victim: Readings in Restitution and Victim Compensation.* Springfield, Ill.: Charles C. Thomas, 1975.

Gardner, Martin R. "The Renaissance of Retribution: An Examination of Doing Justice." *Wisconsin Law Review,* vol. 1976 (1976), pp. 781-815.

Genego, William J.; Goldberger, Peter D.; and Jackson, Vicki C. "Parole Release Decisionmaking and the Sentencing Process." *Yale Law Journal,* vol. 84 (1975).

Kellogg, Frederic R. "From Retribution to 'Desert': The Evolution of Criminal Punishment." *Criminology,* vol. 15 (1977), pp. 179-192.

Krantz, Sheldon. *Corrections and Prisoners' Rights.* St. Paul, Minn.: West Publishing, 1976.

Minnich, Stephen D. *The Planned Implementation of Mutual Agreement Programming in a Correctional System.* College Park, Md.: American Correctional Association, 1976.

Mullen, Joan. *The Dilemma of Diversion.* Washington, D.C.: U.S. Department of Justice, 1975.

Nelson, E.K.; Ohmart, H.; and Harlow, N. *Promising Strategies in Probation and Parole.* Washington, D.C., National Institute of Law Enforcement and Criminal Justice, 1978.

Newman, Graeme, and Trilling, Carol. "Public Perceptions of Criminal Behavior." *Criminal Justice and Behavior,* vol. 2 (1975).

O'Leary, Vincent; Gottfredson, Michael; and Gelman, Arthur. "Contemporary Sentencing Proposals." *Criminal Law Bulletin,* vol. 11 (1975), p. 555.

Prigmore, Charles S., and Crow, Richard T. "Is the Court Remaking the American Prison System?" *Federal Probation,* vol. 40 (1976), pp. 3-10.

Ross, B. *Changing of the Guard: Citizen Soldiers in Wisconsin Correctional Institutions.* Madison, Wis.: The League of Women Voters of Wisconsin, 1978.

Schwitzgabel, Ralph. "Electronically Monitored Parole." *Prison Journal,* vol. 34 (1968), p. 48.

_____. "Limitation on the Coercive Treatment of Offenders." *Criminal Law Bulletin,* vol. 8, no. 4 (May 1972), pp. 267-320.

Shapiro, Michael H. "Legislating the Control of Behavior Control: Autonomy and the Coercive Use of Organic Therapies." *Southern California Law Review,* vol. 47 (1974), p. 237.

Shuman, S.I. *Psychosurgery and the Medical Control of Violence: Autonomy and Deviance.* Detroit, Mich.: Wayne State University Press, 1977.

von Hirsch, Andrew. "Prediction of Criminal Conduct and Preventive Confinement of Convicted Persons." *Buffalo Law Review,* vol. 21 (1972), p. 757.

Wilkins, Leslie T. "Current Aspects of Penology: Directions for Corrections." *Proceedings of the American Philosophical Society,* vol. 118 (1974), pp. 235-252.

Thomas, Charles W. "Prisonization and Its Consequences: An Examination of Socialization in a Coercive Setting." *Sociological Forces,* vol. 10 (January 1977), pp. 53-68.

_____. "Prisonization or Resocialization: A Study of External Factors Associated with the Impact of Imprisonment." *Journal of Research in Crime and Delinquency,* vol. 10 (January 1975), pp. 13-21.

Thomas, Charles W., and Poole, Eric D. "The Consequences of Incompatible Goal Structures in Correctional Settings." *International Journal of Criminology and Penology*, vol. 3 (1975), pp. 27-42.

Toch, Hans. *Living in Prison.* New York: The Free Press, 1977.

_____. *Men in Crisis.* Chicago: Aldine, 1976.

_____. *Police, Prisons and the Problem of Violence.* Washington, D.C.: U.S. Government Printing Office, 1977.

U.S. Law Enforcement Assistance Administration and U.S. Bureau of Census. *Local Jails.* Washington, D.C.: U.S. Government Printing Office, 1973.

Vanaguanas, Stanley. "National Standards and Goals in Corrections." *Criminology*, vol. 14 (August 1976), pp. 223-240.

Ward, David A., and Kassebaum, Gene. *Women's Prison: Sex and Social Structure.* Chicago: Aldine, 1965.

Women Behind Bars: An Organizing Tool. Washington, D.C.: Resources for Community Change, 1975.

Wynne, J.M. *Prison Employee Unionism: Impact on Correctional Administration and Programs.* Washington, D.C.: National Institute of Law Enforcement and Criminal Justice, 1977.

INDEX